REIMAGINING THE NATIONAL SECURITY STATE

Reimagining The National Security State provides the first comprehensive picture of the toll that US government policies have taken on civil liberties, human rights, and the rule of law in the name of the war on terror. Looking through the lenses of theory, history, law, and policy, the essays in this volume illuminate the ways in which liberal democracy has suffered at the hands of policymakers in the name of national security. The contributors, who are leading experts and practitioners in fields ranging from political theory to evolutionary biology, discuss the vast expansion of executive powers, the excessive reliance on secrecy, and the exploration of questionable legal territory in matters of detention, criminal justice, targeted killings, and warfare. This book gives the reader an eye-opening window into the historical precedents and lasting impact the security state has had on America's founding principles.

Karen J. Greenberg is Director of the Center on National Security at Fordham University School of Law. She received her BA from Cornell University and PhD from Yale University. Her books include *The Least Worst Place: Guantanamo's First 100 Days* (2009) and *Rogue Justice: The Making of the Security State* (2016). Greenberg edited *The Torture Debate in America* (2006), coedited *The Torture Papers: The Road to Abu Ghraib* (2005), and is editor in chief of *The Soufan Group Morning Brief*. She is an International Studies Fellow at New America.

To Tim —
the book I am
most proud of to the
son I am, also
proud of !
Love,
Dad

REIMAGINING THE NATIONAL SECURITY STATE

Reimagining The National Security State provides the first comprehensive picture of the toll that US government policies have taken on civil liberties, human rights, and the rule of law in the name of the war on terror. Looking through the lenses of theory, history, law and policy, the essays in this volume illuminate the ways in which liberal democracy has suffered at the hands of policymakers in the name of national security. The contributors, who are leading experts and practitioners in fields ranging from political theory to evolutionary biology, discuss the vast expansion of executive powers, the excessive reliance on secrecy, and the exploration of questionable legal territory in matters of detention, criminal justice, targeted killings, and warfare. This book gives the reader an eye-opening window into the historical precedents and lasting impact the security state has had on American founding principles.

Karen J. Greenberg is Director of the Center on National Security at Fordham University School of Law. She received her BA from Cornell University and PhD from Yale University. Her books include The Least Worst Place: Guantanamo's First 100 Days (2009) and Rogue Justice: The Making of the Security State (2016). Greenberg edited The Torture Debate in America (2005), coedited The Torture Papers: The Road to Abu Ghraib (2005), and is editor in chief of The Soufan Group Morning Brief. She is an International Studies Fellow at New America.

Contents

CAMBRIDGE
UNIVERSITY PRESS

University Printing House, Cambridge CB2 8BS, United Kingdom

One Liberty Plaza, 20th Floor, New York, NY 10006, USA

477 Williamstown Road, Port Melbourne, VIC 3207, Australia

314–321, 3rd Floor, Plot 3, Splendor Forum, Jasola District Centre, New Delhi – 110025, India

79 Anson Road, #06–04/06, Singapore 079906

Cambridge University Press is part of the University of Cambridge.

It furthers the University's mission by disseminating knowledge in the pursuit of education, learning, and research at the highest international levels of excellence.

www.cambridge.org
Information on this title: www.cambridge.org/9781108484381
DOI: 10.1017/9781108676946

© Cambridge University Press 2020

First published 2020

Printed and bound in Great Britain by Clays Ltd, Elcograf S.p.A.

A catalogue record for this publication is available from the British Library.

Library of Congress Cataloging-in-Publication Data
NAMES: Greenberg, Karen J.
TITLE: Reimagining the national security state : liberalism on the brink / edited by Karen J. Greenberg Fordham University, New York.
DESCRIPTION: Cambridge, United Kingdom ; New York, NY : Cambridge University Press, 2019. | Includes index.
IDENTIFIERS: LCCN 2019018563 | ISBN 9781108484381
SUBJECTS: LCSH: National security – Law and legislation – United States. | Terrorism – Prevention – Law and legislation – United States. | Guantánamo Bay Detention Camp. | Counterinsurgency – United States. | Civil rights – United States. | Liberalism – United States.
CLASSIFICATION: LCC KF4850 .R439 2019 | DDC 342.73/0418–dc23
LC record available at https://lccn.loc.gov/2019018563

ISBN 978-1-108-48438-1 Hardback
ISBN 978-1-108-73580-3 Paperback

Reimagining The National Security State

LIBERALISM ON THE BRINK

Edited by

KAREN J. GREENBERG

Center on National Security
Fordham University School of Law, New York

CAMBRIDGE
UNIVERSITY PRESS

Contributors

John Berger is has been involved in international publishing for three decades, first with Wolters Kluwer and then with Cambridge University Press where he was a senior editor. He works in the areas of public international law, human rights, humanitarian law, international criminal law, environmental law, comparative law, law and society, governance, national security, and contentious issues. He is currently at Senior Fellow at the Center on National Security at Fordham University School of Law.

Douglass Cassel is Notre Dame Presidential Fellow Emeritus and Emeritus Professor of Law at the University of Notre Dame Law School. He specializes in international human rights law, international criminal and humanitarian law, regional human rights systems, and business and human rights. Cassel received a BA from Yale and a JD from Harvard Law School, both cum laude.

Joshua L. Dratel is a New York–based lawyer. Dratel has been involved in some of the past three decades' most important cases involving national security, terrorism, international law, and civil liberties. He graduated magna cum laude from Columbia College and from Harvard Law School. Dratel is coeditor with Karen J. Greenberg of *The Torture Papers: The Legal Road to Abu Ghraib* (2005) and *The Enemy Combatant Papers: American Justice, the Courts and the War on Terror* (2008). He also contributed essays to *The Torture Debate in America* (2005) as well as *The Guantánamo Lawyers: Inside a Prison Outside the Law* (2009). Dratel is also a Fellow at the Center on National Security at Fordham University School of Law.

Thomas Anthony Durkin is the Distinguished Practitioner in Residence at Loyola University Chicago School of Law, where he is also cofounder and codirector of its National Security and Civil Rights program. Durkin specializes in the defense of complex federal criminal matters with an emphasis on national security and domestic terrorism–related cases. He received a BA from the University of Notre Dame and also graduated from the University of San Francisco School of Law. Durkin is also a Fellow at the Center on National Security at Fordham University School of Law.

Donald Glascoff is a documentary filmmaker and retired attorney. The major theme of his work is the preservation of human rights and individual liberties. He is a graduate of Yale University and Cornell Law School. He was the executive producer of the 2007 Academy Award–winning documentary, *Taxi to the Dark Side*. He is also a Fellow at the Center on National Security at Fordham University School of Law.

Michael J. Glennon is Professor of International Law at the Fletcher School of Law and Diplomacy at Tufts University. He received a BA and graduated summa cum laude from the College of St. Thomas and received his JD from the University of Minnesota. He is the author of *National Security and Double Government* (2014) and *Foreign Affairs Federalism: The Myth of National Exclusivity* (2016), written with Robert D. Sloane.

John Gray is an English political philosopher. He studied at Exeter College, Oxford, for his BA, MPhil, and DPhil. He is the author of multiple books, including *Straw Dogs: Thoughts on Humans and Other Animals* (2003), *Black Mass: Apocalyptic Religion and the Death of Utopia* (2007), and *The Soul of the Marionette: A Short Inquiry into Human Freedom* (2016).

Karen J. Greenberg is the Director of the Center on National Security at Fordham University School of Law. She received her BA from Cornell University and her PhD from Yale University. Her books include *The Least Worst Place: Guantanamo's First 100 Days* (2009) and *Rogue Justice: The Making of the Security State* (2016). Greenberg edited *The Torture Debate in America* (2006), co-edited *The Torture Papers: The Road to Abu Ghraib* (2005) and is Editor-in-Chief of *The Soufan Group Morning Brief*. She is an International Studies Fellow at New America.

Bernard E. Harcourt is the Isidor and Seville Sulzbacher Professor of Law, Professor of Political Science, Executive Director of the Eric H. Holder Initiative for Civil and Political Rights, and the Founding Director of the Columbia Center for Contemporary Critical Thought at Columbia University. He received an AB from Princeton University, a JD from Harvard Law School, and a PhD from Harvard University. Harcourt's recent books include *Exposed: Desire and Disobedience in the Digital Age* (2015) and *The Counterrevolution: How Our Government Went to War against Its Own Citizens* (2018).

Loch K. Johnson is the Regents Emeritus Professor of Public and International Affairs at the University of Georgia as well as a Meigs Distinguished Teaching Professor. He received a BA from the University of California, Davis, followed by a PhD from the University of California, Riverside. Johnson's recent books include *A Season of Inquiry Revisited: The Church Committee Confronts America's Spy Agencies* (2015) and *Spy Watching: Intelligence Accountability in the United States* (2018).

Mary Ellen O'Connell is the Robert and Marion Short Professor of Law and is Research Professor of International Dispute Resolution, Kroc Institute, University of Notre Dame. She graduated summa cum laude with a BA from Northwestern University. O'Connell then received an MSc from the London School of Economics, a JD from Columbia University School of Law, and a PhD from Cambridge University. She authored *The Power and Purpose of International Law, Insights from the Theory and Practice of Enforcement* (2008) and edited *What Is War? An Investigation in the Wake of 9/11* (2012).

Michel Paradis serves as a senior attorney for the Department of Defense, Office of the Chief Defense Counsel, and is a lecturer in law at Columbia Law School and an adjunct professor of law at Georgetown Law. He received his BA and JD degrees from Fordham University and MPhil and DPhil from the University of Oxford. Paradis is also a Fellow at the Center on National Security.

Laura Pitter interim deputy director for Human Rights Watch's US Program, guides the US Program's work on criminal justice and national security. She has a bachelor's degree from the University of California, Santa Barbara, a master's in international affairs from Columbia University, and a JD from the University of San Francisco. Prior to her work for Human Rights Watch, Pitter worked as a journalist, human rights advocate, and attorney.

David Sloan Wilson is a Distinguished Professor of Biological Sciences and Anthropology at Binghamton University. He received a BA from the University of Rochester followed by a PhD from Michigan State University. His recent books include *The Neighborhood Project: Using Evolution to Improve My City One Block at a Time* (2011) and *Does Altruism Exist?: Culture, Genes, and the Welfare of Others (Foundational Questions in Science)* (2015).

Foreword

Donald Glascoff

Why another book about the national security state? Perhaps, it is really a book on the war on terror, the attack on democracy, illiberalism, and the end of the rule of law. The answer is deceptively simple and disastrously hidden. All of the writing and speeches deploring our current human condition have had minimal impact on the culture of survival that controls our collective subconscious. Torture and extraordinary rendition continue, threats – perceived and real – control the discourse in the United States, and little we have said and done has made a difference. We unconsciously perceive the security state as our only hope for survival.

In his piece, Doug Cassel writes eloquently of the unique public apology of Prime Minister Theresa May for the torture that British and US intelligence services admittedly arranged in Libya for an opponent of the Gaddafi regime. But the apology did nothing to change the reality. Torture has moved offshore from black sites and Guantánamo to the brigs on US warships, which remain immune from basic legal principles or any legal oversight. Rendition continues; the destination for prisoners has changed.

In planning the program that produced this book, I was motivated by how little had changed since 2007 when I produced an Academy Award–winning film exposing the culture of torture, *Taxi to the Dark Side*. I was also struck by a perception that we are not involved in a traditional war but rather a cultural and evolutionary war.

David Sloan Wilson, the distinguished evolutionist, brings our current political and cultural turmoil to a simple conclusion in his piece. Cultures and nation-states – varied, numerous, and incompatible as they now are – become focused on Darwinian survival when they are under constant attack.

What is the mechanism Western culture (to the extent it still exists) has created to survive? The National Security State. The means chosen to assure survival have no limits when our existence is at stake. Values are subjugated to the prime imperative of survival. For some, as for Michael Ignatieff in *The Lesser Evil: Political Ethics in an Age of Terror*, torture becomes a lesser evil than the destruction of the liberal values of the West and perhaps of the West in its entirety. It is a devil's bargain, as compromise on the value of human life itself destroys our values and potentially life itself.

As Michael J. Glennon so clearly shows, we have created a "Trumanite" system, indeed a closed culture of security. Our security institutions have little oversight or control imposed upon them. They are bureaucracies of terrifying size and complexity, which exist in what amounts to a post-democratic vacuum. The nerves of government have been severed as no democratic institution, none of our three traditional branches of government, can withstand this new fourth branch of government. Or, as Glennon aptly names it, "double government."

John Gray will not be surprised by this condition as he long ago abandoned confidence in the idea of progress and failed experiments in liberalism. For him, the future is always uncertain, but he too believes that evolution will occur, without being able to predict its course. Gray may have become a mystic.

Nevertheless, faith in traditional liberal institutions and rational discourse is apparent throughout the volume. The authors in Part II of this volume well summarize the noble traditions of the rule of law and support our democratic traditions. Laws are made, and courts enforce them, aided by the skill of legal advocates. Universities harbor great intellects who see a future far different than mine or Gray's. I applaud their comprehensive treatments and regret that I no longer share their optimism and courage. Joshua Dratel writes most eloquently of a permanent illusion arising from the war on terror. But, which is the illusion? Democracy or terror or survival?

At the beginning, Gray and I thought about inviting a great writer dealing in terror, Cormac McCarthy, to speak and write on our topic. *The Road* and *No Country for Old Men* encompass in pure literary terms the possible futures for a post-terror epoch. We decided, no, we must leave some hope for our readers to clutch.

Acknowledgments

Many people helped to make this book possible. I want to thank Donald Glascoff for his suggestion that the Center on National Security at Fordham Law host a symposium on the long-term consequences of the rise of the national security state. The workshop that resulted led to this collection of essays. His guidance throughout has been invaluable. Jennifer Indig, a long-time colleague, helped give shape and substance to the symposium agenda. Baher Azmy and Steven Simon attended the symposium and offered valuable insights into the questions of liberalism in the context of today's security state. Deepest thanks as well to my long-time Cambridge University Press editor John Berger, who patiently and wisely shepherded this volume through to publication as he has done with me so many times before. CUP's Danielle Menz's editing turned the manuscript into a polished volume. Julia Tedesco, the program director at the Center on National Security at Fordham Law, worked generously on the initial editing of the book and prepared the index.

A Note from the Editor

Karen J. Greenberg

In the spring of 2018, the Center on National Security at Fordham Law School hosted a symposium entitled "Reimagining the National Security State." Participants presented formal remarks on the national security state as it had evolved over the first decades of the twenty-first century. They shared their reflections on the imbalance between liberty and security that has ensued and their thoughts on the viable roads forward for restoring a balance between democratic principles and security aims.

Their presentations, and the rich conversations they inspired, led to the somewhat alarming conviction that expectations that the pendulum would eventually swing back toward liberty and the rule of law were overly hopeful. In fact, the participants suggested that liberal democracy itself was in trouble, its future uncertain as a result of the attack on these foundational democratic principles. Following the symposium, each of the authors delved deeper into their areas of expertise to refine their thinking in light of those discussions. The results, a series of essays, are now collected in this volume. Together, they explore the state of democratic liberalism in today's increasingly unstable world, ever attentive to the impact that the rise of the national security state has had on culture, society, and governance.

Immediately following the attacks of September 11, 2001, the United States instituted reforms in the name of national security that altered the landscape of American democracy. The rule of law was bent to accommodate policies in detention, interrogation, military commissions, criminal justice, targeted killings, and more. Each chapter focuses anew on the challenges to democracy that resulted from the rise of the national security state in response to the attacks. In foreign policy, criminal justice, intelligence strategies, and diplomacy, new policies arose, often in secret, that set aside long-standing norms. The result, in many areas, was the degradation of institutions, law, and governance. Reflecting on the changes that ensued, the contributors to this volume have described the transformations with analytical rigor, placing them in historical perspective while at the same time exploring the usefulness of past philosophers and political theorists for understanding the choices that lie ahead.

In its entirety, this volume is meant to add context and reflection to the scholarly and public discourse that has debated the tension not solely between liberty and security but between liberalism and security as well. The combination of interdisciplinary perspectives is unique to the field; the perspectives, which range from evolutionary biology to political theory and philosophy to legal scholarship and national security expertise, are intended to provide the reader with insights into liberalism and its challengers from both novel and more traditional directions. The result is a compendium that will provide readers in one volume with instructive examples of specific incidents, cases, and policies. As such, it is intended to serve not only as a background for policymakers but as a primer for students and readers who seek a deepened understanding of the perils that have befallen American democracy in the wake of the war on terror.

Taken together, the insights of the volume's authors, though often dire in their analyses, provide a nuanced and fact-driven set of understandings, helpful for informing those who seek to craft a way forward and to fashion a national security strategy that recognizes the importance of constitutional protections, transparency in government, international comity, and a belief in the strength of democracy overall. Ultimately, readers are left to answer for themselves this question: "Is there a way to renew the promise of liberalism amid the realities of twenty-first-century threats?" With the guidance of these essays, readers will be able to consider both the pitfalls of this moment in history and the promises of tomorrow.

The National Security State in Perspective

PART I

The National Security State in Perspective

1

Who's Checking Whom?

Michael J. Glennon

In reimagining the national security state, an initial question is whether we've already been imagining too much. Talk about the "deep state" is now rampant. Even the US president regularly refers to it. A March 2018 poll showed that 74 percent of the American people believe a deep state exists.[1] Are they wrong?

I suggest in this chapter that the national security state is not a product of anyone's imagination. It exists. Second, the national security state emerged in part because the Framers' system of checks and balances has not worked as intended. Third, it is inconsistent with that system for the national security state to check elected officials. I conclude with a thought about the momentous dilemma that confronts the United States today.

First, there is a national security state. It consists of the several hundred managers of the military, law enforcement, and intelligence agencies and departments of our government. It is not deep in that it is not concealed. Quite the opposite: What could speak more loudly of its existence than the five-sided, thirty-acre Pentagon building on the Potomac that is our war department or the J. Edgar Hoover building, an aging concrete fortress that looms over the center of Washington, DC, as did its peculiar former director for whom the building is named? Yet, parts of the national security state are not in plain view. Like the USS Fitzgerald, an Arleigh Burke-class destroyer known for its advanced combat systems and multi-mission capability, we all know it is there, but we are not allowed on board and cannot possibly know everything that is inside.

When I worked for the Senate Foreign Relations Committee in the 1970s, many others and I spent quite a lot of time trying to figure out what was going on inside the national security state. In those days, the security services of some nations – Iran, Chile, the Philippines, and other putative "allies" of the United States – were engaged in some distasteful activities. Some of those activities occurred here in this country, including the detonation of a bomb in a car driven up Massachusetts Avenue that killed a dissident foreign minister and his research assistant (and shattered the windows of the American Society of International Law).[2] This was real foreign intervention in American politics, orders of magnitude beyond retweeting a fake news story. The committee wanted to know what steps were being taken to stop DINA[3] and its ilk from swanking around America as though they were in Argentina.

Getting an answer to that question turned out to be a lot harder than you would have thought.[4] One reason was that it required getting an answer to an antecedent question: **What had we been doing to help them**? These were, after all, American allies. Allies help allies. The answer, it turned out, was extremely sensitive. Civil rights laws impose criminal penalties on governmental efforts to impede the exercise of constitutionally protected rights.[5] Getting to the bottom of this matter required looking into one of the great sources and methods of American intelligence – liaison relationships with foreign services. As such, everything the committee needed and wanted to know was therefore highly classified. I had five compartmented security clearances above top secret. In Langley, Fort Meade, and elsewhere, my colleagues and I took the statements of dozens of security officials. Some were identified only with pseudonyms. We read thousands of pages of classified documents. We ultimately did get a look inside, a pretty good look, I thought, from a vantage point that only a tiny handful of Americans had ever shared. Our view led me to conclude that the US government was very different from the way it appeared from the outside.

What I wrote in *National Security and Double Government*, thirty-five years later, is based on what we observed during that investigation. The book describes a national security bureaucracy that has come to dominate the making of national security policy. In an age of perpetual war against external threats that are both real and inflated, the courts, the Congress, and even the president have had every ambition to defer to its expertise and experience. No judge, senator, or president has wanted to risk responsibility for a devastating national security mistake. The courts have therefore developed an elaborate jurisprudence of non-justiciability, dismissing case after case on grounds of ripeness, mootness, the state secrets privilege, the political question doctrine, or lack of standing. Vast realms of the US Constitution – such as the war power – have become unenforced by the courts, giving the lie to John Marshall's great proclamation in *Marbury v. Madison*[6]: "It is emphatically the province and duty of the judicial department to say what the law is."[7] Congressional oversight became, in the word of the 9/11 Commission, "dysfunctional"[8] – more hindsight than oversight with respect to an array of activities ranging from black site prisons and torture to taps on allied leaders' cell phone conversations. The president, too, has every incentive to defer to the security managers' judgment, with the result that even a president who campaigned on "change we can believe in" ended up continuing the earlier administrations' policies on drone strikes, troop deployments, mass surveillance, covert action, whistle-blower prosecutions, claims of state secrets, and numerous other matters. The upshot has been broad delegation, explicit or implicit, that has resulted in an enormous transfer of authority and movement away from democratic accountability toward autocracy in the making of national security policy. This was not the work of some vast, nefarious conspiracy. The inversion of power has been a response to incentives embedded deeply within the American political system – an incentive on the part of the security managers to resist kibitzers and a corresponding incentive on the part of judges, members of Congress, and presidents to avoid the risk of career-ending misjudgments. The dynamic is more complex – threat inflation, groupthink, and other organizational incentives distort the decision-making process – but that is basically how it operates. The net effect is a structural inducement to evade, rather than honor, constitutional constraints.

Some maintain, in response, that the security managers' policy views reflect a broad consensus on the broad national security and foreign policy that has shaped American policy for decades. The claim is that no accountability problem arises because the managers share in that consensus, particularly in the views of American elites.

Several difficulties attend this assertion. First, it is easy to create a consensus semantically by simply framing issues at a high level of generality. Political pollsters are adept at doing so. When the issues are particularized, however, it turns out that the American public has long been deeply divided on fundamental national security issues. Pew polling data show this on issue after issue, from surveillance to torture to US involvement in the global economy to compromising with allies.[9] There is and has been no broad national consensus on multiple specific security issues.

What policies do the security managers favor? In general, policies that are already in place. Bureaucracies think differently than individuals. Bureaucracies do not like change – they tend toward stasis. They seek to preserve the status quo. That is especially true within the security bureaucracy, given its mission and structural risk aversion. Even when threats fade, the security managers resist lowering levels of protection. Loch K. Johnson, who knows as much about the inner workings of the intelligence world as anyone, puts it well: "The writings of the sociologist Max Weber, an expert on bureaucracy, provide greater insight into the real world of spy organizations than" the writings of Ian Fleming, the creator of James Bond.[10] There is no evidence that the security managers somehow overcome principles of organizational behavior and purposefully shift gears to adopt elites' policy preferences; in fact, it may be the other way around. In 2014, Paul Avey and Michael Desch concluded a study examining where national security decision-makers get information. Far more important than professional journals, academic books or articles, internet blog posts, and news sites were classified US government reports.[11] Few security managers attend meetings of the Council on Foreign Relations or the World Economic Forum or the American Law Institute because they do not need to: They already know what they need to know.

Pause here, in any event, and ponder the argument we have been examining – that the security managers' actions are legitimate not because they carry out the views of the American people or their elected representatives but rather because their policies are favored by elites. What comfort can a believer in democratic government take from that assertion? In a democracy, when voters choose policies different from those favored by elites, the *voters'* policies are supposed to prevail – and (as discussed below) the voters are not supposed to be checked by unelected bureaucrats, even those acting on behalf of elites. If the object is to safeguard democracy, what would be gained by trading external threats for equally dangerous internal threats?

This brings me to the second point. One reason for the emergence of the national security state lies in the failure of the Constitution's system of checks and balances to produce an equilibrium of power. All know the theory on which the Constitution's system of divided government is grounded. "If men were angels," James Madison writes in *Federalist 51*, "no government would be necessary."[12] But men are not angels; they act frequently on base ambitions. Therefore, "[a]mbition must be made to counter ambition."[13] That sentence encapsulates the process that Madison believed would create an equilibrium of power, the equilibrium that would "oblige the government to control itself."[14] By pairing opposite and rival motives against each other, the defect of bad motives could be remedied.

That was the theory, anyway. But the theory could not, and did not, predict the actual turn of events following ratification of the Constitution. In the early days of the Republic, there was no bureaucracy to speak of. When Thomas Jefferson moved into the White House in 1802, the entire executive branch in Washington, DC, numbered 132 officials. His entire White House staff consisted of one person – his personal secretary.[15] When Madison extolled the benefits of setting ambition against ambition, political parties had not yet emerged. Madison's and Jefferson's democratic-republican party did not begin to take shape until three years later, in 1791, with their famous botany expedition to New York.[16] Bureaucracies made it possible to advance one's political career by passing the buck. Parties made it possible to do that by trading favors, sometimes with party members in another branch. The ambition-against-ambition dynamic that was expected to produce an equilibrium of power therefore turned out to be far more complex than Madison had ever supposed.

In the unanticipated political order that emerged, public officials were, sometimes, energized by an ambition to resist encroachments on their own institutional prerogatives, but they were possessed of other ambitions as well. They had ambitions for their political party to succeed, for their careers to progress, and for their policies to be adopted. Party, career, and policy ambitions often align with, rather than clash with, the ambitions of officials in other branches and departments of government. When the House Judiciary Committee, in October of 1973, began consideration of President Richard Nixon's impeachment, Republican members of the committee resisted in straight party-line votes. Democrats who had lamented the demise of congressional war powers fell mute when it was their president, Barack Obama, who joined the attack against Libya without congressional approval. Members of

Congress have come to be invested in the success of a president of their own party. When a colleague of Devon Nunes blurted out, with no irony intended, that Nunes worked for President Donald Trump, he could have been referring to any number of other members.[17] Rather than producing an equilibrium of power, the system has produced a disequilibrium. Party and career ambitions came to prevail over institutional ambitions.

The failure of three-way Madisonian checking to operate as intended opened the door for the modern national security state. But long before then, that failure produced a more mundane problem. That problem was how to deal with corruption and wrongdoing on the part of presidents and their close associates. Madison wrote for a different age and a different peer group. Madison's goal was more to guard against another Caesar than another Crassus. It thus fell to latter-day reformers to improvise a seemingly common-sense remedy to meet the problem. But as would be true of the national security state, that stopgap did not fit neatly into the classic, tripartite Madisonian model of governance. And reliance on it would turn out, years later, to complicate the answer to the emerging question: Who should be checking whom? Its rationale would, indeed, provide the seeds of a justification for an across-the-board challenge to the entire tradition of democratic accountability.

The remedy is the special prosecutor. Contrary to popular impression, the idea did not originate during the Watergate crisis. The first special prosecutor was appointed by President Ulysses S. Grant in 1875 during the Whiskey Ring controversy.[18] At least seven subsequent presidents appointed officials with prosecutorial authority, although their titles varied, to investigate suspected high-level corruption.[19] The most famous case, no doubt, involved Archibald Cox, who was fired during the "Saturday Night Massacre."[20] The most recent is, of course, Robert Mueller, who under Justice Department regulations was denominated an "independent counsel."

Although they have been on the scene for more than 140 years, special prosecutors are still square pegs for the Constitution's round holes. The Constitution assigns to the president the responsibility to "take care that the laws be faithfully executed."[21] It vests executive power in the president.[22] Early presidents thus regarded themselves as the nation's chief law enforcement officer. It was President Thomas Jefferson who personally ordered that Aaron Burr be charged with and tried for treason.[23] The great principle of democratic accountability that permeates the constitutional design requires that voters be able, ultimately, to know where the buck stops. It requires that voters have the final say – not bureaucrats whom neither they nor the president can control. When President Trump lambasted the FBI for not following relevant leads in the Florida school shooting,[24] one might therefore be forgiven for asking: Why do you not do something about it? The FBI does work for you, after all. It's not an independent agency. The FBI is by statute part of the Justice Department.[25] Its functions are vested in the Attorney General.[26] The president can remove its director.[27] Thus, when James Comey testified that President Trump had asked him to go easy on Michael Flynn,[28] it was not without some basis that Comey said that Trump had the legal authority to do that because, as he put it, "all of us ultimately report in the executive branch up to the president."[29] Why should these same principles of accountability not apply to a special prosecutor or independent counsel?

This is a forceful argument, tracing as it does to the Constitution's original intent to place accountability in one of three branches. But democratic accountability is not the only constitutional principle at play, and in a partially unwritten Constitution, original intent is not the only source of constitutional norms. In part as the result of Watergate, another norm has taken on great weight in recent years, even though its origins have no clear textual basis – the principle of prosecutorial independence. That principle flows from the notion that no person can be above the law, from the realization that presidential power to control the investigation and prosecution of executive wrongdoing would confer impunity on the president and his or her associates.[30] It stems from the principle that no one should be the judge of his or her own case, and from the principle of equal justice under law – for the powerful as well as the weak. These are not constitutional rules per se but nascent norms that have taken on a quasi-constitutional status. And they have breathed life into the once-improvisational ideal of prosecutorial independence.

Some managers of the national security state who have coveted bureaucratic autonomy for years but have never been willing to stand up and claim it outright welcome this emerging norm of prosecutorial independence. Of course, we can check elected officials, some now think. Why any longer be coy about it? A number of former prominent officials have very candidly stated their hope or expectation that their successors will be trying to counter Trump. Listen to the recent words of Phillip Mudd, a former top official at both the CIA and FBI:

> So, the FBI people – I'm going to tell you – are ticked, and they're going to be saying, I guarantee it, you think you could push us off this because you can try to intimidate the director, you'd better think again, Mr. President. You've been around for 13 months; we've been around since 1908. I know how this game is going to be played, and we're going to win.[31]

It is, after all, the job of the national security managers to manage – and that includes managing the president. Michael Morrell, a former acting head of the CIA, expressed worry that "the president's advisers have not been able to properly 'manage' [President Trump],"[32] he wrote in the *Washington Post*. For leaders and activists from both parties, the enemy of their enemy has become their friend. Bill Kristol has not been alone in preferring the deep state to the Trump state.[33] Senate Minority Leader Chuck Schumer said, "You take on the intelligence community, they have six ways from Sunday at getting back at you."[34] And *The New Yorker*, after predicting that the intelligence community's managers would challenge Trump before Congress, allowed that this was as it should be: "This is just the sort of thing we want to see happening" as part of "the fabled 'checks and balances' in the U.S. system."[35]

The security managers' weapon of choice has been the leak, as I point out in *Harper's*.[36] *The New York Times* reported that four current and former US officials were behind its story that Trump's campaign had had repeated contacts with senior Russian intelligence officials.[37] The *Washington Post* said that nine senior intelligence sources from multiple agencies had revealed that Trump's first national security adviser, Michael Flynn, had spoken with the Russian ambassador.[38] Later, when Trump accused President Obama of ordering the tapping of his own phones,[39] word leaked that James Comey, the FBI director, had asked the Justice Department to publicly reject Trump's assertion.[40] Add to that list Comey's own, self-acknowledged leak that Trump had suggested to him that he drop his investigation of Flynn.[41]

This tactic inevitably, of course, brings about presidential retaliation. President Trump dismisses the FBI as filled with political hacks;[42] he compares the CIA leadership to the leaders of Nazi Germany.[43] But the greater problem lies in the larger, long-term legitimacy and systemic costs of this open fight. It undermines the legitimacy of the presidency, it undercuts the legitimacy of the security managers, and it subverts the constitutional order. The constitutional structure is an interlocking whole; when one part crumbles, the entire edifice is weakened. "Laws, like houses, lean on each other,"[44] as Edmund Burke reminds us.

Checking by the security managers ultimately undercuts their own legitimacy. The security agencies' credibility rests on their electoral connection. They are deferred to, not simply because they are seen as experts but because they are seen as answerable to elected officials. Once that connection is broken, that traditional source of legitimacy vanishes. To retain credibility, the security state then needs to incubate its own free-standing legitimacy by gleaning support within the general population. That might not be hard. Fewer than 30 percent of millennials believe it is essential to live in a democracy;[45] one of every six Americans now believes it would be a good thing to have the army rule.[46]

Counterchecking by the president undermines his own legitimacy. It makes it appear as though the chief executive cannot control his own security apparatus, feeding deep state suspicions and leading to inferences that a kind of silent coup has occurred. And it detaches the presidency from the experience and expertise of a bureaucracy he needs to assure the nation that his national security decisions are based on more than whim or caprice or personal pique. It hardly bears noting that these agencies are filled with dedicated, smart, hardworking public servants who perform a critically essential job in protecting the nation from external threats that are often very real.

The political implications of this split are the least of it, however. Under the Constitution's system of separated powers, the three branches of the federal government were intended to check, and be checked by, each other – not by an unelected bureaucracy. Power has always been believed to be delegated to the bureaucracy, not by it. To institutionalize the reversal of the intended power flow would be to create a different system of government. Civil liberties and political freedom would require redefinition, for then transgressions of the reigning security managers could be checked, if at all, only by popular opinion – which the self-appointed Platonic guardians could readily manipulate. In those circumstances, the United States could no longer hope to inspire international democracy advocates anywhere; it would instead be dismissed as an example of the dangerous excesses of democracy – of the need for an undemocratic security apparatus to step in, uninvited, to curb those excesses.

I emphasize that I am referring here to the checking of policy initiatives, not law violations. Recall, for example, President Trump's decision to release the Nunes memo, for which the FBI publicly rebuked Trump;[47] or Comey's leak of Trump's alleged request to go lightly on Michael Flynn – which Comey, again, testified that he considered it to be entirely legal;[48] or Comey's reprimand of Hillary Clinton for, in his words, being "grossly negligent" in handling classified information.[49] No one appointed the FBI as the national schoolmarm. The FBI is intended to be a safeguard against law violations, not policy errors. The Constitution does establish institutions to protect elected officials from their unwise policy decisions, but the security bureaucracy is not one of them. The danger of overreaching is ever-present. Effective security agencies are of course essential in today's world, but they are required to operate within a system of democratic accountability, and we have seen how those agencies behave when they do not. The most comprehensive account appeared forty years ago, when the Church committee issued its report,[50] but its central findings are still worth recalling.

Remember COINTELPRO, the FBI's program aimed at exposing and disrupting the activities of thousands of groups and individuals, people who were engaged in constitutionally protected conduct aimed at protesting the Vietnam War or campaigning for civil rights. The FBI mailed hundreds of anonymous letters to civil rights activists; one was sent to Martin Luther King, intending to drive him to suicide. Remember OPERATION CHAOS, the CIA's own domestic spy program, and OPERATION LINGUAL, under which the CIA illegally opened and read thousands of international letters every year to and from American citizens. Remember OPERATION MINARET, under which the National Security Agency (NSA) placed 1,500 individuals on a watch list and listened in on telephone conversations with no court warrants. Remember that even the army engaged in domestic surveillance, spying on political officials, anti war and civil rights activists, and church leaders, and then sharing the information it gathered with the FBI, CIA, and local police departments.

These and other similar operations are not rare one-off pranks undertaken by some lone cowboy. These were painstakingly planned, deliberate operations in which America's most trusted security services, under the direction of their leaders and acting over a period of many years, "turned their dark arts against the very people they were created to protect," as Loch Johnson writes.[51] Their actions represent a violation of the public trust, an attempt to alter the people's form of government without the people's knowledge or consent. We need to remember how easy it is for zealots, acting in secret and freed from the restraints of accountability, to push the nation slowly and silently toward autocracy. Those who do remember will be in no hurry to trade the illiberalism of elected officials for the illiberalism of unelected security bureaucrats.[52]

As though the specter of this potential calamity were not daunting enough, it is even more sobering to realize that the tools available to forestall it are extremely limited. In past crises, defenders of the rule of law have drawn from the standard catalog of remedies provided by our legal system: lawsuits, statutory amendments, tighter standards, inspectors general, independent commissions, more special counsels, new oversight committees, executive orders, special justiciability rules, etc. Today, those remedies are largely unavailable. We cannot realistically call upon the Madisonian institutions to restore power to themselves by exercising the very power that they lack. We cannot expect those institutions, in which any reform must originate, somehow to magically acquire the muscle to force tighter restraints on resistant security managers. Nor can we expect that those managers will for some reason merrily acquiesce in tauter accountability. The forces that gave rise to the national security state are real and continue, and they cannot be wished out of existence.

Why would it be realistic to assume a future, for example, without the same public sense of continuing threat, crisis, and emergency that has nurtured the national security state in the past? Or a future in which established principles of organizational behavior now operate differently within the national security state than in other bureaucracies? Or a future in which voters elect public officials who suddenly begin to place institutional ambition over party ambition and policy ambition? Or a future in which depleted social capital is restored, one in which "pervasive civic ignorance," to use Supreme Court Justice David Souter's phrase, is replaced by intelligence and restraint and deliberation aimed at calmly and rationally trying to identify the common good?

The challenge we confront today is to figure out how to bring the national security state within our system of constitutional restraints while remaining cognizant of the momentous social and political obstacles that stand in the way. Otherwise our most finely wrought reforms will be merely "parchment barriers,"[53] in Madison's phrase – fancier institutional fencing that does not get the bull back into barn. The only other period in American history in which the political system's remedies became unavailable was in the 1860s. What President Abraham Lincoln said then is true again today:

> The dogmas of the quiet past, are inadequate to the stormy present. The occasion is piled high with difficulty, and we must rise with the occasion. As our case is new, so we must think anew, and act anew. We must disenthrall ourselves, and then we shall save our country.[54]

2

The Deep State and the Failed State: Illusions and Realities in the Pursuit of Security

John Gray

The deep state has at least two dimensions. One is the security apparatus that states claim is necessary to deal with threats to their citizens. This refers to intelligence services operating both abroad and at home, together with the armed forces that assist these institutions in their activities. A second dimension of the deep state, arguably more important, is namely the body of institutions that together keep a fixed set of policies in place, excluding them from political contestation. These policies are treated as being part of the permanent framework of government rather than political choices that can be modified or revoked. The attempt to insulate certain policies from political accountability, together with a centrist liberal ideology that underpins these policies with claims about large historical trends these policies supposedly advance, has been central to the deep state in Western countries in recent times.

References to both dimensions of the deep state are common in conspiracy theories that flourish on the far left and right, which assert that it shapes politics in covert ways. Here, the deep state is regarded as being more influential than the rival parties that compete for voters' support in democratic elections. Recently, centrist liberals have displayed more positive attitudes toward the intelligence services and the military, particularly in the United States, where they have been perceived as a counterweight to the Trump administration. Far from posing a threat to liberal values, as generations of liberals used to believe, the deep state has now been embraced by some centrist liberals as a guardian and protector of their values.

A different view is more plausible. Those who regard the deep state as a sinister force and those who view it as a protection against the excesses of populist governments are both overestimating its power. Instead of controlling the range of political choice, the deep state has watched powerless as policies it has long endorsed have been swept aside. Far from shaping the course of events, it has been overwhelmed by them.

A major reason for the fragility of the deep state has been its adherence to an ideology, formulated in hyperbolic terms by Francis Fukuyama at the end of the Cold War, in which the end point of political development throughout the world is the proliferation of political systems akin to those that then existed in the United States and other Western countries. This ideology underpins the view, embedded in the foreign policy establishments of many Western countries, according to which liberal democracies have a responsibility to spread their values by a variety of means including militarily imposed regime change. Though been shaken by a record of consistent failure in Afghanistan, Iraq, and Libya, this view remains the predominant one among professional analysts, opinion formers, and mainstream politicians. In effect, this version of liberal ideology has been an integral feature of the state since the end of the Cold War. Another example of this second dimension of the deep state has been policies on immigration. A consensus among economists and politicians has long asserted that immigration is necessary or beneficial to the recipient societies. Popular opinion has been more skeptical and focused on the potentially disruptive impacts. The tendency among centrist liberals has been to dismiss or belittle these concerns as expressions of ignorance or racism. In fact, they have reflected a wide range of concerns, not only about immigration but also about the impact of globalization, widening inequalities, and adverse effects on the majority of the population of environmental policies that increase the cost of energy. In many European countries, the revulsion against continuing large-scale immigration has resulted in the collapse of the political center as an effective force and the rise of populist parties, some of which are now in government.

With established political classes failing to respond to the concerns of large sections of the population, varieties of populism have spread across much of the continent. Italy is ruled by a coalition, one part of which – Matteo Salvini's Liga – has clear links with interwar fascism. Hungary, Poland, and the Czech Republic are governed by anti-immigrant parties. The rise of the far-right Sweden Democrats is a major factor in the political paralysis of the country following the 2018 elections. In Spain, Vox – the first far-right party to win in a democratic election since the end of the fascist Franco regime in 1975 – won twelve seats in the Andalusian election in December 2018, a result that enabled the party to exercise a potentially decisive influence on the shape of the next regional government. In France, centrist liberals greeted Emmanuel Macron's ascension to the presidency as marking a reversal of the populist advance, but the popularity of Macron's government has slumped. He has been forced to abandon sections of his program of neoliberal reform by the rise of the *gilets jaunes*, or yellow jackets, an amorphous protest movement triggered by rising fuel prices. Perhaps most strikingly, the far-right AfD (Alternative for Germany) has broken through the electoral barriers that were erected in Germany after World War II to prevent extremist parties entering democratic politics. During the 2017 federal elections, the party won ninety-four seats in the Bundestag, where hitherto it had none, becoming the third-largest party in Germany. The attempts to insulate free movement from politics have failed, thus energizing far-right parties in many countries.

Political resistance to continuing mass immigration has unfolded against a background in which free movement of people is one of the fundamental pillars of the European Union. The 1990 Schengen Agreement abolished internal border checks. (Margaret Thatcher secured an opt-out from the Agreement, and Britain has never been part of the Schengen Zone.) The removal of national borders was meant to be an integral part of European institutions, immune to challenge by national governments. But free movement could not be removed from politics in this way. In virtually all European countries, immigration has become a pivotal factor in politics.

Centrist liberals point out that political resistance to immigration conflates several types of migrants – those fleeing war and persecution and those seeking better economic opportunities, for example. Also, there is a difference between resisting inflows of migrants from outside Europe and supporting the reerecting of national borders within Europe. In practice, however, these distinctions are bound to be blurred. Since Europe's perimeters are porous, resistance to immigration has focused on reinstalling national controls – as has been the case in Germany, where even Angela Merkel has suggested instituting border checks. Equally, the distinction between refugees fleeing violence and migrants seeking economic opportunities is less than useful in current conditions. When entire populations have been damaged by war, economic collapse, environmental devastation, and the disintegration of the state, large numbers will try to escape to safer lands. This presents a problem for which liberal democracies have found no solution. When centrist liberals attempt to resist restrictive immigration policies, as Angela Merkel originally did, the result has been to fuel right-wing parties. Political blowback has left the deep state consensus practically powerless.

Here, a neglected feature of the deep state needs to be noted. The migrant crisis and the project of promoting democracy by regime change are interlinked. For those who believe that only liberal democracy can be popularly legitimate, overthrowing tyranny by militarily enforced regime change seems clearly to be a desirable goal. But the most predictable effect has been the creation of failed states, and one of the side effects has been increased flows of migrants. The destruction of any functioning state in Libya, more complete even than in Iraq, has left the country a zone of anarchy fought over by dozens of jihadist groups. Through that ungoverned zone have passed many of the migrants that have ended up in Italy and other European countries. Rather than refugees escaping dictatorial states, these are migrants fleeing states that Western military intervention has destroyed. Salvini's Liga and other rising far-right parties are the political beneficiaries of liberal policies of regime change.

The centrist strategy in the post–Cold War period has been to entrench their policies and values in institutions they believe to be invulnerable to political contestation. Over the past decade, this strategy has shown many signs of foundering. Populist parties, mostly but not entirely of the far right, have continued their advance. Populism is a murky concept, with no generally accepted meaning. But in one of its applications, populism denotes an attempt to repoliticize issues that have been effectively depoliticized. That is part of what happened in Britain during the Brexit referendum. Even though the United Kingdom is outside the Schengen Treaty, successive British governments implemented a centrist consensus on immigration. The benefits of mass immigration were large and obvious, they believed; the costs slight and often disputable. A large section of the electorate did not accept this supposedly self-evident truth. While liberals celebrated increased diversity, they feared diminishing social cohesion, depressing effects on wage levels, and increasing demands on stretched social services.

Centrists like to think of populism as an aberration, which will eventually be followed by a restoration of liberal normalcy. Those who think in this way have not grasped the causes of populist movements. If populism is from one angle an attempt to widen the range of political choices beyond what the deep state has embodied, from another it is a response to the deep state's serial incompetence. The record of American-led military interventions is an obvious case in point. To describe these interventions as ruinous is an understatement. Certainly, they have been enormously expensive, their costs running into the trillions of dollars. They have also been extremely prolonged – in the case of Afghanistan, extending to nearly two decades. At the same time, the purposes these interventions served have always been unclear. Had the goal been to bring democracy to the countries that were invaded? Or to develop them socially – by advancing the rights of Afghan women, for example? Had it been to prosecute a "war against terror," and thereby – it was believed – to enhance Western security? Or had the objective been more specific – to eliminate weapons of mass destruction that were supposedly being developed? If there had been several goals, what were the priorities among them?

To represent these interventions as failures gives them too much credit. By having no definite goals, they could not even fail. The succession of "wars of choice" launched under Western auspices from 9/11 onward has lacked the most basic prerequisite of rational policymaking – an intelligible relationship between means and ends. These wars are better understood as expressions of the bafflement of the deep state when confronted by forces it did not understand, together with its struggle to preserve itself in the face of repeated defeats. In this last regard, the shifting goals of successive interventions did serve a coherent strategy – that of institutional survival. Like any other publicly funded organization, the security state needed to support its continuing claim on resources. The succession of objectives its activities allegedly promoted served this purpose.

But it was a strategy that would prove damaging, even self-defeating, over the medium term of a decade or so. One of the results has been popular disbelief not only in the competence but also in the trustworthiness of government. Disinformation connected with the intervention in Iraq has had an extremely corrosive effect. If the era of fake news has a discernible beginning, it is not with Donald Trump. Rather, fake news started with the manufactured intelligence findings and a "dodgy dossier" that preceded the launch of the invasion by the United States and the United Kingdom.

There are thus some obvious questions about national security institutions that need to be addressed. Are they entrenched bureaucracies that invent new goals in order to justify their existence, or do they respond to enduring needs in society? (They may of course be both.) Should deep states focus primarily on threats to security that emanate from terrorism, or from those that come with intensifying geopolitical competition with other states? Are China and Russia more dangerous to Western liberal democracy than ISIS?

Framing the issue in this way may be misleading, however. Similar in some respects, China and Russia are very different in others. Neither is a liberal democracy, and neither will become one in any foreseeable future. Grandiose theories of history that postulate the eventual convergence of China and Russia to a Western model overlook the fact that this model has morphed out of shape. The "democratic capitalism" that seemed to have triumphed at the end of the Cold War hardly exists as a functioning system. Instead, the future of Western economies depends heavily on China. The impact on Western capitalism of any crisis in the country would be unfathomable. The country faces major problems: The slowing of economic growth, the amassing of vast levels of debt, the rapid aging of the population, and the growing danger of the populist movements of the West could be replicated in a Chinese working-class insurrection. But these fragilities offer no comfort to the West, since unrest in China would increase the fragility of Western political systems as well. Rising unemployment and sliding living standards could only work to fuel the further rise of extremist parties. One of the ironies of the present time is that the future of what remains of liberal democracy may well depend on the continuing stability and economic success of Xi Jinping's authoritarian regime.

This fact points to a radical difference between China and Russia. China is an economic colossus with advancing technologies in many fields and assets spread across the globe, while Russia has a small and shrinking economy reliant on declining extractive industries, with impressive technological advances concentrated in the military sector. More fundamentally, China and Russia embody divergent responses to Western power.

In many of Xi's statements he has stressed the uniqueness and longevity of Chinese civilization and represented his regime as reasserting that civilization in a world shaped over the past few centuries by the West. Yet in some ways China has actively embraced Western ideas and methods of government – not contemporary Western ideas of rights or democracy, but those of an illiberal West that celebrated enlightened despotism. The high-tech surveillance state that Xi is building echoes the all-seeing Panopticon, an ideal prison devised by the early nineteenth-century British Utilitarian thinker Jeremy Bentham and intended by him as a model of a maximally efficient society. (Bentham's younger brother Samuel planned to install a version of the Panopticon in factories in the Russia of Catherine the Great.) Using this model as a basis for penal and social policies, Xi – like Bentham's British disciples – aims to improve the behavior of China's citizens, isolating and reeducating disruptive elements while keeping the entire population under continuous monitoring. The preeminent contemporary example of authoritarian Enlightenment rationalism, Xi's China has applied a way of thinking that originates in the illiberal West.

In contrast, Putin's Russia embodies a counter-Enlightenment project – the vision of a separate civilization founded in Orthodox Christianity, which has haunted the country for centuries and found disciples in writers such as Fyodor Dostoevsky and Aleksandr Solzhenitsyn. Vladimir Putin's assertions that Russia is a "Eurasian" power standing between east and west draws on a long Russian tradition. To be sure, it would be a mistake to take the Russian leader's professions too literally. He is appropriating an anti-Western strand in Russian thinking for his own political purposes. At an earlier stage in his career, Putin was keen to appear as a European modernizer. Moreover, Putin's regime itself owes something to Western thinking. The method of ruling by fear and disinformation that the regime employs and its belief that politics is a form of war are legacies of Bolshevism, which Lenin always believed continued the European tradition of Jacobinism. Even so, Russia under Putin has tilted away from emulating anything like a Western model of government. Neither the longer history of the country nor its current condition suggests that it will pursue a Western path of development. The end point of that path – a well-functioning liberal democratic state, backed up by a stable market economy – has mutated into the divided and floundering Western polities of today. Rather than the end point of history, "democratic capitalism" looks more like a phase of development whose time has passed.

In other words, Frances Fukuyama got things exactly wrong. Writing in October 1989 in response to Fukuyama's original essay "The End of History?" that was published in the summer of that year, I argued that the fall of communism inaugurated a resumption of history in the most traditional sense:

> All the evidence suggests that we are now moving back into an epoch that is classically historical, and not forward into the empty, hallucinatory post-historical era projected in Fukuyama's article. Ours is an era in which political ideology, liberal as much as Marxist, has a rapidly dwindling leverage on events, and more ancient, more primordial forces, nationalist and religious, fundamentalist and soon, perhaps, Malthusian, are contesting with one another. ... If the Soviet Union does indeed fall apart, that beneficent catastrophe will not inaugurate a new era of post-historical harmony, but instead a return to the classical terrain of history, a terrain of great-power rivalries, secret diplomacies and irredentist claims and wars.[1]

In this early formulation, I suggested that with the fall of communism the international system would return to a multipolar or non polar order of the kind that existed before World War I. There would be differences, of course. China and India, which were subordinated to Western power before 1914, would themselves be great powers.

Despite the ambitions of European federalists, Europe would be a bit-player. America would remain pivotal, but it would be nothing like the solitary hyper-power imagined by triumphalist neo-conservatives in the febrile years immediately after the Soviet collapse. I missed some important developments. Although I noted that "the waning of the Soviet system is bound to be accompanied by a waxing of ethnic and nationalist conflicts – just the sort of stuff history has always been made of"[2] – I failed to anticipate the rapid reemergence of Russia as a global player with a powerful presence in the Middle East. Even so, the international system of today is more like what existed pre-1914 than at any time in the second half of the twentieth century.

A key feature of this system is that it is Hobbesian anarchy. By lacking any sovereign power, it also lacks enforceable norms. The ongoing decomposition of the "rule-based" international order that, despite many gray zones and rough edges, has prevailed since the end of World War II is a consequence of this fact. In some ways the emerging anarchy looks more unrestrained than that which existed pre-1914. It is hard to think of precedents from that era for the Salisbury poisonings[3] or the murder and dismemberment of the Saudi journalist Jamal Khashoggi. If we think we live in a more modern world than that which existed before World War I, then we must recognize that we also live in one in which extremes of violence are more common. Despite invoking a mythical past, few contemporary movements are as unequivocally modern as Al-Qaeda and its successor ISIS, which has explicitly adopted violence of the most savage kind as a method of expanding and consolidating its power.[4]

The weakness of the deep state has been demonstrated in the recurrent disasters of regime change and in the deep state's inability to resist populist challenges to its domestic policies. Lying behind both is an intellectual failure. Large-scale institutional defaults are rarely the consequences of theoretical errors. Contingent events, sometimes wholly accidental, are more often crucial. In the case of the deep state since the end of the Cold War, however, a plausible argument can be mounted that its repeated setbacks have been rooted in the ideology that has guided it. Not only has American power been consistently overestimated, but it has also been seen as exemplifying grand historical trends that are much exaggerated, or else fictitious.

How often has it been claimed that the rising middle classes that come with sustained economic growth demand liberal freedoms? On this basis, Xi's authoritarianism is bound to fail. The trouble is that the evidence on this point is at best patchy. The middle classes may have embraced liberal values when they emerged in Europe in the early nineteenth century, as Karl Marx observed. Throughout much of the first half of the twentieth century, on the other hand, large numbers in Europe's middle classes threw in their lot with many kinds of authoritarianism, including fascism. Today, many are strong supporters of populist regimes. This is true not only in Europe but also in the United States, where President Trump's supporters range from the despairing proles of the post industrial rust belt to large sections of the precarious middle classes.

Another strand of deep state ideology asserts that liberal freedoms are required for ongoing economic innovation. Without the incentives of an open market economy, it is claimed, new technologies will not be developed and economic growth will suffer. This may have been true when the alternative to market capitalism was Soviet-style central planning, but in a longer historical perspective it is plainly mistaken. Meiji Japan, Bismarck's Germany, and Tsarist Russia all achieved high levels of economic growth in the nineteenth and early twentieth centuries, while the Hapsburg Empire was an outstanding exemplar of technological innovation. None of them could be described as liberal states.

The belief that an authoritarian regime is bound to lag liberal societies in regard to technological advance is not a falsifiable hypothesis but an act of faith. The origins of this faith are in classical economics – a system of ideas springing from the Enlightenment that asserts a universal link between economic growth and liberal freedoms. Yet one of the greatest thinkers of the Enlightenment was closer to the contingencies of history when he noted that this was a theory falsified by the example of eighteenth-century French absolutism, which presided over a long period of growth in knowledge and wealth. As David Hume put it: "The subjects of an absolute prince may become our rivals in commerce as well as learning."[5] Today this applies to Xi's China, which appears to be leapfrogging the West in many areas of science and technology. Why should China's advance in these areas not continue and even accelerate?

The answer of those who hold to deep state ideology usually involves some reference to stages of economic development. Authoritarian systems may work when the rudiments of an industrial economy are being laid down, it is said, but they do not enable the kind of continuous innovation that is found in developed market economies. This is to beg the question. The idea that economies everywhere must pass through a set of stages terminating in market capitalism is an intellectual relic of Western global hegemony. The world today contains many economies that do not fit into any of the stages identified in Western theories of development. China's economy is a variety of state capitalism, in which markets are not suppressed as they were in the Soviet system and under Maoism but are harnessed to promote politically determined objectives. Why would China renounce this system when it has worked well for them? After all, a large part of the reduction in world poverty that has occurred over the past generation is owed to China. So are an increasing number of cutting-edge technologies. Given this record, the notion that the country would abandon its economic model – which seems to be the ultimate objective of Trump's trade war – is far-fetched in the extreme.

The idea of the deep state encourages many kinds of illusion. One is the belief that deep states can orchestrate the pattern of events, when in fact they are often overwhelmed by them. Another is the belief that the deep state can project a preferred type of polity throughout the world, when that type of polity is morphing out of existence in its countries of origin. Underlying these illusions is the most disabling illusion of all – the ideology that has informed the deep states of Western countries in the period since the end of the Cold War, which asserts a universal process of human development terminating in "democratic capitalism." Originating in secular variations on ideas drawn from Western religion rather than any genuine social science, this system of ideas has repeatedly led the deep states of Western countries into disastrous and self-defeating adventures.[6]

Of course, the deep state is not a peculiarly Western institution. Because of the centrality of former KGB personnel in its ruling elite, Putin's Russia has been described as "an intelligence state." Xi's China has an intelligence apparatus that penetrates every strategically important area of the economy and in one form or another extends its reach throughout the world. These deep states have several advantages over their Western rivals. For one thing, they are not subject to any forms of democratic accountability. More importantly, they are not guided by any ideology of the kind that informs their Western competitors. They may also believe that Western civilization is in long-term decline. To this extent, the deep states of Russia and China can be regarded as instruments of civilization polities – that is to say, political systems that claim to represent a particular civilization, distinct and separate from the rest.

Western deep states have regarded the liberal institutions set in place after World War II as permanent features of the international system, which over time will evolve into a universal order. In contrast, non-Western deep states appear to regard the liberal international order as no more than a power structure, imposed to serve interests and values that are not and never will be universally accepted. Viewing the rivalries of great powers through the lens of civilizational conflict is a stance well suited to an increasingly pluralistic and fragmented world, where common rules are treated as truces in an ongoing Hobbesian struggle.

The mistake of those who fear the deep state is to think of it as an institution that controls the agenda of politics. Liberals that have lately come to see the deep state as a curb on populism make the same error. In the West the deep state embodies a liberal order that is palpably challenged and most likely ending. The deep states of non-Western polities may be better adapted to the anarchic world that is emerging. But both are subject to the shifting forces of politics, which they can neither shape nor escape for long.

3

A Tale of Two Countries: Fundamental Rights in the "War on Terror"

Douglass Cassel

The United States and the United Kingdom are, generally speaking, free societies – despite significant shortcomings in aspects of civil and political rights.[1]

TORTURE: A TELLING EXAMPLE

"It was one of the most shaming, self-abasing apologies ever made in the House of Commons, indeed arguably in any western legislature."[2]

On May 10, 2018, British Attorney General Jeremy Wright read out Prime Minister Theresa May's public apology to Abdel Hakim Belhaj and his wife, Fatima Boudchar. A Libyan dissident, Belhaj had been imprisoned and tortured by the regime of dictator Muammar Gaddafi for six years.

Britain had been complicit in the extraordinary rendition, arbitrary detention, and torture of the couple. The prime minister spoke the following:

> On behalf of her majesty's government, I apologise unreservedly. We are profoundly sorry for the ordeal that you both suffered and our role in it. The UK government has learned many lessons from this period. . . . [W]hat happened to you is deeply troubling. It is clear that you were both subjected to appalling treatment and that you suffered greatly, not least the affront to the dignity of Mrs Boudchar who was pregnant at the time. [Mrs. Boudchar said she was hung from hooks and punched in her womb while in CIA custody] We should have understood much sooner, the unacceptable practices of some of our international partners. And we sincerely regret our failures . . . . We shared information about you . . . [and] we should have done more to reduce the risk that you would be mistreated. We accept this was a failing on our part. Later, during your detention in Libya, we sought information about and from you. We wrongly missed opportunities to alleviate your plight: this should not have happened.

In 2004, the government of Prime Minister Tony Blair had informed the CIA of the whereabouts of the couple. After abducting them from an airport in Malaysia, the CIA spirited them to a secret detention center in Thailand, where they were both brutalized, and then "rendered" them to Libya. Once there, from her separate cell, Boudchar could hear the screams of her husband being tortured. British agents were allegedly present at some torture sessions; they hoped to gain information about Al-Qaeda, to which Belhaj was linked.

In 2018, years of litigation by the family against the United Kingdom finally produced, first, a court order requiring the British government to turn over secret MI6 files on their extraordinary rendition[3] and, second, a settlement in which Belhaj received the prime minister's apology – all he asked for – and his wife was given £500,000.[4]

But what about the United States? If Britain colluded in the extraordinary rendition of the couple to Libya – and its foreseeably grisly consequences – the CIA actually carried out the operation. Would the US government apologize? Would the United States, too, learn from the incident?

Tory MP Andrew Mitchell, a member of Parliament's all-party group on extraordinary rendition, sounded hopeful. He called for the UK government to pass on details of the Belhaj file to US officials who were then examining the conduct of Gina Haspel, recently nominated by President Donald Trump to head the CIA.

"It's important that the attorney general hands his opposite number in Washington the details of this case," said Mitchell. "The next head of the CIA is currently going through an inquiry process. She was in charge of a black site in Thailand where this poor lady [Boudchar] was held."

Haspel had been in charge of the CIA black site in Thailand when, in late 2002, at least one detainee was tortured by waterboarding, and videotapes of the torture of another were erased. But one week after the British government's public apology for torture, the US Senate, by a vote of 54–45 on Haspel's nomination, confirmed a person implicated in torture to run the CIA.

The foregoing is only one illustration of a broader difference in culture, values, and law between Britain and its former colony across the Atlantic. During the post-2001 war on terror, Britain has not generally engaged in torture, extraordinary rendition, or prolonged arbitrary detention.

Instead Britain colluded – but generally only colluded – with American (and in this case Libyan) affronts to human rights. A June 2018 report on *Detainee Mistreatment and Rendition: 2001–2010*, by the Intelligence and Security Committee (ISC) of Parliament,[5] uncovered what the all-party parliamentary group on extraordinary rendition calls "shocking levels of UK complicity in rendition and torture."[6] As summarized by the all-party group, the ISC found:

- Thirteen incidents where UK personnel witnessed firsthand a detainee being mistreated by others.
- Twenty-five incidents where UK personnel were told by detainees that they had been mistreated by others.

- One hundred twenty-eight incidents where agency officers were told by foreign liaison services about instances of mistreatment.
- Two hundred thirty-two cases where UK personnel continued to supply questions or intelligence to liaison services after they knew or suspected mistreatment, and 198 cases where UK personnel received intelligence from liaison services which had been obtained from detainees whom they knew had been mistreated.
- Over seventy cases of UK involvement in rendition.[7]

More information may yet come out; at this writing, the all-party parliamentary group and others are calling for a "judge-led inquiry" into the matter.[8]

Comparably detailed breakdowns are not available for the United States. But a 2014 report by the Senate Select Committee on Intelligence confirms that the CIA used "enhanced interrogation techniques" on at least thirty-nine detainees between 2002 and 2007.[9] The committee rightly described these CIA interrogation techniques as "brutal."[10] Applied with "significant repetition for days or weeks at a time," and in combination, they included, among others, slamming detainees against walls, waterboarding, and sleep deprivation for up to 180 hours, inflicted on detainees "usually standing or in stress positions, at times with their hands shackled above their heads."[11] Especially in combination, such techniques violate the United Nations Convention against Torture.[12]

As later acknowledged by President Obama: "[W]hen we engaged in some of these enhanced interrogation techniques, techniques that I believe and I think any fair-minded person would believe were torture, we crossed a line."[13] In particular, US Attorney General Eric Holder recognized in 2009 that "waterboarding is torture."[14] Unlike Britain, then, the United States did not just collude in torture, it engaged in it.

In the Belhaj case – albeit only after losing court battles and following several changes of government – Her Majesty's Government ultimately confessed to collusion, delivered a public apology, and agreed to a substantial financial settlement. By contrast, the United States did not confess, apologize, or compensate the victims. Instead, Washington elevated a key perpetrator to the top of the CIA.

The point here is neither to praise the Brits (faintly) nor to condemn the Yanks (although condemnation is in order). Rather, the point is to highlight the difference in behavior between the two nations and then to explore this question: Why the difference?

If their differing approaches were evident only in the case of Belhaj and Boudchar, or even only in regard to torture, perhaps the contrast between London and Washington could be written off as episodic or random. In fact, however, in regard to several of the worst forms of human rights abuses in counterterrorism – torture, extraordinary renditions, detention without charge or trial, incommunicado detention, secret detention centers, and military commission trials – the United Kingdom has been systematically and consistently less abusive – albeit collusive – than the United States.

Why should this be? Compared to much of the world, both countries are rule-of-law democracies. If anything, one might expect the United States to do as well or better than the United Kingdom. After all, the United States has a written constitution and Bill of Rights. The United Kingdom has only an unwritten constitution. The United States invented constitutional review by an independent judiciary two centuries ago while courts in the United Kingdom are subject to parliamentary supremacy. Yet, both the law and the courts do a better job in the United Kingdom than in the United States when it comes to protecting fundamental rights in twenty-first-century counterterrorism activities.

One might be tempted to blame the difference on President Donald Trump, whose principal publicly stated objection to US torture of Al-Qaeda suspects was that it was not harsh enough.[15] News accounts report that only the opposition of Defense Secretary (and retired General) James Mattis stood between Trump and a resumption of US torture practices.[16]

But (in this context) Trump is merely an aggravation. The difference between British and American counterterrorism policies after 2001 arose and persisted well before he entered the White House. Something more systematic than a single personality must be at play.

EXTRAORDINARY RENDITIONS

Extraordinary rendition is a euphemism for extralegal, secret, governmental kidnapping of a person from one country to another. It often ends in torture, secret and incommunicado detention, or at least cruel, inhuman, or degrading conditions of detention. It often fits the UN treaty definition of "enforced disappearance," namely

> the arrest, detention, abduction or any other form of deprivation of liberty by agents
> of the State or by persons or groups of persons acting with the authorization, support
> or acquiescence of the State, followed by a refusal to acknowledge the deprivation of
> liberty or by concealment of the fate or whereabouts of the disappeared person,
> which place such a person outside the protection of the law.[17]

In 1999 a British Court of Appeal found that the rendition of a person from Zimbabwe to the United Kingdom to stand trial on terrorism charges, bypassing extradition procedures, was a "blatant and extremely serious failure to adhere to the rule of law" and an "abuse of process."[18] UK government policy since then "has been not to undertake such renditions to the UK."[19]

However, "that policy did not extend to involvement in renditions carried out by others."[20] The United Kingdom supported US extraordinary renditions in post-2001 counterterrorism operations by financing, facilitating, and endorsing renditions; by providing intelligence to enable renditions; and by failing to take actions to prevent renditions.[21]

In contrast, the United States actually carried out extraordinary renditions. Most of the more than one hundred prisoners held at CIA black sites, and of the more than seven hundred detainees held at Guantánamo over the years, were brought there by means of extraordinary rendition.[22]

DETENTION WITHOUT CHARGE OR TRIAL

The United Kingdom is also less tolerant of prolonged detention without charge or trial. From 2001 to 2004 Britain's Home Secretary was authorized to detain indefinitely, without charge or trial, foreign nationals he reasonably suspected of terrorism, if no other suitable country was willing to take them. In 2004 the Law Lords, acting under the Human Rights Act, ruled that such detention was a disproportionate and discriminatory restriction on the right to liberty under the European Convention on Human Rights.[23] Since then, suspected terrorists may be held in the United Kingdom for periods of no more than fourteen days, or twenty-eight days in "urgent" cases, before being charged with a crime.[24]

Even in occupied, postwar Iraq, where the British occupiers acted pursuant to a UN Security Council resolution authorizing internment where necessary for imperative reasons of security, the Law Lords were uncomfortable in a case where a British citizen was interned for three years without charge.[25] Although holding that the Security Council resolution prevailed over the right to liberty granted by the European Convention on Human Rights, the Lords looked for safeguards. In the words of Lord Robert Carswell,

> where a State can lawfully intern people, it is important that it adopt certain safeguards: the compilation of intelligence about such persons which is as accurate and reliable as possible, the regular review of the continuing need to detain each person and a system whereby that need and the underlying evidence can be checked and challenged by representatives on behalf of the detained persons, so far as is practicable and consistent with the needs of national security and the safety of other persons.[26]

The Grand Chamber of the European Court of Human Rights later held that the Security Council resolution merely authorized, but did not require, indefinite internment without charge. Hence, the United Kingdom's three-year internment of its citizen violated his right to liberty.[27]

It is understandable that the European Court – mandated to enforce human rights – might take a narrower view of the intent of a UN Security Council resolution than did the highest court of the United Kingdom, a permanent member of the Security Council. Yet neither court – British or European – thought an internment of three years without charge was compatible with the human right to liberty. If the indefinite detentions of prisoners without charge or trial by the United States at Guantánamo – some now lasting more than 15 years – had come before the Law Lords, it is difficult to imagine that they would uphold them.[28]

The gulf between British and American judicial tolerance of prolonged arbitrary detention of suspected terrorists was made clear as early as 2002, the year Guantánamo opened for business in the war against terror. At that point the Bush administration was holding detainees at Guantánamo, not only without charge or trial but also without access to lawyers, judges, or habeas corpus (judicial review of the lawfulness of a detention). Senior British judges were appalled. Writing for the UK Court of Appeal in a case brought on behalf of Feroz Ali Abbasi, a British citizen held at Guantánamo, Lord Nick Phillips, Master of the Rolls, wrote that "in apparent contravention of fundamental principles recognized by both jurisdictions [the US and the UK] and by international law, Mr. Abbasi is at present arbitrarily detained in a 'legal black hole.'"[29]

Two years later, the US Supreme Court – over dissents by three of the nine justices – ruled that prisoners at Guantánamo are entitled to habeas corpus, in other words, to judicial review of the lawfulness of their detentions.[30] It took four more years and two more Supreme Court judgments to overcome presidential and congressional resistance to ensure this basic right.[31] Even then, in subsequent years, federal judges have been so deferential to executive branch determinations that habeas petitions rarely free prisoners, even when the evidentiary basis for holding them is dubious at best.[32]

As of October 2018, of the forty prisoners reportedly remaining at Guantánamo, twenty-six are still being held indefinitely without charge or trial.[33]

INCOMMUNICADO DETENTION

British law and practice do not allow prolonged incommunicado detention. Even before the Law Lords ruled in 2004 against indefinite detention of suspected foreign terrorists at Belmarsh prison, the detainees could appeal to a quasi-judicial panel, could request and obtain release on bail, and could seek subsequent judicial review. Their detention was subject to periodic administrative review and parliamentary oversight.[34] As Baroness Hale pointedly observed, "Belmarsh is not the British Guantánamo Bay."[35]

Still, a standard of "not Guantánamo" was not good enough, either for Baroness Hale or for other Law Lords. Review of Belmarsh detentions by the Special Immigration Appeals Commission was quite limited, procedurally and substantively. Britain must do better: "We have always taken it for granted in this country that we cannot be locked up indefinitely without trial or explanation."[36]

For the CIA, on the other hand, the Guantánamo standard was too good for its "high value" detainees. At Guantánamo, the identities of prisoners would have to be disclosed to the International Committee of the Red Cross.[37] In addition, the CIA would risk "possible loss of control to the US military and/or FBI"[38] (which preferred to use rapport-building interrogation techniques).[39] At CIA black sites, the identities of detainees would not have to be revealed to anyone outside the US government. Abd al-Rahim al-Nashiri and Khalid Sheikh Mohammed, for example, were detained incommunicado in black sites for more than three years.[40] Detainees could also be kept in complete isolation. Abu Zubaydah was at one point kept in isolation for 47 days straight.[41]

SECRET DETENTION CENTERS

So far as is known, Britain does not operate secret prisons – black sites – for detention and interrogation of suspected terrorists (although there are past reports of a black site and renditions operations on a military base leased by the United Kingdom to the United States on the island of Diego Garcia in the Indian Ocean).[42]

By contrast, the CIA has operated black sites in the past and could potentially open them again. In 2006 President George W. Bush acknowledged the existence of secret CIA detention sites and, at the same time, announced the transfer of the last remaining fourteen CIA detainees to military custody at Guantánamo.[43] However, he ambiguously left the door open: "The current transfers mean that there are now no terrorists in the CIA program. But as more high-ranking terrorists are captured, the need to obtain intelligence from them will remain critical – and having a CIA program for questioning terrorists will continue to be crucial to getting life-saving information."[44]

In 2009 President Barack Obama closed this door, by issuing an executive order barring all CIA detention sites.[45] Eight years later, however, a draft executive order presented to President Trump seemed to open it again. The draft would have revoked the Obama order and reportedly "would clear the way for the C.I.A. to reopen overseas 'black site' prisons."[46] In fact, the Trump order actually adopted in 2018 did not take this step, but it left the door ajar by directing federal agencies to "recommend policies to the President regarding the disposition of individuals captured in connection with an armed conflict."[47]

MILITARY COMMISSION TRIALS

US trials of Guantánamo detainees by military commissions, first authorized by an executive order in 2001,[48] continue as of December 2018, seemingly mired in endless chaos.[49]

Senior British jurists have long taken a dim view of the US military commission trials. In 2003 Law Lord Johan Steyn minced no words in denouncing a "kangaroo court" whose trials implied "a pre-ordained arbitrary rush to judgment by an irregular tribunal, which makes a mockery of justice. ... The only thing that could be worse is simply to leave the prisoners in their black hole indefinitely."[50]

In 2004 the UK government successfully negotiated the release of five British detainees facing military commission trials at Guantánamo. The day following their arrival in Britain, police prosecutors freed them all without charge.[51]

WHY THE DIFFERENCE?

Across a range of serious human rights violations – including torture, extraordinary renditions, prolonged detention without charge or trial, incommunicado detention, secret prisons, and military commission trials – British counterterrorism practices since 2001 are more defensible than those of their American cousins. Why?

Some plausible explanations are, admittedly, accidental. One turns on the person and party occupying the White House at a given moment. Suppose Al Gore had been declared winner of the 2000 presidential election. When the twin towers fell on September 11, 2001, would he personally, and the Democrats, have been as prone to pursue a no-holds-barred war on terror as were George Bush (the incurious) and the Republicans?

Location is another: What if the massive 9/11 attack in New York had occurred in London instead? Would the British public have given Tony Blair the same blank check – please keep us safe at any cost – that a majority of the American public handed to George W. Bush following the attack?

There is no doubt an element of truth in these coincidental explanations. Even so, the divergences in the British and American approaches since 2001 have been so consistent, dramatic, and long-lasting, across the gamut of counterterrorism techniques, that there are likely more complete and compelling reasons why two rule-of-law democracies, both purportedly committed to human rights, and both steeped in the common law, follow such different anti-terrorism rule books.

To explore the underlying reasons, one relevant perspective is a comparative law approach. Upon examination, it turns out that the combination of federalism, common-law jurisdiction, constitutionalism, the manner in which human rights treaties are domesticated, submission to a regional human rights court, and the role and remedies granted to domestic courts in implementing human rights treaties collectively distinguish the British and American legal systems in ways that suggest very different outcomes.

Another viewpoint is historical and geopolitical. The differences in law between the two countries arise from context, including their respective regional and global relations and standing, past and present.

A third perspective views the two together and comes up with more than the sum of their parts. Over time, legal forms and power realities shape collective cultures. Internalized values and priorities become a force on their own.

LEGAL DIFFERENCES

1 *Federalism and the Common Law*

Despite recent partial devolutions, the United Kingdom has been a unitary state for three centuries whereas the United States was born, of political necessity, as a federal state.

For purposes of their approaches to counterterrorism, this difference did not matter until the twentieth century. In 1938, the US Supreme Court ruled that federal courts could no longer create general federal common law.[52] Technically, the ruling applied only in cases in which federal jurisdiction was based on diversity of citizenship, and even then, only to claims based on state law. But the judicial impact was sweeping: The role and mindset of federal judges was no longer to create or discover evolving legal norms. Except in a few discrete areas,[53] US federal judges ceased to be common-law judges.

By contrast, British judges are not constrained by federalism concerns. They remain common-law judges in the traditional sense. This has two crucial effects on human rights issues arising in twenty-first-century counterterrorism cases.

First, British courts have centuries of judge-made common law on which to draw in order to condemn outrages such as torture and prolonged arbitrary detention. This sets them apart from their American counterparts. The US Supreme Court would not feel free to decide cases on the basis of the reasoning of Lord Donald Nicholls: "Torture is not acceptable. This is a bedrock moral principle in this country. For centuries the common law has set its face against torture."[54] Or of Lord Tom Bingham:

> In urging the fundamental importance of the right to personal freedom, ... the appellants were able to draw on the long libertarian tradition of English law, dating back to chapter 39 of Magna Carta 1215, given effect in the ancient remedy of habeas corpus, declared in the Petition of Right 1628, upheld in a series of landmark decisions down the centuries and embodied in the substance and procedure of the law to our own day.[55]

Second, customary international law is part of the common law.[56] British courts can and do draw on international human rights norms to inform their rulings on the common law. In excluding evidence obtained by torture, for example, Lord David Hope noted that Article 15 of the UN Convention against Torture, which bars the use in legal proceedings of statements obtained by torture, had not been incorporated into English law by statute. Still, he continued,

> I would hold that the formal incorporation of the evidential rule into domestic law was unnecessary, as the same result is reached by an application of common law principles. The rule laid down by article 15 was accepted by the United Kingdom because it was entirely compatible with our own law.[57]

2 Constitutionalism

The United States has a written constitution on which the US Supreme Court has the last word (barring amendments). The United Kingdom has no written constitution, and the UK Supreme Court is subordinate to parliamentary supremacy.

One might expect these differences to lead to stronger protections for human rights in the United States than in the United Kingdom. That is doubtless true in some areas of the law. In counterterrorism, however, the reverse may be true. At least since 9/11, passions against terrorism have run so high that US political branches have shown a tendency to push the envelope as far as possible against terrorism and, if there is to be any limit on the techniques employed, to leave it to the courts to draw the line.

This was evident in the battle over habeas corpus for prisoners at Guantánamo. Beginning in 2001, the executive branch attempted to deny them habeas corpus altogether. The Supreme Court struck down this effort in 2004.[58] Congress and the executive then attempted to deny habeas corpus by statute. When the Supreme Court in 2006 strained to interpret the new statute as not clear enough to deny habeas corpus,[59] Congress and the executive passed a new statute that left no doubt. Finally, if habeas corpus was to be ensured, the Supreme Court was left with no alternative but to declare the new statute unconstitutional.[60]

On the one hand, this push-pull between the branches may be seen to reflect credit on the Supreme Court, which held to principle (albeit by divided votes). On the other hand, it can be read as an abdication by the political branches. They chose the politically popular path of denying habeas corpus to suspected terrorists while leaving it to the courts to worry about constitutional rights.

In contrast, in the United Kingdom with no written constitution, there is a lack of clarity, both about rights and about how far the courts will go to protect them. Parliament and government know that they cannot entirely "pass the buck" (or the pound) to the courts. There is a shared responsibility to uphold British rights traditions (even if not all MPs recognize their responsibility). Limits on governmental powers are not merely put on paper and left to someone else to enforce; if they are to be made real, they must be internalized as values and commitments.

It may be no coincidence that the two houses of Parliament have together established a Joint Committee on Human Rights whereas the US Congress has no comparably prestigious and empowered human rights body. Likewise, UK government ministers are obligated by law to attest to the compatibility of their legislative proposals with the European Convention on Human Rights (or, if not, to explain why they nonetheless make the proposal)[61] whereas US officials are under no such obligation.

British judges, too, cannot simply interpret statutes or written constitutional provisions and blame the legislators if they find the result unpalatable. They must study and internalize the history and values of the common law, if they are to apply it. The job of defining and enforcing rights rests on their shoulders, too, and they know it: "Constitutional dangers exist no less in too little judicial activism as in too much."[62]

3 Domesticating Human Rights Treaties

Treaties joined by the United Kingdom have no domestic legal effect unless enacted into domestic law by Parliament. For example, Parliament implemented the UN Convention against Torture by domestic legislation which also authorized judicial remedies for violations.[63] This approach ensures domestic political buy-in, and legitimizes judicial enforcement, if Parliament so decides.

In contrast, treaties are enforceable in US courts if they are either "self-executing" or are implemented by statute. In ratifying human rights treaties, the Senate has a recent practice of attaching a formal declaration that the treaty is not self-executing.[64] Coupled with this is its practice to adopt either no implementing legislation[65] or woefully incomplete implementing legislation.[66]

The result is that UK courts, but generally not US courts, are empowered to rule on violations of human rights treaty commitments.

4 Regional Human Rights Court

As a party to the European Convention on Human Rights, the United Kingdom is subject to the binding jurisdiction of the European Court of Human Rights in Strasbourg, France. Major UK court rulings on human rights regularly parse and attempt to follow the jurisprudence of the European Court,[67] which historically has been as protective or more so of human rights than the British courts.[68] UK courts further pay attention to human rights guidance from the diplomatic organs of the Council of Europe,[69] the regional organization of which the European Court is part.

In contrast, the United States is a party to neither the American Convention on Human Rights nor the Inter-American Court of Human Rights. The United States is subject to nonbinding resolutions by the Inter-American Commission on Human Rights, but almost never complies with them. US courts rarely cite Inter-American jurisprudence or the diplomatic resolutions of the Organization of American States, the regional organization of which the Inter-American human rights bodies are part.

In short, regional jurisprudence and judicial review stiffen the human rights backbones of UK judges (and parliamentarians), but generally not of the US courts or the Congress.

5 Human Rights Act and Domestic Judicial Remedies

The United Kingdom's adoption in 1998 of the Human Rights Act, implementing the European Convention on Human Rights, has enhanced domestic judicial implementation of the convention in at least two main ways. First, British courts are expressly authorized to adjudicate claims of violations of the convention, to provide remedies for government acts violating the convention (where those acts are not compelled by primary legislation), and to make declarations of incompatibility of primary legislation adopted by Parliament where it is inconsistent with the convention.[70] Under these powers, for example, the Law Lords declared the parliamentary law authorizing indefinite detention of suspected foreign terrorists without charge or trial to be "incompatible" with convention jurisprudence requiring that restrictions on rights be proportional and nondiscriminatory.[71]

Second, the Human Rights Act does not empower the courts to dictate the remedies – if any – for incompatibility of primary legislation when they find it.[72] The fix – if any – is left to the UK government and Parliament. While this might seem to weaken defense of human rights by the courts, it may actually have the opposite effect. The courts are freed to "speak truth to power" without being burdened with devising a solution, leaving that instead to the democratically elected bodies. Courts need not hedge their rulings on the law merely because they hesitate over the proper remedy.

In contrast, the United States has no such legislation. US courts rarely rule US government actions or legislation to be incompatible with human rights treaties to which the United States is a party.

HISTORY AND GEOPOLITICS

The differences in British and American law do not arise in a vacuum but reflect underlying history and geopolitics. Some legal differences between the two nations – in federalism and common law, constitutionalism, and the manner of domestication of treaties – have long historical roots, anteceding the development of modern international human rights law in the period since World War II. Although not motivated by attitudes toward international human rights norms, they may nonetheless have a significant impact, as described above, on the extent to which British and American government officials, legislators, and judges choose to respect and follow international human rights law.

By contrast, the differences in regard to regional human rights treaties and courts, and their domestic implementation by law in Britain but not in the United States, owe much to the divergent geopolitical standing and international relations of the two nations in the decades since World War II. In postwar Europe, bounded by fascism in the south and menaced by communism in the east and internally, western European democracies joined to create the European Convention and Court of Human Rights in hopes of erecting a collective shield against erosions of civil liberty in fragile continental States. Britain was content to join a convention that articulated human rights in ways consistent with British traditions of liberty.[73]

As the project of European integration progressed in subsequent decades, the United Kingdom generally respected and complied with judgments of the European Court of Human Rights, even when disruptive of British tradition, or contrary to tenaciously held government policy.[74] In recent years, even as certain judgments of the European Court generated political controversy in the United Kingdom, along with threats by Conservative Party leaders to withdraw from the European Convention,[75] Britain remained in the system and continued to comply with almost all judgments against it by the European Court.[76] Even after the Brexit process began in 2016, the political documents on the proposed Brexit agreement with the European Union (as of December 2018) appeared to commit the United Kingdom to remain in the European Convention.[77]

The geopolitical factors influencing the posture of the United States toward its regional human rights system were markedly different. In the postwar period and up to the present, as a global superpower bathed in hubris, the United States saw itself as the uniquely successful, "indispensable nation."[78] Unlike London, Washington saw no prospect that a collective shield of international judges could preserve democracy and civil liberty in its region, where many of its neighbors to the south were revolving doors of caudillos, military juntas, and corrupt autocracies. Much less would the world's most powerful nation submit to the musings of foreign judges, or bend its legal traditions to fit what it perceived as the inferior civil law systems of its Latin American neighbors. Nor would Washington welcome regional judicial oversight of its various covert and overt interventions in the region. There was no way the United States would join a legally binding regional human rights regime, nor any occasion for it to adopt a law empowering its courts to deploy a regional human rights treaty against the actions of its government or against laws passed by its Congress.

This attitude reflected not only a regional perspective but also a worldview. The United States would no more bow to global than to regional human rights jurisdiction. When Washington finally ratified several major UN human rights treaties in the early 1990s,[79] it did so without accepting their individual complaint procedures. When the International Court of Justice (ICJ) ruled against the United States in cases brought by Nicaragua and Mexico,[80] both involving significant human rights issues, Washington responded by pulling out of the relevant jurisdiction of the court. Meanwhile, the US Supreme Court declared that the United States was not legally bound, as a matter of domestic law, to comply with the ICJ judgment in the case with Mexico.[81]

In short, Washington was a superpower in a region and world populated largely by undemocratic regimes, and in which the United States insisted on freedom of interventionist action. In contrast, London was a former superpower, now reduced to a regional power, in a region of democracies encircled by fascism in the Iberian Peninsula and by communism in the Soviet bloc. In geopolitical terms, their sharply differing approaches to regional and global human rights norms and institutions made sense to each of them from their differing perspectives.

CULTURE

The differing legal institutions and contrasting geopolitical positions of the two nations shaped and reinforced their distinctive legal and political cultures with regard to international human rights law. Invoked over time, endlessly remarked upon and repeated by multiple voices – in legislatures, courts, media and the academy – and confirmed by government practice, the United Kingdom's greater sensitivity to internationally defined limits on acceptable government conduct became a self-perpetuating factor in its own right. The converse was true in the United States. Culture joined law and geopolitics to condition the respective responses of British and American officialdom to twenty-first-century terrorism.[82]

In the United Kingdom, however, cultural and legal forces of self-restraint could succeed only so far. Propelled by its particular mission and by its discrete values and norms, Britain's secret intelligence service, MI6, did not fully accept the publicly stated rules of the counterterrorism game. Political and legal limits might constrain it from actually carrying out torture and extraordinary renditions, and from opening its own black sites, but behind the scenes MI6 could not resist cooperating with its American counterparts who were not comparably constrained. In some instances, MI6 prevailed on political leaders for quiet, even oral authorizations[83] while in others MI6 proceeded on its own behind a cloak of secrecy. Britain thus became complicit in, but generally did not engage in, the gross violations of human rights carried out by the United States.

CONCLUSION

In the event of further large-scale terrorist attacks in Britain and America, how will their public institutions respond? If the analysis in this chapter is accurate or close to it, one may expect far more restraint from London than from Washington. But history is not destiny. Nor is culture. Laws can be changed. The future will be shaped by many moving pieces, both domestically and internationally. Will Britain exit from Europe, and if so, where might that lead? Will the late twentieth-century human rights consensus in Europe continue to unravel, torn by rising populist authoritarianism, economic discontent, and resistance to mass immigration from nearby lands?

In the United States, following the ascension to the Supreme Court of Neil Gorsuch and Brett Kavanaugh, and if the occasion calls for it, will we see again the principled resistance to excesses by the political branches that characterized the jousting over Guantánamo in the first decade of this century?

In the longer run, as American superpower continues to slip in relative terms, and as potential military conflict with China becomes ever more plausible, will Washington rediscover the value of international law and multilateral institutions as mutually beneficial alternatives to armed conflict, and as serving the self-interest of all nations? Or, in the face of a weakened West, will the repressive values of the Chinese Communist Party triumph? Will international human rights law be downsized to little more than a turn-of-the-century memory?

None of these outcomes – good or bad – is inevitable. Those who embrace the values of human rights are well-advised to study the past, if we are to strengthen our cause in the future. The long tradition of the defense of liberty by the common law teaches that, despite all obstacles, principled progress is possible.

Tracking the Decline of Liberalism

PART II

Tracking the Decline of Liberalism

4

The National Security State Gone Awry: Returning to First Principles

Loch K. Johnson

INTRODUCTION

Open societies seem to have lost much of their luster, as the lamplights of democracy flicker around the globe. China has achieved economic miracles while eschewing democratic principles, and the country has relied on a centralized government to conduct effective foreign aid programs in Pakistan, India, nations throughout the African continent, Latin America, and elsewhere. With apparent insouciance, Russia routinely conducts disinformation-and-deception cyberattacks against the democracies, revealing the vulnerability of open societies to the clandestine operations of secret agencies dancing on the strings of autocratic governments. The President of Russia, Vladimir V. Putin, bears all the trappings of a czar.

In Germany, an unsteady coalition government faces the rise of anti-immigrant, right-wing groups and political factions reminiscent of the days preceding the fall of the Weimar Republic. In Italy, a right-wing, nativist government has come into power. Turkey's Recep Tayyip Erdogan looks more and more like a standard dictator, as do Hungary's Viktor Orban and Egypt's Abdel Fattah el-Sisi, while Iran's Ali Khamenei has embraced the title of "Supreme Leader." Authoritarianism haunts modern-day Poland, too, and in the United States the presidential election outcome in 2016 yielded Donald J. Trump, a politically inexperienced and erratic chief executive. His antics, especially an unrelenting stream of tweets that denigrates everything from the Central Intelligence Agency (CIA) and the Federal Bureau of Investigation (FBI) to individual members of Congress and the media as well as private citizens who draw the president's wrath, have distracted daily life in America while festering acrimony and discontent across the land. Periodic school shootings and a raging opioid epidemic further plague the nation, causing erstwhile allies around the world to question the value of following the leadership of the United States, the world's most prominent democracy.

It has not always been this way. At the end of World War II, the United States and the other democracies were widely viewed as beacons of hope for the future. Washington, DC, became the focal point of aspirations for freedom and liberty around the globe. The Truman (1945–1951) and the Eisenhower (1952–1960) administrations constructed a worldwide web of alliances to defend and promote democratic regimes, with great success in Europe and Japan (along with other key nations in the Far East). The United States was admired across the latitudes not just because of its imposing military might but even more for its good example: its freedom of religion, independent media, fair elections, and – though imperfect, as procedures in Guantánamo have illustrated – a judicial system remarkable for its reliance on due process and impartiality.

More than 200 years earlier, America's founders initiated this unprecedented trajectory toward a government based on liberty and equality, with elections, representative government, the rule of law and a presidency held in check by a system of shared powers and other safeguards against the abuse of authority. These beginnings in Philadelphia at the Constitutional Convention of 1787 were marred by incongruities, though, as slavery continued, women were denied the right to vote or hold public office, and the sense of national unity remained tenuous. The country would split apart in a civil war that began in 1861 and ended five years later after 618,000 battlefield deaths.[1] Since then, America's experiment in democracy has moved forward, step-by-step, toward vastly improved rights for blacks, women, and other previously disadvantaged segments of society. Waves of new citizens from abroad have enriched life in the United States, although – as in other nations – powerful anti-immigrant reactions have surfaced recently and other imperfections still abound, as underscored by important movements like Black Lives Matter (protesting police violence against blacks) and #MeToo (countering sexual harassment) as well as support for immigrants. Disquieting, too, is the political polarization that grips citizens and their leaders alike. Moreover, poverty, racism, and inequality persist in the United States, as the gap between the rich and the poor not only endures but also widens.

Yet, until recently, the broad public sense has been that America will continue to move forward in its quest for a fair and equitable society, making progress (if fitful) and still being a worthy example for other nations. Optimism has remained the coin of the realm. Even after the shock of 9/11, Americans regrouped as the nation's soldiers have hunted down the terrorist perpetrators and waged warfare against global terrorism, while successfully rebuilding the national economy after a wrenching housing mortgage crisis and financial meltdown during the Great Recession of 2008. The United States was on the march again, with ever greater hopes for an America at home that matched the dreams of its citizens, coupled with aspirations that the nation would also remain an important force in the international affairs of the twenty-first century.

Beneath the surface, however, this idealism has begun to unravel. President George W. Bush (2000–2008) failed to overcome the polarization ripping at the fabric of American society, and he led the United States into a costly and unnecessary war in Iraq. His successor, Barack Obama (2008–2016), deepened America's involvement in military conflicts in Iraq, Afghanistan, Libya, and Syria. The fighting in Afghanistan has become the longest war in US history (at eighteen years and still counting). Obama seemed to career from one crisis to another, extending America's military presence in the Middle East and Africa. President Donald Trump (2016–) has had a similar approach; he initially threatened war, against a nuclear-armed North Korea while thumbing his nose at traditional allies. The Trump administration is planning as well to develop an expensive new set of nuclear weapons, including small and mobile warheads designed for tactical warfare (a controversial new direction in the esoteric domain of nuclear planning).

A savvy Congress-watcher, Stephen R. Weissman, looks upon the post–Vietnam War period in the United States as the last era of congressional activism in foreign policy and security affairs. He notes a marked backsliding by lawmakers in the early 1990s during the Bill Clinton presidency and, as demonstrated by initiatives related to Libya and Syria during the Obama years, Congress came to a point of largely absenting itself from debate over foreign military interventions.[2] In a dangerous undercurrent inside the United States, public officials often seem to forget the genius of America's original constitutional design. All too frequently, the president and many lawmakers have rejected the prescriptions of the founders for divided power, robust congressional involvement in foreign policymaking, and a White House checked by the law and fellow power-sharers in Congress. The United States has drifted during the Bush II, Obama, and Trump administrations toward a system of government that has belittled the nation's founding principles and exhibited a willingness to permit excessive presidential discretion over national security and foreign policy.

This trend toward a renewal of the "imperial presidency," once practiced extensively by Richard M. Nixon as encouraged by his Secretary of State Henry Kissinger, can be seen vividly in three of the most important instruments of international relations exercised by the federal government: the war power, the treaty power, and the spy power (i.e., the use of secret agencies to accomplish policy goals). This chapter examines the erosion of constitutional safeguards within these domains during the Bush II, Obama, and Trump administrations, and it attempts to reimagine a national security state that commits anew to the nation's first principles.

KEY NATIONAL SECURITY POWERS IN THE UNITED STATES

The war power, the treaty power, and the spy power – each plays an important part in America's relations with the world. The first two were central to the writing of the Constitution; the third remained outside the normal framework of government at the time and, indeed, until 1975 when the Church Committee, led by Senator Frank Church (D-Idaho), persuasively argued in Congress (in the wake of a domestic spy scandal) that the nation's spy agencies should be brought in from the cold and subjected to the same checks and balances laid out in the Constitution for the rest of the government. A brief review of these powers underscores their volatile nature, as their meaning and base of authority has ebbed and flowed over the course of America's history.

The War Power. The Constitution lodges the war power primarily in the hands of Congress (Article I, Section 8). No governmental power so concerned the founders as the right to draw the United States into a war. They were loath to turn the "Dog of War," as Thomas Jefferson put it, over to the discretion of a single individual, even the much-admired George Washington. If this beast had to be unleashed, a representative assembly should be responsible, they argued – not the president alone. The founders made clear that, naturally, a president would be expected to use military force for the purpose of repelling a sudden attack against the United States; a delay to consult with lawmakers could prove suicidal. When it came to initiating hostilities, however, the president was clearly forbidden from unilateral action. As Senator Sam Ervin Jr. (D-North Carolina), a constitutional sage in the modern era, once put it: ". . . use of the Armed Forces for any purpose not directly related to the defense of the United States against sudden armed aggression, and I emphasize the word 'sudden,' can be undertaken only upon congressional authorization."[3]

On the eve of the Korean War in 1950, the Truman administration balked at this long-standing limitation on presidential power. Its State Department opined that "the President, as Commander in Chief of the Armed Forces of the United States, has full control over the use thereof," adding that an inherent constitutional right allowed "the President to use the Armed Forces of the United States without consulting Congress."[4] The president's constitutional status as commander-in-chief, along with the Constitution's injunction that the nation's chief executive "shall take Care that the Laws be faithfully executed," allowed Harry S. Truman – so went the claim of his administration – the implicit right to use US troops as the White House alone saw fit. At the time, GOP lawmakers recoiled at this interpretation. As Mr. Republican himself, Senator Robert Taft (R-Ohio), said, looking back at this stance: "The President simply usurped authority, in violation of the laws and the Constitution, when he sent troops to Korea to carry out the resolution of the United Nations in an undeclared war."[5]

During the 1950s, the Eisenhower administration felt uncomfortable with President Truman's raw assertion of president war-making power. It turned to a middle ground between the view of the Truman administration and the constitutional requirement for a formal declaration of war by Congress, as mandated by the founders. President Dwight D. Eisenhower requested that members of Congress grant him authority to conduct war, if necessary, by way of broad congressional resolutions whenever a conflict began to simmer, as illustrated by the Formosa Resolution of 1955. In this case, the Eisenhower administration feared a mainland Chinese invasion against the off-shore island of Formosa (Taiwan), protected by a bilateral treaty with the United States. President Eisenhower believed that a congressional resolution would provide him with authority to use military force to protect the island nation, which had split off from China and allied itself with the United States, and thereby deter a Chinese invasion from the mainland.

Such resolutions required a majority vote in each chamber of Congress, just like a declaration of war; the problem, though, was that lawmakers fell into the habit of providing the president overly broad grants of authority – resolutions "so general and imprecise," concluded a review by the Senate Foreign Relations Committee, "[as to] amount to an unconstitutional alienation of its war power on the part of the Congress."[6] With respect to the Formosa example, historian Arthur S. Schlesinger Jr. concluded: "It committed Congress to the approval of hostilities without knowledge of the specific situation in which the hostilities would begin."[7] Granted, Congress had more of a say with the use of resolutions on questions of war – but not much more – than it did when President Truman simply dismissed the legislative branch outright; but now lawmakers succumbed to a habit of passing along its war powers (by way of broad resolutions) into the hands of the executive branch.

The risks of relying on vague foreign policy resolutions passed by Congress eventually became self-evident with the Gulf of Tonkin Resolution, approved by Congress in August 1964. This congressional authority allowed President Lyndon B. Johnson (1963–1968) to counter suspected North Vietnamese attacks against US naval vessels in international waters off the coast of Vietnam (which later proved never to have happened). Over the next year, President Johnson's short-term concern over these suspected attacks grew, without serious debate on Capitol Hill, into a long-term war in Indochina that cost the lives of more than 58,220 US troops and civilians by the time the war ended in 1973.[8] At the beginning of the war, a senior official in the Johnson administration, Undersecretary of State Nicholas Katzenbach, publicly referred to the Gulf of Tonkin Resolution as the "functional equivalent" of a declaration of war by Congress. Yet a senior member of the Senate Committee on Foreign Relations later recalled that "Congress neither expected nor even considered at the time of the debate on the resolution that the President would later commit more than half a million American soldiers to a full-scale war in Vietnam."[9]

This struggle between the legislative branch (Article I) and the executive branch (Article II) reached a climax during the Cold War with enactment of the War Powers Resolution (WPR) in 1973. Lawmakers embraced this initiative as a means for placing obstacles in the pathway of presidential attempts to commit US forces abroad without meaningful debate and formal approval by the legislative branch of government. No more Vietnams. The statue required that the president "in every possible instance shall consult with Congress" before introducing armed forces "into hostilities or into situations where imminent involvement in hostilities is clearly indicated by the circumstances."

Further, the president had to report to the Congress within forty-eight hours regarding the deployment of troops; if hostilities were imminent, the president's report would start a sixty-day clock (which could be extended to ninety days in an emergency). When this time period elapsed, the new law required the White House to obtain congressional approval for continuation of the military involvement. The WPR also permitted lawmakers to force the withdrawal of US troops from a region at any time by a concurrent resolution, that is, by a simple majority vote in both chambers without the need for the president's signature or possible veto. (This provision was later rendered null and void by a 1983 Supreme Court decision, *US Immigration and Naturalization Service v. Chad.*) Moreover, if Congress refused to endorse the president's use of force within sixty days of the initial reporting, the president had to withdraw the US troops. Congress could grant a thirty-day extension, if necessary, to assure an orderly and safe exit.

During debate on the measure, Senator Jacob Javits (R-New York) spelled out the significance of the resolution: ". . . after 200 years, at least something will have been done about codifying the implementation of the most awesome power in the possession of any sovereignty and giving the broad representation of the people in Congress a voice in it." He continued, "This is critically important, for we have just learned [with the war in Vietnam] the hard lesson that wars cannot be successfully fought except with the consent of the people and their support. At long last . . . Congress is determined to recapture the awesome power to make war."[10]

Since its enactment, the WPR has been hounded by controversy. Its lack of a clear definition of what it means to enter into "hostilities" overseas has led to disputes between the branches about when – or even whether – the sixty-day clock should begin ticking. Moreover, presidents have been inconsistent in their willingness to report automatically to the Congress when US troops have entered what by all accounts had the earmarks of a hostile region in the world. Unlike Robert Taft, more recent members of the GOP – in both the executive and legislative branches – have latched on to Truman's "inherent powers" interpretation as a rationale to undermine the role of lawmakers in war-making. During the Ronald Reagan years, for example (1980–1988), an aide to the president maintained that the White House had the "constitutional and historical power" to ignore the War Powers Resolution altogether and guide American foreign policy according to presidential designs.[11] These inconsistencies and renewed pronouncements of inherent presidential authority for war-making increased during the Bush II, Obama, and Trump administrations (examined below). So did disputes between the branches of government over the treaty power.

The Treaty Power. The astute journalist William Pfaff once noted that "international law is not 'law' at all. It is a system of treaties, conventions, precedents and other commitments."[12] In the Constitution, the only explicit reference to diplomacy and the making of international agreements is in Article II, Section 2, which states that the president "shall have power, by and with the advice of the Senate to make treaties, provided two-thirds of the Senators present concur." As a prominent legal authority has observed, "The Founders made it unmistakably plain their intentions to withhold from the President the power to enter into treaties all by himself."[3] The president, too, was given a central role to play in the treaty process, including the final right of ratification (a word often attributed wrongly in the media and even in scholarly journals to the prior, penultimate step of an approval vote in the Senate).

Early in the nation's history, the government found the treaty-making procedure too cumbersome for the negotiation of all international agreements, some of which dealt with routine matters.[14] The United States began to carry out its formal agreement-making by way of two additional and less formal instruments of diplomacy: the statutory agreement and the executive agreement (including secret understandings between nations on matters related to intelligence liaison as well as clandestine military support). Statutory agreements, often loosely worded and typically employed for trade measures, are permissions by majority votes in both chambers of Congress for the executive branch to move ahead on a pact with another nation (or nations) without seeking an extraordinary two-thirds approval in the Senate. The second method, executive agreements, involves diplomatic transactions that are devoid of any meaningful consultation with either chamber of Congress; they are carried out by the White House and (often without White House involvement) one or another executive agency that deals with international relations.

Sharply criticizing this unilateral executive branch approach to US diplomacy, the Senate Foreign Relations Committee has warned that the making of commitments abroad "by means of an executive agreement, or a military memorandum, has no valid place in our constitutional law, and constitutes a usurpation of the treaty power of the Senate."[15] The committee understands that executive agreements make sense for the many quotidian international arrangements entered into by the United States, say, allowing Canadian military aircraft on training missions to land at Wyoming airports under proper liaison arrangements. Yet, when executive agreements have been resorted to by presidential administrations (sometimes in complete secrecy) as a way of bypassing Congress on important diplomatic commitments – say, the establishment of military bases abroad – lawmakers cry foul.

In 1962, for instance, Secretary of State Dean Rusk issued a joint statement with the Foreign Minister of Thailand, in which Rusk expressed "the firm intention of the United States to aid Thailand, its ally and historic friend, in resisting Communist aggression and subversion."[16] By this executive agreement, the joint US-Thai communique converted the Southeast Asian Treaty Organization (SEATO) – which provided only that member nations would "consult" in times of military peril – into a much stronger bilateral defense pact, with military aid to Thailand subsequently skyrocketing from $24 million in 1960 to $88 million in 1962.

To ensure executive agreements were being used appropriately, the Congress enacted the Case-Zablocki Act in 1972 and further strengthened the law in 1976. The statute requires the executive branch to report to lawmakers on all executive agreements, so members of Congress can judge whether the proper instrument of diplomacy has been selected, or whether a statutory agreement or a treaty would be more in order. As with the war power, controversies between the executive and legislative branches over the proper approaches to diplomacy have festered anew during the administrations of Presidents Bush II, Obama, and Trump. Tensions over the spy power have similarly risen.

The Spy Power. Since its early beginnings, the United States has deployed secret services to advance the nation's interests. Today, seventeen major organizations (the CIA and FBI among them) make up the so-called Intelligence Community. From 1787 until 1975 – a span of 188 years – policymakers viewed America's spy agencies as an exception to normal oversight procedures; the dark side of government would be exempted from the "auxiliary precautions" (checks and balances) successfully advocated by James Madison at the Constitutional Convention. The CIA domestic spy scandal, which leaked to the media in 1974 and triggered the Church Committee inquiry, challenged the notion of intelligence exceptionalism and brought the espionage services into the framework of government accountability that is the hallmark of US democracy.

As Madison might well have predicted in 1787, allowing America's secret agencies to operate free of checks and balances spelled out in the Constitution would eventually lead to the abuse of power. The Church Committee uncovered, among other stunning revelations, CIA espionage operations directed against anti–Vietnam War protesters (Operation CHAOS); covert FBI schemes to ruin the lives of these dissenters, plus individuals involved in both the Civil Rights Movement and far-right groups (Operation COINTELPRO); and National Security Agency (NSA) surveillance aimed at the telephones of American citizens (Operation MINARET) and their international cables (Operation SHAMROCK). The CIA accumulated files on 1.5 million American citizens; infiltrated media, academic, and religious groups inside the United States; and plotted assassinations against foreign leaders in third-world countries. The FBI's smear tactics were intended to blacken the reputations of lawful political activists, from the lowliest volunteers to the top leaders; the NSA leaned on flimsy executive orders from the days of the Truman administration to pursue MINARET and SHAMROCK targets throughout the next five presidencies (1953–1977: Eisenhower, Kennedy, Johnson, Nixon, and Ford) without obtaining renewed authority from any of these leaders or from Congress.

In the aftermath of the CIA spy scandal, lawmakers moved dramatically and largely in a bipartisan manner to stretch America's constitutional canvas over the full framework of government, open and hidden. The Hughes-Ryan Amendment, passed in the waning days of 1974, forced the president to shed the doctrine of plausible deniability and henceforth formally approve all significant covert actions – the means by which the CIA attempts to manipulate foreign nations and non-state actors through the use of secret propaganda, political and economic machinations, and paramilitary (warlike) activities around the globe. Further, covert actions approved by the president have to be reported to the Senate and the House "in a timely fashion" (two days was the understanding, but that requirement was tightened to "prior notice" in the language of the Intelligence Oversight Act of 1980). Further, at the end of its inquiry in 1976, the Church Committee successfully advocated the creation of a permanent standing committee for intelligence account-ability, known as the Senate Select Committee on Intelligence (SSCI, pronounced "sis-see"). The next year the House followed suit by establishing the House Permanent Select Committee on Intelligence (HPSCI, or "hip-see").

In addition, the Congress soon passed legislation to give SSCI and HPSCI meaningful authority, as with the enactment of the Intelligence Oversight Act of 1980, which requires the executive branch to report to Congress not only on covert actions but all other significant intelligence activities prior to their implementation – powerful *ex ante facto* reporting rather than the earlier Hughes-Ryan standard of *ex post facto*. Lawmakers had become genuine partners in the realm of intelligence, just as the Constitution had prescribed for every other domain of government. The vigor and success of congressional accountability over intelligence activities fluctu-ated throughout the next four administrations (1977–2001: Carter, Reagan, George H. W. Bush, and Clinton), with a series of high points during the Carter years (the 1980 Intelligence Oversight Act among them) and low points during the Reagan years (most prominently, the Iran-Contra affair), followed during the second Bush administration by NSA violations of surveillance laws and the CIA's adoption of a torture program – both occurring in the crucible of fear in the United States that followed the terrorist attacks of September 11, 2001.[17]

Overcoming setbacks like Iran-Contra, by the advent of the George W. Bush administration in 2000, Congress was well established in the intelligence oversight business. The difference between the pre-Church Committee era of benign neglect toward the nation's secret agencies and the post-Church Committee existence of SSCI and HPSCI made the contrast in the levels of intelligence accountability between the two periods as stark as night is to day, occasional setbacks notwithstand-ing. Exactly how well this experiment in bringing democracy to the hidden side of government – unprecedented in the United States and around the world – would play out during the Bush II, Obama, and Trump administrations, however, has remained in doubt. As events have unfolded from Bush II through Trump, relations between the branches have proven as fraught in the realm of spy power as they have been with the war and treaty powers.

NATIONAL SECURITY POWERS IN THE BUSH II, OBAMA, AND TRUMP ADMINISTRATIONS

George W. Bush, Barack Obama, and Donald J. Trump have all led administrations that have been, for one reason or another, less than robust in their embrace of the constitutional framework for the sharing of national security powers – often referred to eponymously as the Madisonian model of governance, since James Madison played such a major role in drafting democratic safeguards into America's founding document. Both Bush II, and Trump even more so, pushed the boundaries in a manner designed to enhance unilateral presidential control over America's foreign and security policies.[18]

THE BUSH II ADMINISTRATION

The War Power. The key event in the second Bush administration was the terror- ist attacks against the United States on 9/11. A central personality in the administration, in the context of this study, was Vice President Dick Cheney, a longtime and unalloyed proponent of strong – practically exclusive – presidential authority when it came to foreign or security affairs and a leading critic of the WPR. As a result of the terrorist attacks, the administration immediately (and understandably) geared up for retaliation against those responsible for the tragedy: Al-Qaeda and its Afghani hosts, the Taliban regime. George W. Bush's father, George H. W. Bush (president from 1988 to 1992) had himself initially displayed no qualms about using the war power as the White House saw fit. Before invading Iraq in 1990, he claimed (Truman-like) an inherent constitutional right as the commander-in-chief to engage in war. He also pointed to a resolution from the United Nations that, he maintained, granted him authority to invade Iraq – as if decisions made by the United Nations could hold sway over the US Constitution. Dick Cheney served as White House chief of staff under the first President Bush and urged this radical Article II stance.

The Congress, prodded by the Senate Armed Services Committee, balked at both the "inherent" and the UN claims for unilateral presidential action against Iraq. Leading lawmakers insisted that George H. W. Bush seek an "affirmative approval" before the White House launched an invasion against the Saddam Hussein regime. After a rousing debate in the Senate on January 21, 1991, the Congress delivered a verdict in favor of the president: 52-47 in the Senate and 250-182 in the House. President Bush had achieved his war-fighting goal, but only after bowing to full participation by lawmakers, including vigorous debate and a vote.

Now, after 9/11, it was the son's time to address the question of war against Iraq, this time with Vice President Cheney at an even higher perch in the White House. In 2001, Congress formally voted for Bush II's invasion of Afghanistan against the 9/11 perpetrators. Fully aware of his father's initial and failed initial attempts to bypass the Congress in his attack against Iraq, the second President Bush chose to seek authority from lawmakers from the beginning, despite steady counsel from Cheney that the administration already had all the authority it needed in the second article of the Constitution.

The example of Bush II provides a reminder to students of the war power that there is more than one way to achieve presidential predominance in Madison's framework of shared powers; as in this instance, a president can greatly increase the odds of having his or her way by simply frightening the Congress and the American people into support for the use of military force against Iraq. In the months leading up to the vote in Congress on the proposed military intervention, Bush II and his administrative team engaged in a steady public drumbeat on the theme that weapons of mass destruction (WMDs) were likely possessed by Iraq. The president and his national security adviser, Condoleezza Rice, went so far as to give public speeches in 2002 that raised the possibility of "mushroom clouds" appearing on America soil as a result of nuclear attacks from Iraq – a preposterous scenario at the time, given the difficulty of directing such weapons against far-away US territory from Iraq, even if Saddam possessed nuclear warheads.

Despite the facts that major US allies (most notably Germany and France) refused to accept the WMD hypothesis in 2002 or enter into warfare against Saddam Hussein until additional UN inspections had been carried out in Iraq, and that the intelligence supporting the hypothesis remained soft (see below), the administration alarmed Congress into adopting overwhelming support for an Iraqi invasion, without meaningful hearings or floor debate on the topic and only a perfunctory vote guided by the shrill rhetoric emanating from the White House. The Bush II administration didn't need Article II; it had successfully spooked a deferential Congress.

Only after the invasion did it become apparent that Saddam's WMDs were a myth, and that the administration had other reasons for attacking Iraq – extending from revenge by Bush II against an earlier Iraqi assassination plot against his mother and father to a desire by neoconservatives ("neocons") in the administration to remove Saddam as a thorn in Israel's side, along with their pipe dream of establishing a democratic beachhead in the Middle East by transforming Iraq into a flowering republic – all supposedly paid for by Iraqi oil reserves. The war summed up, in the words of a recent Bush II biographer, to "easily the worst foreign policy decision ever made by an American president."[19]

The Treaty Power. Bush II understood the advantage that executive agreements held for presidents: no debate on Capitol Hill, no naysayers, no political capital wasted in lobbying lawmakers – just the consummation, sometime secretly achieved, of a foreign policy goal the White House or some executive agency found useful. An example is this president's outreach to King Abdullah of Saudi Arabia. Working through the Commerce Department, Bush II sent a letter to the King recommending that he purchase forty-six Boeing jets, including three for the use of his own family. The deal would mean 11,000 new jobs in the United States, big profits for Boeing, and ongoing good will between oil-rich Saudi Arabia and its multiple clients in Texas – not to mention further solidifying the long-standing family ties between the Abdullahs and the Bushes. Yet, Airbus of France was in pursuit of this deal, too. The president moved quickly, meeting the King's one demand: that his personal Boeing plane be equipped with the same advanced telecommunications and security equipment enjoyed by the US President on Air Force One. By letter exchange, as reported in the media at the time, the deal was struck—an approach firmly within the circle of the Cheney theory of unilateral presidential policymaking, free of congressional involvement.

On other occasions, Bush II followed the traditional treaty route, with the Senate approving twenty-two of the administration's twenty-six foremost treaty initiatives (none of great moment). On average, though, only about 5.14 percent of this administration's international agreements were pursued in the form of treaties, which is below the average of 6.04 from 1949 to 2008.[20] As with other administrations, most of Bush II's formal diplomacy rested on statutory agreements, with the executive branch moving forward toward an international agreement only after the Congress had given broad approval by a formal vote. Yet, as the Saudi case illustrates, this White House was prepared to bypass lawmakers when it saw fit. As it built a coalition to help the United States invade Iraq, for example, this Bush administration cut deals right and left, straight from the White House, the Pentagon, and the State Department. At the time, Senator John Kerry (D-Massachusetts) observed that the wheeling and dealing – a spate of executive agreements, most of them hidden from sight – had produced a "coalition of the bribed, the coerced, the bought, and the extorted."[21]

Spy Power. The Bush II White House displayed a stark institutional aggressiveness within the realm of the espionage agencies, with its responses to suspected Iraqi WMDs providing several examples. The administration:

- attempted to influence the CIA to adopt the view that Iraq clearly possessed WMDs, with Cheney visiting the agency eleven times in the lead-up to war, arguing on behalf of the hypothesis (no other vice president has ever visited the CIA even close to this number of times);
- placed into the State of the Union address in 2002 a reference to Saddam's alleged purchase of forty tons of yellow-cake uranium from Niger to build nuclear weapons, even though CIA research had debunked this notion and urged the president to drop the reference in the speech; and, in revenge for the CIA's criticism, improperly revealed the name of a senior agency officer – in violation of the Intelligence Identities Act of 1982 – whose husband, a former US ambassador to Niger, had written a report on the subject (at the CIA's request) that scoffed at the idea of a Niger uranium connection with Iraq;
- never ordered the writing of a National Intelligence Estimate (NIE) on Iraq before the invasion, which should have been standard protocol (and was finally demanded by lawmakers, but the NIE was hastily prepared and too ambiguous to affect public opinion at the last minute on the proposed war against Iraq);
- too readily accepted the pro-WMD testimony of Iraqi émigrés in the United States who had escaped the Saddam regime and offered their help to the CIA, one of whom claimed to have personal knowledge of Iraqi WMDs – only to be

revealed late in the war-planning as an ambitious politician-in-exile who hoped the United States could bring about regime change in Iraq so that he might become president of the new government;

- failed to listen to important intelligence agencies in the Departments of Defense, Energy, and State who had significant misgivings about some of the "evidence" supporting the WMD argument that should have been further explored before an invasion;

- ignored a CIA report, originally prepared in 1995 and updated (and dismissed by the Clinton administration as well), that warned – displaying remarkable prescience – that "aerial terrorism" might come to the United States, with terrorists hijacking and flying US commercial airliners into city skyscrapers; and

- belittled further warnings by the outgoing Clinton administration that Al-Qaeda had become Threat No. 1 to the United States – failing to hold a National Security Council meeting on this subject until nine months later (on September 4, 2001, just days before the 9/11 attacks).[22]

Another aspect of the administration's reaction to 9/11 was to encourage the NSA director to flaunt the Foreign Intelligence Surveillance Act (FISA) of 1978, a Church Committee initiative. Here again, Vice President Cheney played a major role in guiding the president (and the NSA) toward the stance of unilateral White House action in security affairs – an extreme interpretation of the unitary theory of the presidency.[23] For scholars, the word "unitary" in this phrase implies that all officials in the executive branch are firmly under the direct control of the president. In Cheney's use of the term, though, the meaning is extended further still: the president is considered able to concentrate in the White House all national decisions, including use of the war power – what historian Arthur S. Schlesinger Jr. referred to as the "imperial president" in his famous book title of 1973, or what is referred to in this chapter as the "unilateral president."

With Article II of the Constitution as his brief, Cheney ordered the NSA's chief to return to his agency and unleash its surveillance powers against suspected terrorists, with no need for FISA warrants beforehand. The director returned to NSA headquarters and informed his legal staff: "The President is going to do this on his own hook. Raw Article 2, commander-in-chief stuff. No new legislation."[24] Neither the director nor his lawyers bothered to object that this order from the White House flew directly in the face of existing law – FISA – and was, therefore, illegal.

All of these failures of law and protocol stemmed from hubris in the White House, fueled by the belief of Cheney and his fellow neocons that they knew best and the president could proceed with war and illegal surveillance, other considerations (such as Article I of the Constitution and FISA) to the contrary notwithstanding. Throughout the buildup to this second invasion of Iraq, the Congress was of little more use to the body politic than the vermiform appendix is to the human body.

Like his father, an outspoken critic of the Church Committee reforms, Bush II evidently preferred the era before lawmakers became equal partners in the use of, and supervision over, the nation's secret agencies – a time of benign neglect when presidents could blithely direct, or ignore, their intelligence agencies according to the whims and wishes of the White House (an approach revived by President Trump; see below).

THE OBAMA ADMINISTRATION

The War Power. In the commission of his duties, President Barack Obama, a graduate of Harvard Law School and a now-and-then professor of international law, usually paid lip-service to the founders and their scheme for a government based on power sharing among the branches of government. His actual approach to carrying out the war, treaty, and spy powers was, however, sometimes a different story.[25] With respect to war-making, he committed the use of US military forces against ISIS terrorist forces in Libya solely on the basis of Article II and UN Security Council authority, without ever acquiring approval from Congress. It was the first time any great power had gone to war against a stateless, borderless group.[26] As a former senior attorney in the Obama administration has noted, "a president who had signaled as a candidate this wariness about engaging unilateral executive war-making would, by the end of his second term, find himself accused of doing just that."[27]

At first, the president labeled his military actions against ISIS as a limited, humanitarian intervention and, admirably, he exercised caution and constitutional restraint. He even requested from the Congress, on December 8, 2015, a war authorization for the use of military force against the terrorist faction – an increasingly rare request by American presidents. "I think it's time for Congress to vote," said Obama, "to demonstrate that the American people are united and committed to this fight."

In the spirit of the unilateral president acting alone, though, the Obama White House made it clear that the president enjoyed full authority to use armed force regardless, should Congress prefer to stay out of the decision loop. Obama said he would "welcome support for this effort" but, pointing to Article II, he continued: "I have the authority to address the [ISIS] threat."[28] His top lawyers at the Pentagon and the Justice Department urged him to follow the procedures of the WPR, but Obama went his own way.[29] As Louis Fisher noted, "Military force would last seven months, exceeding the 60–90-day limit of the WPR."[30]

This operation, supposedly of short duration, soon morphed into the wider use of ground troops and air support in Iraq and Syria against ISIS targets, in what appeared to be an endless cycle of escalating warfare. The bombing of the Iraqi city of Tikrit in 2015 provided a stark illustration of the escalation. Conflating ISIS with Al-Qaeda and – a vital turning point – relying on AUMF (Authorization for the Use of Military

Force, legislation passed by Congress to greenlight Bush II's retaliation against Al-Qaeda and the Taliban in 2001 in Afghanistan and extended in 2002 to cover an invasion of Iraq) to fight both terrorist factions "fueled the criticism," recalled a former attorney in the Obama administration, "that the president was a unilateralist after all."[31]

The trigger word "hostilities" in the WPR seemed to have followed the dinosaurs on the road to extinction. Fisher has noted that "according to the analysis by the Obama administration, if the United States conducted military operations by bombing at 30,000 feet, launching Tomahawk missiles from ships in the Mediterranean, and using armed drones, there would be not 'hostilities' in Libya (or anywhere else) under the terms of the War Powers Resolution, provided that US casualties were minimal or nonexistent." Noting the slipperiness of this slope, Fisher observed further: "Under that interpretation, a nation with superior military force could pulverize another country – including the use of nuclear weapons – and there would be neither hostilities nor war."[32]

The GOP leaders of the House and Senate chose to stand on the sidelines when it came to the war powers, with Senator Mitch McConnell (R-Kentucky), the majority leader, maintaining that repeal of AUMF would simple confuse matters and jeopardize the safety of America's fighting men and women in the field of battle. This docile response to Congress's responsibilities reminded observers anew that the aggrandizement of power in the White House can be just as much a function of congressional negligence as unbridled presidential initiative. Even many Democrats in the Congress were wary of officially granting President Obama authority to escalate the nation's war against foreign terrorists, sensing that the Obama strategy in Syria was muddled. Some of these Democrats were still feeling the sting of remorse from their votes for the Bush II war in Iraq. So, the blame for the concentration of the war power by the president should not be placed on Obama alone. When he sought congressional approval for the use of force to strike against the chemical weapons of the Bashar al-Assad regime in Syria, for instance, lawmakers balked (with the exception of some Republicans whose default position was to oppose Obama on anything he requested, though they were happy later to let President Trump do as he may with the war powers). The president pulled back in light of this congressional dithering. Only subsequently did he resort to reliance on AUMF to confront the evils of ISIS in Syria.

Nonetheless, despite a passive Congress, a president – especially a former professor of international law – should arguably have felt compelled to honor the Constitution and the WPR, even if lawmakers remained docile. Obama could have resisted the urge to seek refuge in outdated AUMF authority. A man of his enormous persuasive and oratory skills could surely have made this constitutional position more compelling than he did on Capitol Hill and to the public. In contrast, Senator Tim Kaine (D-Virginia) was one senator at least who refused to take casually the imperative to repeal AUMF, with its overly board assertions of presidential authority for war-making – or any other fresh war-fighting assertions of unilateral powers that might emerge from the White House, whether the president happened to be a Democrat or a Republican. "The current interpretation of the authorization [AUMF] essentially allows an American president, without any approval from Congress," Kaine argued, "to wage war anywhere against any terrorist groups for however long they want to."[33]

Senator Kaine was correct: Both the Congress and the presidency have been far too lax in relying for war-making authority on counterterrorism laws passed in the immediate aftermath of 9/11, especially AUMF but also the broadly worded vote for Bush II's war in Iraq. Passed in a time of great anxiety, these congressional actions provided insufficient standing for the White House to engage in battles against terrorists around the world decades later. Under the Obama and Trump administrations, the United States pursued not only Al-Qaeda and the Taliban, but also ISIS and other terrorist factions in Libya, Somalia, Yemen, Pakistan, Mali, Niger, and several other locations – often by way of military and intelligence operations hidden from the American people and even their representatives in the Congress. When jihadists gunned down American Special Forces troops in Niger in 2018, Senator Lindsey Graham (R-South Carolina, and a member of the Armed Services Committee) said plaintively, "I didn't know there was [sic] 1,000 [American] troops in Niger."[34] Today, there are some 1,200 Special Operations forces in Africa, although in the wake of this controversy, military brass contemplated cutting the number by half over the next three years.[35]

A polarized, sometimes paralyzed Congress – riven by partisan strife and even disdain toward members of the opposition party – has usually been unable to enter effectively into this debate on the war power, although a few lawmakers (like Senator Kaine and Representative Adam Schiff, D-California) have attempted to bring the Constitution to bear on the use of military force in the twenty-first century. Kaine worried not only about the tendency on Capitol Hill to set the Constitution aside, but also the more practical matter that the lack of a congressional vote undermined the sense overseas that the United States stood united against its terrorist enemies. "You don't ask people [US troops] to sacrifice their lives until the nation has debated and committed to the mission," the senator said in an interview, adding: "It's immoral."[36]

To its credit, the Senate Foreign Relations Committee voted on a resolution in 2017 to limit presidential authority for military operations against ISIS to three years, and the panel demanded careful definitions from the Pentagon about the scope of the war-fighting. The measure never made it to the floor, however, blocked by the GOP Senate leadership, which evidently preferred to let the White House struggle on against ISIS by itself without drawing Senate Republicans into the war powers controversy. (In March 2018, during the Trump administration, the Senate leadership would again block a Senate Foreign Relation Committee resolution designed to limit US involvement in foreign wars, this time in Yemen.)

President Obama, eventually guided less by constitutional theory and more by the realities of political gridlock in Washington, finally sidestepped the Congress and unilaterally pursued his administration's objectives on distant battlefields – a posture forced upon the president by a dysfunctional legislative branch. The end result was a national security policy slipping dangerously away from constitutional moorings. "Legislative paralysis only reinforces the executive branch's inclination to stretch the law," observed *New York Times* constitutional specialist Charlie Savage.[37]

For Yale University law professor Bruce Ackerman, Obama's reach went too far in Libya and Syria. He viewed the president's approach as "a decisive break in the American constitutional tradition," arguing that "nothing attempted by his predecessor, George W. Bush, remotely compares in imperial hubris."[38] A fundamental problem with Obama's unilateral use of the war power is that it set precedents for later, perhaps less thoughtful and ethical commanders-in-chief – even inviting an opportunity for presidentially ordered, preemptive strikes against suspected terrorists anywhere: the Middle East, South Asia, West Africa, maybe even the hills outside Los Angeles. Or perhaps a first strike against nuclear-armed North Korea.

Despite his occasional Madisonian rhetoric, Obama may well have breathed a sigh of relief that he did not have to engage in a major donnybrook with the Congress over the applicability of the WPR to counterterrorism efforts against the likes of Al-Qaeda and ISIS. Also, no doubt he remembered the pain of an earlier embarrassing situation when the Congress had refused to authorize his request for airstrikes against President Assad of Syria in 2013. The Constitution, though, is not about making life easier for presidents by granting them carte blanche authority for war-making, or easier for lawmakers and judges by allowing them to look the other way; rather, it is about, as former Supreme Court Justice Louis Brandeis once put it, "saving the people from autocracy."[39] The bottom line: presidents must explain to Congress why a military conflict is important – perhaps, as journalist David Brinkley once suggested in the context of the failed war in Vietnam, with a press conference held in Arlington Cemetery, the president standing among the crosses that mark the graves of those who paid the ultimate sacrifice in past American wars.[40]

The Treaty Power. When it came to international agreements, the centerpiece of the Obama years was a deal with Iran to curb its nuclear weapons program in exchange for relaxing economic sanctions against the regime. Here, the administration went to great lengths to avoid the treaty process, which might have led to the strangulation of the initiative by a GOP majority in the Senate. He even eschewed the use of a statutory agreement in this instance. "The White House has made one significant decision," reported the *New York Times*: "If agreement [with Iran] is reached, President Obama will do everything in his power to avoid letting Congress vote on it."[41] This strategy failed, though, as lawmakers – Republican and Democrat alike – bristled at this attempt to bypass them. In a letter to the president dated March 12, 2015, the chairman of the Senate Foreign Relations Committee, Bob

Corker (R-Tennessee), wrote that a nuclear deal with Iran absent a congressional vote would be "a direct affront to the American people and seeks to undermine Congress's appropriate role."[42]

While the president had an executive agreement in mind, the Congress insisted on, if not a treaty, at least a statutory agreement. Chairman Corker introduced a bipartisan bill known as the Iran Nuclear Agreement Review Act, which mandated a congressional review of the nuclear pact before it was consummated. The bill passed overwhelmingly in both chambers on May 22, 2015, giving lawmakers thirty days to examine America's negotiating position. Obama had vowed initially to veto any such attempt by Congress to "encroach on traditional presidential prerogatives" – a phrase that seemed to come directly from the Dick Cheney playbook – but the Corker Act had sufficient support to be veto-proof. The Congress now had a chance to review the US stance and offer improvements in the language. By the end of the thirty-day period, it was clear that lawmakers would allow the agreement to move forward as, essentially, a hybrid statutory agreement: No formal vote was taken on the actual final agreement wording, but at least the Congress had been involved (by formal vote) in a review process with an opportunity to make changes in the pact. The White House retreated from its opposition to a congressional review and supported the modest pushback by lawmakers as a legitimization of its plan to complete the deal with Iran.

The Obama administration also locked horns with the Senate on fast-track trade authority, whereby the president's proposal for the use of statutory agreements dealing with trade negotiations would be allowed an up-or-down decision on the Hill, without lawmakers adding amendments here and there and thus complicating the commercial foreign policy objectives of the executive branch. Majority leader Harry Reid (D-Nevada) proved reluctant to grant this approach (used by previous presidents) because labor unions and environmental activists had grown wary of how President Obama's initiatives might affect their interests. Eventually, the president backed away from a fight with the Congress on trade and agreed to full legislative debate on major trade proposals. The president's Trans-Pacific Partnership (TPP) also drew widespread criticism in the Congress, demonstrating that presidents may have more success in their attempts to exert unilateral control over the war and spy powers than the treaty powers. With the latter, members of Congress are willing to go to the mat with a president because trade agreements can have an immediate effect – positive or negative – on their districts. Lawmakers demonstrated, too, that they still had a pulse on another matter: the gross Russian annexation of Crimea in 2014. In retaliation, the Congress moved quickly to pass strong trade sanctions against Russia, with the White House following after.

The quiet buildup of US Special Forces troops in Niger during the Obama administration probably (the facts remain secret) also included an executive agreement with the local government to allow the construction of a $110 million American drone base on its soil.[43] This was the preferred approach used by the

Johnson administration in Thailand, recall, to support US military operations in Southeast Asia, leading to deep commitments by the United States to the defense of Thailand – all without formal congressional debate and approval.[44]

The Spy Power. President Obama displayed ambivalence toward working with the Congress when it came to matters of intelligence. As with other administrations, much of the time, the Obama team provided documents and witnesses for hearings held by SSCI and HPSCI (the Senate and House Intelligence Committees), knowing that subpoenas would be forthcoming if the administration failed to cooperate. On other occasions, though, the Obama White House proved recalcitrant during some key intelligence controversies – for example, stiff-arming Democrats on Capitol Hill who questioned the administration's record number of prosecutions against journalists accused of publishing leaked classified information.

Moreover, when Democrats on SSCI investigated the CIA's use of torture against suspected terrorists, the president time and again resisted providing documents for the inquiry. Indeed, the White House helped the CIA and the Committee's Republican members keep buried more than 10,000 pages of pertinent documents. The president never once had a discussion about CIA torture with the Senate's chief investigator on the topic, fellow Democrat Dianne Feinstein (California). He also resisted at first declassifying even an executive summary of the panel's findings, let alone the full report, electing to bottle up these important documents away from public light.[45] President Obama finally relented, somewhat, by allowing the release of a much-abbreviated – though still shocking – executive summary of the full report. To his credit, though, Obama did halt the further use of torture, requiring the CIA to follow more humane interrogation procedures enumerated in the Army Field Manual (a position enacted into law by the Congress).

In addition, President Obama was slow to work with Capitol Hill on developing proper practices for the use of drones in warfare, including the establishment of appropriate approval procedures for placing suspected terrorists on the "kill list" – despite the fact that the use of drone-fired missiles had become the tip of the spear in America's struggle against terrorists. At the CIA, drones had evolved into its most lethal form of covert action, with attacks in the Middle East, South Asia, and North Africa – all without a partnership role with the Congress or the courts in deciding when and where these pilotless aerial robots would be deployed. Absent congressional authority, President Obama ordered drones to track down Muammar al-Qaddafi, the Libyan leader. When a US drone found him hiding in the desert of his own country, he was executed by local rebel forces. The Obama administration also authorized via White House decree the killing of American citizens abroad who were suspected of terrorist activities against the United States, but were never tried in a court of law.[46]

THE TRUMP ADMINISTRATION

The War Power. President Donald Trump has been in office for less than two years at the time of this writing, so an evaluation of his use of the national security powers must be more tentative. Some early indications of his approach to the war, treaty, and spy powers can be discerned, nevertheless. Standing at the center of his time in office so far is the fact that he has concentrated power in the Oval Office beyond what any other modern presidency has displayed. As the unilateral president personified, Trump is the most anti-democratic of the presidents examined here. For example, both his Secretaries of Defense and State observed in October 2017 that AUMF was sufficient authority for the president to use the war power, worldwide, against suspected terrorists and, in fact, that tampering with this source of authority would cripple America's counterterrorism efforts. In the manner of the Bush II and (however more reluctantly) Obama administrations, the Trump administration claimed a blank check for this power, at least when it came to ISIS, Al-Qaeda, and other terrorist threats.[47]

Without congressional debate, President Trump allowed a US military buildup on the Saudi Arabian-Yemeni border, with Army commandos helping to destroy missiles controlled by Iranian-backed Houthi rebels in Yemen. In addition, the number of American soldiers engaged in poorly defined operations in an unknown number of the fifty-three countries of the African continent continued to increase (according to the Defense Department).[48] Much of the time, the president seemed content to let the Pentagon run its own course; in the twenty months since he has been in office (at the time of this writing), for example, Trump failed to meet even once with the American commander of the United States and NATO forces in Afghanistan, General John W. Nicholson Jr.[49]

Some lawmakers balked at this blatant expansion of presidential war-making. For example, Senator Kaine and his colleague, Jeff Flake (R-Arizona), cosponsored a bill to provide new legal authority in the counterterrorism war. "Congress needs to weigh in," said Senator Flake, who retired from the Senate in 2018. "We have to make sure our adversaries, and our allies, and most importantly, our troops know that we speak with one voice."[50] This proposal went nowhere. Kaine would try again in 2018, this time joining forces with Senator Corker, the Foreign Relations Committee Chair (see below).

According to Chairman of the Joint Chiefs of Staff General Joseph F. Dunford Jr., the Trump administration had added Syria to its list of locations where it believed AUMF already provided sufficient authority for war-making.[51] In April 2017, without going to Congress (or the UN), President Trump ordered airstrikes against Syrian government forces for its use of chemical weapons against Syrian rebels. These airstrikes should have set off the WPR sixty-day clock. It was, noted Bruce Ackerman, the first time this president had to confront the language of the resolution. Ackerman argued that Trump had some right to use AUMF authority against terrorists, but that an attack against the Syrian regime was a different kettle of fish.

Would the president comply with the WPR requirements? So far Trump has ignored this law, relying on his own supposed presidential authority. Ackerman warned that this behavior would force the country "to the verge of a profound constitutional crisis."[52] Senator Cory A. Booker (D-New Jersey), writing with Yale University law professor, Oona A. Hathaway, sounded an alarm, too, that the next possible step of inserting US troops on Syrian soil would be not only "bad policy, it is illegal under both the Constitution and international law."[53] Within the Trump administration, then-Secretary of State Rex Tillerson opined vaguely that "our military mission in Syria will remain conditions-based" – a pronouncement the *New York Times* interpreted to mean "without any end date or public benchmarks for success."[54] The prospect: open-ended presidential warfare against jihadists in Syria, and quite likely wherever else they might crop up around the world.

On April 14, 2018, President Trump ordered a second military strike against Syria, hitting that nation with even more firepower – fifty-nine Tomahawk missiles aimed at chemical weapons facilities – in response to a suspected chemical attack President Assad launched against Syrian rebels. Some lawmakers complained that Trump had exceeded his authority again, since he had no authorization from the Congress for this attack either.[55] In a press conference that provided an *ex post facto* explanation of the attack, Defense Secretary Jim Mattis claimed simply and laconically that the president's authority stemmed from Article II of the Constitution.[56] In line with the recent trend, Secretary Mattis seemed to embrace the arguments of White House counsels that if a president only uses military force for a short duration and in the national interest, he is on firm legal ground – quite contrary to the WPR requirement for a report to the Congress on any US venture into "hostilities," thereby starting the sixty-day clock.

Beyond counterterrorism warfare, President Trump spoke of using force to halt North Korea's testing of nuclear weapons and long-range missiles. Again, the administration made no mention of seeking prior authority from lawmakers. Whether the president thought that AUMF covered even this topic, or that he possessed inherent constitutional authority for his potential strikes against a nuclear-armed North Korea, remained unstated.

In the House of Representatives, lawmakers considered one of the Trump administration's war-related ventures too much to swallow. On November 13, 2017, they passed a nonbinding resolution by a vote of 366-to-30, stating that US military assistance to Saudi Arabia for its war in Yemen lay beyond AUMF authority. Such nonbinding measures had virtually no effect, however, on the approach of the Trump administration to the Middle East. Adding to the public perception that this administration would be oriented toward war not diplomacy, the president sought record-high defense budgets for the Department of Defense while simultaneously slashing spending for the Department of State. While the Department of Defense received a 15 percent budget increase (boosting troop levels by some 20,000 personnel), the State Department suffered a 30 percent cut. By late 2017, forty-eight US ambassadorships abroad remained vacant, and only three assistant secretary positions (out of twenty-one) had been filled.

The president's reckless talk about possibly attacking North Korea led, for the first time in decades, to renewed discussion of whose finger should be on the nuclear button in the United States – a subject in which the theory and practice of the unilateral president takes on a particularly sobering dimension. The Senate Foreign Relations Committee held its first hearing in forty-one years on the topic. Chairman Corker said that he saw no immediate legislative solution to this question, but at least his panel was taking a serious look into the risks of nuclear war-making by presidential decree.

Adding fuel to the fire, President Trump announced a massive nuclear weapons upgrade (a continuation of an Obama administration initiative, with a $1.2 trillion price tag), including the development of small, low-yield warheads that could be more readily used in modern-day skirmishes – even in retaliation for nonmilitary grievances (such as a cyberattack from abroad). Experts pointed out that the traditional line between nuclear and conventional forces would be blurred, making it quite tempting for the White House and the Department of Defense to cross that once-sacrosanct boundary. Nuclear war would become, cautioned Andrew C. Weber, an assistant secretary of defense during the Obama years, "a lot more likely."[57]

In April 2018, Senator Corker joined forces with Senator Kaine to advocate on behalf of an AUMF replacement: a formal congressional authorization for US military operations, in line with the WPR, against the likes of Al-Qaeda, the Taliban, and ISIS. "For too long, Congress has given Presidents a blank check to wage war," said Kaine. "Our proposal finally replaces those authorizations and makes Congress do its job by weighing in on where, when, and with who [sic] we are at war."[58] The proposed law included a reporting requirement that forced the president to let the Congress know within forty-eight hours if he had launched attacks against any new terrorist group or its host country. In addition, the initiative contained a sunset provision: every four years, lawmakers would be required to review extant war-making authorizations and approve, modify, or terminate them as necessary. Passage of the measure looked like an uphill battle, though, since Corker and Kaine could boast only four other co-sponsors among their twenty-one colleagues on the Foreign Relations Committee. As James Goldgeier and Elizabeth N. Saunders have observed, "the status quo actually suits many members of Congress. It lets them avoid voting on military operations – always risky, since they can be held accountable for their decisions on the campaign trail."[59]

Even senators favorably disposed toward greater congressional involvement in the war power were troubled by weaknesses in the Kaine-Corker draft bill. The measure would have approved military operations already underway (based on AUMF) against terrorists in at least fourteen countries, among them Afghanistan, Eritrea, Iraq, Kenya, Niger, the Philippines, Somalia, and Yemen. The proposed law also extended the number of terrorist organizations from the original listing of Al-Qaeda and the Taliban in AUMF to include ISIS; Al-Qaeda in the Arabian Peninsula; Al-Shabab in East Africa; Al-Qaeda in Syria; Al-Qaeda in the Islamic Maghreb; and the Haqqani Network in Afghanistan and Pakistan. Further, the proposal would have allowed a president to widen these operations with minimal congressional involvement.

Moreover, the language was sufficiently vague to open the door for the comman-der-in-chief to attack any country (say, North Korea) under the pretext of fighting global terrorism, simply by designating them as "associated forces" allied with one of the existing terrorist organizations on the authorized list. Under the WPR, the onus was placed on a president to muster majority support for the continued use of force abroad; under the Kaine-Corker initiative the Congress would have to muster a majority to halt a military operation – or, quite likely, a supermajority if some lawmakers chose to conduct a filibuster to shield the president's war-making activ-ities. Professor Ackerman warned that enactment of Kaine-Corker would have the effect of repealing the War Powers Resolution.[60] The bottom line: Unintentionally, the measure seemed more likely to expand presidential war powers and spread rather than confine America's global military operations against terrorists. More work on the useful Kaine-Corker proposal appeared in order.

Worrisome, too, was another dimension of the war power related to the round-ing up and sequestering of individuals in the United States considered to be a threat to national security. The most notorious instances of such actions are this nation's handling of Native Americans early in its history and, more recently, President Franklin D. Roosevelt's forced removal of Americans of Japanese des-cent from their homes during World War II and their placement in internment camps in Utah, Montana, and elsewhere. Today, the Trump administration's treatment of migrant families along the border with Mexico who have sought asylum in the United States is shockingly reminiscent of these earlier tragic errors, as upwards of 20,000 "unaccompanied alien children" have been separated from their parents and housed apart on military bases. In June 2018, Laura Bush (wife of George W. Bush) referred to this policy as "one of the most shameful episodes in U.S. history."[61]

Finally, as 2018 came to an end, President Trump – who enjoyed close personal ties with the government of Saudi Arabia and its leader, the youthful Crown Prince Mohammed bin Salman – dismissed conclusions reached by the US Intelligence Community that the prince had been behind the grisly killing of a dissident Saudi journalist, Jamal Khashoggi, while he was visiting the Saudi Consulate in Turkey. Khashoggi was a contributing writer to the *Washington Post*. Angered by this denial of the widely accepted belief in the complicity of the Crown Prince in the murder, the Senate voted symbolically 56-to-41 to end America's military assistance to the Saudi war in Yemen, a conflict that was already rising in controversy because of the profound humanitarian crisis it had created. During the Senate debate, lawmakers accused President Trump of violating the War Powers Resolution by way of America's assistance to the war (providing armaments and intelligence). It was an unusual effort by senators to curb the presidential use of the war powers and seemed to presage further interbranch conflict ahead, especially since the Democrats had won control of the House in the 2018 bi-elections.

The Treaty Power. When it came to international agreements, the Trump administration demonstrated how a president can be as powerful reinterpreting existing agreements – or abandoning them altogether – as they are when fashioning new ones of their own making. The administration remained vague on how well it would honor the New Start Treaty with Russia (ratified by President Obama and designed to keep long-range nuclear arsenals at lower levels), while at the same time it began a new arms race with the Russians by developing the low-yield weapons mentioned above. President Trump referred to the New Start Treaty as "just another bad deal" and moved forward with a novel and, critics maintained, destabilizing set of weapons innovations, from nuclear cruise missiles to submarine-launched low-yield warheads. "The new plan is a fiction created to justify the making of new nuclear arms," cautioned an expert. "They'll just increase the potential for their use and for miscalculation."[62]

More immediately, in 2018, the Trump administration also sacked – unilaterally – the Obama administration's nuclear deal with Iran. Concerned about presidential overreach in the realm of international agreements, even some staunch Trump supporters (such as Senator James Risch, R-Idaho) applauded a guarantee from Secretary of State Mike Pompeo that any arrangements reached with North Korea on nuclear weaponry, trade, or other matters would be pursued through the treaty procedure, not by way of an executive or even a statutory agreement.[63] In the context of diplomacy with North Korea, President Trump muted his initial harsh criticism of Kim Jong-un and met with him in an affable summit conference to discuss making the Korean peninsula free of nuclear weapons and otherwise improving relations between the two nations. Trump left the summit expressing optimism about its success, but critics noted the absence of any tangible outcomes beyond handshakes, grins, and cheerful rhetoric.

Another approach to international agreements that can be powerful when exercised unilaterally by presidents is simply to do nothing. President Trump signaled an abandonment of the international order by refusing to join other nations in the Paris Accord of 2017 on climate change, a pact six years in the making. By retreating from the promise of the Obama administration to seek a lowering of global greenhouse gas emissions by 26–28 percent below 2005 levels by 2025, Trump essentially dissolved – again unilaterally – America's commitment to join with this global community of 195 nations to protect the planet's environment. The decision satisfied his political base perhaps but alienated nations around the world, including the United States's top allies. Further, in a meeting with NATO members in 2018, he chastised the other heads of state in that venerable organization for failing to pay higher dues to the organization, even though they have been moving in that direction as well as supporting with their own troops America's wars in Iraq and Afghanistan.

President Trump left members of NATO – America's top allies, including the United Kingdom, Germany, France, Canada – with the sense that he had little appreciation for the collective alliance that had helped keep the Soviet Union at bay throughout the Cold War. A few days later, he more warmly embraced Russian President Vladimir Putin, an acknowledged foe of the United States, at a meeting. Nations in the European Union began to scramble for more reliable allies than Washington DC – Japan, for one, which signed sweeping trade agreements with the European Union in the aftermath of Trump's rudeness toward NATO.

In August 2018, Senator Bob Menendez (D-New Jersey) and Lindsey Graham (R-South Carolina) led a rare bipartisan legislative attempt to prevent the president from attempting a unilateral US withdrawal from NATO (should that prove to be the goal of the White House). It was, the *New York Times* noted, "one of the biggest efforts to date by the Congress to wrestle back some authority to shape foreign policy."[64]

Moreover, as is often the case when it comes to arms sales, members of the Congress displayed some further (rare) willingness to play hardball with President Trump. Such matters can affect local districts where weapons are manufactured. In addition, the selling of arms to Arab nations in the Middle East immediately presses the "AIPAC" button. The American-Israeli Public Affairs Committee is one of the most dominant interest groups in the United States, rivaling the National Rifle Association in its effectiveness. When the Trump administration sought a statutory agreement to sell $500 million in precision-guided munitions to Saudi Arabia, the Senate flexed its muscles and demanded a more thorough debate on the proposal. The Senate finally allowed the measure to move forward as a statutory agreement, but by a narrow margin of 53–47. On another arms issue, the sale to Turkey of F-35 stealth fighter jets, senators moved to block the transaction unless Ankara abandoned an arms deal with Russia to purchase S-400 missile-defense systems. As Senator Chris Van Hollen (D-Maryland) of the Appropriations Committee explained, "The concern is that the F-35 is the most advanced aircraft, the most advanced NATO aircraft, and if Turkey goes forward with the acquisition of the S-400, it will allow Russians to collect information on how to best attack an F-35 fighter."[65]

Trade matters, too, occasionally mobilized lawmakers to abandon the president. In 2017 and 2018, for instance, the Congress raced ahead of the Trump administration to advance stronger economic sanctions against Russia (including painful banking restrictions), in an escalating response from Capitol Hill against Moscow's meddling in America's elections. Within the realms of arms sales and trade – autos, cheese, milk, sugar, grain, pharmaceuticals – Madison's model of congressional involvement in policymaking seemed to still have some life.

Presidents, though, enjoy some unilateral powers when it comes to international trade – indeed, as granted by the Congress. Bush II, for instance, relied on the Trade Act of 1974 to impose tariffs on the import of foreign steel. Moreover, the Trade Expansion Act of 1962 allows presidents to raise tariffs when this might be necessary to strengthen national security. In March 2018, President Trump imposed further tariffs on foreign steel as well as on aluminium. He could resort to such methods close to home, if he decided – unilaterally – to abrogate the North American Free Trade Agreement (NAFTA), which had been negotiated by Presidents George H. W. Bush and Bill Clinton as a statutory agreement and approved by both chambers of Congress in 1993 (234–200 in the House, and 61–36 in the Senate).

In 2018, the president also adopted a worldwide use of trade tariffs to punish other nations. From January to July 2018, the Trump administration went from imposing tariffs on eighteen products to 10,000 products, raising the possibility of a potentially devastating global trade war with China and other nations, which the legislative branch proved unable or (especially on the Republican side) unwilling to stop. Yet, lawmakers proved less passive on the NAFTA renewal debate. Even though President Trump warned via his favorite means of communication, Twitter, that "Congress should not interfere w/ these negotiations or I will simply terminate NAFTA entirely & we will be far better off," various trade experts anticipated in early fall of 2018 a bipartisan pushback against the White House on this measure.[66]

Another illustration of how the treaty power can be eviscerated by presidents simply by the White House doing nothing is the challenge of cyberattacks on the United States from the around the globe. The expanding electronic war in cyberspace cries out for treaty limitations, but so far the Trump administration has failed to seek a treaty remedy – or, for that matter, even to order the NSA to take strong secret actions against specific cyber-adversaries in China, North Korea, Russia, and elsewhere.

The Spy Power. No president has engaged in political warfare against the nation's intelligence agencies to the extent that President Trump has: indeed, a steady, two-year-long attack against these organizations. He has castigated the espionage agencies for everything from alleged spying against him to suggesting that their analysis of world events is often useless. The president complained, too, that intelligence officials were leaking rumors that Russian manipulation of the 2016 presidential election may have led to his victory over Hillary Clinton. (Trump even rejected the incontrovertible evidence from the US Intelligence Community, as well as from the investigation led by special prosecutor Robert S. Mueller III and another inquiry conducted by the Senate Select Committee on Intelligence, that Russian intelligence tried to influence the election.)

The president's verbal fisticuffs with the nation's spies were most apparent in his denigration of FBI Director John B. Comey, whom he accused of disloyalty. In turn, intelligence chiefs like Comey, John O. Brennan at the CIA, and James R. Clapper (the Director of National Intelligence or DNI) accused the president of trying to "delegitimize" the intelligence agencies.[67] The president, in retaliation, let it be known that he might strip the security clearances of Comey, Brennan, Clapper and other former national security figures who had been critical of him – an unprecedented threat from the White House to intimidate critics and an assault on First Amendment protections afforded every US citizen. The relationship of the White House with former key intelligence leaders had clearly ruptured, as the president's personal vendettas threatened to have a chilling effect on free expression in the United States.

While this unheard-of public wrangling between the White House and retired senior intelligence officers continued to play out, many of the nation's officials proved capable of engaging simultaneously in a more dispassionate debate about the spy agencies and the state of justice and liberty in America. For instance, even though HPSCI had fallen into partisan disarray, its Senate counterpart (SSCI) moved forward with an impressively nonpartisan probe into the allegations concerning Russian electoral interference, reporting in July 2018 that Moscow had indeed tried to interfere with the presidential election, even if the president didn't want to admit it. More prominently, the preliminary findings of the special counsel inquiry led by Mueller also pointed to Russian influence in the election.

The pluralism of American government was on display, with a range of entities in the government – the White House, the Congress, the special counsel, the intelligence agencies, federal law enforcement (not to mention outside interest groups, the media, and public protest movements) – taking various and sometimes conflicting positions on questions of national security and privacy in the United States. The overall result was an encouraging national conversation about politics and policy in Washington that one would hope for in a democracy, with the stark exception of the president's attacks against critics and his establishment of an enemies list (à la Nixon and the Watergate scandal) of former intelligence and national security officials who would be threatened by the White House for their comments as private citizens.

The spy power requires the application of basic democratic tenets to the hidden side of government, not just to the more open agencies and departments. Even before the dramatic intelligence oversight reforms of the Church Committee in the mid-1970s, certain norms of integrity and honesty guided most intelligence professionals. Although some unfortunately strayed into illegal domestic surveillance operations (CHAOS, COINTELPRO, MINARET, SHAMROCK), the vast majority obeyed the law and sought to provide presidents and other policymakers with accurate, timely, and objective intelligence. Yet, President Trump began to dismiss even these important professional intelligence contributions to the nation's security.

His first dubious position came during the 2016 presidential campaign when he rejected traditional CIA daily briefings accorded leading candidates – a sensible development from the 1960s based on the notion that a successful presidential victor ought to arrive at the White House knowledgeable of world affairs and ready to guide the United States on day one. Trump apparently found the briefings unhelpful. In fact, sometimes they do repeat what one can learn in the newspapers or on CNN, but they usually include additional useful information as well, derived from clandestine sources, that government leaders can benefit from knowing.

The president then selected as director of the CIA (D/CIA) a right-leaning politician from Kansas, Republican Congressman Mike Pompeo. He had been a leader of the Tea Party faction in the House and the fieriest critic of Hillary Clinton when she was secretary of state. Pompeo had an attractive resume: first in his class at the US Military Academy, a degree from Harvard Law School, and experience as a tank commander and subsequently as a lawyer at a prestigious firm in Washington DC; yet, the CIA was known for its stance above politics, serving as a neutral, fact-finding organization that prided itself on analysis free of ideology. Compounding this problem of mixing politics and intelligence, President Trump selected another professional politician, Senate Dan Coates (R-Indiana), as DNI.

Pompeo and Coates have not been the first politicians to head the CIA, but the number has been few and the results almost always regrettable. Examples from the past include George H. W. Bush, a former director of the Republican National Committee and a member of the House (R-Texas), appointed by President Gerald R. Ford (1976); William J. Casey, the former national presidential campaign director for Ronald Reagan and appointed by him (1981); George J. Tenet, a Democrat and former SSCI staff director, appointed by President Bill Clinton; Porter J. Goss, another former House member (R-Florida), appointed by President Bush II; and, finally, Leon E. Panetta, a former House member (D-California), appointed by President Obama – five out of a total of twenty-five CIA directors since the Truman administration created the agency in 1947.

Of these men, George H. W. Bush and Panetta usually kept true to the neutrality principle, but Casey was rabidly political, Tenet fell into excessively cordial relations with the White House over its plans for war in Iraq, and Goss used the CIA as a bully pulpit to carry on his long-standing public loathing of Hillary Clinton. With the Trump administration, Pompeo often appeared to be more of a White House aide and policymaker than he was an unbiased intelligence director, even calling for regime change in North Korea, as if he were secretary of state or defense rather than D/CIA (he would soon replace Tillerson as secretary of state).[68]

President Trump went so far as to send CIA Director Pompeo to North Korea in 2018 to engage in preparations for a diplomatic summit conference between Trump and the leader of North Korea, an unprecedented blurring of CIA and State Department roles. Richard Helms, one of the more widely admired intelligence directors, once observed that in high-level meetings at the White House what was needed was someone in the room "who was not trying to formulate a policy, carry a policy, or defend a policy; someone who could say: 'Now listen, this isn't my understanding of the facts.'"[69] Pompeo's extreme political views exhibited as a Tea Party member and his policy pronouncements as CIA director, ran contrary to the notion of a neutral fact provider in the room.

Further, unlike any other president, Donald Trump lambasted the CIA and the FBI (in particular), but also the Intelligence Community writ large, soon after he settled into office. From time to time, other presidents have complained about the intelligence agencies, especially when they brought bad news ("The war in Vietnam is failing") or were unable to anticipate a major calamity (9/11), but they had not done so as publicly – or as viciously – as President Trump. He accused America's intelligence agencies of leaking a secret dossier that alleged he had engaged in sexual improprieties while in Moscow in 2013 (these charges have yet to be substantiated); that the Obama administration and the FBI had carried out illegal surveillance against him during the campaign (denied by Obama and the Bureau); and, when Trump visiting the CIA in early 2017, that the intelligence agencies were involved in behind-the-scenes plots against him that reminded the president of approaches used by Adolf Hitler to defame adversaries during the Third Reich – a comparison that stunned intelligence officers throughout the government.

At first, Trump rejected the *President's Daily Brief*, presented each morning by the CIA to top government officials, then he later relented but said he preferred to have an oral briefing rather than read the actual document (thereby losing the detail and texture of intelligence reporting from around the world). He also declared early in his administration that neither the Chair of the Joint Chiefs of Staff, the D/CIA, or the DNI would be welcome at most sessions of the National Security Council, where their presence had been routine in previous administrations. The president later changed his mind about these exclusions, but he still paid only marginal attention to his top national security advisers, except for Pompeo, who appeared to have become his Polonius. Moreover, while the CIA had sworn off waterboarding against suspected terrorists (a key subject of a searing investigative study by SSCI's Democratic staffers), President Trump sang praises to "enhanced interrogation" as a method of intelligence gathering. He proclaimed during the presidential campaign: "I would bring back waterboarding, and I'd bring back a hell of a lot worse than waterboarding."[70] In the spring of 2018, he nominated CIA Deputy Director Gina Haspel to succeed Pompeo as D/CIA, even though she had been involved at high levels in the agency's torture program. The Senate confirmed her appointment. Near the end of the year, Trump would again shun, and stun, the Intelligence Community by questioning its conclusion that the Crown Prince of Saudi Arabia had arranged the death of journalist Jamal Khashoggi.

So, by past measures of strict political neutrality among intelligence chiefs, Pompeo was a sharp departure in the manner of William Casey (chief architect of the Iran-Contra scandal); moreover, the president was over the top in his denigration and jousting with the intelligence services. The world of America's spies under Trump had fallen into turmoil, and that is just when judged by the pre-Church Committee standards of basic intelligence integrity and commitment to neutrality. When turning to the question of how well the Trump administration measured up to the post-Church Committee precepts of strong intelligence accountability, the story grows even more grim.

The House Intelligence Committee, created in 1976 to stand as a check against the abuse of spy power within the executive branch, witnessed its chairman, Devin Nunes (R-California), become an errand boy for the Trump White House. According to newspaper reports, he met regularly with White House staff to plan how he might best divert the attention of HPSCI away from a thorough investigation into possible collusion by Trump with the Russians in derailing Hillary Clinton's presidential campaign. The House Committee was being torn asunder by this coordinated jockeying between the White House and Nunes. At least on SSCI, its Democratic and Republican leaders were attempting to remain bipartisan in their committees' separate investigations into these topics – both inquiries supplementary to the one being pursued by special counsel Mueller.

Perhaps the most astonishing intervention by President Trump into the world of intelligence activities occurred in August 2018, when he ordered the revocation of John Brennan's security clearance. Brennan had served as CIA Director for President Obama from 2013 to 2017 and, upon retirement, he became a sharp public critic of Trump's national security policies as a CNN consultant on that topic. On July 15, 2018, Brennan went so far as to call Trump's uncritical acceptance of Putin's assurances that Russian intelligence had not tampered with the presidential election in 2016 – exactly the opposite conclusion reached by America's intelligence agencies – as nothing less than "traitorous." That conclusion earned him the president's wrath and no doubt led to the withdrawal by the White House of Brennan's access to classified intelligence as a consultant to the government.

No US official has ever had his or her clearance stripped before, unless suffering from extreme alcoholism, drug, or mental health problems, or found guilty of violating rules related to the unauthorized disclosure of classified information, such as leaking information to the Hill or to journalists. (One exceptional case: J. Robert Oppenheimer, the head of the Manhattan Project, was stripped of his security clearance during the 1950s, wrongly accused – as it turned out, in the era of McCarthyism – by rival physicist Edward Teller of having Communist leanings; the Kennedy administration later exonerated Oppenheimer.) Brennan was never accused of any of these charges, nor were the nine other former national security officials the White House reportedly planned to strip of security clearances, among them DNI Clapper, CIA Director Michael V. Hayden, and National Security Adviser Susan Rice, each with a long record of impeccable public service, but all critics of President Trump's presidency. Like Brennan, both Clapper and Hayden had strongly suggested that Trump's statements seemed to point to his collusion with Russia in its "active measures" (covert action) against the 2016 US elections and candidate Hillary Clinton.

The White House action against Brennan struck most observers as purely an exercise by the president to silence critics, raising the question of who would be next on Trump's "enemies list." Perhaps members of the Mueller panel investigating his possible collusion with the Russians in defeating Hillary Clinton in 2016? Those who denounced the president's unprecedented use of the spy power, including seventy former senior CIA officers, wondered about the chilling effect his attack against Brennan would have on the staff of the National Security Council, the CIA, and others in the intelligence business.

It is important for retired senior intelligence leaders to maintain their security clearances for those occasions – and they are frequent – when top National Security Council and intelligence officials (particularly the current DNI Dan Coats, CIA Director Gina Haspel, and FBI Director Christopher A. Wray, none of whom were consulted in advance of the Brennan decision) would like an old hand with whom they can discuss dicey intelligence operations as they face sensitive decisions. Or when the private sector, which has many government contracts dealing with classified intelligence topics, requires advice from experienced consultants who are now retired from government. Individuals like Brennan, Clapper, and Hayden are an ongoing "corporate memory" with considerable experience to share with incumbent intelligence leaders. Clapper alone accrued fifty years of service in the Intelligence Community. The government will soldier on without this outside counsel, but a useful – perhaps even, in some cases, vital – resource was being taken away from them by the president. Brennan has had enormous experience with counterterrorism; Clapper, with space-based surveillance capabilities; and Hayden, with signals intelligence (SIGINT). These kinds of consultations have gone on for decades and now the United States was about to abandon them, partially blinding the nation as a result.

With respect to the spy power, then, President Trump was acting in a more unilateral and anti-intelligence manner than any previous president. Arguably, this exercise of authority was less dangerous than President Nixon's adoption of the Huston Spy Plan in 1970 against anti war dissenters, in clear violation of several laws;[71] but the relationship of the White House with Nunes was chilling, too, bordering on what might be the beginnings of a cover-up regarding ties by the president and his family to the Russian government. In addition, the president's advocacy of torture; his renewal of an indefinite imprisonment of suspected terrorists at Guantánamo (with plans to send more detainees to the island fortress); his running verbal sparring with prominent former intelligence chiefs; and his dramatic increase in the number of drone attacks against suspected terrorists in Somalia, northeastern Niger, southern Libya, Yemen, and elsewhere all raised questions about a White House that appeared overly aggressive in its exercise of the spy power.[72]

While SSCI displayed a devotion to seeing its Russia probe through to completion without partisan ranker, HPSCI continued to disintegrate along party lines (even constructing a wall inside its offices between Democratic and GOP staffers). Furthermore, the Congress passed the USA Liberty Act in 2017 with little debate and a willingness to grant the president use of broad delegate discretion over the surveillance of suspected terrorists inside the United States, often without a warrant requirement. This law represented a return to the same "the president knows best" philosophy that haunted a supine Congress and led to Operation CHAOS and the other horrors uncovered by the Church inquiry.

THE WAR, TREATY, AND SPY POWERS IN SUSPENSION

The three administrations examined here each displayed a tendency toward rejection of the Madisonian model of constitutional government. Each pushed Congress away and embraced a more unilateral presidential approach to foreign and national security policy. For each of the administrations, the exercise of presidential hubris was most evident with the war and spy powers, but at times these presidents skirted (or tried to skirt) the procedures for treaty-making as well, or even the instrument of statutory agreements, on some important matters. In the instances of Bush II and Trump, these tendencies toward presidential aggrandizement seemed tethered to a fervent belief in the virtue of a presidency acting alone in foreign and security affairs. Even President Obama, the constitutional law scholar, ended up in this camp, too, from time to time, but more by necessity when a GOP-dominated and polarized Congress made a policy partnership between the executive and legislative branches unlikely, if not often impossible. While Obama's heart and legal mind seemed to bend toward Madison, his actions remained more in the camp of Article II devotees. Further, all too many lawmakers in both parties seemed content to avoid their constitutional obligations as a check on the executive branch.

What would a return to first principles have meant for these three presidencies? It would have required fealty to the Constitution's basic requirement of sharing power between the Congress and the president, with the courts as arbiters. Presidents would have been more insistent on replacing the initial authorities of AUMF in 2001 (and the vote to invade Iraq in 2002) with up-to-date and more specific laws related to contemporary counterterrorism activities, from Syria to Niger. Congress would have insisted on this, too, and taken the lead to restore its war powers.

With the treaty power, both branches would have turned to the treaty process for measures of great import (such as the Iranian nuclear deal). Should a two-thirds majority have proved impossible, then so be it. The nation's leaders could then try another drafting in search of more acceptable treaty language in the Senate; or, if the wisdom of lawmakers so decreed, drop the matter altogether and seek some other

accommodation with Iran, perhaps through trade measures. With other less significant but still important international pacts, statutory agreements would have been
the rule, and only with low-level, routine matters would the president and his
agencies have been permitted to move forward with executive agreements.

With the spy power, these presidents should have named nonpolitical figures to
head the intelligence agencies instead of the politicians each chose – with Pompeo
an especially dubious outcome, permitting a Tea Party stalwart to lead the nonpolitical CIA. At every opportunity, the presidents should have placed intelligence
above politics as usual. Further, these presidents could have cooperated with
lawmakers to craft improved procedures for drone kill lists, especially when
American citizens were in the crosshairs. Above all, the presidents could have
worked more closely with SSCI and HPSCI on the torture inquiry, NSA accountability, and the development of cyber-defenses – and Trump could have stayed far
away from trying to co-opt HPSCI Chair Nunes or otherwise interfere with the work
of the congressional Intelligence Committees. These are all serious flaws for each of
the administrations.

Which direction will the United States take in the future when it comes to these
vital national security powers? Will the constitutional model advanced by Madison
and his colleagues attract the respect it enjoyed for most of the country's history; or
will the Richard Nixons, Dick Cheneys, and Donald Trumps of the world hold
sway, allowing presidents to become ever more imperial? Perhaps, it may one day
even follow the Chinese example, set in 2018, of removing term limits for an
incumbent president so he or she can rule indefinitely, eventually with "emergency powers" that have no time constraints. It is easy to scoff at such drastic
possibilities, but consider how effortlessly the Roman Caesars stole powers away
from an unsuspecting senate and how quickly the democracy of the Weimar
Republic crumbled when Hitler sought emergency authority to defend the
Reich against terrorists and other alleged rabble-rousers. A security-obsessed coalition government gave the Nazis power over war-making and treaties, over budgets
and law-making, and perhaps most fatefully over the Gestapo. Similarly, today, in
a time of terror, overheated rhetoric from Trump, and collapsing liberal norms
around the globe, democratic institutions here and abroad seem increasingly
fragile.[73]

In his magisterial study of the Roman Empire, the British historian Edward
Gibbon cautioned that "constitutional assemblies form the only balance capable
of preserving a free-constitution against enterprises of an aspiring prince."[74]
America's founders understood this principle and enshrined it in the Constitution;
that document's safeguards against the abuse of power were their greatest innovation, and their most important gift to subsequent generations of Americans. Whether
we and our progeny will appreciate and honor these safeguards is a matter of ongoing
debate in the United States. The unitary theory of the presidency always hovers near,
with its strident worship of centralized authority that often extends into the unilateral

or imperial range, a philosophy of governance that sometimes controls the White House and, ironically, is beguiling even to many members of Congress – the very institution created by the founders to guard America's freedoms against the accumulation of powers into the hands of one institution or individual. We must rein in the reckless misuse of the war, treaty, and spy powers, or America's noble experiment in democracy will disappear down the rathole of what the founders feared most: autocratic rule.

5

The Illiberal Experiment: How Guantánamo Became a Defining American Institution

Michel Paradis

A generation has now grown up with the penal colony in Guantánamo as a permanent fact. Those in college cannot remember a time before it. As an institution, it is older than Facebook and Twitter. It is older than the International Criminal Court. And it is older than the Department of Homeland Security, whose very name – with its connotations of the *Volksgemeinschaft* – echoes the illiberal era that Guantánamo's permanency both helped to create and reflects.

Plenty has been written, filmed, and produced on Guantánamo. It is notorious and it was designed to be so. This essay focuses on its peculiar role as a self-conscious experiment: a liberal democracy's test of whether it could create a place in which it could behave as an illiberal one while still retaining its liberal self-identity.

A principal motive for this experiment was the desire by elements within the George W. Bush administration to use torture against terrorism suspects after the attacks of September 11, 2001. But Guantánamo involved far more than a lawyering around the laws of torture. The use of torture was merely a central aspect of a broader experiment, specifically the creation of an institution that was in between the laws. Those detained there were helots, like the captured enemies of Sparta, having no rights or privileges except for those granted as a matter of political grace.

The public creation of this "legal black hole"[1] and the inability of liberal actors and institutions to ultimately close it resulted in a slow, but decisive, shift in national identity, such that a generation later, Guantánamo's continued existence seems less extraordinary than it did the day it opened. Now, mainstream US politicians, including the president of the United States (Donald J. Trump), openly advocate for torture and against international law and institutions, and defend the legitimacy of their exercise of political power solely by their success in having exercised it. Guantánamo's permeance as an institution has, in other words, contributed to the delegitimization of liberalism as a political theory and the flourishing of illiberal politics in the second decade of the twenty-first century.

1 THE PRISONER IN WAR

The detention facility at Guantánamo Bay was opened in January 2002 and would ultimately hold approximately 780 men from more than three-dozen countries.[2] Starting in May 2002, the Central Intelligence Agency began operating numerous black sites around the world, small-scale Guantánamos, where at least 119 men would be held until 2008 when the last of the black site prisoners were publicly transferred to Guantánamo.[3] As of this writing, Guantánamo remains open and continues to house approximately forty men.

The detention of the enemy population during armed conflict is neither new nor illiberal, or at least no more illiberal than warfare itself. While its origins likely had more to do with ransoming high-value captives, the large-scale detention of the enemy population supplanted the millennia-old alternative of mass summary execution. The duty to detain those who have surrendered or are otherwise incapable of fighting is a bedrock norm of international humanitarian law, which has itself spun off numerous additional protections for enemy captives, such as those contained in the Third and Fourth Geneva Conventions.

If we use John Gray's tenets of liberalism (individualism, egalitarianism, universalism, and meliorism) as a benchmark for evaluating the consistency of a state's policies with its self-identification as liberal,[4] there was nothing inevitably illiberal about the creation of places like Guantánamo and the black sites to detain individuals captured in the war in Afghanistan or the associated armed conflicts the United States initiated against Al-Qaeda after the September 11th attacks. Captives had to be held somewhere. And, the investment in capture and detention instead of homicide (e.g., by drone strikes) was arguably within the finest traditions of warfare conducted by self-identified liberal states.

In that spirit, President George W. Bush could have declared that, regardless of their technical legal entitlement, individuals captured in the so-called War on Terror would be treated as prisoners of war. This would have relied upon the liberal tradition, avoided the subsequent legal battle over the Guantánamo detainees' right to habeas corpus, and guaranteed the established standards of prisoner treatment that the Geneva Conventions provide.

President Lyndon B. Johnson chose a similar path in the context of the US-backed counterinsurgency against the Viet Cong. Though arguably not entitled to prisoner of war status, the Johnson administration voluntarily opted to treat captured Viet Cong fighters as prisoners of war.[5] The legacy is that US detention operations in Vietnam were largely uneventful and now are mostly forgotten. In fact, to the extent that prisoner abuse is remembered at all from that war, it is in the form of the "Hanoi Hilton," the infamous prison run by the North Vietnamese, who classified any US personnel it captured and held there – such as the late Senator John McCain – as unlawful combatants.

But Guantánamo and the black sites were not mere detention facilities.[6] Instead, the Bush administration seemed to go out of its way to affront the liberal tradition, in particular, with its embrace of torture.

One could certainly argue that the use of torture at Guantánamo was itself sufficient to sustain the argument that the United States broke in a fundamental way from its liberal values and traditions there. Since at least the Enlightenment jurist Cesare Beccaria,[7] the governmental resort to torture has been a paradigmatic act of illiberalism. Torture necessarily turns the individual into an object stripped of human dignity, a mere repository of information to be extracted whatever the cost. One could argue that Guantánamo itself was not the problem. It was what was done there.

But, legal policies that admit the use of torture, or at a minimum, that create flexibility so that torture might be used, need not require the systemic illiberalism that this essay contends renders Guantánamo peculiar. Legal policies admitting the use of torture by state actors can and often do exist within a liberal state without fundamentally compromising the state's claim to being liberal. Such policies may be immoral. But they need not jettison the principles of universal equal dignity that define the liberal state.

Darius Rejali has done the most comprehensive historical analysis of torture's use in liberal states.[8] He strictly describes his focus as the use of torture in "democratic" states, which I would argue he uses interchangeably with liberal states, insofar as he intends the term "democratic" to be juxtaposed with authoritarian states. The principal trends he identifies are that liberal states use "clean" techniques (i.e., forms of torture that leave no obvious and permanent physical traces) and go to great lengths to maintain secrecy around the use of torture, generally denying its use altogether.

The United States' use of torture in the post-9/11 period generally fits Rejali's pattern. The authorized torture techniques, euphemized as "enhanced interrogation techniques," are all examples of the "clean" torture techniques Rejali describes. What is more, when interrogators varied from them, there were at least reprimands, a recognition of impropriety. For example, in the torture of Abd al-Rahim al-Nashiri, an interrogator menaced him with both a drill and a handgun. Neither were used to maim al-Nashiri. But seeing as those techniques had not been authorized, the interrogator's behavior was post hoc deemed impermissible.[9]

Similarly, President Bush repeatedly denied that the United States was engaging in torture of any kind, both in denying that "enhanced interrogation techniques" were torture and using the classification system to keep even the use of these "not torture" techniques hidden from public view. In fact, in response to a reporter's question, President Bush seemed to make both arguments simultaneously.

Part of a successful war on terror is for the United States of America to be able to conduct operations, all aimed to protect the American people, *covertly*. However,

I can tell you two things: one, that we abide by the law of the United States; we do not torture.[10]

In other words, the government is not engaging in torture but whatever it is doing is secret. Indeed, the United States government continues to conceal the details surrounding the use of torture at Guantánamo and the black sites and the very use of these places protected this secrecy.

Both of Rejali's features – the use of clean torture techniques and secrecy – reflect, what I would call, hypocritical decency. They reflect the liberal state's acknowledgement that liberalism is incompatible with torture, even if it is used. Bernard Harcourt identifies a similar concept when he describes counterinsurgency by liberal states as "Janus-faced." On the one hand, the state engages in brutality to the point of terror against the enemy elements within the population, while ostentatiously espousing liberal ideals in a play for the hearts and minds of the broader population from which those elements come.[11]

One could certainly argue that the very fact that it is hypocritical renders any claim of decency illegitimate. It is certainly the implication of Harcourt's description of it as two-faced, a subterfuge to mislead the broader population about the state's true illiberal nature. But this would be a mistake. The hypocrisy both recognizes and brands the illiberal act as aberrational, which in turn prevents it from becoming institutionalized even when widespread. It seeks to preserve the liberal national identity. It acknowledges a fall from grace, a sin against the state's liberal ideals. It does not hail the infernal world.

The euphemism "enhanced interrogation techniques" demonstrates this just as forbearance in only applying clean torture techniques creates the opportunity to deny that any torture is being used because what is being done is not technically within the definition of torture. In a now-notorious August 2002 memorandum, the Office of Legal Counsel postulated that to be torture, the "victim must experience intense pain or suffering of the kind that is equivalent to the pain that would be associated with serious physical injury so severe that death, organ failure or permanent damage resulting in a loss of significant body functions will likely result."[12] Such a contortion of the existing legal standards is arguably corrupt and blameworthy for that reason. But, the very attempt to claim, however implausibly or cynically, that the conduct was not torture by virtue of not being the kind of acts that the law prohibits, necessarily recognizes – indeed reaffirms – the binding force of the torture prohibition and the liberal order of which it is a central part.

To Rejali's two features, I would add a third that depends on the liberal states' exploitation of their own liberal institutions, specifically the legal system. In order to fit the possibility of torture within the liberal order, states may continue to recognize the binding force of the torture prohibition but nevertheless embrace subsidiary legal doctrines, such as the defense of necessity, which admit that torture will occur.

This was famously floated in the Israeli Supreme Court's decision on torture, where Chief Justice Aaron Barrack wrote:

> [T]he "necessity" defence has the effect of allowing one who acts under the circumstances of "necessity" to escape criminal liability. The "necessity" defence does not possess any additional normative value. In addition, it does not authorize the use of physical means for the purposes of allowing investigators to execute their duties in circumstances of necessity. The very fact that a particular act does not constitute a criminal act (due to the "necessity" defence) does not in itself authorize the administration to carry out this deed, and in doing so infringe upon human rights. The Rule of Law (both as a formal and substantive principle) requires that an infringement on a human right be prescribed by statute, authorizing the administration to this effect. The lifting of criminal responsibility does not imply authorization to infringe upon a human right.[13]

To be sure, the *ex ante* advertisement of this defense is guaranteed to encourage the use of torture. And, it may be difficult in practice to distinguish from a formal abandonment of the torture prohibition altogether.[14] Exigency is in the eye of the beholder and human nature inevitably leads one to overestimate how extraordinary the circumstances of one's own life really are.

But even more than hypocritical decency, such as accepting miserly definitions of what constitutes torture and maintaining embarrassed secrecy, letting it be known that existing legal defenses will be looked upon favorably is well within the traditions of liberal government. Assuming it is not institutionalized as a nonprosecution policy, it preserves the universal character of the torture prohibition and the protection of human dignity that the prohibition protects. It recognizes that the acts of the torturer are a legal wrong. And it affirms the individual and equal dignity of the torturer and his/her victim alike, insofar as it at least facially purports to adjudicate the individual culpability of the torturer vis-à-vis the individual victim status of the tortured. The liberal tradition does not demand perfection, it merely specifies that government must be a certain kind of rule-bound institution that is preserved so long as there is genuine accountability for breaches of the rule.

2 THE PRISONER WHO CANNOT BE TORTURED

What made Guantánamo uniquely and perniciously illiberal was not that it admitted the use of torture as such. It was how it did so. Guantánamo institutionalized illiberalism. And while much of the specific details of what occurred were secret, seemingly satisfying the demands of hypocritical decency, the institution itself was public and choreographed from the orange jumpsuits to the dog kennels to be literally notorious. Its rationales as an institution were publicly defended within the legal system. And it became a rule.

The initial legal authorization that led to using torture was President Bush's September 17, 2001, covert action memo authorizing the CIA to detain terrorism suspects in the secret prisons that became the so-called black sites.[15] This was three days after Congress adopted the Authorization for the Use of Military Force (AUMF), recognizing the September 11th attacks as precipitating a state of war.[16]

As the open-ended text of the AUMF made plain, precisely where this war would take place and precisely whom this war was against were by no means clear. It would be another month before President Bush would invoke the AUMF to initiate hostilities in Afghanistan.[17] It would be almost a year before the alleged mastermind of the attacks was identified as Khalid Sheikh Mohammed, who, in turn, would not be taken into custody until March 2003.[18] Indeed, it would be more than four months before any inmates were taken to Guantánamo[19] and apparently more than six months before anyone was taken into CIA custody under the auspices of this covert action memo.[20]

The covert action memo and the policy process it initiated were, in short, anticipatory. The embrace of torture before there was anyone to torture made the problem hypothetical. And hypothesizing the circumstances under which torture can and should be used required a programmatic approach. It took what Harcourt aptly described as "a slow, bureaucratic, deliberate negotiation, fully reasoned, regarding the government regulation of prohibited conduct at a time when a deep international consensus – including international treaties and customary law – held that actions like waterboarding would violate sovereign responsibilities."[21]

Put differently, because the decision to use torture preceded any ostensible need to use torture, the crafting of legal policy could not simply tailor exceptions to existing laws to meet the concrete circumstances that demanded it. Instead, legal policy had to be crafted _ex ante_ to accommodate any circumstance in which hypothetical "ticking time bomb" scenarios might arise. And to do that, torture had to be institutionalized.

To evade the laws prohibiting torture, therefore, the Bush administration did not limit itself to narrow definitions of torture and strict secrecy, or to broad definitions of the necessity defense (though it did all of those things too). Instead, it embraced a theory of who the individuals being tortured were. The men held in Guantánamo and its satellite black sites, by virtue of their so-called alien unlawful enemy combatant status, were reasoned not to have had any rights at all, not the least to individual and equal dignity. Just as it is impossible to torture a stone, the United States, it was maintained, did not violate the legal prohibitions on torture because it was impossible to commit a crime against individuals against whom no act was illegal. The unlawful enemy combatants were individuals who could not be "tortured" because they had no right not to be tortured.

To reach this conclusion, presidential-level policy documents from November 2001 and February 2002, and supporting legal analysis,[22] proceeded from five premises: 1) because the United States was at war, domestic and international human rights law constraints did not apply to the enemy population abroad, supplanted by the *lex specialis* of the law of war; 2) Guantánamo was abroad; 3) the enemy population was not defined by nationality, rendering the conflict not international for Geneva Convention purposes, and thereby disentitling enemy fighters to lawful combatant status; 4) the enemy population was also not confined within a single national border, rendering the conflict not non-international for Geneva Convention purposes, thereby disentitling the enemy population of the conventional protections contained in Common Article 3 and the aspects of the Additional Protocol II the United States had accepted as reflecting customary international law; and 5) the executive's declaration that an individual bore enemy status was dispositive.

These five premises led to two conclusions that came to form the legal pillars of Guantánamo as a special place where a liberal government was free to behave as an illiberal one. And while the second and fourth premises would be later undermined by the courts, the pillars themselves, once in place, proved immovable.

The first legal pillar was that the enemy population fell in between the laws. If they lacked the rights afforded by both domestic and international law, then the enemy population had no rights under any law, not the least against torture or lesser forms of abuse in the course of interrogation. Guantánamo was consciously designed to be "the legal equivalent of outer space."[23] Indeed, former policymakers have been candid that the ultimately successful search for what I would call the "black loophole" in the Geneva Conventions, in particular, was motivated by the desire to deregulate the treatment of prisoners.[24]

In place of the Geneva Conventions, the president stated that as a matter of *policy* the United States would "treat detainees humanely, including those who are not entitled to such treatment … and to the extent appropriate and consistent with military necessity, in a manner consistent with the principles of Geneva."[25] Explicitly then, inmates in Guantánamo had no legal right to humane treatment and even the prerogative to treat them humanely was qualified by the demands of military necessity.

The second legal pillar was that because the enemy population was not defined by national status, an individual's designation into this rights-less enemy combatant status was a function of his alleged connections to Al-Qaeda, the Taliban, or what came to be called "associated forces."[26] And this designation was a stigma in the truest sense of the word. It was a classification that, once made, by sheer force of *ipse dixit*, marked one as a member of the helot class that fell between the laws.

Assessing an individual's connections to one of these groups, however, was not a well-defined task. To some extent, Al-Qaeda and the Taliban maintained fairly traditional organizational structures. But formal membership was rare and encompassed only a small minority of the detainees taken into US custody. Even indicia of de facto membership, such as the swearing of loyalty to Osama bin Laden personally, was not universally shared, not the least by individuals who seemed to fall at the paradigmatic end of the targeted enemy class.[27]

This was more than a pragmatic problem. As Phillip Bobbitt argued, a liberal state – what he termed a "state of consent" – faces a profound legitimacy problem when attempting to wage war against non-state actors. While supportive in principle of the concept of the terrorist as "enemy combatant," Bobbitt argued that the use of war powers invited lawlessness if readily available for the suppression of ordinary criminality. The only solution, he concluded, was for liberal states to make such designations via rule-of-law institutions such as the judiciary. "It is not a civil libertarian's conceit," he insists, "but rather an essential element in the arsenal of the states of consent."[28] Otherwise, the state of consent (to use his terminology) jeopardizes its liberal character by doing precisely what the Bush administration did: "a refusal to follow existing law or create new law that is more responsive to our new situation."[29]

Lacking any ready means of identifying membership, the Bush administration treated enemy status as a political question incapable of judicial review.[30] The bare fact of having been transferred to Guantánamo (or the black sites) was sufficient to establish one's enemy combatant status. Even when pseudo-hearings were later created for the ostensible purpose of making individual status determinations of the Guantánamo inmates, the so-called Combatant Status Review Tribunals, the question the tribunal had to decide was whether the inmate was an enemy combatant or should "no longer be classified as an enemy combatant."[31] There was no option of "is not and never was an enemy combatant." There was no option, in other words, of being absolved of one's rights-less status – of being released – except by political grace.[32]

3 THE BATTLE LAB

When brought together, these two legal pillars made Guantánamo an extreme form of what the sociologist Irving Goffman has called a "total institution." As Goffman described them, such total institutions are defined by the bureaucratic satisfaction of all or most human needs of all those within it. The institution, in turn, is primarily populated by the institutionalized (or "inmates"), who live in an antagonistic stereotypical relationship with the supervisory staff, whose chief activity is discipline. This, in Goffman's view, made the total institution a kind of factory, where people were the product. But drawing upon the unique status of persons, at least in a liberal society, Goffman made a core presumption about the relationship between the inmates and the total institutions:

> Persons are almost always considered ends in themselves, according to the broad moral principles of the institution's environing society. Almost always, then, we find that some *technically* unnecessary standards of handling must be maintained with

human materials. This maintenance of what we call humane standards comes to be defined as part of the "responsibility" of the institution and presumably is one of the things the institution guarantees the inmate in exchange for his liberty.[33]

What Goffman failed to account for, or at least treated as implausible, is the situation Guantánamo presented. To be sure, Goffman cited the POW camp and the concentration camp as examples of total institutions. And at first blush, Guantánamo could at least be described as a kind of concentration camp. But Goffman presupposed that the institutional goal of the camp was simply "to protect the community against what are felt to be intentional dangers to it, with the welfare of the persons sequestered not the immediate issue."[34]

Guantánamo, however, was not created to perform this kind of incarceratory function. Those places certainly did exist in the post–September 11th period. The Bagram Theater Internment Facility in Afghanistan largely fit this description, insofar as this was the place where the military detained thousands of suspected terrorists caught during hostilities in and around Afghanistan. Even Abu Ghraib in Iraq, despite its notorious reputation, was a mass detention facility with a high volume of inmates believed to pose a danger to the US-led occupation.

Guantánamo was different. It did not exist to protect a community. This was evident from its comparatively small population, even at its peak, and by the fact that most of the inmates in Guantánamo were drawn in one way or another from the otherwise securely detained inmate population of Bagram. Instead, Guantánamo's purpose from its inception was to create a total institution whose "factory" purpose was intelligence collection.

To be sure, Guantánamo, like any governmental project, was always administered by a patchwork of overlapping and often conflicting governmental actors and entities. But from the outset, bureaucratic priority was given to any governmental entity with an intelligence mission. This spanned the gamut from civilian agencies such as the FBI and CIA to military entities such as CITF, NCIS, and Guantánamo's indigenous military intelligence group, Joint Task Force 170 ("JTF-170").[35]

When it was first opened, the basics of detention administration were technically segregated into a pre-existing group ("JTF-160"), which had administered the internment of refugees and migrants who had been held at the base over the previous decade. But in its War on Terrorism incarnation, JTF-160 was subservient to the intelligence agencies. It took principal direction from the intelligence agencies in the granting/withholding of detention privileges or in manipulating the detention environment, for example, by moving an inmate from cell to cell every couple of hours to induce disorientation and sleep deprivation (colloquially called the "Frequent Flyer Program"). And even this formal distinction was erased in the first year of Guantánamo's operations, when JTF-160 and JTF-170 were merged into JTF-GTMO (or "Joint Task Force – Guantánamo"). In all meaningful respects, therefore, the detention facility was designed to foster and facilitate the collection of intelligence on the inmates.[36]

In reflecting upon this description of Guantánamo's objectives and how the entire facility was designed to carry it out, it is tempting to think of Guantánamo as simply one of the stricter implementations of Jeremy Bentham's panopticon. And that, at least facially, counters the notion that Guantánamo was uniquely illiberal. In other words, the implementation of a penitentiary design created by an intellectual founder of liberalism could hardly be described as an exercise in flagrant illiberalism. But this would be a mistake.

The disciplinary panopticon of the Benthamite variety is devoted to creating a particular kind of subjective relationship between the institution and the inmate. Its use of surveillance, in particular, is necessarily overt. Its very purpose is to impress its presence upon the inmate. Only by being visible are the apparatus of surveillance capable of triggering the endogenous regulation of behavior, which, in turn, fosters discipline. As Michel Foucault described it, the feeling that everything one does is observed helps to preserve basic order within an institution, a force multiplier for a guard staff that is vastly outnumbered by the inmate population.[37] And in its idealized form, panoptic surveillance serves a penological function as the self-regulation it instills becomes habitual even its absence, leading to the rehabilitation of the inmate.

Guantánamo's panoptic properties, however, were neither disciplinary nor penological. This was in part because Guantánamo was not a penological institution. To be sure, the courts would ultimately afford Guantánamo's administrators the deference afforded to prison wardens, subjecting the detention facility's often arbitrary and changing rules to the "legitimate penological interest" test.[38] But it was never designed to serve any penal purpose.[39] Even if the conditions of confinement were often made deliberately unpleasant, Guantánamo was designed neither to punish nor to rehabilitate its inmate population.

Its panoptic properties served no disciplinary purpose either. For one, the detainees' capacity for self-regulation was presumed, at least at the outset, to be impossible. They were, in what became a mantra for the Bush administration, the "worst of the worst."[40] As the first planes were landing in Guantánamo, General Richard Myers, then the chairman of the Joint Chiefs of Staff, described them as so inherently dangerous that "these are people that would gnaw hydraulic lines in the back of a C-17 to bring it down." He continued, "These are very, very dangerous people, and that's how they're being treated."[41] The very language, therefore, abandoned any pretense that the men taken to Guantánamo had any liberal individuality or equality. Human beings with individual dignity and subjectivity do not gnaw. Animals gnaw, typically their own limbs in order to escape traps. And we treat such animals humanely out of noblesse oblige, since nearly any instrumental end is sufficient to overcome the moral weight of their primitive suffering and gratuitous cruelty is distasteful.

Panoptic discipline also offered no force multiplier. In the typical prison, each guard would, on average, be responsible for dozens if not hundreds of inmates. The guard force in Guantánamo, by contrast, has consistently numbered approximately 2,000, even after the number of inmates had fallen below 100.[42] Even when Guantánamo's inmate population was at its height, therefore, the inmate to guard force ratio was at least 1:3, an extraordinary inversion of the ratio of a typical prison. In fact, certain inmates in solitary confinement were often subjected to "line of sight," a practice in which one or two guards could observe the inmate in close proximity twenty-four hours a day for weeks on end.[43]

What made Guantánamo different, therefore, what made it an extreme and uniquely illiberal kind of total institution, and what makes comparisons to Bentham's panopticon inapt, was that the inmates held there were wholly instrumental resources. The inmates were not ends in themselves. They were the raw materials for the institution's work. Guantánamo was not the total institution of the prison or even the concentration camp (and it was certainly not a POW camp). It was rather the total institution of the laboratory. The inmates were its experimental resources and its regime of panoptic surveillance was an earnest effort at data collection.

If this description appears overwrought, a since-declassified intelligence policy review conducted soon after Guantánamo opened was explicit about this. The review breathlessly began with the exhortation that "operations at GTMO must be viewed as 'America's Battle Lab' in the Global War on Terrorism." The repeated use of "Battle Lab," routinely capitalized as a term of art, reflected the phrase's necessary implication that the men held there were in fact its "resources," whose instrumental value was providing "insight into a world whose stated goal and intention is the destruction of the United States."[44]

Guantánamo's laboratory model is also reflected in how the use of torture was both crafted and explained. Lacking institutional experience in using torture, government psychologists theorized that the use of torture might be able to preserve "capture shock"[45] and induce "learned helplessness"[46] to render inmates believed to be messianic in their willingness to suffer any hardship compliant under questioning. Learned helplessness, in particular, was consciously derived from experimental psychology and the work of Martin Seligman, who studied how arbitrary cruelty leads to submissiveness in dogs in the 1960s.[47]

Further highlighting this experimental orientation was the fact that both concepts – capture shock and learned helplessness – were theorized hypothetically. They were proposed and then adopted in order to enable the use of torture on yet unknown inmates possessing yet unknown information and a yet unknown willingness to provide it. And in the absence of an actual problem to be solved, the experimental methods ultimately devised were used to varying degrees on the resources made available to the Battle Lab. Hence, relatively marginal figures believed to be associated with Al-Qaeda, such as Abu Zubaydah, Abd al-Rahim al-Nashiri, and Mohammed al-Qahtani, were subjected to meticulously supervised and chronicled regimens of torture and abuse over prolonged periods, abuse that continued despite its failure, noted in real time, to extract otherwise unavailable human intelligence.[48]

Now, this characterization of Guantánamo's experimental design risks being overstated. Both generals responsible for Guantánamo at the time it was conceived of as a "Battle Lab" later denied to Senate investigators having ever used the term.[49]

Most of the proponents of the illiberal features of Guantánamo would also not have described their intentions this way. Rather, they would have said that they were faced with the murder of 2,977 people in single well-coordinated terrorist attack from abroad. The imperative to prevent another similar attack (or worse) compelled them to view the then-standard law enforcement paradigm as inadequate to effective counterterrorism policy, indeed one that had proven itself inadequate. Hence, they would argue that the machinery of government turned to the war paradigm, which is simply more permissive in matters of individual rights, and it did so at the direction of a democratically elected president, the acquiescence of the Congress, and minimal popular resistance.

Guantánamo's experimental design, in other words, was neither illiberal nor nefarious. It was, to repurpose a cliché, a liberal balancing of the individual security of millions of ordinary people against the individual liberty of a relatively small number of individuals, who were in good faith believed to be intent on doing serious harm. Guantánamo, in this view, was intended to be the moral and legal equivalent of a counterterrorism quarantine.

There are two problems with this counterargument, however. The first is that, it underdetermines the known evidence. The opening of Guantánamo, the crafting of the legal framework of those who would be held there, and – in particular – the embrace of torture as policy were not solutions to existing problems. Rather, the historical record shows that most of these policies were put in place *ex ante*, prior to the capture of any individual who demonstrated any resistance to the standard methods of questioning. They were fashioned to create flexibility should hypothetical scenarios involving imagined terrorism suspects arise. And, in practice, they became solutions in search of a problem, tools that were subsequently used in large part to justify the transgression and the considerable moral, political, and economic cost of the process that created them in the first place.

The second and more significant problem with this counterargument, though, is that the motives of those who devised and implemented what would become Guantánamo are irrelevant. The cumulative removal of legal constraints – even if the removal of each one was done in good faith for individually defensible reasons – created a public institution whose illiberalism was greater than the sum of its individual legal exceptions. It was a place in which a liberal state asserted the ability to act as an illiberal one and thereby compromised its claim of being a liberal state at all.

4 THE LOOPHOLE BECOMES THE RULE

Guantánamo would not have posed as profound a threat to the legitimacy of liberalism as it ultimately has if the other institutions of the US government succeeded in stopping or reversing it. Instead, both the judicial and political institutions of government proved largely unwilling and unable. The government's public assertion that it was free to act without any legal restraint in Guantánamo was probably the clearest challenge to the notion that the United States was a government of "laws not men" since the battle over habeas corpus in the earliest months of the Civil War. Yet, with the exception of one decision from the US Court of Appeals for the Ninth Circuit,[50] the lower courts proved accommodating to the notion that Guantánamo was outside the laws completely.[51] And with rare and short-lived exceptions, the courts generally confirmed and then formalized the view that the Guantánamo detainees lacked any substantive legal rights at all, against torture or otherwise.

Indeed, the only permanent success for liberalism that the Guantánamo litigation arguably yielded had nothing to do with torture or any substantive right that a Guantánamo detainee might have. Rather, the only issue the Supreme Court was willing to insist upon was habeas corpus. This did nothing to alter the Guantánamo detainees' rights-less status. It rather limited itself to the question of whether they had the procedural right to have their rights-less status reviewed by the federal judiciary.

In a series of decisions that culminated with *Boumediene v. Bush* in 2008,[52] the Supreme Court confirmed that the detainees could challenge their rights-less detention status before a federal judge in a habeas corpus proceeding. This was a decision, ultimately, about process, not substance. To be sure, the opinion written by then-Justice Anthony Kennedy waxed poetic about the "Constitution grants Congress and the President the power to acquire, dispose of, and govern territory, not the power to decide when and where its terms apply."[53] But the court steered clear of any argument respecting their individual dignity, legal equality, or universal human rights.

Instead, what troubled the court were separation-of-powers principles, the question of when the political branches could strip the judicial branch of its authority to decide legal questions. It expressly provided no answers to those questions, specifically holding that "questions regarding the legality of the detention are to be resolved in the first instance by the District Court."[54]

Following this restoration of habeas corpus, the district courts held hearings and in the earliest days, those hearings resulted in a few Guantánamo detainees' status being reevaluated.[55] But in short order, the viability of habeas corpus as a means of even challenging one's right-less status was limited by the DC Circuit Court of Appeals. One series of decisions loosened the standards the executive had to meet in order to demonstrate a detainees' enemy combatant status, meaning that no one could actually escape the designation, no matter how circumstantial the evidence or to which international law protections they may be entitled (e.g., as press or medical workers).[56] And another series of cases held that the judges could not actually order the release of anyone previously designated as an enemy combatant even erroneously.[57]

The Supreme Court ceased using its discretionary docket to hear Guantánamo cases after its *Boumediene* decision. And cumulatively, habeas corpus became a hollow process that, as Jack Goldsmith has argued, both ratified and solidified the executive branch's freedom of action.[58] In one decision, DC Circuit Court of Appeals' Judge Lawrence Silberman stated the outcome explicitly. The Guantánamo detainees remained helots, unentitled to liberty, which made the habeas corpus proceedings "a charade prompted by the Supreme Court's defiant — if only theoretical — assertion of judicial supremacy . . . sustained by posturing on the part of the Justice Department, and providing litigation exercise for the detainee bar."[59]

The only substantively significant decision the Supreme Court issued relating to Guantánamo was its 2006 decision in *Hamdan v. Rumsfeld*.[60] While the decision was technically an invalidation of the military commissions system the Bush administration had established to prosecute Guantánamo detainees, the most significant part of the court's decision was its holding that the so-called War on Terror was a non-international armed conflict for the purpose of the Geneva Conventions.[61] This assertion that the Geneva Conventions and by extension the prohibition on torture did in fact apply was not essential to the court's ultimate decision. But now-retired Justice John Paul Stevens, who had served in the US military during World War II, went out of his way to make it a holding of the court.

This closing of the black loophole was short-lived, however. The Bush administration immediately recognized that the court's reaffirmation of the Geneva Conventions put a broad array of counterterrorism policies at risk. As President Bush argued around the fifth anniversary of the September 11th attacks, "Now, the Court said that you've got to live under Article III of the Geneva Convention, and the standards are so vague that our professionals won't be able to carry forward the program, because they don't want to be tried as war criminals."[62] And so the administration succeeded in persuading Congress to pass legislation restoring Guantánamo's pillars.[63] Specifically, the law narrowed the terms of the Geneva Conventions, made the Geneva Conventions unenforceable in court, and stripped anyone ever designated as an enemy combatant of any right to sue in US courts for any claim.[64]

The courts, in turn, were compliant in the restoration of Guantánamo's two pillars, going so far as to hold that anyone to have ever been detained in Guantánamo, whether their enemy combatant status was accurate or not, had no substantive rights in US courts, including for claims of torture.[65] The courts' embrace of the notion of the rights-less helot went so far that in one case, the DC

Circuit held – over the objections of then-Judge Janice Rogers Brown – that Guantánamo detainees were not legally "persons" at all.[66]

Similarly, though it looked as if the liberal traditions of American politics would ultimately prevail in rolling Guantánamo back, political institutions proved equally incapable of limiting anything but its most obvious illiberal excesses. By the middle of 2006, American political leaders from all sides of the partisan divide accepted as conventional wisdom the need to close Guantánamo. A month before the Supreme Court's decision in *Hamdan v. Rumsfeld*, President Bush stated in an interview with the German media that "I very much would like to end Guantánamo; I very much would like to get people to a court. . . . And we're waiting for our Supreme Court to give us a decision as to whether the people need to have a fair trial in a civilian court or in a military court."[67] This careful phrasing said nothing about the CIA's black sites, which were still operating around the world. And a highly influential faction in the Bush administration remained convinced that Guantánamo had not only been a correct policy but remained so.[68] But President Bush's acknowledgement that Guantánamo should close – at least as an aspiration – created a break in the partisan divide that had prevented the vast majority of Republican politicians from withdrawing their support from Guantánamo.

Over the next two years, a bipartisan consensus formed around the closure of Guantánamo. When former Secretary of State Colin Powell said in 2007, "I would close Guantánamo not tomorrow, but this afternoon," he seemed to be speaking for a resurgent majority committed to America's long-standing liberal ideals.[69] And by the fall of 2008, one of the few political points upon which both Senators John McCain and Barack Obama agreed in their presidential campaigns was that Guantánamo would be promptly closed upon either of their taking office. In a 2007 policy speech, then-candidate Barack Obama promised to "close Guantánamo, reject the Military Commissions Act, and adhere to the Geneva Conventions."[70] Then, on his first full day in office, he signed executive orders directing the closure of Guantánamo within a year and rescinded the 2001 covert action memo that had led to the CIA's torture program.[71]

A year later, however, Guantánamo remained open. The Obama administration embraced a notionally reformed military commission system that all but ensured Guantánamo would remain necessary for the foreseeable future.[72] Attorney General Eric Holder's plans to move the September 11th suspects to federal court for prosecution were politically thwarted. The Obama administration lawyers pressed positions in the courts that were not substantively different than those the Bush administration had used to justify Guantánamo from its outset. And while torture was no longer used, the Obama administration blocked accountability initiatives for those who had perpetrated torture.[73]

For the reasons discussed in the next section, the Obama administration's failure to close Guantánamo has been profoundly damaging to liberalism's credibility as a viable theory for the governance of a complex modern state. But it was also during the Obama administration that the legal architecture that had been previously quarantined in Guantánamo, which made Guantánamo a discrete illiberal laboratory within an otherwise liberal state, proliferated. It formed the basis of the Obama administration's "targeted killing" program, asserting the unilateral prerogative to assassinate individuals, including US citizens, anywhere around the world.[74] It has made it nearly impossible for noncriminal prisoners to seek legal redress for torture in US custody.[75] It created the legal ground work that has allowed the Trump administration to act arbitrarily in immigration matters.[76] It has supported the discretion of Border Patrol agents to shoot unarmed Mexicans across the border.[77] And it continues, to borrow from former US Supreme Court Justice Robert Jackson's dissent in *Korematsu*, to lay about "like a loaded weapon ready for the hand of any authority that can bring forward a plausible claim of an urgent need."[78]

5 GUANTÁNAMO, AN AMERICAN INSTITUTION

Charlie Savage has done the most comprehensive reporting on the Obama administration's failure to close Guantánamo or to reverse the policy framework that supported it. Savage's conclusion was that the Obama administration was not actually committed to liberal values, what Savage calls "civil liberties." Rather, the administration's concern was limited to what Savage described as the "rule of law," ensuring that there is a legal process supporting any policy. This, according to Savage, showed that the key policymakers in the Obama administration were basically indifferent to liberal values, as such. Rather, "with very few exceptions, like torture, they were far more likely to criticize Bush for violating the rule of law than for violating civil liberties."[79]

There is certainly counterevidence to suggest that those within the Obama administration were troubled by Guantánamo's illiberalism, but nevertheless felt powerless to stop it. I would contend that this was on its most naked display in the context of a 2013 hunger strike by Guantánamo detainees that returned the issue to the national news cycle for the first time in many years and, as history would show, for the last time of any significance. When asked at a press conference, President Obama lamely stated:

> I continue to believe that we've got to close Guantanamo. I think – well, you know, I think it is critical for us to understand that Guantanamo is not necessary to keep America safe. It is expensive. It is inefficient. It hurts us in terms of our international standing. It lessens cooperation with our allies on counterterrorism efforts. It is a recruitment tool for extremists. It needs to be closed.

***

I mean, the notion that we're going to continue to keep over a hundred individuals in a no man's land in perpetuity, even at a time when we've wound down the war in Iraq, we're winding down the war in Afghanistan, we're having success defeating al-Qaida core, we've kept the pressure up on all these transnational terrorist networks, when we've transferred detention authority in Afghanistan – the idea that we would still maintain forever a group of individuals who have not been tried – that is contrary to who we are, it is contrary to our interests, and it needs to stop.[80]

This, in turn, prompted lengthy segments on that week's satirical news programs, where it was doubted whether Obama knew, in fact, that he was the president of the United States.

The reasons for the Obama administration's failure to close Guantánamo, whether earnest or cynical, are ultimately irrelevant for the purposes of this essay, however. What they demonstrate is the inability of liberal institutions of the US government to defend liberal values against a patent threat – be it the courts or even the election of a president who made a thinly veiled criticism of Guantánamo part of his inauguration speech, when he "reject[ed] as false the choice between our safety and our ideals."[81]

One of the principal criticisms of liberalism is supposedly liberal governments' hypocrisy. This is most clearly reflected in the "what-about-ism" deployed by illiberal actors in Putin's Russia. When President Vladimir Putin gave his unprecedented third inaugural press conference in 2012, he made a point of drawing the world's attention to the continued existence of Guantánamo. "Not only are those prisoners detained without charge, they walk around shackled, like in the Middle Ages," he said. "Can you imagine if we had anything like this here? They would have eaten us alive a long time ago."[82] If the self-proclaimed liberal governments of the world, with all of their military and economic resources, were truly convinced of the durability of any government that acted consistently with liberalism's virtues, they would not act so illiberally so often. They would not have their Guantánamos.

This is not a criticism of liberalism's supposed virtues. It is a critique of liberalism's practical feasibility as a form of governance, and therefore its descriptive force philosophically. For example, radical egalitarianism has a certain sentimental appeal (at least to college undergraduates). But whatever its theoretical virtues, one can make a compelling case that it is utterly bankrupt as a political philosophy in light of the rapid collapse of the Paris Commune and communism's consistent devolution from revolutionary populism into famine-prone authoritarian terror-states. A theory must withstand the available evidence.

Liberalism must demonstrate the success of a real-world government committed to its principles. If the United States, the world's leading champion of liberalism in the twentieth century, readily abandons these tenets whenever – to borrow Dick Cheney's formulation[83] – there is a 1% chance of danger to public safety, then how robust can these principals be in describing the bases of a practical form of government? If liberal states go beyond hypocritical decency to unembarrassed hypocrisy, then they simply do not function as liberal states (whatever they may profess). This, the what-about-ists argue, makes movements that pursue liberal values at best naive, since even under the best material conditions (conditions far better than those prevailing in Russia, etc.), self-described liberal governments are the same as the more candidly illiberal.

It is therefore difficult to overstate the damage Guantánamo did to the perception of liberalism as a viable political philosophy. When Turkey's President Recep Tayyip Erdogan pressed for repressive internal security laws a year after a failed coup attempt, he rallied crowds by advocating that when coup plotters appear in court "let's make them appear in uniform suits like in Guantánamo."[84] When ISIS dressed its mass execution victims in orange jumpsuits, they were drawing a vivid and immediately recognizable moral equivalence. And when President Trump ran for office as a proponent of illiberalism, he was simultaneously able to promise that he would fill up Guantánamo with "bad dudes" and to criticize President Obama for failing to close it.

Guantánamo has become, simultaneously, an icon for the need to exercise illiberal power as well as for liberalism's inability to preserve itself. It has become a defining American institution and a reference point for the dispensability of the nation's liberal identity.

6

National Security and Court Deference: Ramifications and Worrying Trends

Laura Pitter

In reimagining the national security state, US institutions would see threats realistically and characterize them fairly, and courts would end the excessive deference given to government national security claims. In the nearly two decades since the September 11, 2001, attacks, these claims have undermined fair process for defendants and others detained by the United States in a myriad of ways.[1] Courts have rejected valid claims brought by US victims of torture on grounds that litigating the cases would interfere with national security or expose state secrets,[2] and they have permitted national security exceptions to normal procedural protections in criminal cases that reinforce secrecy, *ex parte* communications, evidentiary restrictions, and onerous conditions of pre-trial detention.[3] Entire treatises have been written about various aspects of these developments[4] but in the space of this limited article, I am going to focus on two.

The first discusses the detention standard developed by the DC Circuit in the Guantánamo Bay habeas litigation and expands upon what has been learned about how it was applied and to whom, in the nearly a decade since the standard was first articulated. Though many scholarly articles and books were written about the standard at the time it was developed,[5] more information has come to light in recent years about many of the detainees to whom it was applied, illuminating to an even greater degree the harm done and mistakes made in using this standard to indefinitely detain men at Guantánamo. It is important to take a fresh look at this standard now because it is possible that it could be applied to future detainees; and Brett Kavanaugh, newly appointed to the US Supreme Court, is one of the judges most responsible for adoption of a core element of the standard.

The second discusses the development and attempted normalization of a two-step interrogation process, known to have only been used in a few cases thus far. In this two-step process, the government delays informing individuals charged with crimes in their custody of their right to remain silent and to a lawyer, holding them in military detention aboard ships and interrogating them for intelligence purposes first before US law enforcement personnel read them their rights, as required in the criminal context by *Miranda v. Arizona,* and then interrogating them for the purposes of criminal prosecution. This approach provides US law enforcement and intelligence agencies with flexibility when carrying out overseas counterterrorism operations, but circumvents long-standing procedural protections put in place in the criminal context, as well protections in the military context, to help guard against government abuse, incommunicado detention, mistreatment, and torture.

The United States already circumvents these protections regularly when arresting individuals in international waters in drug interdiction cases.[6] In hundreds of cases since 2012, the United States has held defendants in incommunicado detention for long of periods of time on board US Coast Guard boats before bringing them to US shores and prosecuting them. In many cases, the defendants have reported serious mistreatment, but because defendants in most of these cases plead guilty shortly after the United States brings them to US shores, the defendants, as explained below, have no real opportunity to challenge the abuse. These drug interdiction cases have received much less public attention than the US overseas counterterrorism cases, but they are an example of why judges should be wary of finding this two-tier interrogation process permissible.

I   GUANTÁNAMO DETENTION STANDARD – A FRESH LOOK

After hundreds of detainees had been held at Guantánamo Bay for roughly six years, the US Supreme Court, in *Boumediene v. Bush,* finally granted those held there the right to habeas corpus, allowing them to challenge their detention in federal court.[7] The Supreme Court did not articulate any particular standard of review that lower courts should use but merely stated that review should be "meaningful."[8] The review standard that the US Court of Appeals for the DC Circuit came up with, however, was not meaningful. While district courts granted many Guantánamo detainees habeas relief, the DC Circuit Court reversed nearly all of those decisions that came before it and imposed upon lower courts a standard of review that made it virtually impossible for detainees to win their cases.[9] The standard was justified, the DC Circuit wrote, because it is permissible to "plac[e] a lower burden on the government defending a wartime detention – where national security interests are at their zenith and the rights of the alien petitioner at their nadir."[10] One District Court judge, citing this passage, made no secret that he disapproved but was nevertheless bound:

> [O]ne might reasonably ask, how can Guantanamo detainees – locked up for years on a remote island, cut off from the world, without resources, with only such access to intelligence sources and witnesses as the government deigns to give them – how can such people possibly carry the burden of rebuttal, even against weak government cases? The answer, unfortunately for detainee petitioners, is that they are indeed at a considerable disadvantage, and that successful rebuttals of credible

government cases will be rare events. The Court of Appeals has acknowledged this imbalance and approved it.[11]

This approval first came in *Al-Bihani v. Obama*, when the DC Circuit required lower courts to use a preponderance of the evidence, or a "more likely than not" standard, in evaluating whether detainees were members of al-Qaeda, the Taliban, or associated forces or purposefully and materially supported such forces.[12] A preponderance of the evidence standard is already one of the lowest standards of proof permitted for evidence in US cases.[13] But next in *Al-Adahi v. Obama*, the DC Circuit went further to note that though they believed an even lesser standard of just "some evidence" would be permissible, they were left with no choice but to impose a preponderance of the evidence standard since the government had not requested any lower standard be applied.[14] In fact, there is reason to believe that the court may have even applied this lower standard of "some evidence," in later cases even though the government had not asked for it.[15] Under the *Al-Bihani* and *Al-Adahi* line of cases, of which the newest US Supreme Court justice Brett Kavanaugh was a part, the court held that the government can rely on facts derived entirely from hearsay[16] and courts must apply a "conditional probability," also known as a "mosaic theory" analysis. The mosaic theory is a tool of analysis that the intelligence community did not use much prior to September 11, 2001, but afterward federal agencies began asserting it aggressively, mostly in the context of Freedom of Information litigation.[17] Under this theory, disparate items of information, though individually of limited or no utility, can take on added significance when combined with other information. Combining this information "illuminates interrelationships and breeds analytic synergies, so that the resulting mosaic of information is worth more than the sum of its parts."[18] The DC Circuit Court adopted this theory of analysis as part of its detention standard holding that the court could not discard pieces of evidence merely because they deem them unreliable; they must look at all the evidence as a whole, even if on its own some pieces of evidence may be unreliable.[19]

Using this standard, with one exception,[20] the DC Circuit denied every case that Guantánamo detainees brought before it, claiming that they were being unlawfully held, including claims that had been won at the lower court level.[21] Later in *Latif v. Obama*, the DC Circuit further lowered the review standard by requiring courts to presume the accuracy of the government's evidence, subject to rebuttal, prompting dissenting Judge David Tatel to ask what was left of *Boumediene*'s requirement that federal court review of detentions at Guantánamo be "meaningful."[22] Since *Latif*, the DC Circuit has continued to deny all unlawful detention claims brought by Guantánamo detainees. Use of the "conditional probability" analysis in Guantánamo cases have also been cited in other cases, not related to detention at all, in support of similar lenient evidentiary standards.[23]

The decision to give the government's evidence great deference is particularly troubling given that over the years the US government has detained inmates at

Guantánamo based on inaccurate analysis of evidence,[24] misinformation,[25] evidence derived from torture or that is unreliable in other ways,[26] and mistaken identity.[27] An independent assessment of US government intelligence files on Guantánamo detainees in 2011 showed that much of the information used against 235 detainees there at the time was obtained from just eight other detainees that themselves were deemed unreliable by US intelligence agencies.[28] We now know that as a result of the Obama administration arguing for, and the DC Circuit Court applying its Guantánamo detention standard, the United States held hundreds of men for years based on an exaggerated threat of the danger posed by their release, and discouraged others to even pursue their habeas cases.

This includes men like Mohamedou Ould Slahi whom the United States once claimed was one of the most dangerous men held at Guantánamo[29] but who we now know was held based on evidence derived from torture, and objectively overstated claims about his dangerousness.[30] While still held in Guantánamo, after fighting for years for release, his lawyers were able to get a manuscript Slahi wrote that deftly conveyed how overstated claims of his dangerousness were, which eventually was published as *Guantanamo Diaries*, a *New York Times* best-selling book.[31] Slahi initially won his habeas case but the DC Circuit Court remanded after the Obama administration appealed.[32] Slahi remained at Guantánamo for 14 years until the US government finally released him in October 2016. It also includes men like Adnan Latif, a Yemeni who maintained that he did not train or fight with the Taliban as claimed but traveled to the region to seek medical treatment from a charity for problems stemming from a head injury he had sustained in a car accident.[33] A District Court judge found Latif's claims "supported by corroborating evidence provided by medical professionals" and granted him habeas,[34] but after the Obama administration appealed, the DC Circuit Court reversed, holding that the lower court was required to presume the government's evidence countering Latif's claims was accurate.[35] Latif had gone on hunger strikes repeatedly at Guantánamo and had been placed on suicide watch.[36] Three months after the US Supreme Court refused to hear the DC Circuit Court's denial of his habeas case, he committed suicide. By that point, Latif had been held at Guantánamo for more than ten years. "Every hope held out to him was dashed," Latif's lawyer David Remes said. "He felt that his spirit was dying, that he couldn't continue to bear his conditions."[37]

Slahi and Latif are just the tip of the iceberg. In addition to these two who had their habeas cases rejected, many others, like Sharqawi al-Hajj, one of forty men still held at Guantánamo, stopped pursuing their habeas claims after the DC Circuit Court precedent was set.[38] Though a District Court judge had ruled that statements al-Hajj made in Jordan or at a US prison in Afghanistan were coerced, unreliable, and could not be used against him,[39] al-Hajj lost faith in the US judicial process after the *Latif* decision, dropped his habeas case, began regular hunger strikes, and became depressed and physically weak.[40] In fall 2017, his lawyers reported that al-Hajj was frail and in despair.[41] He was hospitalized in August 2017 after he fell unconscious in his cell and his lawyers reported at that time that he weighed 104 pounds. In September 2017 his lawyers filed an emergency motion seeking an outside medical examination and his medical records.[42] In January 2018, at the urging of his counsel, al-Hajj joined many other detainees in filing a new mass habeas appeal – an appeal that gives US courts a chance to revisit the legality of Guantánamo detentions.[43] Others, though no longer at Guantánamo, like Mustafa al-Shamiri, who was just 16 or 17 when initially detained, and Abdul Zahir, both of whom were cases of mistaken identity, were only released from Guantánamo after fourteen years of detention.[44] Comprehensively assessing the full failure of Guantánamo is difficult because citizens of forty-nine different countries[45] have been held at Guantánamo, and the US has released detainees slowly over the course of the past two decades to fifty-nine different countries around the world.[46] Although with each release new facts come to light about their cases,[47] this happens piecemeal. Unlike the Japanese Americans wrongly detained during and following World War II, former Guantánamo detainees have no constituency in the United States and no network connecting them.

Still, the US government and the courts need a post–*Korematsu v. United States*[48]-style reckoning about what has gone on and continues to go on at Guantánamo – though they do not need to wait sixty years to have it. They need to acknowledge that the standard used in Guantánamo cases was wrong and resulted in the unlawful, prolonged detentions of hundreds of men who would have been released had courts applied the fairer and more just standards of the lower courts. My organization, Human Rights Watch, has long taken the position that the vast majority of the 800 men held at the facility since 9/11 were never legitimate "law of war" detainees to begin with and should never have been held there.[49] Clearly, the US government disagrees with this position and given that current US policy, under President Donald Trump, is to keep Guantánamo open and possibly send even more men there,[50] such a reckoning is important both for the forty men who remain at the facility and for potential future detainees.

II NORMALIZING TWO-TIERED INTERROGATIONS

A trend developing in national security cases is the government's use and attempted normalization of a two-tiered method for interrogating defendants. Under this method the government first holds a suspect in military detention and interrogates them for intelligence purposes without informing them they have a right to remain silent and to an attorney under *Miranda v. Arizona*.[51] Afterward, law enforcement sends in a civilian law enforcement so-called clean team, unconnected to the prior intelligence-gathering team to conduct a second interrogation during which the defendant is given *Miranda* warnings. Law enforcement only intends that the information obtained from this second set of interviews be introduced as evidence in the prosecution's case against the defendant (though prosecutors generally also attempt, and have been largely successful at, preserving the right to use the information for impeachment purposes).

The argument in support of using this system is that the government needs to obtain information for intelligence purposes – information about the alleged armed group or associations the person is a part of, its membership, structure, and means of generating income and support, for example – and that warning the individual of their rights and permitting them to consult a lawyer ahead of such an intelligence interview would interfere with that process.

Many professional military and law enforcement interrogators argue that informing individuals that they have a right to remain silent – which, other than being required to provide basic information about their identity, law of war detainees are entitled to do[52] – and also that they have the right to an attorney, would not significantly impede the ability of intelligence teams to gather such information.[53] But putting that argument aside for the moment, one problem with this method is that unless suspects challenge the admissibility of evidence derived from these clean team interviews or challenge their delay in being brought to court – challenges only available at later stages in their criminal cases – it permits interrogators and prosecutors to circumvent procedural protections put in place to guard against government abuse, such as mistreating defendants in custody, keeping them in incommunicado detention, or delaying their being presented before a neutral arbiter or a judge without delay.[54] Even when individuals bring such challenges, they are substantially delayed and often do not result in sanction when it should.

The US government used these clean teams before the September 11, 2001, attacks but mostly to assist prosecutors in obtaining evidence for prosecution from people previously detained and mistreated by other governments.[55] After September 11, 2001, US agencies used them to try to obtain statements from people that the United States had mistreated and tortured in US military or Central Intelligence Agency custody. They did so in the hopes that courts would find the clean team statements sufficiently attenuated from the torture that they would be admissible in US federal courts that normally bar use of evidence derived from coercion. More recently, the two-tiered method using clean teams has been preplanned – integrated into operations to apprehend and detain someone suspected of terrorism offenses that the United States also wishes to interview for intelligence purposes.[56] It is cases involving this more recent use that I intend to focus on here. US officials have said that this preplanned two-step process is a new approach to overseas counterterrorism operations.[57]

Only three individuals are publicly known to have been subjected to this new two-tiered approach: Ahmed Abdulkadir Warsame, Abu Anas al-Liby and Ahmed Abu Khatallah. All three were apprehended by US forces overseas, detained onboard US military ships for prolonged periods, interrogated by intelligence officials, and then interviewed by US law enforcement before being transferred to US federal court.[58]

Not much is known about how Warsame was treated during the nearly three months he was held on board a US Navy vessel because he pled guilty shortly after he was transferred from the ship to a US federal court. That was when the public first learned about his apprehension and detention. He has been cooperating with US officials against other defendants and on intelligence matters ever since.[59] For this reason, he never challenged the admissibility of any statements or evidence obtained from this interrogation period, or the delays in being brought to court – the main means available to criminal defendants to test the legality of their detentions and treatment in the US judicial system.

After US forces apprehended him on April 19, 2011, in international waters between Yemen and Somalia, he was held aboard a US Navy vessel for nearly three months in secret detention. After two months, Warsame's interrogators gave him a four-day break and let the International Committee of the Red Cross have access to him before letting a clean team on board to conduct a second interrogation for law enforcement purposes.[60] This team informed him of his right to remain silent and to an attorney, rights which he waived, and he continued to talk to his then law enforcement interrogators. On July 5, 2011, he was transferred to the United States and made a brief appearance in a federal court in New York on July 5, 2011.[61] In December 2011 he pled guilty to terrorism-related charges.[62]

Unlike Warsame, Abu Anas al-Liby alleged he was mistreated during the course of his criminal case.[63] Al-Liby was apprehended in a surprise early morning raid by US forces outside his home in Tripoli, Libya, on October 5, 2013.[64] A US Defense Department press release on that same day said he was being held under the laws of war but also mentioned allegations from a 2000 criminal indictment charging him and nineteen other people with involvement in the 1998 bombings of the US embassies in Kenya and Tanzania.[65] After his apprehension, he was taken to the USS Antonio and held on board for eight days from October 5 to October 12.

According to court papers, al-Liby's allegations of mistreatment included the United States using excessive force during his arrest and holding him incommunicado without access to a lawyer, family, or anyone other than his interrogators for eight days in a windowless cell with no furniture, including a bed, with lights on 24 hours per day.[66] He said he did not know when a day ended and began because he was not exposed to sufficient natural light, creating disorientation and confusion. His guards forced him to sleep on a blanket on the floor and interrogated him constantly. They gave him a blanket to cover himself and he was able to use another blanket as a pillow but said he was cold the entire time. The US forces did not provide him with a Koran or tell him which direction was east to enable prayer. They warned him that their initial questioning would be the easiest part and that things would get progressively harder. He said he saw little to no distinction between his CIA and FBI interrogators. He was aware that the United States had tortured prisoners in CIA and Guantánamo detention facilities and therefore was in "morbid fear of [his] imminent death where its only precursor would be torture."[67] Whenever he was moved, his interrogators repeatedly placed ear muffs, blindfolds, and hand-cuffs on him.[68] Al-Liby filed a motion to suppress statements obtained from him during the course of his interrogations, but he died from complications related to liver cancer, hepatitis C, and other medical conditions before the court ruled on the motion, which was just one week before his trial was set to begin.[69] For this reason, his allegations of mistreatment were never addressed by the court.

Khatallah is the only one of the three held and questioned in this way who raised the legality of his detention and treatment aboard a US warship and litigated his claims.[70] He was apprehended in Benghazi, Libya, in a surprise raid on June 16, 2014, for his alleged role in the September 11, 2012, US Benghazi Embassy attack where four people were killed, including US Ambassador Chris Stevens. Khatallah was blindfolded, hooded, gagged, and fitted with special noise-blocking headphones and then transported by different vessels to a larger Navy war ship, the USS New York, where he was held for the next 13 days. He was beaten badly during the operation, allegedly because he resisted, causing a two-inch cut to his head requiring staples and leaving his face bloodied and black and blue.[71] Once on the ship, he was placed into a windowless seven-foot by eight-foot cell, with lights on continuously, and told not to address his captors with any words other than "bathroom" and "water."[72] His access to a shower and meals were limited and he was not allowed continuous sleep—roused or moved every two hours for five days. Khatallah was masked for any movement outside his cell, even to the bathroom, so he could not see his guards' faces. He was continuously shackled. He was held in these conditions for five days and interrogated by an intelligence-gathering team.[73]

After five days, his conditions changed and a new FBI team, intended to be separate from the first intelligence-gathering team, led the questioning. Khatallah got a mattress, pillow, prayer rug, and writing materials.[74] He went from two meals a day to three, was allowed to shower, and got a tracksuit as a change of clothes. He was told that the new FBI team had no knowledge of what was learned during the prior interrogation. After this, he was read his *Miranda* warnings for the first time and told he had a right to remain silent and to a lawyer. He then repeatedly asked if a lawyer was present on board, but each time was told that one was not. He answered the FBI's questions anyway, but each day on a form he indicated he was only doing so "due to there not being a lawyer available."[75] Khatallah had been charged in a secret indictment in July 2013,[76] which was unsealed the day after he was apprehended. On June 26, 2014, a federal grand jury issued a new indictment.[77] He was arraigned in a Washington DC federal District Court on June 28, 2014.[78] On November 28, 2017, he was ultimately convicted at trial on terrorism charges but was acquitted of multiple counts of murder. On June 27, 2018, he was sentenced to 22 years.[79]

Prior to his conviction, in a motion to suppress, Khatallah alleged that the statements he made after his military detention were coerced – the product of his mistreatment during the intelligence phase of his 13-day detention on a US warship – and in violation of his right to a lawyer, which he argued he was entitled to and had requested.[80] District Court Judge Christopher Cooper rejected Khatallah's claims finding that his treatment did not rise to a level that would require exclusion. Prior cases where coercion had been found, he wrote, involved a "substantial element of coercive police conduct" such as "physical beatings, and the use of drugs akin to truth serum."[81] By contrast, Khatallah was treated "respectfully and humanely while in custody," Cooper wrote.[82] On his request for a lawyer, Cooper found that Khatallah did not unequivocally ask for one.[83]

It is hard to understand how Judge Cooper came to his decision. Perhaps the key to this is contained in a classified annex referenced in his opinion but not publicly available. Still, many facts about the way Khatallah had been treated came out during a hearing and in the press.[84] Not permitting Khatallah to get more than two hours of consecutive sleep every day for five days should be enough to constitute mistreatment, leading to sanction. But that, coupled with incommunicado detention and, lack of access to family or to a lawyer, certainly seems to warrant such a step. When informed of his right to a lawyer, only halfway through his detention on the ship, it seems clear that he wanted one, and only continued to answer questions without one because he assumed that one was not available. Regardless, if these circumstances do not rise to the level of warranting sanction, it should.

The purpose of issuing the warnings required by *Miranda* is to deter police abuse, guard against the inherent coercive nature of incommunicado detention, and ensure that statements obtained from the accused were voluntary.[85] Impermissible coercion, the *Miranda* court warned, can be "mental as well as physical ... the blood of the accused is not the only hallmark of an unconstitutional inquisition."[86] "Without proper safeguards," the court had warned, "the process of in-custody interrogation of persons suspected or accused of crime contains inherently compelling pressures which work to undermine the individual's will to resist and to compel him to speak where he would not otherwise do so freely."[87] Setting this kind of precedent undermines the safeguards that have been put in place to protect against this abuse in future cases.

Khatallah also argued that holding him on board a ship for 13 days violated his right to be promptly brought before a judge and informed of the charges against him – commonly referred to as the "right to presentment." Under Rule 5 of the Federal Rules of Criminal Procedure, an arresting officer must "take the defendant without unnecessary delay before a magistrate judge."[88] The rule does not specify what constitutes "unnecessary delay" and one purpose of the rule is to "avoid all the evil implications of secret interrogation of persons accused of crime."[89]

Courts can consider the means of transportation and the distance that needs to be traveled but delay for the purpose of interrogation "is the epitome of [an] unnecessary delay."[90] Like the *Miranda* rule, the remedy for a presentment violation is also exclusion of the evidence derived from the period of delay, even if the statements were voluntary.[91]

The United States had admittedly planned the Khatallah two-step interrogation months in advance. However, Cooper accepted prosecution arguments that they had exhausted all other options in trying to get him to court earlier. Transporting Khatallah by air, prosecutors argued, would have required the cooperation of other governments – cooperation that they could not obtain in the one request they made. Other requests would have compromised national security or the mission itself, they argued.[92] Ordering the nearest aircraft carrier, which at the time was in the Arabian Gulf, to Khatallah's location, or transporting Khatallah to the carrier, was untenable.[93]

The fact that the only way for defendants to challenge the lawfulness of these detentions is through a motion to suppress or challenges to presentment is a problem that, if left unaddressed, leaves open the possibility for serious government abuse without recourse. It is already happening in other contexts and, in at least one case, with reliance on *US v. Khatallah* for support.

Last year the *New York Times* reported that the United States had apprehended hundreds of individuals suspected in drug-smuggling crimes off the Pacific coast, and the United States was detaining them in conditions the newspaper alleged were inhumane for weeks or months on board mostly US Coast Guard ships.[94] Over the past six years, the United States has arrested roughly 2,700 people in such operations. Two of those apprehended, Johnny Arcentales and Carols Quijije, from Ecuador, said they were held on board various US ships for seventy-seven days, at one point with twenty others, before they were brought to the United States for trial. According to their accounts, and the accounts of others collected from court cases, detainees held as part of these operations are shackled by their ankles to the decks of ships for weeks, sometimes months, at a time, often exposed to the rain and sun, forced to defecate in buckets and sleep when they could on rubber mats, and deprived of food.[95] Arcentales said during this period he lost twenty pounds. Another detainee held with Arcentales and Quijije for a period of time said he lost 50 pounds.[96] During this period, they were not charged with crimes, held incommunicado, not read *Miranda* rights, and not permitted to speak to friends or family members, who in many cases were not informed of their loved ones' whereabouts or whether they were alive or dead.[97]

These types of detentions and arrests are becoming more common. Between 1990 and 2000 such detentions averaged about 200 per year.[98] Then, in 2012, the Department of Defense's Southern Command launched "Operation Martillo," or operation hammer, aimed at shutting down drug-smuggling routes.[99] This effort was largely ushered in by Trump's former Chief of Staff John Kelly who, from 2012 to 2016, served as the head of the Southern Command and in that position also oversaw Guantánamo Bay.[100] In 2016, the United States arrested 585 suspected drug smugglers and brought them to the United States to face charges, up by a third from 2012, 80 percent of whom were taken to the United States to face charges. In the 12 months that ended in September 2017, the Coast Guard captured more than 700.[101] Prior to 2012 the United States would send most of those apprehended in international waters and suspected of drug smuggling back to their home countries for prosecution, but since 2012, they have been sending more to the United States for prosecution.[102]

The vast majority of those apprehended in these operations appear to plead guilty at early stages of their cases, which never reach a point where they would file motions challenging their conditions of confinement and extended detentions. All seven of those interviewed for the *New York Times* story, for example, pled guilty and filed no such motions.[103] A search for cases filing such challenges turned up few results.

In one case, *United States v. Mero,* in which a defendant did file such motions, Judge Kimberly C. Priest Johnson, citing *US v. Khatallah,* rejected the defendant's motion to suppress due to his twelve-day delay in presentment but expressed concern about what she said was credible testimony about the conditions in which the defendant was held.[104] Like Arcentales and Quijije, the defendant, Byron Mero, was "cable cuffed" to either the vessel or other detainees and held on the top deck where he was "exposed to the elements at sea"[105] the entire time he was on board US boats. He was never told where he was being taken, even after asking, and did not learn of his destination until he finally arrived at Guantánamo Bay from where he was flown by air to the United States. Further, after being detained for twelve days at sea, a special agent interviewed him and told him that if he spoke to him, Mero would receive a lower sentence. "Precedent dictates that although these conditions may reasonably put a defendant in a stressful, uncomfortable, and/or vulnerable position, the distance between the site of the arrest and the nearest magistrate judge leads to unavoidable delays in presentment," Judge Priest Johnson wrote, citing *Khatallah.*[106] If the United States had the capacity, she suggested that it should consider arranging appearance by video for these defendants. "If the government is determined to detain defendants found in international waters and spend a long journey to bring them to the United States in order to prosecute them, some adjustments arguably should be made – particularly with the advancements in available technology."[107]

In another case, *United States v. Cheme-Ibarra,* the defendants made not only a motion to suppress, but argued a new theory that conditions in which the government held the defendants constituted "outrageous government conduct" such that the entire case should be dismissed.[108] Judge M. James Lorenz said he was troubled by detainees' accounts of "inadequate nutrition, weight loss, lack of privacy for toilet use and lack of sufficient protection from the elements." Even so, he said, the conditions were not sufficient to meet the "steep burden" of demonstrating outrageous government conduct sufficient to dismiss the indictment.[109] "This is not to say that such treatment of detainees is condoned by this court," he added. "Far from it."[110] But whether "the physical discomfort, and psychological challenges could be avoided by the government agencies working to provide better accommodations is a question for another forum," he wrote.[111]

The following year, in *United States v. Giler et al.,* several other defendants, who had been detained on US ships for 31 days in similar conditions without charges being filed, tried to get their cases dismissed on speedy trial grounds, arguing that they were entitled to such relief because charges had not been filed within 30 days of their arrest as required.[112] The prosecution argued that the time to start counting the 30-day requirement did not start until the defendants were brought to the United States. The court, apparently for the first time in such a case, found the indictment had been filed 37 days after the arrest of the defendants and granted their motion to dismiss the charges.[113] However, the judge did so without prejudice, and as a result, prosecutors were able to refile the charges so that the 30-day deadline was met.[114] Still, Judge James I. Cohn noted a concern that should be apparent in these drug interdiction cases. "If government's argument is taken to its logical extreme, an individual could be detained indefinitely for a federal crime as long as the government did not file a formal complaint."[115]

Federal courts have been granting longer and longer delays in these drug interdiction cases, cases upon which Judge Cooper in *Khatallah* relied to find no presentment violation. Five days in the Caribbean in 1985, sixteen days in 2006, and nineteen days in 2012.[116] The average detention time is now eighteen days and an official told the *New York Times* that men have been held up to 90 days.[117]

US treatment of prisoners on board these ships may violate US and international law, including treaties to which the United States is a party, requiring the country to treat prisoners humanely.[118] International law also bars incommunicado detention and US law contains safeguards to prevent use of the practice.[119] Canada's navy and air force provide support for US drug interdiction missions in international waters, though Canadian officials say they do not detain any prisoners on board their ships.[120] After the *New York Times* exposed abuse on board US Coast Guard ships, high-level Canadian military officials opened an investigation into Canadian complicity but ultimately found that no Canadian forces had witnessed or been involved in abuse. Still, they issued a statement that the allegations of mistreatment were "of grave concern to us."[121] Under international law anyone subjected to this kind of abuse is also entitled to an effective remedy.[122] But if the only way to challenge the treatment is through motions to suppress or motions challenging presentment, an effective remedy in the United States does not exist.

Over the course of the past several decades, US courts have permitted a greater number of exceptions to the right to presentment and *Miranda* requirements. These carve-outs increase the risk that prisoners in US custody will be subjected to abuse. The United States should consider whether denying defendants these rights is necessary and worth potentially creating a space for abuse to foster without recourse. As stated above, it is not clear that failing to read defendants their *Miranda* rights or presenting them to a court in a timely fashion really inhibits interrogation and intelligence gathering to any degree at all, let alone one that would justify, even for practical reasons, removing these safeguards against abuse. In the alternative, however, the United States should consider, at least in cases where intelligence gathering is not the reason to delay, reading defendants their *Miranda* warnings at earlier stages. It should also consider the alternative proposed by the judge in *United States v. Mero* – arranging for defendants to appear via video conference from the ship, or going further, permitting defendants to consult with a lawyer or family via video or phone conference. Some scholars, who have written about the two-tiered interrogation process, suggest that bolstering habeas rights by not mooting petitions upon a detainee's transfer to criminal process, applying speedy trial rules more robustly and genuinely, and recognizing clearer damage remedies, currently woefully inadequate in a variety of government abuse contexts, are other solutions.[123] Bolstering the possibilities for dismissal in the case of mistreatment is another.[124] Regardless, current remedies are inadequate; and without reform, a dangerous loophole exits that is clearly too permissive of abuse.

III CONCLUSION

Courts have permitted the US government to assert national security claims in a variety of ways that have eroded rights for those in the criminal justice system and others detained for different reasons. Nearly two decades after 9/11 it is important that US government institutions and the courts evaluate some of these decisions and policies and consider fairer alternatives. This article has only touched on two discrete aspects, but a more thorough review is long overdue and required.

7

The Zealotry of "Terrorism"

Thomas Anthony Durkin[*]

Have we become the zealots we vowed to defeat with the Global War on Terror in response to 9/11? Could it be that our repeated and careless domestic use of nationalistic war rhetoric and the numinous apocalyptic imagery associated with it has led to the same zealotry in our national security policies and our courts, substituting one form of evil for another?[1] Sadly, I fear, the answer to both is a resounding yes. But to get to the root of this much-debated topic,[2] and perhaps begin to right our course, we might first do well to come to a better understanding of the nature of the psychology of terrorism itself and the juridical concept of the "state of exception." Odd as it may seem, the two – zealotry and apocalyptic emergency powers – may be seen to go hand-in-glove; and, we ignore these concepts at our continued detriment, at least insofar as we wish to maintain any credible belief in what is left of our faith in the rule of law.

As for terrorism and its zealotry, rather than merely continuing to search statutes, Office of Legal Counsel memoranda, treaties, law review articles, or appellate opinions, we would do best to consider it through the lens of depth psychology as advocated well before 9/11 by the Jungian psychologist Edward Edinger. Likewise, the juridical concept of the state of exception is better understood not through legal scholarship per se but through the philosophical writings of the Weimar (and Nazi) jurist Carl Schmitt and the modern Italian ethicist Giorgio Agamben. Woven amid this trio of unlikely bed fellows – Edinger, Schmitt, and Agamben – is the unappreciated, and perhaps unintended, sense of apocalyptic and existential fear or foreboding triggered by our careless tapping into the numinosity of archetypal religious imagery when we resort to nationalistic war rhetoric as a political tool. This volatile and incendiary mixing of the apocalyptic with the political has seriously undermined our collective sense of normalcy and permitted unremitting judicial acquiescence to the executive. It has also created the suspension of any plausible reliance on the rule of law to provide us with any sense of normalcy.

If there is any hope of reversing this trend – which I fear there is not – such an understanding of the dynamics of the use of these emotionally laden and anger-provoking concepts is critical.[3] The Editor's Preface to Edinger's pre-9/11 book, *The Archetype of the Apocalypse: A Jungian Study in the Book of Revelation*,[4] includes a letter Edinger penned to an editor of a local paper in response to the 1995 bombing of the Oklahoma City Federal Building, where 168 men, women, and children were killed.[5] At the time, this bombing was the nation's worst terrorist attack. Commenting that the bomber, Timothy McVeigh, viewed civilians in the federal building as being part of an "evil empire"[6] that had killed eighty members of an apocalyptic cult in Waco, Texas, two years earlier, Edinger proposed that it was necessary to understand terrorism in order to deal with it effectively. Edinger explained that "terrorism is a manifestation of the psyche" and that it was time that "we recognized the psyche as an autonomous factor in world affairs."[7] He went on to explain that "the psychological root of terrorism is a fanatical resentment – a quasi-psychotic hatred originating in the depths of the archetypal psyche and therefore carried by religious (archetypal) energies."[8]

Edinger proposed a new category to understand this phenomenon. He suggested that "these individuals are not criminals and are not madmen although they have some qualities of both." Instead of being criminals or madmen, Edinger said we should call them "zealots."[9] Their goal is a collective one, not a personal one, Edinger pointed out; and, in "the name of a transpersonal, collective value – a religion, an ethnic or national identity, a 'patriotic' vision, etc. – (these zealots) sacrifice their personal life in the service of their 'god.'"[10]

My entry into the puzzle box created by these dynamics, illuminating my understanding of Edinger's insight into the psychology of terrorism, began in 2008 in a small attorney interview room at Guantánamo Bay Naval Base. There, a Yemeni Muslim, shackled, chained, and facing capital punishment, was said to be resisting legal representation. His alleged participation in helping orchestrate the attacks on the World Trade Center and the Pentagon was contended to be an act of jihad that would supposedly grant him martyrdom. If convicted, it would most certainly result in his execution.[11] So, the first question I put to him to break the awkward silence was this: "If you are a warrior, why do you want to let George Bush kill you by lethal injection? That's the way we kill common criminals in this country. If you are a warrior, let us represent you so that we can, at least, get you executed by a firing squad."

His answer is beside the point and classified, but the surrealism of the situation is not. What is this about? How had this attack supposedly caused so much global mayhem without being part of a traditional nation-state military operation? What is it that is really behind the horrendous strike witnessed on live television that has caused such collective American anger and made our world so that it would never be the same again? While sensing that things might never be same while watching the attacks, little did I suspect on 9/11, or even in my 2008 meeting at Guantánamo, that our courts would never be the same either.

Since then, however, by participating in the Military Commissions, Guantánamo habeas corpus litigation, and a myriad of domestic national security criminal prosecutions in federal courts throughout the country, I have witnessed such substantial changes in fundamental procedural due process protections that it has caused me to conclude that we have reached the point where it can plausibly be said that in federal criminal prosecutions there is now a two-tiered system of justice at play – one for regular Title 18 prosecutions, i.e., general criminal cases, and another for national security prosecutions.[12] Worse yet, it has caused me to seriously question whether, based upon our misunderstanding of the psychology of terrorism, our use of war rhetoric and its numinous religious imagery have not played squarely into the hand of these zealots. It has also caused me to question whether our reliance upon emergency powers and executive authority has not caused us to reach the point of what can fairly be described as a permanent state of exception.[13]

The state of exception is a term coined by Carl Schmitt, the Weimar (and Nazi) jurist, in his classic work *Political Theology*.[14] The first sentence of Schmitt's 1922 treatise says it all: "Sovereign is he who decides on the exception."[15] The identification of who makes the decision in a "situation of conflict" of "what constitutes the public interest or interest of the state, public safety and order, *le salut public*, and so on" is of the utmost importance insofar as its "concrete application" is concerned.[16] Schmitt's answer, for present juridical purposes, is that a "case of extreme peril" or "a danger to the existence of the state" "cannot be circumscribed factually and made to conform to a preformed law."[17] The sovereign, therefore, is the one who "decides *whether* there is an extreme emergency *as well as what must be done to eliminate it.*"[18] This necessarily includes "whether the constitution needs to be suspended in its entirety."[19]

Schmitt's thinking was informed by Article 48 of the Weimar Constitution,[20] which, in the event of a "serious disturb(ance)" of "public security and order," allowed the president to "take measures to restore them" without consent of parliament and included "the assistance of the armed forces," suspending, as needed, fundamental rights, liberties, and freedoms guaranteed in the constitution.[21]

This, Schmitt argues, is the core mechanism by which the Nazis gave the creation of their dictatorship a semblance of legality.[22] Schmitt makes clear that in his conception of sovereignty, the sovereign cannot be specified by a rule of law.[23] For Schmitt, this becomes a matter of personal dictatorship, a view he approvingly ascribes to Hobbes.[24] This conception of sovereignty, it seems, leaves little space for judges as interpreters of law, except perhaps to shoehorn the exceptions into some articulable semblance of the law.

The idea that this Schmittian shoehorning of exceptions into a semblance of law has eroded much faith in the rule of law, no matter how much lip service we continue to pay to it, can also be found in Agamben's short, dense book *State of Exception*.[25] Agamben poignantly comments on the use of the metaphor or rhetoric of war by US presidents in the twentieth century as "being an integral part of the presidential vocabulary whenever decisions of vital importance are being considered."[26] After discussing President Franklin D. Roosevelt's use of war rhetoric regarding the use of extraordinary executive powers in a series of statutes culminating in the 1933 National Recovery Act, Agamben considers President George W. Bush's similar claim to sovereign powers in emergency situations after 9/11. As is obvious, however, such use of sovereign emergency powers has hardly been limited to the Bush Administration. Presidents Barack Obama and Donald Trump have each seized upon this mechanism so fluidly that it can plausibly be said to be a continuous seamless policy.[27]

Agamben, commenting upon the November 13, 2001, executive order authorizing the indefinite detention of enemy combatants, points out that "what (was) new about President Bush's order is that it radically erases any legal status of the individual, thus producing a legally unnamable [*sic*] and unclassifiable being."[28] As if to predict a controversial 2013 opinion of Judge Royce C. Lamberth, of the US District Court for the District of Columbia, which explained that a former Taliban detainee at Guantánamo could not be released even after President Obama declared publicly on multiple occasions that our combat mission had ended in Afghanistan,[29] Agamben calls the detainees "object(s) of a pure de facto rule, of a detention that is indefinite not only in the temporal sense but in its very nature as well, since it is entirely removed from law and from judicial oversight."[30] A shock to our American sensibilities, Agamben goes on to state that "the only thing to which it could possibly be compared is the legal situation of the Jews in the Nazi *Lager* (camps), who, along with their citizenship, had lost every legal identity, but at least retained their identity as Jews."[31] Even more to the point, Agamben cites with approval the American philosopher and gender theorist Judith Butler's assertion that "in the detainee at Guantánamo, bare life reaches its maximum indeterminacy."[32] An alarming, but quite to the point descriptor for any lawyer who has encountered the legal black hole that Guantánamo has become.

Agamben goes into considerable detail discussing Schmitt and ultimately disagrees with him over the place of the state of exception in the law or juridical order of things. Agamben first points out that the state of exception in Schmitt's *Political Theology* must be understood in the context of Schmitt's earlier book *Dictatorship*.[33] Agamben shows that Schmitt first places the state of exception in the context of dictatorship, and that Schmitt then distinguishes between "commissarial dictatorship" and "sovereign dictatorship." A commissarial dictatorship, Agamben explains, "has the aim of defending or restoring the existing constitution," while a sovereign dictatorship becomes "a figure of the exception" that reaches its critical mass or melting point.[34] Essentially, Agamben parts company with Schmitt's use of dictatorship insofar as it becomes a means within the law or structure of a constitution so as to permit the sovereign to declare a state of exception to preserve the existential survival of the state itself. More poignantly for our purposes, especially in a nation whose constitution does not contain express provisions for the declaration of emergency powers, Agamben goes on to explain that the state of exception is really "a zone of indifference," neither external nor internal to the juridical order.[35] Agamben, referencing the "unstoppable progression" of the war on terror, bluntly asserts that "the state of exception tends increasingly to appear as the dominant paradigm of government in contemporary politics."[36]

Whether or not our post-9/11 national security policies have deteriorated into a *permanent* state of exception is something fellow panelist Bernard E. Harcourt – who spoke at the symposium that gave rise to this volume of essays and whose essay is included herein – takes on in his thought-provoking new work, *The Counterrevolution*.[37] Harcourt criticizes the state of exception view for mistaking mere tactics for what he describes as the "overarching logic of our new paradigm of governing and, in the process, fails to see the broader framework of (what he identifies as) The Counterrevolution" i.e., a revolution without an actual revolution.[38] Harcourt goes on to claim that the framework of the state of exception "rests on an illusory dichotomy between rule and exception" and what he boldly asserts is a "myth that idealizes and refines the rule of law."[39] Harcourt argues that the 9/11 use of emergency powers in areas such as torture at CIA black sites, bulk collection of telephone metadata, and drone warfare cannot be said to be "exceptions" to the rule of law. Instead he advocates the proposition that they "were rendered fully legalized and regulated practices – firmly embedded in a web of legal memos, preauthorized formalities and judicial or quasi-judicial oversight."[40] As such, these processes cannot be said to exist in a space "outside the rule of law." Harcourt posits that rather than being the exception, these policies are legitimized as "all encompassing, systematic, and legalized."[41] Harcourt borrows the fitting of virtually every use of emergency powers within a legal framework from a concept called *illégalismes*, advanced in Michel Foucault's 1973 lectures at the Collège de France on the punitive society.[42] Harcourt bluntly and correctly insists that this practice, particularly the Office of Legal Counsel memos, "sanitizes the political decisions (and) cleans the hands of the military and political leaders" by producing what he and Foucault would call *legalities*.[43]

Harcourt's counterrevolution paradigm and the turning of illegality into legality, of course, turns traditional concepts of procedural due process on their head – and it is procedural due process or the fundamental sense of fairness that provides the underpinning of our very sense of justice. What procedural processes we afford to someone risking the loss of liberty at the hands of a criminal prosecution, truth be told, is all that we have available in our everyday criminal justice system. In commenting upon the deviations from what we would consider to be traditional due process principles, Harcourt cites approvingly of Karen Greenberg's thorough and provocative historical analysis of the legal battles in the war on terror.[44] Greenberg's succinct and seminal premise, repeated by Harcourt, is to the point: "The institutions of justice caught up in the war on terror have gone rogue."[45]

No matter how one describes it – rogue justice, illegalisms, states of exception, emergency powers, or the exercise of raw political power through "legal" means – the result remains the same: In lieu *of* the rule of law, we end up with rule *by* law. This concept, on which I trust Harcourt, Greenberg, Schmitt, and Agamben, who would all agree on this point, fits the everyday reality in the federal courts. To borrow the definition supplied by the Canadian legal theorist Stephen Dyzenhaus: rule by law is the "use of law as a brute instrument to achieve the ends of those with political power" as opposed to "the rule of law," which he defines as "the constraints which normative conceptions of the rule of law place on the instrumental use of law."[46] Dyzenhaus pointedly suggests as well that attempts by academics in the United States "to respond to an allegedly different post-9/11 world turn out to support (Carl) Schmitt's view (that law cannot govern a state of emergency or exception)."[47] Dyzenhaus further warns that academics who do this might well make things worse "in much the same way as do judges who claim to be upholding the rule of law when there is merely rule by law."[48] Eighteen years and counting, I fear this is exactly where we find ourselves these days.

Perhaps a few examples from my current caseload can make this point. First, the convoluted habeas corpus litigation involving the Guantánamo detainees in the US District Court for the District of Columbia, in which our law firm has been participating now for more than ten years. In the summer of 2018, I participated in an oral argument before Judge Thomas Hogan of that court. As one of several lawyers, I was arguing an emergency motion on behalf of our Moroccan Guantánamo detainee client who has been detained without charges since he arrived in GTMO with the initial plane load of detainees in February 2002.[49] Worse yet, our client and five others had been cleared for release by the Periodic Review Board instituted by the Obama Administration as a means of providing return to their home countries on a finding that they were no longer a national security threat. Due to a paperwork error, our client could not be released within thirty days of Obama's leaving office. He is now stuck at Guantánamo in legal limbo, as the Trump Administration has created no process for any further release of detainees.

In the course of that oral argument, a high-ranking Department of Justice (DOJ) lawyer told Judge Hogan that the government believed it could continue to hold all the remaining detainees for the "duration of the hostilities," which is the current status of the law under the 2001 Authorization for Use of Military Force (AUMF),[50] the current legal foundation for the Global War on Terror and the legal thread permitting the detention of these men without charges as prisoners of war – or as they are legally known, "enemy combatants." Noting that the government was ignoring our argument that the very duration of these novel hostilities with no end in sight constituted a due process violation unto itself, Judge Hogan asked if the Department of Justice had any idea when these hostilities might end. The DOJ lawyer replied that he did not since "[y]ou cannot tell when hostilities end until they have ended."[51]

This circular response led Judge Hogan to ask whether the lawyer was familiar with the English Hundred Years' War, and whether DOJ thought that they could hold these men that long without charges. The DOJ lawyer responded without hesitating, "Yes, we could hold them for one hundred years if the conflict lasted one hundred years."[52] Judge Hogan merely shrugged, and at the end of the hearing went into a self-described soliloquy,[53] in which he bluntly told the DOJ lawyer that these cases were very troubling to the many judges involved in them, and that the judges would greatly appreciate it if the government would solve this problem for them.[54] Judge Hogan appeared weary of having to keep providing the government a Schmittian shoehorn for such absurdity.

Another personal case in point is the Chicago case of *United States v. Adel Daoud*, a case that has garnered some national attention because of a pretrial ruling by Judge Sharon Johnson Coleman that the defense team be permitted access to a search warrant application filed with the Foreign Intelligence Surveillance Court. No defense lawyer, before or since, had ever been granted permission to access such a document in the now forty-year history of the Foreign Intelligence Surveillance Act ("FISA"), notwithstanding express provisions in the act permitting defense access under certain circumstances.[55] The long and short of this complex proceeding was that our victory was short-lived because the government successfully brought an interlocutory or immediate appeal to the US Court of Appeals for the Seventh Circuit Court. In an opinion authored by Judge Richard Posner, a three-judge panel of the Seventh Circuit unanimously agreed that national security concerns overrode any concerns Judge Coleman had that due process required that the warrant application be provided to the defense who possessed security clearances to otherwise be able to review classified information.

What is remarkable about the opinion is not that the defense lost, which is virtually a given these days in national security cases. Instead, two things stand out. First, the court took evidence presented by the government in a closed courtroom in which the defense was excluded by law – much to the shock and amazement of the press corps that was unfamiliar with the practice that is becoming rather routine in national security cases. Second, Judge Ilana Diamond Rovner wrote a separate opinion that, while agreeing with Judge Posner's result, had the courage to admit that by doing so, the court was essentially ruling out a time-honored Fourth Amendment constitutional principle that the defense be given access to search warrant applications so as to pose a challenge as to any material misstatements or omissions to the warrant application under Supreme Court precedent. Put another way, Judge Rovner had the intellectual honesty to concede that shoehorning in a national security exception under these circumstances meant that judges could not do their traditional job with respect to the Fourth Amendment.

But this is exactly where we are these days, and it is the problem with emergency powers, states of exception, *illegalismes*, or whatever one chooses to call it. Rather than trying to shoehorn these emergencies into the rule of law, judges might do the country a far better service by following Judge Rovner's lead: conceding that they cannot do their job in some instances involving domestic national security prosecutions while the country goes through these emergencies or states of exception.[56] But now after continuing to watch spineless judicial acquiescence to the Department of Justice and its National Security Division,[57] I can only conclude we have crossed the line permitting any real semblance of credible belief in the rule of law.[58] Worse yet, is this acquiescence going to reach the point where Guantánamo's endless detention without charges is imported onto US soil? Will the continued judicial deference to the government's national security assertions result in domestic Military Commissions or National Security Courts? Will we one day soon be invoking the ex parte proceedings and secret evidence routinely invoked in domestic national security prosecutions in routine criminal prosecutions? It takes little imagination to theorize ways to invoke national security concerns in virtually any federal criminal prosecution. These are hardly hysterical hypothetical questions.[59]

More importantly, though, do these very domestic procedural due process concerns take us into a far murkier philosophical and political underbelly that Edward Edinger was getting at after the Oklahoma City bombing? Could it be that the United States might need to examine its own reliance upon a form of nationalism under the mythical guise of American exceptionalism? If I may go back to the Guantánamo interview room, these very fear-related calls for emergency measures grounded under the guise of national security and forever wars have the ring of the apocalyptic that Edinger warned against. Matching the apocalyptical language of Osama Bin Laden's declaration of war against the "crusaders and infidels,"[60] much of the rhetoric in the aftermath of 9/11 focused on an apocalyptic "clash of civilizations." President Bush could not have put it more evidently when he said in 2006 on the fifth anniversary of 9/11:

> Since the horror of 9/11, we've learned a great deal about the enemy. We have learned that they are evil and kill without mercy, but not without purpose. We have learned that they form a global network of extremists who are driven by a perverted vision of Islam: a totalitarian ideology that hates freedom, rejects tolerance and despises all dissent. And we have learned that their goal is to build a radical Islamic empire where ... terrorists have a safe haven to plan and launch attacks on *America and other civilized nations*. The war against this enemy is more than a military conflict. It is the decisive ideological struggle of the 21st century and the calling of our generation.[61]

It is here that Edinger's warning of tapping into the numinosity of religious symbolism should give us "pause," since this type of nationalist war rhetoric is every bit as dangerous as the calls for unveiled religious fanaticism. Using numinous religious imagery in a uniquely American secular context does not make its psychological impact less so. Nationalism, as the wars of the twentieth century remind us, can trigger the same fanaticism.

Sounding like Edinger in his psychological analysis of terrorism, nationalist scholar Gregory Jusdanis points out to us that nationalism itself "works through people's hearts, nerves, and gut."[62] At its very core, nationalism cannot be separated from the classical ideal of dying for one's country – *pro patria mori*. Another formidable nationalist scholar, Peter Sahlins, tells us that *pro patria mori* can be traced from Virgil and Horace to Machiavelli (via the Christian paradigm of the martyr), Jean-Jacques Rousseau, the French Revolution, and modern nationalism.[63] This concept of dying for one's country can also be shown to have very deep Christian roots, relating back as early as the teachings of the early Church Fathers, who borrowed the Roman idiom of *patria* to make reference to the fact that the Christian had become a citizen of another world, the Kingdom of Heaven or the celestial city of Jerusalem.[64]

Thus, while providing a theological or sacred basis for elevating dying for the fatherland to martyrdom concededly may not equate itself with nationalism, it certainly must be said, for better or worse, to be a considerable part of the package. The same, for that matter however, can be said to be true with respect to revolution and the terror often associated with it. In a very relevant pre-9/11 work, Arno Mayer makes a similar point with respect to the French and Russian revolutions, commenting upon this confrontation between the state and the monopolistic official religion of both countries in 1789 and 1917, respectively. Mayer points out that "in its uphill battle to desacralize the hegemony of the throne and altar, the revolution eventually spawned a secular or political religion of its own."[65] Arno also references Jules Michelet's *Histoirie de la Révolution Française* and the *idee patrie* as a "first crystallization of the new religion of the *patrie* and of humanity."[66] Arno goes on to comment, however, that Michelet believed that one of the French Revolution's great shortcomings was that "it failed to realize that 'it carried the embryo of a religion and . . . was itself a church.'"[67] Fellow panelist speaker and contributing author, John Gray, also makes the same observation in his excellent work *Seven Types of Atheism*.[68] In a chapter entitled "Atheism, Gnosticism, and Modern Political Religion," Gray poignantly comments upon the fact that "partisans of revolution, reform and counterrevolution think that they have left religion behind, when all they have done is renew it in shapes they fail to recognize."[69]

These renewed shapes of religious imagery in our post-9/11 secular context should not blind us to the same unconscious psychological response Edinger warns against. As with nationalism, the emotional impact of these archetypal psychological issues on the collective unconscious should be a concern of national security policymakers. As Edinger also goes on to say in the *Archetype of the Apocalypse*:

> [Archetypes] are not metaphysical facts, but psychic facts. And it does no good to fuss about whether they should or should not be a certain way – that is the way they are. Everyone who goes within deeply enough will discover these same facts, because they are part of the collective psyche. We are all grounded in that same foundation.[70]

If one wishes to get to inside zealotry, therefore, and alter our current headlong dive into our war-driven permanent state of exception, Harcourt's *illegalismes* or Greenberg's "Rogue Justice" we might well consider following Edinger's warnings about getting a better grip on an understanding of the psychology of terrorism. This will be no easy task, however, since, as Mayer and Gray warn, modern Western man seems to exult in its Enlightenment illusion that we are free from the myths of religion and religious imagery. But this is a fool's mission as our endless war on terror seems certainly to be proving. As early as 1988, Edinger was telling us that Western society no longer had a viable and functioning central myth with the disappearance of what he called a "trans personal reality (God)."[71] This loss of a central myth, Edinger bluntly warns, "brings about a truly apocalyptic condition . . . [which] is the state of modern man."[72] Referencing W. B. Yeats' 1921 classic poem, "The Second Coming," and its reference to the center not being able to hold because the "falcon cannot hear the falconer," Edinger suggests that the chaos we are now experiencing is the release of the "primitive levels of the unconscious from control."[73] Does this sound familiar to our post-9/11 ears?

But to free ourselves from the unconscious requires a coming to consciousness, which is no easy task either. However, Edinger warns it is quite critical for a sufficient number of people to reach this level of consciousness. If not, Edinger bluntly suggests we might very well end up attempting to write the history of another world war that may finally become the war to end all wars.[74] While our nationalism myth is most certainly here to stay, globalization notwithstanding, it may well be worth coming to grips with the task at hand. In addition to the debunking of our national myths, there is an urgent need to suffer consciously through the restructuring of the architecture of the collective psyche that is no longer "contained" by an "operative religious myth."[75] This, rather than a relatively small number of unstable zealots – ironically seeking a society with a governing principle based upon a religious text – may very well be the root of our collective sense of unease over what we feel is the lack of normalcy since 9/11.

Old habits die hard, but perhaps it is time for us to consider an alternative to reaching for the apocalyptic and the existential exception as a way of governing. Perhaps, too, we may then avoid blowing each other off the face of the earth as Edinger warns. If nothing else, with a sufficient level of consciousness, we may begin to retreat from the cliff of apocalyptic zealotry in our governing and recover some sense of normalcy. But retreat is not usually in our American vocabulary – at least insofar as wars go. But this misguided and endless war on terror has already caused far too many casualties. Retreat is worth the try. And maybe, just maybe, our courts might then find the backbone to resist the increasing usurpation of its authority by our ever-expanding national security state.

8

Reimagining the National Security State: Illusions and Constraints

Joshua L. Dratel

There are indeed existential threats to US national security, and this chapter will identify those that are most important, and the challenges they present. It will also separate them from those threats that are not nearly as serious, but which may occupy more attention – and with it, the expenditure of disproportionate investment of emotional reaction and tangible resources. The most dangerous threats to national security are income inequality and race, followed by cyber-vulnerability and climate change, with nuclear conflict and its catastrophic capabilities perhaps looming more ominously. Yet, they are all overshadowed in popular discourse by less serious threats that, contrived for political purposes, are artificially magnified in significance.

The most popular threat, but which is not existential, that nevertheless occupies an inordinate amount of time and space in the media, political rhetoric, people's psyches, and – most of all – budgets is terrorism, particularly Islamic terrorism. A preoccupation with terrorism is natural. It is, indeed, the purpose of the exercise itself: to intimidate a population and government on a disproportionate level in relationship to the acts of terrorism themselves. Also, the randomness of terrorism is a factor. The vulnerability and helplessness that civilians feel – after all, what precautions can a person adopt to insulate themselves completely from being victimized by a terrorist incident? – are manifested in fear, and can be ameliorated by the comfort – whether deserved or not – in believing that the government is doing everything possible to prevent an attack.

As Robert Malley and Jon Finer, two former Obama administration officials, explain,

> [t]he combination of seeming randomness of the target and the deliberateness of the offender helps explains why terrorism inspires a level of dread unjustified by the actual risk. At any given time and place, a terrorist attack is extremely unlikely to occur – and yet, when one does happen, it's because someone wanted it to.[1]

Yet that uncertainty does not transform sporadic, episodic jeopardy into an existential threat. As President Barack Obama reassured in 2016, terrorism generally, and

ISIS in particular, does not present an "existential" threat to the United States.[2] That conclusion is echoed in a study by the Washington DC-based think tank New America, which states, "The threat is not existential."[3]

The divide between what is perceived as an existential threat to national security and what in fact constitutes such a threat is the product of certain illusions and constraints. The illusions can be divided into two categories: (1) those stemming from American civic mythologies that dominate public perception, and which operate as constraints because they impair the ability to recognize or acknowledge problems as well as their seriousness and depth; and (2) those that are the product of the *less* important threats to national security, but nevertheless create a level of anxiety that drains resources on an unjustifiable scale and that, in turn, imposes constraints on the ability to confront the genuine threats. Reality also imposes constraints, both in the availability of resources to address authentic threats and in confining public expectations to what is practical and possible rather than what is politically expedient and bureaucratically defensible.

A INCOME INEQUALITY

A society in which the wealthy, whether 1 percent or some slightly higher percentage, persistently and by the design of the political and economic system attain the vast proportion of new wealth, while the middle and lower classes are economically marginalized on an increasing scale, is unsustainable. That is simply a historical fact, regardless of how long that state has endured or how impregnable it seems.

As reported by the Economic Policy Institute:

> Income inequality has risen in every state since the 1970s and, in most states, it has grown in the post–Great Recession era. From 2009 to 2015, the incomes of the top 1 percent grew faster than the incomes of the bottom 99 percent in 43 states and the District of Columbia. The top 1 percent captured half or more of all income growth in nine states. In 2015, a family in the top 1 percent nationally received, on average, 26.3 times as much income as a family in the bottom 99 percent.[4]

And if you want an ominous statistical parallel, the United States's top 1 percent accumulated 22.03 percent of all income in 2015, just 1.9 percentage points below the peak of 23.9 percent – reached in 1928.[5] Unsurprisingly, given the Great Depression a year later and the changes in economic and fiscal policy it augured, the trend moved decisively in the opposite direction for nearly 50 years: Between 1928 to 1973, the top 1 percent's share of income declined in every state for which data exist.[6] During that 45-year period, the top 1 percent families in the United States acquired only 4.9 percent of income. Yet that pattern reversed between 1973 and 2007, when that top echelon captured 58.7 of all income growth.[7] According to a United Bank of Switzerland study, billionaires increased their wealth by 19 percent in 2017, their best performance ever recorded.[8]

If the "haves" believe that because the "have nots" have not yet staged a revolt means that that they – the "haves" – can continue with impunity to reap nearly all the material benefits available in the United States at the expense of the remainder of the populace, they are putting national security at grave risk. Presently the "haves" control not only the financial system but also, through the campaign financing system, the political system, which provides the means for controlling, regulating, and changing economic and financial policy and practice. However, again, history proves that security is in many respects an illusion when tested by increasing – and increasingly insensitive – income inequality. Peter Georgescu asks, understandably, "How long is this sustainable?"[9] What he also finds "genuinely astonishing" is that "the private sector doesn't see the immense danger in all this – not simply the prospect of a collapse from enormous household debt loads, but the prospect of civil unrest after another huge correction like the one in 2008."[10] Thus, he concludes, "[o]ur current course is unsustainable."[11]

Even such committed and successful – and in many respects ruthless – capitalists as Joseph Kennedy, patriarch of the United States's preeminent late twentieth-century political family, recognized the danger of ignoring income and wealth inequality. Asked why someone like himself, with a reputation as a stock speculator, would support Franklin D. Roosevelt's New Deal to confront the Depression, Kennedy remarked that he "would give up half his wealth in order to be assured his family could enjoy the other half in peace and safety."[12] That prudence among the economic elite – and the politicians they purchase – appears to be missing today. Also, the impact of income inequality transcends a poor person's lack of purchasing power in the marketplace. As Eduardo Porter of *The New York Times* has pointed out, "[s]eventeen percent of Americans are poor by international standards – living on less than half the nationwide median income. That's more than twice the share of poor people in France, Iceland or the Netherlands."[13]

Newborns in the United States also have a shorter life expectancy than their counterparts in Australia, Austria, Belgium, Britain, Canada, Chile, Denmark, Finland, France, Germany, Greece, Iceland, Ireland, Israel, Italy, Japan, Luxembourg, the Netherlands, New Zealand, Norway, Portugal, Slovenia, South Korea, Spain, Sweden, Switzerland, and other countries.[14] Conversely, the United States's infant mortality rate is higher than every nation in the Organisation for Economic Cooperation and Development with the exceptions of Chile, Mexico, and Turkey.[15] Also, as Porter notes, "[b]lack males born in the United States today will probably live shorter lives than boys born in Mexico, China or Turkey."[16]

While Porter has "suggested that my compatriots might come to a consensus that inequality is harmful when they [realize] how vast inequities could gum up the cogs of economic and social mobility[,]" he learned that "interestingly, Americans still don't care that much."[17] In fact, while polls have found that "two-thirds say they are dissatisfied with the way income and wealth are distributed . . ., more than three out of five – compared with just over half six years ago – are satisfied with 'the opportunity for a person in this nation to get ahead by working hard.'"[18]

Here, the illusion itself creates the constraint; as long as the American public clings to the now mythical notion of the American Dream, that stubborn resistance to reality stifles any chance to revive it (or afford it meaning for the first time for many, such as blacks and women, for whom it has never delivered its stated promise of reward for hard work and merit). In understatement, Porter characterizes these figures as "problematic," and cautions that the United States "risks its prosperity by leaving so many Americans behind."[19]

Global income inequality presents a national security threat as well. If, as a result of income inequality, other nations experience either unrest or economic distress, implement repressive or other measures that create the prospect for revolution, or even adopt policies contrary to US interests, US national security would be adversely affected. In today's interconnected global economic system, instability anywhere – whether economic or political, or both – has a tendency to exert a ripple effect on markets and economies elsewhere. The World Inequality Report cited by Eduardo Porter "finds that the richest 1 percent of humanity reaped 27 percent of the world's income between 1980 and 2016. The bottom 50 percent, by contrast, got only 12 percent."[20] And "[n]owhere has the distribution of the pie become more equitable."[21] Porter also warns:

> If the evolution of income inequality in every country remains on the same path it has been since 1980, the plateau in global inequality since 2000 will prove to be but a temporary blip: by 2050, the bottom half of the world's population will draw only 9 percent of the world's income, a percentage point less than today. One-percenters at the top, by contrast, will reap 24 percent of the global income pie, up from 21 percent in 2016.[22]

On a national level, the US contains the most billionaires, 585, while China, which had only 16 twelve years ago, now has 373.[23] The top 1 percent of the United States owns approximately 42 percent of the nation's economy; in China, the portion is 30 percent.[24] Globally, according to a 2017 Credit Suisse report, the top 1 percent owns approximately half the world's economy; the planet's poorest inhabitants – 3.5 billion persons, comprising 70 percent of the world's workforce – possess only 2.7 percent of global wealth.[25] Income and wealth inequality also interact with the other national security threats discussed below. They certainly have had an adverse impact on climate change issues and contribute significantly to institutional degradation and public confidence in those institutions.

All of this has not necessarily led to introspection by the 1 percent, but certainly to judgment from the remainder. In *Current Affairs*, A. Q. Smith concludes, "It's Basically Immoral to Be Rich."[26] Smith presents his case as follows:

> If you possess billions of dollars, in a world where many people struggle because they do not have much money, you are an immoral person. The same is true if you

possess hundreds of millions of dollars, or even millions of dollars. Being extremely wealthy is impossible to justify in a world containing deprivation.[27]

In summarizing Stanford University economics professor Walter Scheidel's *The Great Leveler: Violence and the History of Inequality from the Stone Age to the Twenty-First Century*,[28] *The Economist* writes that "throughout history, economic inequality has only been rectified by one of the 'Four Horsemen of Leveling': warfare, revolution, state collapse and plague."[29] Scheidel does maintain hope that today's inequality can be resolved by peaceful means, but insists that it "requires us to be more creative in dealing with inequality[,]" and that "[a]bove all we must think harder about feasibility."[30] Certainly the money exists to achieve greater equality: "Last year, the world's billionaires made over $462 billion combined – enough money to end extreme poverty around the globe seven times over[,]" according to a 2018 report from Oxfam.[31]

The issue is not quantity; rather, it is distribution and retention. Until those who have garnered, and continue to garner, a disproportionate share of wealth and income in the United States (and in the world at large) accept that construct and implement changes that promote economic equality, the current deteriorating situation presents an urgent existential threat to national security.

B RACE

Arguably the most serious existential national security threat in US history – the Civil War – was grounded in race. Unfortunately, progress has been dampened by not only resistance in some quarters, but also the broader popular illusion of greater advancement than has, in fact, been realized. The deep fissures caused by a history of dysfunctional race relations in the United States still exist. In many respects, they have deepened recently and retain a capacity for producing hostility and violence. Thus, race remains a fundamental problem for US national security.

The United States's race problem is not unrelated to income equality, as economic inequity is most profound along racial lines. For example, white families average sixteen times the wealth of black families.[32] A 2016 report by CFED (formerly the Corporation for Enterprise Development, and now known as Prosperity Now) and the Institute for Policy Studies, which studied trends in wealth accumulation from 1983 through 2013 and projected those trends 30 years into the future, demonstrates that racial inequality persists across the entire economic spectrum, and will only worsen absent changes in government and social policy.[33]

The CFED/IPS report explains:

> While housing has been a major driver in the growth of the racial wealth divide, black and Latino households have also faced numerous other economic inequities that are impacting their wealth position. At the root of this are a number of discriminatory practices – including, among others, employment discrimination,

racial discrimination in the criminal justice system, housing segregation and unequal access to educational opportunities – that have continued into the present even as some acts of past discrimination decline.[34]

That analysis is supported by startling statistics: It would require 228 years for black families to accumulate the wealth of white families today; for Latino families to reach that level, it would take 84 years.[35] By 2043, when people of color are projected to attain the majority of the US population, the chasm of wealth between white families and black and Latino families will double on average the $500,000 difference that existed in 2013.[36] In fact, the richest 100 entrants on the Forbes list own approximately that of the entire black population; the top 186 equal the wealth of the entire Latino population.[37] The disparity those statistics manifest is not surprising considering the obstacle race presents for black employment. In *Race at Work – Realities of Race and Criminal Record in the NYC Job Market*, Devah Pager and Bruce Western analyze the data and reach discouraging conclusions:

- "Black job applicants are only two-thirds as successful as equally qualified Latinos, and little more than half as successful as equally qualified whites."[38]
- A "white applicant with a felony conviction appears to do just as well, if not better, than his black counterpart with no criminal background. These results suggest that employers view minority job applicants as essentially equivalent to whites just out of prison."[39]

Thus, "[i]n contrast to public opinion that assumes little influence of discrimination on labor market inequality," *Race at Work* determines that "[d]iscrimination continues to represent a major barrier to economic self-sufficiency for those at the low end of the labor market hierarchy."[40] Consequently, "Blacks, and to a lesser extent Latinos, are routinely passed over in favor of whites for the most basic kinds of low-wage work."[41] Distressingly, "discrimination has not been eliminated in the post-civil rights period as some contend, but remains a vital component of a complex pattern of racial inequality."[42] *Race at Work* punctures illusions about equality and color blindness in hiring under a legal system that prohibits it as a matter of law: Despite the fact that white and black (and Hispanic) "applicants presented equivalent credentials and applied for exactly the same jobs, race appears to overtake all else in determining employment opportunities."[43] Yet that illusion is powerful and pervasive even among experts. In Professor Pager's obituary in November 2018, *The New York Times* points out that William Julius Wilson, a Harvard University sociologist and author of *The Declining Significance of Race*, in reaction to her groundbreaking revelations, admits that even as a scholar on the subject, he would not have anticipated her report's findings.[44]

There is one circumstance in which blacks do receive more, though: punishment. Black students are suspended and expelled far more than white students,[45] and that unsurprisingly carries over into criminal sentencing, in which federal judges impose longer prison sentences on black defendants. For example, a 2017 US Sentencing Commission report states that black male offenders continued to receive longer sentences than similarly situated white male offenders. Black male offenders received sentences on average 19.1 percent longer than similarly situated white male offenders during the [] period (fiscal years 2012–2016), as they had for the prior four periods studied.[46]

The race problems that permeate and threaten the fabric of US society extend beyond even the extensively documented cradle-to-grave oppression and discrimination that start with historical and modern voter suppression, are geographically institutionalized through redlining,[47] and continue with underfunded and underserved public education and public health systems. That oppression and discrimination exercise their punitive powers through the war on drugs and mass incarceration, and are reinforced through felony disenfranchisement that completes and restarts the cycle. The precarious position that blacks occupy in the United States is a matter of national security because it means that 13.4 percent of the population is insecure for very good reason – and that does not include the 18.1 percent Hispanic and the 2.1 percent Muslim who also have reason to feel unsafe.[48] Indeed, white mass shooters – such as Robert Bowers in Pittsburgh, Gregory Bush in Kentucky, Dylan Roof in South Carolina, Nikolas Cruz in Florida – who do not kill themselves have a better chance of surviving the subsequent police encounter than an unarmed black committing no crime at all.

Race is an extraordinarily important issue for national security not only in the context of equality – economic and social – but also in the context where resources are devoted. For example, it is discouraging to read that when the FBI considers domestic terrorism legislation, it is concentrating not on white supremacist/nationalist organizations and individuals who have been responsible for the vast majority of fatalities from domestic terrorism incidents, but instead on what the FBI characterizes as Black Identity Extremism, a term and movement the FBI has itself created.[49] Nor is it just a matter of white supremacist rhetoric and brutality, or overt, conscious racism. Leaving aside the 20 percent of Trump supporters who disapprove of "the executive order that freed all slaves in the states that were in rebellion against the federal government" – Abraham Lincoln's 1863 Emancipation Proclamation[50] – or the large segments of state and congressional district electorates that voted for candidates running expressly racist campaigns,[51] the problem of implicit bias fuels racism in its own pernicious, if unsuspecting, fashion.[52]

Convincing even well-meaning people that suffering from implicit bias does not make a person racist is a challenge.[53] Just as difficult is getting white people to concede the power that racism still exerts today despite equality under the law, and how it materially impairs black opportunity. Ultimately, the future of the United States's race problem – and whether it can be solved – can be distilled down to two essential questions:

- Will white people recognize and acknowledge that racism still exists, and that it disadvantages African Americans on a broad scale?
- Will white people be willing to sacrifice *anything* they currently have, or aspire to, in order to implement the equality that the Declaration of Independence is supposed to embody for "all men"?

Part of the difficulty in achieving a "yes" answer to both questions[54] – prerequisites to commencing the process of achieving racial equity – is the illusion that slavery is a stain of the distant past. It is not. In historical and generational terms, and most certainly in economic terms, it is rather recent – roughly the consecutive life expectancies of two adult women. Thus, in considering black economic performance, "[m]any of those included in the calculus are a single generation away from the systematic extraction of their parents' wealth (and their parents' parents, etc.)."[55]

Etched in stone at the Lincoln Memorial is a renowned passage from his second inaugural address, with the end of the Civil War in sight: "with malice toward none, and charity for all." Less popularly quoted is another section of that speech, confronting the United States's legacy of slavery, and it resonates profoundly today:

> If we shall suppose that American slavery is one of those offenses which in the providence of God must need to come but which, having continued through this appointed time, He now wills to remove and that He gives to both North and South, this terrible war as the woe due to those by whom the offense came. Shall we discern therein any departure from those divine attributes which the believers in a living God always ascribed to? Fondly do we hope, fervently do we pray, that this mighty scourge of war may speedily pass away.
>
> If God wills that it continue until all the wealth piled by the bondmen's 250 years of unrequited toil shall be sunk and until every drop of blood drawn with the lash shall be paid by another drawn with the sword. As was said 3,000 years ago, so it still must be said the judgments of the Lord are true and righteous altogether.[56]

Whether the United States can transcend the inhumane inequality it tolerated at its origin and for so long thereafter, as well as reconcile its accounts to overcome the "bondmen's 250 years of unrequited toil," remains an open question that poses a distinct existential threat to national security.

C CYBER-VULNERABILITY

Entire library sections are now devoted to the perils of inadequate cybersecurity, which has been amply recognized as a national security threat.[57] Cyber-vulnerability represents an extraordinary threat, not only systemic in terms of power grids,[58] hospitals, and similar essential civic and social services,[59] but also economic and political. The modern dependence on computers and the Internet, and their interconnected nature, makes any cyber-weakness potentially catastrophic.[60] As James Patchett, president and chief executive of the New York City Economic

Development Corporation declared in an April 10, 2018, letter to *The New York Times*, "without question, cybersecurity is a public safety issue; it is panic-inducing to think about the damage an attack similar to Atlanta's could inflict on New York City's 8.6 million residents."[61]

The entire banking community could be riven instantly by a serious cyber-intrusion.[62] Cyber-intruders pilfered $800 million from a bank in Bangladesh.[63] It does not require much imagination to contemplate the level of systemic harm hackers – whether independent or state sponsored – could inflict on any country's, or even the global, banking system. Even purely commercial hacks – which in some instances can be functionally indistinguishable from traditional political espionage, thereby blurring boundaries[64] – can adversely affect public confidence, or create liability that can cripple even a large, successful business. As Mr. Patchett warns, a "sustained, targeted attack on these economic engines could send us into a recession, or worse."[65] Thus far, even the hackers have not been as malevolent as they could be, as most attacks have been motivated by greed and pranksterism rather than disruption. Avarice has been a moderating force in that sense, because instead of creating complete chaos in the banking industry, people just want to steal money.

Also politically, electoral integrity and legitimacy are at stake. That applies to the voting process itself as well as the dissemination of information and disinformation, primarily on social media platforms, during political campaigns.[66] That elections are subject to some element of corruption is not necessarily a new phenomenon in the United States, even on a national level. In the 1960 presidential election, questions were raised regarding the validity of the tally in Illinois (and how it was secured) that provided John F. Kennedy a narrow victory there, and of course the repeated Florida fiascos from 2000 forward are fresh in the public's mind.[67] The difference now is that the potential for cyber-interference creates an opportunity in every election for the loser to delegitimize results in partisan fashion. That is very difficult to overcome. The inability to prove a negative – that interference with votes did not occur – has the capacity to compromise any and all results with which the vanquished (and their supporters) is dissatisfied.

In fact, information has been weaponized in the cyber context, either to disclose secrets, as in the Panama Papers disclosures,[68] or Edward Snowden's revelations, or WikiLeaks document releases, or even for purposes of extortion. For example, the hacking of personal information of persons applying for security clearances from the US Office of Personnel Management in 2015 presents the prospect of blackmail and other solicitations by foreign intelligence services seeking access to US classified information. Conversely, disinformation is also powerful, and the capacity for fakery now eclipses the ability of the average, or even sophisticated, consumer to detect.[69] The exploitation of Facebook in Myanmar to incite anti-Rohingya violence provides an object lesson in the potentially direct, fatal consequences of an orchestrated disinformation campaign.[70]

Technological advances also raise the likelihood of additional exposure to cyber-interference. Cybersecurity expert Bruce Schneier's most recent book, *Click Here to Kill Everybody: Security and Survival in a Hyper-Connected World*[71] portends a future – or even present – in which a "world of 'smart' devices," such as pace-makers, driverless car systems, or even simply thermostats, can be hacked and manipulated, which "means the Internet can kill people." Given that terrifying and even paralyzing prospect – if you cannot trust your pacemaker, can you even risk getting out of bed? – it should be apparent that comprehensive, categorical cybersecurity is itself an illusion. Hackers dedicated to penetrating computer systems will always be sufficiently ahead of cyber-defenses to do damage to systems that contain any weakness.[72] Cyber-defenses may constitute a series of modern, virtual Maginot lines that offer a false sense of security because they are not adaptable to the next phase and methodology of cyber-intrusions.[73]

Instead, as a national security imperative, cyber-reactivity and cyber-recovery and mitigation may well be far more realistic and productive and merit far more resources than a defense system that is only as strong as its weakest link – an undisciplined person at whatever level within an organization emailing or gaining access to a server or other Internet portal from a personal, unsecured phone or other electronic device as a matter of convenience or even urgency.[74] In addition, malware and other destructive cyber-weapons and techniques are likely already embedded within various important systems – public and private – and are lying dormant until and unless the foreign government or criminal organization, or bored 14-year-old, activates them. Cyber-defense at that point is the electronic equivalent of locking the barn door after the enemy's horse is already inside.

Also, the United States's relaxation of the rules of engagement controlling its offensive cyber-operations in 2018 makes a mistake, if not a deliberate attack, much more likely and certain to produce retaliation or even preemptive action.[75] As *The Wall Street Journal* notes, the policy shift "has prompted questions about how the military will carry out offensive digital strikes, and whether hostilities with foreign adversaries will rapidly escalate."[76]

D CLIMATE CHANGE

Climate change presents a national security threat on several levels. As a threshold illusion, denial that it exists – at existentially critical levels such as in the Trump White House, and in the leadership of the agencies, such as the Environmental Protection Agency and the Department of the Interior, as well as among influential members of Congress – and that energy and other policies are responsible constitute a grave national security threat. It is also related to income inequality because to the extent wealthy, powerful interests are responsible for the failure to implement policies that could arrest or moderate climate change, economic imbalance sustains climate imbalance. Also, the poor generally suffer more from the disequilibrium attending climate change.

Ignoring the impact of climate change was not always US policy, although currently climate change denial is, if not the official US policy, at least the practical attitude as references to climate change and its dangers are wiped from US government websites, reports, agendas, and funding.[77] In 2014, the US Department of Defense released its *Climate Change Adaptation Roadmap*, which begins with the recognition that "[a]mong the future trends that will impact our national security is climate change."[78] In addition to listing the implications peculiar to the military, the Pentagon's *Roadmap* also catalogs the broader effects of climate change that affect national security and the military's role therein:

> Rising global temperatures, changing precipitation patterns, climbing sea levels, and more extreme weather events will intensify the challenges of global instability, hunger, poverty, and conflict. They will likely lead to food and water shortages, pandemic disease, disputes over refugees and resources, and destruction by natural disasters in regions across the globe.[79]

In that context, "[t]he military could be called upon more often to support civil authorities, and provide humanitarian assistance and disaster relief in the face of more frequent and more intense natural disasters."[80] The *Roadmap* adds that in the Pentagon's "defense strategy, we refer to climate change as a 'threat multiplier' because it has the potential to exacerbate many of the challenges we are dealing with today – from infectious disease to terrorism."[81] Also, like a serious cyber-infiltration, climate change events can exert a ripple effect – maybe even of tsunami magnitude – on the economy. The US government's November 2018 Fourth National Climate Assessment, prepared by thirteen federal agencies, warns that unless substantial measures are adopted to curb global warming, the US economy could suffer as much as a ten percent reduction by 2100.[82]

The climate-induced crises described in the *Roadmap* constitute a devastating, incremental national security threat. Each successive climate event – whether serial hurricanes in a single season, or periodic rampant wildfires – stretches the limits of emergency response with respect to both personnel and money and inflicts costly long-term damage to infrastructure.[83] The increasing frequency and severity also collide with "demographic and economic changes," such as residential and other development in coastal areas and flood plains, that, according to experts, "are exacerbated by rising sea levels and more powerful hurricanes due to climate change[.]"[84] That causes more and costlier damage, weakens more infrastructure for longer periods, and reduces government's ability to respond effectively within a reasonable period of time.[85]

In this instance, again, national security threats converge to amplify their negative impact. For example, in North Carolina, where "tourism and real estate interests along the coasts hold considerable political power[,] . . . a state commission report [in 2010] estimated that sea levels could rise by up to 39 inches by the year 2100."[86] However, "rather than adjust the state's plans for coastal development, the Republican-controlled legislature passed a law in 2012 that banned state and local agencies from using sea-level estimates that 'include scenarios of accelerated rates of sea-level rise.'"[87] Consequently, due to control of the legislature by powerful economic interests, "[t]he law required predictions to stick to historical trends, despite scientific evidence that sea levels are rising at an accelerated rate due to climate change."[88] The results – the extensive damage from Hurricane Florence in 2018 – were both largely "man made" and avoidable.

These episodes also further aggravate geographic, race, and class inequities because they often cause worse damage in underprivileged and underserved areas, and because they divert resources that cannot be used to rectify the ordinary, daily inequality that requires attention. For example, Hurricane Katrina ravaged the poorer sections of New Orleans worse than any other neighborhoods, and the reclamation of those areas took considerably more time, too.[89] Thus, climate change incidents act as a "threat multiplier" in concert with other national security concerns.

Climate change also presents a health issue that implicates national security. *The New York Times* characterized a recent "wide-ranging scientific report" by *The Lancet* as presenting "stark findings" regarding "the growing risks of climate change for human health and predicts that cascading hazards could soon face millions more people in rich and poor countries around the world."[90] Among the threatening trends reported, "[c]rop yields are declining. Tropical diseases like dengue fever are showing up in unfamiliar places, including in the United States. Tens of millions of people are exposed to extreme heat."[91]

The threat posed by climate change incidents is not just from domestic events. As the *Roadmap* points out, natural disasters across the globe can destabilize populations and governments, destroy economies, and create refugee crises that affect neighboring nations – all with ramifications for US national security.[92] Also, as extreme weather associated with worsening climate change reduces the amount of habitable land – eliminating certain coastal areas, for instance – the competition for scarcer viable living space will likely also provoke conflict.[93] Indeed, the 2006 drought, for instance, is one of the principal roots of the conflict in Syria, as farmers migrated to urban centers, setting the stage for political unrest.[94] A paper in the *Proceedings of the National Academy of Sciences* ("PNAS") explains:

> Before the Syrian uprising that began in 2011, the greater Fertile Crescent experienced the most severe drought in the instrumental record. For Syria, a country marked by poor governance and un-sustainable agricultural and environmental policies, the drought had a catalytic effect, contributing to political unrest.[95]

Elaborating, the authors note that the decreased precipitation, rising sea levels, warming trends, and reduced soil moisture constituted trends for which "[n]o natural cause is apparent[,] . . . whereas the observed drying and warming are consistent with model studies of the response to increases in greenhouse gases."[96] The authors conclude that "a drought of the severity and duration of the recent Syrian drought, which is implicated in the current conflict, has become more than twice as likely as a consequence of human interference in the climate system."[97] Yemen, too, is suffering from a similar confluence of war and climate change that has transformed it into the current principal global humanitarian crisis.[98]

Recent history, as well as the historical record from antiquity, teaches that the escalation of these crises portends not only more severe and frequent climate change incidents, but also, with them, regardless of where they occur, more resounding repercussions for US national security.[99]

E NUCLEAR WAR

Nuclear conflagration has been a national security threat since the inception of nuclear warfare. It demands rapt attention not because of its probabilities – in almost 75 years there have been perhaps a handful of genuine instances in which nuclear conflict was even an authentic possibility – but because of the categorical stakes should there be any resort to nuclear weapons by anyone. Following the end of the Cold War, the likelihood of nuclear war diminished even further. However, three recent developments have raised the specter of a nuclear incident to a level not present in decades. The first is that US President Donald Trump appears not to possess his predecessors' allegiance to the policy of nuclear restraint that marked US policy for more than a half century.

As reported during the 2016 campaign, "a foreign policy expert on the international level went to advise Donald Trump. And three times [Trump] asked about the use of nuclear weapons. Three times he asked at one point if we had them why can't we use them," according to Joe Scarborough on his MSNBC "Morning Joe" program.[100] Compounding that astonishing lack of understanding of unswerving US policy since World War II, once elected, the president has engaged in unprecedented nuclear saber-rattling with another nuclear power, North Korea. That attitude and rhetoric are themselves a threat to national security. Not only do they represent a reckless approach to a subject that demands the utmost care and caution, but also they send exactly the wrong messages to other nuclear powers: That use of nuclear weapons could be acceptable, and, more troubling, that in a conflict the United States might use nuclear weapons first, which could motivate a nuclear-capable opponent to launch a preemptive strike.[101]

The second development is the US president's cavalier approach to negotiations with North Korea. By treating his summits with Kim Jong Un like public relations opportunities instead of serious and precise substantive negotiations, and afterward announcing a vague "agreement" that neither party had any intention of honoring, President Trump trivializes a matter of paramount importance. In this instance, phony diplomacy is perhaps even more dangerous than none at all. It promises the illusion of a false sense of security (without any means of achieving it) and sets the stage for failure that will generate pressure for more severe measures – perhaps conventional war, or even nuclear conflict.[102] It also confuses allies who might rely on the bogus claims of rapprochement, and therefore adapt their policies accordingly.

The third development is the president's stated intention to withdraw from the 1987 Intermediate-range Nuclear Forces treaty ("INF") between the United States and Russia, signed by Ronald Reagan and Mikhail Gorbachev, and which banned ground-launch nuclear missiles with ranges from 500 km to 5,500 km.[103] While that move has been criticized by essentially every expert outside the current US administration, the Trump administration has not relented.[104] Renewal of a nuclear arms race would increase substantially the chance that nuclear weapons would be used. Just because there has been a 75-year hiatus since the advent of nuclear arms does not mean that will continue in the face of nuclear proliferation in a world in which nationalism is trumpeted over international cooperation and pursuing common interests, including peace.

F INSTITUTIONAL DEGRADATION

Another threat, albeit less tangible, is institutional degradation, which affects and encompasses all of the threats discussed thus far because civil society institutions – the legislature, the courts, media, and the executive branch – that function in the manner in which they were designed can identify threats and react in an effective manner to reduce or eliminate them. There has been a gradual deterioration of the public's perception of institutional capacity and sincerity, and consequent declining confidence. As conservative columnist Peggy Noonan has noted, "all the polls show and have for some time what you already know: America's trust in its leaders and institutions has been falling for four decades."[105] Noonan points out that "trust in the federal government has never been lower[,]" citing a 1958 Pew Research poll that found that 73% trusted the government to do what is right "always" or "most of the time" compared with just 18% in 2017.[106] Stating the obvious, Noonan observes that is not "healthy."[107] She adds that "other institutions have suffered, too – the church, the press, the professions[,]" and finds that "disturbing because those institutions often bolster our national life in highly personal ways," and "when government or law turns bad, they provide a place, a platform from which to stand, to make a case, to correct."[108]

This diminution in public confidence is not a sudden phenomenon. Distrust of a centralized government is deeply rooted in the American psyche, and was exploited successfully by Republicans anxious to dismantle the regulatory systems that had been implemented since the New Deal. Recall one of Ronald Reagan's presidential campaign catchphrases: "The nine most terrifying words in the English language are 'I'm from the government and I'm here to help.'"[109] From the other political direction, the Vietnam War, Watergate, and the United States's perceived role as the prevailing imperial/colonial power in the world have caused disillusionment.[110]

Currently the institutions that are reflexively relied upon for solutions and corrective measures have not responded effectively or at all because they have been rendered dysfunctional by decades of degradation. Thus, Congress has abdicated its authority to the executive in multiple areas – particularly war and foreign policy. The legitimacy of the courts has been eroded gradually over time by partisanship, but more rapidly by petulant criticism from President Trump that compromises the integrity of future court rulings and politicizes them in the minds of the public – most recently and more dramatically by the Kavanaugh confirmation, which, regardless of how any observer wanted it to turn out, constituted a debacle that only accelerated the damage to the integrity of court rulings and deliberations, and further normalized politicization of the judiciary. The media, too, have been under assault by President Trump, and the proliferation of disinformation on social media platforms has impaired the ability of news consumers to trust what they read, hear, and see, and the sources that provide information. The media's longstanding penchant for tabloid sensationalism and prurience has contributed as well, as has its willingness to be seduced by soap opera at the expense of substance.[111]

The inability of these institutions to perform their functions has produced a vacuum, not only with respect to authority and initiative in policymaking, but also regarding the accountability that the system of checks and balances is designed to ensure. Since President Trump's inauguration, neither Congress nor the courts nor the media have stymied him. The only effective activity to halt his policies has been in the streets: opposition to the travel ban, to family separation at the border, and to repealing the Affordable Care Act in 2017–2018. Those early successes provided protestors the impetus to apply that model to other contexts: Now there are high school students as the vanguard in the campaign for gun control. Not legislators, not pundits. And those students were a factor not only locally, where Florida passed at least some gun control measures in response, but also nationally in registering young voters and urging them to vote.

When government is paralyzed by partisanship and obstinance, and civic institutions fail to pick up the slack, that is a recipe for the rise of facile and often extreme solutions with substantial emotional appeal, but little practical feasibility to correct the problems. Rather, those solutions are prone to scapegoating and political opportunism that amplify the underlying fundamental deficiencies, and their threat to national security. The failure of public and private institutions to address threats both existential and situational is also reflected in the US economic system, which has accommodated and even enabled a concentration of capital and commerce that defies the many federal and state laws that are designed to prohibit and inhibit monopolization. Ultimately, the consolidation in so many industries affects not just pricing and labor rights, but also the fabric of society as a whole.

Tim Wu, a professor at Columbia University, cautions that among the factors that lead to fascism – although "often overlooked" – is "the threat to democracy posed by monopoly and excessive corporate concentration."[112] He warns that "[w]e must not forget the economic origins of fascism, lest we risk repeating the most calamitous error of the 20th century."[113] Wu identifies that mistake by citing post–World War II observers like West Virginia Senator Harley M. Kilgore, who "argued that the German economic structure, which was dominated by monopolies and cartels, was essential to Hitler's consolidation of power." Today, Wu admonishes, "we have cast aside the safeguards that were supposed to protect democracy against a dangerous marriage of private and public power."[114] As a result, according to Wu, "we are conducting a dangerous economic and political experiment" because "extreme economic concentration does create conditions ripe for dictatorship."[115]

That connection exists because "[t]here is a direct link between concentration and the distortion of democratic process."[116] Naturally, "the more concentrated an industry – the fewer members it has – the easier it is to cooperate to achieve its political goals."[117] In contrast, a "group like the middle class is hopelessly disorganized and has limited influence in Congress."[118] Yet "concentrated industries, like the pharmaceutical industry, find it easy to organize to take from the public for their own benefit."[119] Here, again, the impact of economic inequality is profound, and the decreasing regulation of political contributions has only enhanced the wealthy's influence on the structure of the state with respect to law, politics, and, ultimately, the ability for the majority to effect change. One commentator places particular blame on "dark money,"[120] which "can be seen as the underlying corruption from which our immediate crises emerge: the collapse of public trust in politics, the rise of a demagogic anti-politics, and assaults on the living world, public health and civic society."[121]

In addition, a recent paper published by several academic institutions (Columbia, Harvard, and the University of Chicago) finds a connection between concentration in industries and wage inequality and economic stagnation due to the reduced power of labor in industries with fewer employers and therefore reduced labor competition.[122] The paper adds that government has done little, despite legal tools such as antitrust laws, to mitigate this trend, and private litigation has been rare and mostly unsuccessful.[123] The mutually reinforcing impact of money in politics and the functional disenfranchisement of those classes below the uppermost tier have produced an electorate that is alternately apathetic and agitated. As Tim Wu remarks, in the United States "we have witnessed the anger borne of ordinary citizens who have lost almost any influence over economic policy – and by extension, their lives."[124] As a result, "[t]he middle class has no political influence over their stagnant wages, tax policy, the price of essential goods or health care. This powerlessness is brewing a powerful feeling of outrage."[125]

Is all this a prelude to a popular uprising that will culminate in angry citizens wielding pitchforks, chasing elites through the countryside? Perhaps, if these institutions do not recover, and presently there is little indication they will do so on their own, or cooperatively. The other alternative is that aggressive, intact institutions, such as the executive or the military, exert inordinate control. A precondition for recovery, though, would be acknowledgment by the populace and leadership that these institutional deficits exist, and that they desperately need reform and correction. Yet there does not appear to be unified momentum, much less agreement, in that direction.[126] This institutional abdication and failure present harmonic convergence of a potential resolution of two national security threats not only to the nation that elites should ponder. If a solution to climate change involves dramatically reducing reliance on coal, wood, or petroleum-based energy, and a solution to income inequality involves somehow divesting economic elites of their wealth and political power, it is worth noting that the guillotine does not run on fossil fuels.

G COUNTERTERRORISM AND THE STATE OF PERPETUAL WAR AND ARMED CONFLICT

Terrorism, and 9/11 in particular, punctured many Americans' notion that they could lead an essentially risk-free life. Existential fear was such an abstract concept for most Americans that television shows like "Fear Factor" were created to provide ersatz terror for national audiences. That changed with 9/11; Americans did not need fear manufactured for entertainment by Hollywood writers and producers any longer. And Americans have yet to recover from that traumatic and dramatic puncturing of their post-threat idyll. Prior to 9/11, the United States was basking in its status as the preeminent, unchallenged world superpower for more than a decade. External threats were effectively nonexistent. Capitalism had prevailed, and unlike during the 1930s, there were not any alternative economic systems to compete. In addition, all manner of scientific and technological advances had removed many of the environmental hazards that a hundred years earlier had regularly decimated populations. Dramatic improvements in product and occupational safety, in food, personal, and institutional hygiene in the decades before 9/11, and the development of remarkably reliable transportation options, have all contributed to the substantial diminution of fatalities associated with those aspects of daily life US residents take almost entirely for granted. For millennia humans were vulnerable to a host of diseases and dangers that science, medicine, and engineering eliminated by the end of the twentieth century: various plagues, the 1919 flu pandemic. But now, no more smallpox. No more polio. Vaccines wiped out fatal diseases that previously ravaged communities. Anyone know anyone who has gotten diphtheria? When was the last time your neighborhood had a cholera outbreak?[127] By the 21st century, even AIDS patients began to lead surviving longer and fuller lives.

Prior generations of Americans lived with that jeopardy without panic, but the public seems to lack stamina for such fortitude now.[128] If people constantly have to congratulate themselves on their "resilience," perhaps it is not as hardy or natural as they claim but more to convince themselves. The practical solution to overcoming that nagging fear is the illusion that the United States can attain complete, airtight security, reinforced by the corollary illusion that if enough money is spent on security, it can be achieved. Politicians, law enforcement, and intelligence professionals occupy an unenviable position in which the demands are impossible to satisfy: No lapses are tolerable, or unavoidable. Accountability is not based on fault, but simply on responsibility – You had one job, government: Reinstate our modern risk-free life. Any single failure is impermissible, as Malley and Finer recognize:

> By tacit consensus, American society has adopted a zero-tolerance policy toward terrorism, such that any administration on whose watch an attack were to occur would immediately face relentless political recrimination. The United States has become captive to a national security paradigm that ends up magnifying the very fears from which it was born.[129]

Like many societies currently and through history, the United States is, and should be, capable of weathering occasional acts of terrorism without orienting disproportionate resources toward eliminating it altogether. Nor has anything changed since 9/11 that would alter that conclusion; indeed, statistically and logistically, Islamic terrorism has diminished as an existential threat. A study by New America concludes that while "[e]ach of those deaths [caused by terrorism] is a tragedy ... the attacks are not national catastrophes of the type the United States experienced on 9/11."[130] Rather, "the death toll has been quite similar to other forms of political- and even non-political-violence Americans face today."[131]

As a matter of purely gross numbers, even including 9/11, which involved 2,996 fatalities, terrorism has accounted for 4,085 US civilian deaths through 2016.[132] Between 9/11 and 2017, Islamic terrorists killed 103 people inside the United States.[133] In a perverse irony, since 9/11 6,951 US military personnel have died in combat prosecuting wars in Afghanistan, Pakistan, and Iraq.[134] Since 9/11, a substantially larger number of US military veterans – more than 6,000 each year since 2008 – have committed suicide than died in combat through 2018.[135] During a slightly shorter period (2001–2014), 440,095 Americans died as a result of gun violence;[136] the number who have perished from opioid overdoses has increased annually for twenty years, with 20,000 in 2016 from fentanyl alone;[137] deaths from auto accidents rose to more than 40,000 in 2017 alone (exceeding 40,000 for the second consecutive year after a decade-long decline).[138] Indeed, suicides and opioid abuse are believed to have shortened US life expectancy in measurable fashion.[139]

Between 2008 and 2015, during which period 113 Americans died as a result of terrorist acts,[140] animals killed 1,610 people in the United States.[141] Thus, from 2008 through 2015, the probability of being killed by an animal in the United States was 1 in 1.6 million per year, compared with 1 in 30.1 million for a terrorist attack – 1 in 43.8 million per year for a US-born person committing a terrorist act, and 1 in

104.2 million per year for a foreign-born person doing so.[142] Nor is Islamic terrorism even the most common fatal form of terrorism in the United States. For example, in 2017, right-wing extremists were responsible for the majority of all extremist-related deaths in the United States.[143] Yet the federal government has not appeared eager to assuage the public's outsized fears of Islamic terrorism. Rather than provide data that would illustrate the relative dangers of Islamic terrorism compared to right-wing extremism, the federal government does not maintain such data, and has even defunded certain programs designed to monitor violent right-wing extremism.[144] The numbers that do exist – culled in part from a list of international terrorism-related convictions that the Justice Department releases periodically – illuminate the issue: Foreign-born Muslim extremists have committed forty-three out of 260,000 murders in the United States since 9/11, or 0.002 percent.[145]

Yet Islamic terrorism – and the fear thereof – nonetheless dominates the news, policy discussions, political debate, academic study, and, of course, again, budgets. Robert Malley and Jon Finer observe that "there are costs to this singular preoccupation and approach that are seldom acknowledged[,]" and that "[a]n excessive focus on this issue disfigures American politics, distorts US policies, and in the long run will undermine national security."[146] For them "[t]he question is not whether fighting terrorists ought to be a key US foreign policy objective – of course it should."[147] Instead, it is whether "the pendulum has swung too far at the expense of other interests and of a more rational conversation about terrorism and how to fight it."[148]

The human costs alone have been overwhelming. A November 2018 report by Brown University's Watson Institute for International and Public Affairs calculated that between October 2001 and October 2018, US military fatalities numbered 6,951 (of which 4,550 were in Iraq) in three theaters: Afghanistan, Pakistan, and Iraq. For those three countries, though, civilian deaths totaled between 244,124 and 266,427, and total deaths – military (US and other), civilians, aid workers, and others – was between 479,858 and 507,236.[149] That is the equivalent of wiping out the entire population of Sacramento, California. Moreover, the report acknowledges that its civilian death figures represent an "undercount" because there is "great uncertainty in any count of killing in war."[150] Nor does the tally include "indirect deaths," defined by the Watson Institute report as follows: "when wars' destruction leads to long term, 'indirect,' consequences for people's health in war zones, for example because of loss of access to food, water, health facilities, electricity or other infrastructure."[151]

The report estimates that the "[s]everal times as many have been killed indirectly as a result of the wars – because, for example, of water loss, sewage and other infrastructural issues, and war-related disease."[152] In addition, the total "does not include the more than 500,000 deaths from the war in Syria, raging since 2011, which the US joined in August 2014[,]" or civilian or other fatalities in Somalia, Yemen, or other conflict zones traceable to the war on terror.[153] That number would add to the carnage the entire population of Fresno, California. Adding US veteran suicides back home, and the refugees created by these conflicts, only multiplies the unconscionable human toll manifold.[154]

The financial costs are also staggering. According to the Watson Institute report, "[t]he United States has appropriated and is obligated to spend an estimated $5.9 trillion (in current dollars) on the war on terror through Fiscal Year 2019, including direct war and war-related spending and obligations for future spending on post 9/11 war veterans."[155] The report maintains that those expenditures and obligations "pose a national security concern because they are unsustainable" – there is that word again – and that "[t]he public would be better served by increased transparency and by the development of a comprehensive strategy to end the wars and deal with other urgent national security priorities."[156] Nor does the Watson Institute report even include costs – or profits – related to security, intelligence, investigations, and surveillance since 9/11, from the simplest identification requirements for entering public and private office buildings to the most sophisticated forensic equipment.

Government spending alone on counterterrorism since 9/11 has been estimated at $2.8 trillion.[157] While such spending peaked at $260 billion in 2006, and the height of the wars in Afghanistan and Iraq – a 16-fold increase over 2001 levels – the $175 billion expenditure in 2017 still eclipsed the 2001 total by eleven times.[158] However, despite the decrease from 2006, the Stimson Study Group "found no indication that [counterterrorism] spending is likely to continue to decline."[159] Nor is the spending transparent. As the Stimson Study Group points out, "[i]ncomplete data on spending poses a challenge to objective and rigorous assessments of the efficacy and efficiency of US counterterrorism strategy."[160] In fact, "[i]n recent years, billions of dollars in spending unrelated to the wars has been characterized as" overseas contingency operations in order to exempt that money from statutory budget ceilings imposed by 2011's Budget Control Act.[161] That bureaucratic budgetary shell game "makes it more difficult to identify spending that is truly dedicated to [counterterrorism] and to evaluate potential trade-offs."[162]

In the private sector, "fueled by voracious government and private sector demand," the US market for homeland security products and services was already $23.8 billion by 2006, and has continued to expand.[163] The money and focus dedicated to this multibillion dollar industry have also spawned a colossal public and private – and powerful – bureaucracy. In 2010, *The Washington Post* reported that there were 1,271 government organizations and 1,931 private firms related to counterterrorism, intelligence, or homeland security in some 10,000 locations around the US.[164] That massive financial and institutional component also presents an apparently irresistible incentive to continue on the present, although ultimately self-destructive, path. Twentieth-century German jurist and political theorist Carl Schmitt, discussing the political implications of departure from democracy in an emergency, or "state of exception," famously declared, "Sovereign is he who decides on the exception."[165]

Today, though, considering the overwhelming economic investment by everyone – governments, politicians, the military, media, businesses, academics, pundits,
consultants, lawyers, and the justice system – in the state of exception, the United
States has arrived at what appears to be a permanent state of exception. Indeed, it is
the exception itself that is sovereign. It dictates budgets, which in turn dictate
bureaucratic career advancement, media attention, political rhetoric, legislation,
and persistent popular concern that fan the flames for the exception to continue. As
Malley and Finer observe, "[t]he fact is that many US political leaders, members of
the media, consultants, and academics play a role in hyping the threat. Together,
they form what might be described as a counterterrorism-industrial complex – one
that, deliberately or not, and for a variety of reasons, fuels the cycle of fear and
overreaction."[166] In addition, "[o]fficials quickly learn that they stand a better
chance of being heard and carrying the day if they can argue that their ideas offer
the most effective way to defeat terrorists."[167]

While twenty years ago counterterrorism was a career dead-end, now it is the
avenue to promotion, and swiftly. It is a significant challenge to get any of the
disciplines involved – which are all profiting handsomely from a continued obses-
sion with terrorism as an existential threat – to leave the trough voluntarily just
because the facts do not support such expenditure. After all, how many actors turn
down the $25 million offered for the fourth sequel that is almost guaranteed to be
awful? The result is a "'permanent-war complex,' which is now engaged in conflicts
in at least eight countries across the globe, none of which are intended to be
temporary."[168] Also, it has been reported that US Special Forces operate in 149
nations (there are only 196 recognized sovereign states)[169] – 150 percent more than
even during the George W. Bush administrations.[170] In fact, the United States's war
on terror has now also involved seventy-six countries in the ongoing campaign.[171] Yet
this proliferation is barely covered by the US media.[172]

This "permanent-war complex" has "justified its enhanced power and control
over the country's resources primarily by citing threats to US security posed by
Islamic terrorists."[173] However, like the military-industrial complex from which it
evolved, and which it has now enveloped, "it is really rooted in the evolving relationship between the national security institutions themselves and the private arms
contractors allied with them."[174] As a result, private contractors, especially those
who supply, manage, and control drone warfare, "have both a powerful motive and
the political power, exercised through its clients in Congress, to ensure that the wars
continue for the indefinite future."[175]

The United States's commitment to perpetual war has been enshrined in the
Department of Defense's revised mission statement, which now reads: "The mission
of the Department of Defense is to provide a lethal Joint Force to defend the security
of our country and sustain American influence abroad."[176] That amended the prior
version by removing the words "to deter war" while adding that it is the Pentagon's
responsibility to "sustain American influence" overseas.[177] It is also manifested in US

armed activities, many of which fly under the radar of a generally disinterested US public and media – and Congress – that do not demand notice of or accountability for the United States's military adventures abroad. For example, in 2017, "[w]hen a Navy SEAL was killed and three others injured during a raid in Central Yemen in early 2017, Americans asked, 'What are we doing there?' When three US Army Special Forces troops were killed in an ambush while on patrol in Niger, folks back home said, 'What are we doing there?'"[178]

Describing that as "the iceberg beneath the surface[,]" *The American Conservative* laments that "US military activity – in particular, airstrikes and raids in the Middle East and Africa, not to mention Afghanistan – has not only accelerated under the Trump administration, but targeted killing campaigns are reportedly operating under fewer constraints and with less transparency than even under the notoriously secretive Obama administration."[179] Regarding aerial bombing, *The American Conservative* adds that "[o]f this we have only troubling glimpses[,]" and that according to the Bureau of Investigative Journalism, "the Trump administration launched over 160 strikes in Yemen and Somalia in 2017—that's 100 percent and 30 percent more, respectively, than the drone-loving Obama administration launched the year before."[180] Also, "[e]qually frustrating, the congressional mandate only covers US military strikes – we still have no idea how many CIA drone operations have been conducted in each of these countries under Trump."[181]

The expansion of the United States's deadly overseas military operations illumi-nates another illusion under which the United States – both its officials and public – labors: that counter-messaging can prevail against anti-US sentiments and ideology that manifest in violence. That ignores the reality that the solution is not counter-messaging, it is counter-*conduct*. Even President Lyndon B. Johnson, while escalating the United States's involvement in the Vietnam War to unprecedented heights, recognized in 1965 that "[t]he more bombs you drop, the more nations you scare, the more people you make mad."[182] The United States has lost that recognition entirely in its counterterrorism policy. It does not matter what the United States says about its peaceful intentions, when it drones a Pakistani village and a family is killed, those benign words are without effect. When someone gets their chain ripped off their neck on the street, their first reaction and their second reaction and their third reaction, is not to say, "It's the system, it's economic inequality, it's a failure to educate, it's a failure to provide resources that caused that crime." Rather, they blame *the person who took the chain*. If US officials or its populace think in Pakistan, a villager or a family that gets droned is going to blame the Taliban as opposed to the person responsible for the deadly drone strike, they are making a critical mistake.

In fact, Malley and Finer note that "[o]ne possible explanation for the resilience of the terrorist threat is that an overly militarized approach aggravates the very conditions on which terrorist recruitment thrives."[183] They explain that "[t]he destruction of entire cities and the unintentional killing of civilians, in addition to being tragic, serve as powerful propaganda tools for jihadists[,]" adding that "[s]uch incidents feed resentment, grievances, and anti-Americanism. Thus, while "[n]ot everyone who is resentful, grieving, or anti-American will turn to violence" – indeed, "[t]he vast majority will not" – "invariably, some will."[184]

Savvy military professionals understand that as well. For example, "[i]n a secret May 2009 assessment leaked to the Washington Post, General David Petraeus, then commander of the Central Command, wrote, 'Anti-US sentiment has already been increasing in Pakistan, especially in regard to cross-border and reported drone strikes, which Pakistanis perceive to cause unacceptable civilian casualties.'"[185] Similarly, a 2013 Council on Foreign Relations report on drone war policy "found that membership in *al Qaeda* in the Arabian Peninsula in Yemen grew from several hundred in 2010 to a few thousand members in 2012, just as the number of drone strikes in the country was increasing dramatically – along with popular anger toward the United States."[186] The same inadvertent but completely predictable recruitment is being accomplished today by the United States's support of Saudi Arabia's (and the United Arab Emirates') military campaign in Yemen.[187]

Yet despite these quite rational and clinically supported assessments, the United States persists in the illusion that when it announces, in the 149 countries in which its military operates, "We come in peace," that the United States can overcome the fatal and devastating effects of its conduct on indigenous communities abroad. It is impossible for the US to assume any moral high ground until it reconciles its conduct to match its message. Thus far, the US has failed to do so, and the world knows it and knows it full well. Nor can the US continue to resort to an invocation of 9/11 as an excuse for every military intervention and infliction of casualties. Is the United States going to break even at some point? As the figures cited above demonstrate, the United States has killed, or shares responsibility for killing, hundreds of thousands of people, and for destabilizing numerous countries and regions. How many civilians are homeless and dead, or refugees? It is vastly more than 3,000 by considerable orders of magnitude. Is it a sufficiently breathtaking number that the United States can now forever shelve 9/11 as a justification for war and violence?

In that context, a cynical observer would not be too harsh in characterizing the United States's definition of "collateral damage" as "not white people." They are defined as "collateral damage," and not as casualties, not as victims, not as humans. Unless and until the United States recognizes the paramount importance of protecting civilians and not treating those considered non-Americans or nonwhite people, or however "the other" is identified, as deserving of less protection than Americans are, the United States will fail to stem the tide of anti-US attitudes no matter how much counter-messaging it purveys.

Domestically, the effectiveness of counter-messaging is further offset by the government's focus on law enforcement through sting operations rather than countering violent extremism through methods that do not involve prosecuting and imprisoning young Muslim men and women. If all the money and other resources the FBI has devoted to turning ambivalent young Muslims into would-be terrorists for purposes of arresting them were instead directed at encouraging those same persons to work for NGOs, to become politically active, to receive a authentic Islamic education, or to do something legal and productive so their protests could be channeled positively, as opposed to simply treating it as a law enforcement problem, perhaps that is a counter-message that would resonate with its target audience.

Terminology of counter-messaging is also important. It is another mistake to define the objective as "de-radicalization." It is not unlawful to be radical. It is unlawful to commit crimes, including those that are violent outside the concept of legal justification. However, if people are denied the right to their own political views – which may very well be different than the majority's, or the government's, but which may very well have merit – and they are denied their First Amendment rights to dissident expression however radical it might be, the United States will not only continue to fail to arrest anti-US sentiment, but also will have repudiated its fundamental constitutional principles. If the United States is intent on engaging in perpetual war, a better objective would be that proposed by David Love, an editorial board member of BlackCommentator.com, and a contributor to the Progressive Media Project and theGrio: "If we are to have a perpetual war, it must be a war against injustice and deprivation at home and abroad. We need to get our own house in order, rather than demolish and rebuild other nations that did not invite us there."[188]

Another obtuse illusion is that the United States's immersion in perpetual war and counterterrorism operations is worth the suffering of those who implement that strategy: military and other personnel. The physical toll is obvious; modern ordnance combined with modern trauma medical care means that the lives of many who sustain devastating injuries are able to survive. The mental toll is less apparent, but no less profound. Post-traumatic stress disorder (PTSD) has a purely emotional component, but in the context of the unprecedented explosive power of today's munitions, research is discovering neurological damage caused by their concussive power.[189]

These psychological issues, aggravated if not caused by neurological damage, also provide a troubling counterpoint to the illusion that the United States's war on terror occupies the moral high ground. Indeed, it is now common to hear veterans' psychological struggles expressed as a by-product of "moral injury" – a term used by the National Center for PTSD and defined as an extreme and unprecedented life experience, including the harmful aftermath of exposure to such events that "transgress deeply held moral beliefs and expectations."[190] According to Aaron Pratt Shepherd, a philosophy professor who for a time served as a chaplain at a Veterans Affairs Medical Center, "[t]he term 'moral injury' was popularized in the mid-1990s by Jonathan Shay, a staff psychiatrist at a Department of Veterans Affairs outpatient clinic in Boston who was working with veterans suffering from psychological trauma[,]" and who "describes moral injury as a result of being ordered to do something in a 'high-stakes situation' that violates an individual's deeply held beliefs about what is right.[191] Closing in on a second complete decade of continuous war on multiple fronts, the US public's failure to appreciate what Shepherd calls "[t]he problematic disconnect between the American public and its military and veteran community" can be characterized only as willful ignorance designed to permit that public to persist in its illusions about the purposes and effects of the United States's military activities abroad.[192]

Also, the resources that counterterrorism drains from US society reflects another illusion: that the United States possesses infinite capacity to pursue the zero-tolerance policy with respect to terrorism that the public ostensibly demands. That exists in tandem with the illusion that technology will solve all problems related to security, or that acquiring all intelligence available is somehow superior to targeted collection. Again, both illusions constrain the United States's ability to direct those resources to confront other, more serious threats. Collection that overwhelms the capacity of human analysts to evaluate intelligence adequately is counterproductive, and intelligence professionals have realized that dragnet surveillance and intelligence inundation limit rather than expand intelligence productivity.[193] In the mid-2000s, when the FBI had only a few Arabic-speaking agents, there was a backlog of years in translating and transcribing intercepted conversations and other electronic communications.[194] That is not an effective means of gathering intelligence or investigating crime. Resources are finite; every false positive pursued forecloses the ability to track a genuine threat.

The singular focus on counterterrorism, in tandem with the United States's commitment to perpetual war on a global scale – military operations in 75% of the planet's nations – has exacted other costs, some unquantifiable and others intangible, within the United States. It has materially skewed the way in which the United States evaluates the other threats that are existential. As a commentator has pointed out, "[t]he small chance of being murdered in an attack committed by foreign-born terrorists has prompted expensive overreactions that do more harm than good, such as the so-called Trump travel ban, but address smaller risks than those posed by animals."[195] Yet "nobody suggests banning bees, dogs, or other animals just because they have killed 7,548 people since 1975."[196] In contrast, "[b]ut it is common for people to argue for banning immigrants due to the manageable hazard posed by infrequent terrorist attacks by foreign-born individuals."[197]

While "[c]ertain precautions do make sense[,]" they do so "only if they pass a cost-benefit test that counter-terrorism spending is guaranteed to fail."[198] Ultimately, "[e]valuating small and manageable threats such as that from terrorism relative to other small and manageable threats from homicide or animal attacks is a useful way to understand the world and where we should focus our energies and worries."[199] Conversely, "just because terrorist attacks strike randomly and infrequently does not mean that the fear that those attacks create needs to be addressed through new public policies that spend trillions of dollars and kill many people in addition to making daily life just a little more inconvenient for little to no benefit."[200]

A disproportionate concentration on counterterrorism also disorients policy imperatives, as "it's not just American politics that suffers from an overemphasis on counterterrorism; the country's policies do, too."[201] While "[a]n administration can do more than one thing at once, ... it can't prioritize everything at the same time."[202] As a result, "[t]he time spent by senior officials and the resources invested by the government in finding, chasing, and killing terrorists invariably come at the expense of other tasks: for example, addressing the challenges of a rising China, a nuclear North Korea, and a resurgent Russia."[203]

The ultimate illusion is that despite these existential threats, everything will continue just as it always has because, after all, this is America. That complacency – that these threats to national security will resolve themselves without effort, intervention, and vigilance – is a threat in itself and a by-product of the United States's global hegemony since the demise of the Soviet Union. Even if the institutions that people relied on in the past were self-executing in their ability to confront problems, the current circumstances demonstrate they no longer retain that capacity.

Only by recognizing these national security threats that the United States has in many respects itself created and cultivated, and reconciling them honestly and courageously with the values the United States professes to embody, can there be optimism for the future.

PART III

The Future Imagined

9

Beyond the Counterinsurgency Paradigm of Governing: Letting Go of Prediction and the Illusion of an Internal Enemy

Bernard E. Harcourt

What, if any, are viable and constructive ways forward to reconfigure the American national security state? The question itself, like any well-posed question, is loaded in the sense that it implicitly injects the concern of national security into the matter of statecraft. It would be easy to avoid the question by arguing that statecraft need not privilege security or national security – in effect, that we should not design a national security state, but instead a well-educated citizenry and an egalitarian, compassionate democratic society, all of which would inherently promote greater security and national security. (This undoubtedly is correct and highlights a problem in American politics today, namely the fetishization of security at the expense of other foundational values of the Republic as well as the instrumental deployment of a rhetoric of security to govern and exercise social control.) It is also important to explore whether the concept of the nation – implicit in the term "national security" – is worth holding on to, if we are truly interested in reimagining statecraft or our larger political condition. But all of these responses merely deflect the question, resist the hypothetical, and in the process fail to address the kernel at the heart of the original question presented: Assuming that national security is a genuine and worthwhile priority, then how should those aspects of the American state that are intended to promote national security be reimagined? In examining the aims of the national security state, it is important to focus on the "genuine" goals as opposed to those deployed so often by US political leaders who see national security more as a vehicle for reelection and enrichment than as an authentic concern. If we authentically care about the national security of the United States – defined in terms of its protection from foreign influence or invasion – how do we reconfigure the apparatus of the national security state?

The answer I propose is as narrow and candid as the reformulation of the question: by ceasing to govern on the model of counterinsurgency warfare and stopping to project the counterinsurgency vision of society on other populations and on our own. This entails, as the first and perhaps most important step, giving up on the prediction of who is going to become our next enemy. The prediction of internal and external enemies is a self-fulfilling prophecy that justifies and reinforces a form of governing through counterinsurgency warfare that is, itself, detrimental to our politics and security. The answer, then, entails replacing our predictive forms of security with a combination of preemptive forms of solidarity and judicious enforcement of penal laws. To give a concrete example, it means not executing suspected terrorists on the basis of prediction, but instead preemptively providing support and solidarity to them, to their region, or to their group, and simultaneously administering due process penal justice to anyone who has been convicted of engaging in acts of terrorism. It means, in essence, restraining from predicting future behavior, but punishing past bad acts judiciously. This approach would render our Republic more respected by foreign nationals, morally righteous at an international level, less targeted for attacks, faithful to our ideals, and ultimately more secure. We need, in sum, to hit the reset button on how we relate to others abroad and to our targeted minorities at home and discard the counterproductive strategies of prediction of future behaviors that have backfired in the struggle against terrorism.

In order to spell this out, it is essential, first, to properly understand what the American national security state looks like today and on what forms of rationality it currently operates. So, in Part I of this essay, I will demonstrate the extent to which the national security state has gravitated toward a counterinsurgency warfare paradigm, and Part II will expose the underlying logic and rationality of the "internal enemy." Then, in Part III, I will set out to debunk the vision of society upon which the counterinsurgency paradigm rests. Following that, in Part IV, the essay will argue that the path forward is to shed the vision of society embedded in counterinsurgency, which means simultaneously letting go of prediction. It will respond to critics, and then in a short conclusion raise reflections on the ethical dimensions of these matters.

I THE AMERICAN NATIONAL SECURITY STATE

Since 9/11, the institutions, organizations, practices, and members of the national security state apparatus (NSSA) have coalesced around a counterinsurgency warfare paradigm, both in terms of their functioning abroad and their governing at home. The different components of the NSSA now work together in furtherance of the three-prong strategy of counterinsurgency theory developed by Western powers during the anti-colonial wars of the 1950s and 1960s. The heart of the strategy is the identification and elimination of an insurgent minority – whether an insurgent enemy abroad (the Taliban, Al-Qaeda, ISIS) or an internal enemy that is constructed in order to mobilize counterinsurgency tactics. Given the absence of an insurgent minority on domestic soil in the United States, the internal enemy is fabricated by the NSSA through a process of prediction and projection. The turn to counterinsurgency as a mode of governing is the product of a decades-long history of prediction.

During the wars in Iraq and Afghanistan, American political and military leadership recuperated, refined, and harnessed the counterinsurgency practices that had been developed in Indochina, Malaya, Algeria, Vietnam, and elsewhere. America's political leaders and conservative intelligentsia embraced counterinsurgency methods including torture, indefinite detention, and targeted drone assassinations. Its military leaders rewrote counterinsurgency theory, notably by means of General David Petraeus's 2006 US Army and Marine Corps Field Manual 3–24 on counterinsurgency, and began implementing it widely across the Gulf. Through these practices, the NSSA pivoted toward the three-part strategy of counterinsurgency: total information awareness via surveillance of the entire population in order to identify and then eradicate the insurgent minority, with a focus on the larger ambition of winning the hearts and minds of the passive masses.

The first prong, total information awareness about the total population, has become the guiding compass of American signal intelligence agencies, with the goal of identifying and separating the small insurgent minority from the larger mass of the passive population. This ambition has been made possible thanks to new digital technologies that allow intelligence agencies to capture total information about the total population at a fraction of earlier costs. Before, intelligence programs like the FBI's COINTELPRO were so expensive in terms of manpower and resources that they had to focus on particular targets, suspects, and suspected groups – civil rights leaders and organizations. But the advent of digital splicing and collection technologies have made it possible now, at practically no cost, to target entire populations, including the US population. Those advancements have made it possible to attempt to parse the radical insurgent minority from the passive masses of individuals.

The second prong builds on the purported identification of the insurgent minority and aims to eliminate them through any means possible. In Algeria in the 1950s and 1960s, this was achieved through torture and summary executions, often by throwing suspects out of helicopters into the Mediterranean Sea. Shortly after 9/11, the NSSA began pursuing this second core strategy through practices of life-threatening torture and indefinite detention, and the NSSA gradually evolved toward the use of targeted drone strikes and special operations, first within and then outside the war zone. Tortured interrogations fit within both the first prong as a way to achieve total information, and the second, as a way of eliminating and creating fear to dissuade insurgents. It also served the third prong by terrorizing the general population into submission (while radicalizing others).

The third prong is the traditional strategy of "winning the hearts and minds" of the passive majority – as it was called in Vietnam. There are several approaches to this third effort – from more to less punitive. There are the carrot and stick approaches. There are, for instance, some efforts that involve providing basic needs and services to targeted populations, or sometimes just offering cash and contracts. At the other extreme, there are forms of terrorizing the population into submission with the frequent use of drones and strikes that often involve innocent casualties. And then, in between, there are multiple strategies, such as methods of deradicalization using targeted digital propaganda. Increasingly, the NSSA is involved in forms of distracting populations, especially the US population, through social media and reality TV–type governing.

In a three-step movement of historical proportion, America's political and military leadership embraced the counterinsurgency warfare paradigm as its mode of governance. It started abroad in the wars in Iraq and Afghanistan, when the US military retooled counterinsurgency tactics from the colonial wars of the 1950s and 1960s and implemented those very strategies – waterboarding and stress positions, indefinite detention at Guantánamo, targeted drone killings, and total surveillance of suspected enemies –primarily on Muslims in the war zone and at secret prisons and black sites around the world. In a second step, the US government extended those counterinsurgency strategies more widely throughout its foreign policy, using targeted drone strikes outside the war zone, rendition of suspects to countries around the globe, and total information awareness on all foreigners. Third, American leaders then brought these techniques home. They hyper-militarized local police forces with excess counterinsurgency equipment – military-grade assault weapons, armored vehicles, night scopes, and grenade launchers. Local police departments deployed counterinsurgency tactics to infiltrate mosques and student groups and to surveil Muslim businesses – all without individualized suspicion. The NSSA also turned its total surveillance apparatus on ordinary Americans, bulk collecting their telephony metadata, social media, and other digital traces.

The surprise election of Donald Trump crystalized this new mode of governing and propelled it to its ultimate and final stage, sanctified in June 2018 by the US Supreme Court's decision that upheld the Muslim ban: a perfect model of domestic government through a counterinsurgency warfare paradigm despite the absence of an active insurgency at home. A counterrevolutionary method of governing *without* a revolution. A counterinsurgency *without* an insurgency. We are now living in an epoch, in the United States, that can only be described through a counterinsurgency paradigm. Few grasp the magnitude of this historical transformation.

II THE CONSTRUCTION OF AN INTERNAL ENEMY

At the heart of this American counterrevolution is the preemptive identification of foreign enemies abroad and of internal enemies on domestic soil. The former raises problems of prediction, the latter compounds those problems given that, in the absence of an internal enemy, one has to be invented and sustained. And that is exactly what has happened under the Trump administration.

The creation of an internal enemy has been achieved through the deliberate construction of Muslims, including Muslim Americans, Mexicans and Mexican Americans, and more broadly Hispanics and immigrants, as internal enemies. The

Muslim ban, signed as an executive order within days of Trump's inauguration, was a centerpiece of that effort. "Islam hates us," Trump declared. "We can't allow people coming into this country who have this hatred of the United States . . . and of people that are not Muslim." With his campaign pledge for "a total and complete shutdown of Muslims entering the United States," his unambiguous Islamophobic propaganda and his crystal-clear innuendos about "political correctness," Trump methodically turned Muslim Americans and Muslims into internal enemies who need to be contained and eliminated. Trump's suggestion of a Muslim database or, even worse, for the registration of Muslims on American soil and for the renewed infiltration of mosques, demonized an entire population.

Other groups as well have been constructed into internal enemies. The FBI's designation of "Black Identity Extremists" converted ordinary peaceful black protesters and the #BlackLivesMatter movement into a dangerous internal threat. Trump's derogatory remarks about Mexicans and Hispanics and his persistent effort to build a wall on our southern border turned Latinos into criminal social enemies. This was especially true during the midterm elections in 2018 when Trump demonized the "caravan." His decision to exclude trans persons from military service also served to vilify sexual minorities.

To make matters worse, the US Supreme Court constitutionally immunized this new way of governing when it authorized the Muslim ban in June 2018. The Supreme Court failed to censure patently discriminatory tactics, to acknowledge religious animus, or to cut through the pretextual charade that Trump himself mocked ("We all know what that means" in Trump's words, or "Let's stop being politically correct"). "We're having problems with the Muslims, and we're having problems with Muslims coming into the country," Trump said, before enacting his Muslim ban on entry from predominantly Muslim countries. Replace Muslim with any other religious minority – Jews, for instance, or Catholics – and history would shudder. But not anymore. We now live in an era marked by the regularization of torture and indefinite detention, of ultra-militarized police forces and counterinsurgency policing, of total NSA surveillance, and now of a constitutionally approved religious ban – in a country originally founded on entirely different ideals of equality, freedom, and due process. And our highest court has placed its imprimatur on this historical transformation in how the NSSA governs abroad and at home: The United States's political and military leaders now rule through the willful demonization of religious and ethnic minorities and through the deliberate construction of phantom internal enemies – in essence, through a counterinsurgency warfare paradigm of government.

This way of governing through an internal enemy traces to a unique way of conceptualizing society that goes back to Mao Zedong. The genealogy is fascinating, and the consequences are deeply paradoxical. The fact is this: The French commanders in Indochina and Algeria who developed counterinsurgency warfare practices – which they called *la guerre révolutionnaire* or *la guerre moderne* – steeped themselves in Mao's writings in order to better anticipate and combat Maoist insurrections in their colonies. Mao's vision of society thus highly influenced military strategists, especially the French commander David Galula, who would then serve as the intellectual role model for General Petraeus and his counter-insurgency field manual.

The Maoist view of society was tripartite: there was, first, a small minority of active insurgents. These were Mao's soldiers and sympathizers. Then, second, there was a set of counterinsurgents, who represent essentially the guardians of the state. In Mao's time, these were the Kuomintang; in today's context, this would be the NSSA. Third, there were the passive masses: the bulk of the population. The central Maoist strategy was for the small minority of active insurgents to gain the allegiance of the masses in order to seize power from the counterrevolutionary minority.

What is particularly interesting, and somewhat unexpected, is that the Western commanders who developed counterinsurgency theory to fight Maoist insurrections adopted Mao's view of society. Rather than embrace some other view of social divisions or classes, the counterinsurgency theorists essentially adopted Mao's views and strategies and just decided to implement them better. The central tenets of counterinsurgency theory drew on the Maoist vision: populations – originally colonial populations, but now *all* populations – are made up of a small active minority of insurgents, a small group of those actively opposed to the insurgents, and a large passive majority that can be swayed one way or the other. Thus, the most important battle is over the hearts and minds of the general population. This requires separating the active minority from the general population – isolating them, containing them, and ultimately eliminating them. The key to victory is to keep the passive masses just that: passive, by weeding out and extracting the small revolutionary minority or, even better, by turning the neutral masses against the insurgency. And all of this turns on total intelligence: Collecting information on *everyone* in the population is vital to sort friend from foe, to identify and extract the small revolutionary minority, and ulti-mately to pacify the masses. Only total information awareness makes it possible to cull the dangerous minority from the passive majority.

The French commander and pioneer of *la guerre révolutionnaire*, David Galula, embraced precisely Mao's tripartite vision of society. Galula learned his Mao well. He studied closely Mao's writings in the late 1940s based on their English translation in the *Marine Corps Gazette* and, according to people close to him at the time, "spoke of Mao and the civil war 'all the time.'" From Mao he drew the lesson that societies were divided into three groups and that the key to victory was to isolate and eradicate the active minority in order to gain the allegiance of the masses. The battle was over the general population, Galula emphasized in his book on *Counterinsurgency Warfare*, and the first line of offense was total intelligence.[1]

Galula italicized in his writings that the central strategy of counterinsurgency theory "simply expresses the basic tenet of the exercise of political power":

In any situation, whatever the cause,
there will be...

An active minority for the cause

A neutral or passive majority

And an active minority against the cause.

FIGURE 9.1 Support for an Insurgency
Source: Figure FM I-2 from General Petraeus's Field Manual

In any situation, whatever the cause, there will be an active minority for the cause,
a neutral majority, and an active minority against the cause.
     The technique of power consists in relying on the favorable minority in order to
rally the neutral majority and to neutralize or eliminate the hostile minority."[2]

Notice that Galula not only wholeheartedly embraced Mao's vision of society, he
also universalized and generalized it, so that, for him, it applied in every situation
and it simply expressed "the basic tenet" of how political power is exercised.

     After 9/11, General David Petraeus would return to Galula's words and adopt them
verbatim. Widely recognized as the leading American thinker and practitioner of
counterinsurgency theory, eventually responsible for all coalition troops in Iraq and
the architect of the troop surge of 2007, Petraeus followed Galula's words perfectly.
General Petraeus's edition of the US Army and Marine Corps Field Manual 3–24 on
counterinsurgency,[3] published and widely disseminated in 2006, reiterated Galula's
lesson and reduced it to a concise paragraph in the very first chapter, under the
header "Aspects of Counterinsurgency":

     In almost every case, counterinsurgents face a populace containing an active
     minority supporting the government and an equally small militant faction oppos-
     ing it. Success requires the government to be accepted as legitimate by most of
     that uncommitted middle, which also includes passive supporters of both sides.
     (See figure 9.1.)[4]

The referenced figure captured the essence of this way of seeing the world, echoing
Galula's words exactly: "In any situation, whatever the cause." From Mao and
Galula, Petraeus derived not only the core foundation of counterinsurgency, but
the central political vision of society. This is a political theory, not simply a military
strategy. It is a worldview, a way of seeing, a way of dealing with all situations –
whether on the field of battle or off it.[5]

     On this Maoist vision of society, General Petraeus's manual established the three
key pillars discussed earlier – what might be called counterinsurgency's core

principles: total information awareness, elimination of the insurgent minority, and pacification of the masses.

In effect, our NSSA adopted Mao's way of imagining society as composed of a small active insurgency, a counterinsurgent minority, and a mass of passive citizens who can be swayed one way or the other. Based on that Maoist vision of society, the NSSA has begun to govern abroad and domestically, on American soil, deploying Mao's brilliant warfare tactics: Gather all the available intelligence, weed out the dangerous insurgents, and seduce the passive masses. Mao's three-prong military strategy, which first mesmerized French colonial commanders like Roger Trinquier and David Galula, has now come home to roost. This is the greatest paradox: American political and military leaders have become Maoist.

III UNVEILING THE ILLUSION

The problem is, this vision of society is an illusion, and it makes us see counter-insurgents even when there are none. By projecting outward an internal enemy, citizens begin to map onto that specter a pattern when there are in fact only isolated incidents. They begin to see patterns where there are none. In the United States, this illusion makes citizens believe that there is an insurgency in this country. By creating a fictitious insurgency, citizens begin to see it. This is what is so remarkable and so different about the current political situation in the United States versus what was happening in Algeria or Vietnam in the 1950s and 1960s. In Vietnam, there was the Viet Cong, and in Algeria there was the FLN (National Liberation Front). Those were armed revolutionary insurgents. But in the United States today, there is no insurgency. There are acts of extreme violence that claim certain extreme ideologies – white supremacism for instance, and sometimes Islamic fundamentalism – but those tend to be isolated acts by unstable individuals who are not part of an insurgency. They may gravitate toward extreme ideology as an explanation or as something that is attractive to them, especially white supremacy or radical Islam, but they do not form part of an insurgency.

Paradoxically, we have all drunk the Kool-Aid. It is not just the NSSA that sees internal enemies when there are none. It is not just the foreign affairs hawks. The doves as well have begun to see the NSSA itself as that active minority of counter-insurgents. In other words, those who are most skeptical and critical of the excesses of the Global War on Terror have themselves internalized the Maoist vision of society and begun to think of the different components of the NSSA as the counterrevolutionary minority. Whether under the rubric of the double government or even possibly the deep state, many on both sides of the political spectrum have begun to believe in an inner core of guardians against insurrection. Many, again on both sides of security debates, have also started to think of the general population as a passive mass that can be swayed either way. This has become, perhaps, a dominant way of thinking about American society today.

Instead of embracing the Maoist vision of society, however, the only viable way forward is to struggle against this way of thinking, not to adopt the same vision of society and do better, as counterinsurgency theory surprisingly did, but rather to abandon the illusion. The reason is that these categories are phantasms.

The deceit of hegemonic ideas is that we begin to believe them and internalize them. That's certainly true of counterinsurgency governing. We have begun to think that the masses are passive and can be swayed one way or the other. Or that there is only a small minority that is prepared to actively resist – or a small guardian class that is maintaining an oppressive system. Part of what makes these ideas so powerful is that we begin to absorb them, to internalize them into our own thinking about how to resist. We begin to believe them or to stop asking questions. But the truth is, they are just myths. That counterrevolutionary vision of society – of a tripartite division of society, with the passive masses in the middle – is pure fiction. It is far too simplistic and misleading.

The passive masses is a phrase that completely misleads. Nothing could be further from the truth. The masses have never been passive. And they are not passive today. They know what they want, and they know what they are doing. Today, the majority of Americans are content: With their digital devices and their online shopping, reality TV, and opinionated news shows, most Americans are enjoying life. And that's what most people want – to simply enjoy life. For many of us, as long as we have a modicum of pleasure, we are content, basically. It is what allows us to go on with our lives even when our president, Donald Trump, makes a mockery of the White House. Even when, in the words of a disgruntled anonymous official in the Trump administration, the president "engages in repetitive rants, and his impulsiveness results in half-baked, ill-informed and occasionally reckless decisions that have to be walked back."[6] It is only when there is a direct affront to our way of life – when for instance our way of life and retirement savings were threatened by the Great Recession of 2008 – that people, or at least a number of people, take to the streets to occupy the public space. The election of Trump did not cause a constitutional crisis or a political revolt because most people did not believe he would fundamentally destabilize their way of life. That is not passivity, it is deliberate. It is intentional.

The Germans chose fascism. The American people allow Trump. These are not passive decisions but active ones. And they need to be understood by recourse to desire, even possibly libidinal, impulses. As Gilles Deleuze and Félix Guattari reminded us, in the context of German support for fascism at mid-century, these moments demand "an explanation that will take their [citizens'] desires into account, an explanation formulated in terms of desire: no, the masses were not innocent dupes; at a certain point, under a certain set of conditions, they *wanted* fascism, and it is this perversion of the desire of the masses that needs to be accounted for."[7]

The masses are not passive. When they are quiet, they tolerate. They might tolerate because they are scared, or because they think the alternative would be worse, or because they have been taught to tolerate. But it is not because they are inherently passive. Nor is it because they have become brainwashed by an ideology. Again, as Deleuze and Guattari forcefully told us, "It is not a question of ideology. . . . It is not an ideological problem, a problem of failing to recognize, or of being subject to, an illusion. It is a problem of desire, and desire is part of the infrastructure."[8] Whether in an authoritarian or democratic regime, the political system always depends on the authorization and legitimacy of the people. That is, surprisingly, what Gandhi made clear through his inspiring acts of nonviolent resistance: A regime, even an oppressive regime that wields all the military force, cannot survive if it does not have the backing or support of the citizens. And the citizens grant or withhold that authorization – or resist – based on their deliberate decisions.

Domestically, there is no insurgency. Even the few men and women on American soil who wreak terroristic damage do not form an insurgency. For the most past, they are unstable individuals who gravitate to radical forms of Islam (or to the KKK) because it is the new fringe. We are not facing, in the United States, a radical insurgency so much as the Islamification (as well as the white supremacization) of a few radically violent individuals. As the political scientist Olivier Roy argued, in summary, we are witnessing not so much the radicalization of Islam as the Islamification of radicalism[9]: Radicalism and extremism have found their new causes. This surely seems true with regard to the number of unstable individuals who seem to gravitate toward Islam at the height of their psychoses (such as, for instance, the truck driver in Nice, France, and possibly also the shooters in San Bernardino or Miami).

There isn't a dangerous radical minority in the United States – so much as a handful of troubled individuals who drift toward the latest form of extremism (to which we need to add "domestic terrorists," such as the Charleston church shooter, who drift toward white supremacist ideology and have caused a greater number of fatalities). American history is replete with the false demonization of interior enemies – from the Red Scare, to the Japanese internment camps, to the juvenile predators. It is crucial that we ourselves avoid doing that again.

If anything, the logic of an internal enemy is a self-fulfilling prophesy insofar as it encourages unstable individuals – such as the San Bernardino shooter or the Chelsea pressure-cooker bomber – to embrace the most recent radical discourse, and then allows us to assemble them into an active minority, when in fact they are mostly lone wolf, unstable individuals who gravitate to Islam as the most attractive radical discourse on offer today (i.e., alongside the KKK and other white supremacist ideologies).

Internationally, there are of course individuals and groups that are enemies. But we should define them by their acts, not their propensities or likelihood of future dangerousness. It is too easy to get caught up in this way of thinking about society. That is in part why it is so contagious. But to move forward viably means giving up on the very bases of these ideas and recognizing that we are facing a constructed way of thinking about society. That may mean, at the same time, escaping a logic of double government. It means giving up the idea of extreme minorities and a passive population in the middle. In the process, we would also be letting go of a lot of prediction, because the principal mechanisms of the NSSA are based on preemptively identifying foreign or internal enemies and eliminating them before they can harm anyone. If we are to dismantle the punitive excesses of the NSSA, we need to get rid of those notions of prediction on both sides.

IV BEYOND PREEMPTION, AGAINST PREDICTION

Most importantly, we need to refrain from preemptively identifying enemies and attacking, torturing, detaining, or killing them – to forcefully enforce the law against those who act, to be sure, but not to preemptively punish those we suspect. That foments enemies and destroys our moral standing.

I have argued elsewhere that the use of prediction and profiling is generally counterproductive to the goal of security. In *Against Prediction: Profiling, Policing, and Punishing in an Actuarial Age* (University of Chicago Press, 2007), I offer two principal reasons why actuarial prediction likely backfires, and both reasons are relevant here in the context of predicting internal enemies. First, the reliance on predictions of future dangerousness may undermine the primary goal of law enforcement, namely enhancing security, because it may increase the overall amount of the targeted phenomena – whether it is criminal activity or terrorism – depending on the relative responsiveness of the profiled suspects (in comparison to the responsiveness of those who are not profiled) to the shift in the level of law enforcement. The ultimate effect will depend on how members of the two different groups – purported internal enemies and others – react to changes in policing or punishment. If we assume elasticity in both groups, and if the purportedly higher-offending profiled population of internal enemies are *less* responsive to the policy change, then the overall amount of the targeted conduct will *increase* in society. This is because the more elastic response of the non-profiled will outweigh the less elastic response of the profiled suspects. In other words, profiling on higher past, present, or future offending may be entirely counterproductive to the central aim of the NSSA – increased national security. I have demonstrated this in the terrorism context as well as in the ordinary criminal context.[10]

Second, if we assume complete inelasticity, the reliance on predictive methods will produce a distortion among the punished population that will likely have cumulative detrimental effects on society in the long term. It creates an imbalance between, on the one hand, the distribution of demographic or other group traits among the actual offending population and, on the other hand, the distribution of those same traits among the population of persons with national security traces, such as arrest, conviction, probation, incarceration, parole, or other forms of punishment. Simply put, the profiled population for purposes of internal enemies – say, for instance, Muslims – will become an even larger proportion of the punished population (larger in relation to its representation among suspected persons) than the non-profiled population. This in turn aggravates and compounds the difficulties that many of the profiled individuals have obtaining employment, pursuing educational opportunities, or simply leading normal family lives. These are significant social costs that are often overlooked but tend to have widespread detrimental effects within the community of those who are profiled. There are, naturally, other costs to consider as well. Psychologist Tom Tyler has demonstrated how perceptions of the legitimacy of justice affect the willingness of citizens to abide by the law.[11] Lawrence Sherman has also discussed the need to better minimize defiance through fair and just procedures that do not stigmatize the profiled populations. Other commentators have properly emphasized the link between targeted enforcement – particularly in the case of racial profiling – and increased law enforcement misconduct. So, for instance, the implementation of a targeted policing strategy that focused on increased misdemeanor arrests on the streets of New York City in the 1990s was accompanied by disproportionate effects on black and Latino citizens as well as a sharp rise in the number of civilian complaints of police misconduct, including brutality.[12] Still others have focused on the direct costs on families and the incarcerated.[13] All of these are important, but it is equally important to consider as well the negative consequences associated with a potential ratcheting effect on the profiled population.

These arguments should severely temper our embrace of predictive methods aimed at national security. The most important point – at least for those who find themselves inclined to support the NSSA – is that the use of prediction is likely counterproductive to the national security interests.

Some skeptics will respond that prediction in and of itself does not necessarily have the negative effects I attribute to it here – in terms of discrimination and so on. Also, that prediction can be useful to alleviate, rather than exacerbate, social, racial, or economic inequalities when used carefully. The use of informed statistics in the bail context, or in the context of releasing arrested undocumented immigrants, some will respond, may reduce the number of persons harmed by government policies. Accurate predictions, they might add, can be used effectively, and our prediction technologies are getting better. They are often better than the fly-by-the-seat-of-your-pants intuitions – and racially discriminatory intuitions at that – that would replace them.

But not every statistical fact needs to be turned into a prediction or needs to be understood through the prediction lens. The fact that undocumented immigrants with children may not abscond at high rates may itself justify a policy of release-on-recognizance, without being labeled a "prediction." Even if we do, though, it is important to recognize that those policies will likely have detrimental effects for undocumented immigrants who do not have children. It would be blinking reality to ignore those negative effects, even if the predictions are used for progressive ends. Prediction is costly. My point is, it generally entails costs that outweigh the advantages – and this is generally unrecognized. In the end, letting go of prediction is likely to support the goals of security, not to undermine them.

CONCLUSION

Imagine a world in which we do not construct internal enemies or target suspected foreign enemies, but instead treat them in such a way as to demonstrate genuine humanity and compassion. I would like to suggest that, over the long term, we end up more secure. Perhaps fewer people are radicalized against us, and fewer think of the United States as an evil force. These may sound like instrumental arguments, but what is important is that they support the larger point that the creation of an internal enemy is a dangerous illusion. Perhaps the most virtuous argument, in the end, is that it is simply unethical to do so.

This then raises the more important issue of ethics. As I mentioned earlier, American history is rife with the false demonization of internal enemies, from the Red Scare to the Japanese internment camps to the "juvenile superpredators" of the 1990s. In fact, the seeds of all this may have been planted long before, at the birth of the Republic, when black slaves and indigenous peoples became the country's first internal enemies. And the gestational period surely extended over decades or centuries – from the Trail of Tears to the demise of Reconstruction, through Jim Crow and the era of lynching, through the Asian Exclusion Act and quotas on Arabs, Italians, and Jews.

It is crucial, not just as a political matter but as an ethical matter as well, that we do not repeat that dark history, that we avoid turning Muslims, peaceful protesters, and other minorities into our new internal enemies. That, I contend, means letting go of prediction and of Mao's tripartite vision of society.

Let me end, then, on one of my favorite passages from Nietzsche, one that I return to again and again. It is from the more aphoristic writings in the Second Essay of his *Genealogy of Morals*, and it occurs in the middle of his discussion of punishment. Nietzsche writes:

> It is not unthinkable that a society might attain such a consciousness of power that it could allow itself the noblest luxury possible to it – letting those who harm it go unpunished. "What are my parasites to me?" it might say. "May they live and prosper: I am strong enough for that!"[4]

10

Reestablishing the Rule of Law as National Security

Mary Ellen O'Connell

Since the founding of the United States, presidents have cited law compliance and promotion as primary rationales and justifications for foreign and defense policy. The practice continued until the end of the Cold War when a subtle but significant change occurred. Instead of citing actual law, presidents and their advisers put forth self-serving interpretations only loosely based on authentic principle. Two infamous examples include the "Torture Memos" of the Bush administration and the "Targeted Killing Memos" of the Obama administration.[1] Upon taking office in 2017, Donald Trump took the next logical step. He largely abandoned legal fig leaves. He has authorized military force without providing legal justification, has shown disdain for the law and institutions of world order, and has asserted a right to invoke national emergency powers in the absence of a national emergency.[2] His actions expose the depths of a crisis long in the making and one not restricted to foreign and defense policy.[3] Contempt for the rule of law in these important areas is undermining respect for law in general.

In the United States, undermining the law is an existential threat. The United States was founded as a nation under the rule of law. This was a revolutionary concept in 1776, one that countered the reigning model of a supreme monarch or parliament. The Founders placed the concept of law in the leading position of society. They looked to international law, which was well-known to them,[4] for a model of law superior to government. International law provided this model as well as a common bond for disparate peoples.[5] The Founders wagered that law – international and other categories – could play the same role in a country that lacked not only a monarch, but a shared history and ancestry.[6] Law supplied the new society's supreme authority, common bond, and place in the world. To protect and defend the United States, therefore, has always meant more than simple physical protection of the borders from invading armies. American security requires protecting and defending the rule of law.[7] Assertions that it is necessary to violate the law in the interest of national security or in order to pursue military power are, in the US context, contradictions in terms.

This understanding of the essential role of law in the United States has been challenged at various points in US history. The most enduring and severe test, however, began at the end of the Cold War and is ongoing. Responding to the crisis of the current moment requires a look back at the founding period to confirm that the goal of securing the United States has been coextensive with promoting the rule of law at home and abroad. The move away from the rule-of-law paradigm began during the Cold War, then plummeted when US political and intellectual leaders lost the mirror to US policy provided by the Soviet Union. The most important factor in the law's decline has been the ideology of realism.

Realists teach that to achieve security, a US president should be free of legal constraints in the use of military of force.[8] They rely on faith in force above all else. This faith has appealed to holders of other perspectives, particularly American neoconservatives and many liberals.[9] Outside the United States, groups involved in liberation struggles of all kinds have largely abandoned the Gandhi/Martin Luther King/Nelson Mandela model of peace through law in favor of armed conflict.[10] Traditional realists complain that liberal and neoconservative policy-makers have been misusing military force but overlook their own success in undermining respect for the law on resort to force.[11] The consequences have been overwhelmingly negative and have sparked discussion about rising authoritarianism, risks to democracy, and even civil war.[12]

I LAW, IDENTITY, SECURITY

All societies need law. Even brutal dictators who rely on violence and fear need some law to keep order as a practical matter. The United States is, however, uniquely reliant on law. The United States needs law not only to support order without the high cost of ruling through force alone but in order to define itself and much more. In 1776, international law provided the reasons why a rebel movement with limited military resources could claim equality with long-established sovereign powers. It was a normative argument that appealed to states with larger militaries capable of conquering or disregarding a small and squabbling newcomer. International law provided the normative basis for arguing that British colonies had a right to be independent from Britain. The realization of the right could only happen when the new state received recognition from other states.[13] Law provided the rationale and the language that persuaded France and other European states to accept the United States into the club of states as a fully sovereign coequal. James Madison explained that "independent nations" are "subject to no law, but the law of nations."[14] Put affirmatively, all sovereign, independent states are under the rule of international law. International law existed prior to the establishment of the United States and was essential to its creation and its survival. As Benjamin Franklin observed, "The circumstances of a rising state make it necessary frequently to consult the law of nations ."[15]

Once a member of the state system, the United States could and did demand respect for the principles of territorial integrity, nonintervention, the prohibition on resort to force, and other protections that states owe to other states.[16] The arguments did not always work but did so enough of the time to allow the United States to survive. America repaid the debt by promoting international law for much of its history.[17]

US reliance on law extends beyond its place in the world. The United States was the first society to be organized around the supremacy of law as an alternative to the supremacy of a monarch, parliament, or religion. The government is limited by and therefore subject to the law.[18] One of the most important functions, if not the most important, of law is to control the use of force. Government is a tool of legal control over force; it maintains a monopoly over the lawful use of force.[19] In a rule-of-law society, only the government has the legal authority to use force. The allowance for force in self-defense by individuals is excused, not affirmatively permitted. These are fundamental precepts of the American design. John Adams declared in the founding period: "We are a nation of laws, not men."[20]

With independence, the first citizens of the United States began developing law for governing the new state, agreeing first to the Articles of Confederation, then to the Constitution of 1789. The Constitution replaced the Articles in part to better capture the "international advantages of a stronger form of national sovereignty and a uniform approach to treaties and the law of nations."[21] James Madison, John Jay, and Alexander Hamilton all argued in their commentary on the new Constitution, collected in *The Federalist Papers*, that a stronger central government would adhere more closely to the international rule of law than had the weaker form of central government under the Articles of Confederation. Jay wrote in *Federalist No. 3* that the new Constitution would provide for a government in which "treaties, as well as the law of nations, will always be expounded in one sense and executed in the same manner, whereas adjudications on the same points and questions in thirteen states, or in three or four confederacies, will not always accord or be consistent."[22] International law was essential to a new small state that aspired not only to independence and self-governance but to moral leadership. It required a government that could speak with one voice regarding international legal issues. It was plain that promoting international law needed to be among the United States's most important foreign and security policies. Americans had some sense that they were lucky to win the War of Independence, and they turned to law to secure their success.

This is not to say that the United States was a model of legal compliance or even moral rectitude. The treatment of blacks, Native Americans, and other ethnic groups is proof to the contrary. In the nineteenth century, treaties with China were disregarded out of blatant racism by members of Congress.[23] The point here is that the idea of law was held in high esteem and did in fact guide policy in many respects. Major pillars of foreign policy for the nation's first 150 years revolved around principles of international law.[24] "Non-intervention in the domestic affairs of other countries, prompt recognition of established governments, a respect for treaty obligations, the peaceful settlement of international disputes, and a reluctance to wage war indicate . . . some of the ideals which the United States tried to live up to in dealing with other nations."[25]

US presidents and diplomats did more than use international law as a shield; they sought to advance it as a moral imperative. Benjamin Franklin negotiated a Treaty of Amity in 1785 with Prussia that included the first known treaty provisions promising to treat captured enemy soldiers humanely.[26] In its long-running policy of neutrality, the United States made a "novel and satisfying contribution to international law" by demonstrating "to the cynical eighteenth century that neutrality could be true impartiality, not a thinly disguised device to give covert aid to one of the belligerents."[27] The Jay Treaty of 1794 that settled outstanding issues with Great Britain ushered in a golden age of arbitration.[28] George Washington said that the United States needed the treaty, explaining that a small, new nation could not afford to go to war with Britain or any other state.[29] The Treaty of San Lorenzo of 1796 with Spain settled issues of the United States's southern border and provided commercial benefits as well.[30]

Throughout the eighteenth century, the United States promoted compliance with international law in a variety of ways. It was a major proponent of neutrality law, adhering to its neutral duties even when European states did not reciprocate. The United States took strong measures to prevent Americans from traveling abroad to join, support, or profit from civil wars and rebellions in Latin America and the Caribbean.[31] One of the greatest US contributions came at the behest of Abraham Lincoln. When the Civil War broke out, President Lincoln, a lawyer by training, understood the importance to the possibility of a future national reconciliation of soldiers showing restraint on the battlefield. He ordered the drafting of a written code of the law of war, which became known by the name of its drafter, Franz Lieber.[32] It is the foundational document on which today's Geneva Conventions were built.

When the Civil War ended, the United States charged Britain with violating the United States's neutral rights.[33] The most egregious violation was the sale by British ship makers of warships to the Confederacy. The US government proposed arbitration to decide whether Britain owed the US compensation. The tribunal ruled for the United States, and Britain paid the $15.5 million award.[34] The *Alabama Claims* arbitration electrified the American peace movement, inspiring its members to campaign for a world court that could play the same role internationally as the US Supreme Court played within the country.[35] The platforms of US political parties in the late 1800s included an arbitration plank promising that the United States would commit to a standing arbitration treaty for the resolution of any disputes with Great Britain. Following his election, President William McKinley presented the treaty to the Senate, which failed to approve it by the required two-thirds majority. Too many senators wanted each dispute with Britain to be the subject of a specific agreement that the Senate could approve or reject.[36]

Despite this set back, most political leaders and the population in general supported peace through international law as a principal goal of US foreign policy. As the nineteenth century ended, however, the United States's wealth combined with developments in science, technology, and ideology began to win people away from the cause of peace. Theodore Roosevelt stands out as an adopter of new theories around the importance of fighting wars to build national character.[37] He advocated the Spanish-American War of 1898, even interfering with the investigation into whether Spain caused the explosion that sank the USS Maine in the harbor of Havana, Cuba.[38] Spain had nothing to do with the explosion, but Roosevelt wanted to use it as a pretext, a *causus belli*, for declaring war.

The resulting Spanish-American War came just as the American peace movement was succeeding in becoming a global peace movement.[39] National peace societies convinced Tsar Nicholas II to expand his disarmament conference into a peace conference – the First Hague Peace Conference in 1899. The US delegation had instructions to propose the establishment of a permanent international court.[40] The conference did not create a court but did establish a permanent arbitral facility that paved the way for today's United Nations International Court of Justice. In 1901, McKinley was assassinated, and Theodore Roosevelt succeeded him. Roosevelt chose a prominent New York trial lawyer, Elihu Root, as secretary of state. Root was a pragmatist and promoted international law, not out of commitment to the moral principle of peace, but because it made sense to resolve disputes in court rather than in combat when possible. Root cofounded the American Society of International Law in 1906,[41] and Root attended the Second Hague Peace Conference in 1907. He again proposed a world court but met opposition, particularly from Germany. He succeeded in founding an international court in the Americas, the Central American Court of Justice, but when World War I broke out, Root became an early advocate for US entry into the war on the side of Britain.

By then, Woodrow Wilson was president, and he kept the United States out of the war – at first. Wilson's first secretary of state was also a lawyer, William Jennings Bryan. Bryan worked tirelessly to move the world toward compulsory dispute resolution through binding, bilateral commitments that relied upon arbitration and other means of peaceful settlement from 1913 until his resignation in June 1915. In that period, Bryan negotiated twenty-nine treaties between the United States and European and South American states.[42] He resigned when he could not continue to serve Wilson, believing that Wilson was failing to honor America's neutral duties as World War I broke out in August 1914.

Bryan, together with most of the still massive peace movement, wanted Wilson to mediate a peaceful resolution of the war. The United States had strong and close ties to both Britain and Germany, but Wilson was not a peace-through-law proponent. Indeed, Wilson had little regard for lawyers and no prominent lawyer, such as Root, was included in the US delegation to the Paris talks on a postwar settlement.[43] After campaigning on the boast that he had kept the United States out of the war, soon after he was reelected the United States joined the British and French, turning the tide of the war decisively in their favor. After the war, Wilson began his experiment in social engineering, redrawing national boundaries based on guesses about cultural affinity. The realist scholar, John Mearsheimer, is right to critique the effort, though Mearsheimer fails to note that Wilson's approach was also a radical departure from international law.[44]

US entry into World War I was a significant marker on the road to a foreign and security policy that has left behind the American commitment to the rule of law. Wilson ignored international law principles concerning neutrality, maritime embargoes, respect for sovereignty, boundaries, and the equality of states.[45] His theories of nationalism ignored the fact that the United States itself had no claim to be a nation built on common ancestry, language, religion, or folkways. By the time of the Paris talks, Root had become a senator from New York and led the opposition to Wilson's plans. The Senate refused to consent to US membership in the Versailles Treaty or the League of Nations. Root did support a world court and was selected in 1918 to be a member of the commission tasked with drafting a treaty to finally establish the Permanent Court of International Justice.[46] Despite Root's significant role in creating the court and a bipartisan effort lasting through the 1930s, the Senate never reached the two-thirds majority needed to join.

The campaign to join the court suffered from its association with the League of Nations, which Root had rejected. In addition, the American peace movement went into steep decline during the war. Americans did not want to hear that the war was avoidable or that the United States's role in it was unlawful when tens of thousands of family members, friends, and neighbors were risking their lives. The cause had to be a noble one for the cost to be worthwhile. The United States emerged from the war set to become a major military power that put faith in weapons over rules.

Still, the American commitment to the rule of law in the world was deep. In addition to their continuing interest in joining the World Court, a small group promoted a treaty to end the use of war as an instrument of foreign policy.[47] They persuaded US diplomats to join with their French counterparts to create the Treaty for the Renunciation of War, known as the Kellogg-Briand Pact of 1928.[48] No treaty was actually needed to prohibit resort to war. Restricting force is the purpose of law and is certainly the reason modern international law arose. Nevertheless, by the 1920s and the rise of science, international lawyers sought to adopt treaties codifying in written agreements the principles long understood to be based on natural law theory.[49] Enforcing the Kellogg-Briand Pact became a major concern of US foreign policy for the next ten years.

When the pact failed to prevent World War II, US President Franklin Roosevelt ordered the development of a postwar order that would succeed in preventing another world war. At the heart of the plan, which became the United Nations Charter, is the prohibition on the use of force. The prohibition is supported by four pillars: renewed commitment to international law, a powerful Security Council to enforce the prohibition, renewed commitment to the use of mechanisms for the peaceful settlement of disputes, and a new effort at preventing armed conflict through promoting human rights and economic development.[50]

II REALISM, LIBERALISM, NEOCONSERVATISM

When World War II ended, not only did the United States lead in creating the new United Nations, it was the United States that insisted on the trials for international law violations by high-ranking officials and military officers of the Axis powers at Nuremberg and Tokyo.[51] The United States oversaw the drafting of clauses in the new Japanese Constitution and the German Basic Law requiring that foreign policy comply with international law.[52] The US Senate agreed to accept the optional compulsory jurisdiction of the new International Court of Justice – successor to the PCIJ – and Eleanor Roosevelt chaired the committee drafting the Universal Declaration of Human Rights.[53] It was an extraordinary time for the United States and international law. Political leaders and scholars alike spoke movingly of a future of peace through the rule of law. Realists opposed the vision even before the war ended, and fifty years later it was their view that dominated attitudes in US foreign and domestic policy not the traditional commitment to law.

The story of realism's rise to dominate US policy is multifaceted. A few highlights must suffice here but should serve to support the point that realism supplanted the promotion of and adherence to law. The men who shaped early realist thought aimed precisely at undermining the place of international law in the new field of international relations. International relations developed as a combination of the existing study of government together with the only existing academic discipline focused on foreign affairs, international law. For followers of the seventeenth-century British political theorist Thomas Hobbes, it was simply impossible for international law to exist, given the absence of a world government. At the interstate level, there is only constant competition for military power to deter or defeat attack by others. A British political theorist of the inter-period, E. H. Carr railed against international law in his book, *The Twenty Years' Crisis 1919–1939*. He found it impossible to accept the international legal principle that states enjoy equal status under international law, given the asymmetries of material power.[54] Carr found this a "fiction [that] contradicted the inherent logic of international politics, where the strength of the individual states had to be considered a crucial factor in the solution of conflicts of interest."[55]

Carr plainly knew little about the nature of law, domestic or international, and the fact that all law is, if not a fiction, a human construct that relies on acceptance of normative concepts such as equality. Carr could not see that all law, domestic and international, requires imagination. The idea of equality before the law is essential whether in reference to individuals and domestic law or states and international law. The principle of equality does not rest on material power but on a moral concept.

Nevertheless, the idea that material strength might matter more than the ideas of law appealed to many in the United States as the country amassed extraordinary military assets. The promise of scientific and technological research to keep Americans ahead in the developing arms race coincided with the suppression of natural law theory in favor of simple positivism, based on material evidence alone. Knowledge of the theoretical and normative basis of law was also being lost.

US leaders shifted their interest in international law and institutions to the promises of the realists. As early as 1951, the prominent American diplomat George Kennan urged abandoning the "legalistic-moralistic approach" in American foreign policy at the University of Chicago.[56] He was the architect of US containment policy aimed at the Soviet Union, which urged entrance into the arms race and proxy wars, regardless of the law, in order to counter the communist threat to the American way of life. The American way of life, however, was founded on the moral preference for the rule of law. In positing physical survival as more important than law, Kennan and fellow realists aimed at preserving the country's form over its substance.

The German refugee and international law scholar, Hans Morgenthau, did as much as any one person to give US leaders and scholars permission to reject the place of law, especially international law, for realism. Despite being a student of the great Hans Kelsen, Morgenthau meticulously explained why international law cannot really be law worth respecting in important matters of state. Morgenthau placed the sanction for law violations ahead of belief in the rule of law. International law, in his opinion, lacked sanctions that could enforce the law against a powerful state like the United States, ergo the United States was free of legal restraint in military affairs. Reciprocal niceties such as exchanging ambassadors or trade in goods might attract US compliance. American presidents, however, not only could but must ignore international law in military competition. Morgenthau supported the theory of the strongman leader, inspired by the Third Reich's chief legal theorist, Carl Schmitt.

Morgenthau was forced to flee Germany in the 1930s because he was Jewish. This only served to reinforce his support of realism and rejection of international law. In 1940, Morgenthau wrote an article highly critical of the expectations people had for international law.[57] He worked to weaken respect for international law in his new homeland and was highly effective, knowing international law as well as he did. He could discuss the weaknesses of international law with real authority. He singled out the apparently weak sanctions and inadequate theories of international law. Morgenthau wanted the United States to build up military power and remove legal obstacles to the president's ability to deploy it as he saw fit. Morgenthau, someone with little personal experience of the robust rule of law, almost single-handedly moved the United States away from its founding principles.[58]

By 1943, he was a professor at the University of Chicago where he would teach and write until 1973. His 1948 book, *Politics Among Nations*, continues to be read by every student of international relations in the United States. It is a fact unparalleled in the academy.[59] His 1961 book, *The Restoration of American Politics*, points to "the incompatibility between the rational requirements of sound foreign policy and the emotional preferences of a democratically controlled public opinion." Knowing his views of international law, it should come as no surprise that Morgenthau rejected domestic legal restraints on the strongman president's exercise of military power.[60] Such radical thinking might have remained on the margin, but for the efforts of a very few individuals in addition to Morgenthau. First, the Protestant theologian, Reinhold Niebuhr, and then the Columbia University political scientist, Kenneth Waltz, presented arguments that suppressed religious objections to realist militarism as well as realism's antidemocratic tendencies.

Niebuhr, like Morgenthau, was a convert to realism. He came from the world of Christian anti war teaching.[61] After the catastrophe of World War I and the rise of authoritarian militarism in Germany, Italy, and Japan, however, Niebuhr concluded that preparing to do battle with the forces of evil was essential. He blamed World War II in part on Christian pacifists, not the harsh, one-sided terms of the Versailles peace settlement. Subsequently, he became a war advocate and, from his position at New York's Union Theological Seminary, formulated his theory of "Christian realism." Just as Morgenthau argued against adherence to the international law prohibiting the use of force, Niebuhr did the same respecting Christian nonviolence. He, like Morgenthau, believed that human beings are overwhelmingly selfish, and while humanity has developed some checks on this tendency for individuals, among groups the only option is striving for military superiority. States must constantly threaten other states to achieve international order. "Peace among nations 'is gained by force and is always an uneasy and an unjust one.' Conflict is inevitable, and ... power must be challenged by power.'"[62] Niebuhr persuaded many that the military struggle against evil was morally ordained. If law stood in the way, it was logically immoral law, deserving of no respect.

Kenneth Waltz, in his 1959 book *Man, the State, and War* and his 1979 *Theory of International Politics*, also promoted the realist contention of human life as a struggle for survival.[63] Waltz presented his views as having a rational, scientific basis.[64] Thus, realism played to the rising dominance of scientific materialism over extra-positive cognition that long lay at the base of law and morality. The shift to science helps account for the turn to faith in military and market forces. Realists hold not only that it is the leader's duty to increase material strength but also that the result of doing so will be perceived as threatening to others who will react by increasing their own strength. This competition, known in security circles as the "security dilemma," is held to be a factual statement about reality because it is supposedly based on scientific principles of human nature.[65] The American foreign policy establishment found realism far from being a discrete theory propounded by some particularly antidemocratic, war-loving intellectuals with little regard for humanity's capacity beyond self-preservation, but instead as merely an accurate description of state relations in the international system. Moreover, Waltz did not openly reject law and legal institutions, as some of his realist predecessors had done. He just obscured realism's anti-legal/antidemocratic pillars using abstract terminology, analogy, and hypothetical constructs in place of plain language respecting his views.

The long US tradition of commitment to law did not disappear quickly or easily, however. It was bolstered after a fashion by competition with the Soviet Union. So long as the Soviet Union existed, US government officials took some care to present credible arguments to justify US conduct as complying with international law. Both superpowers tended to manipulate the facts rather than argue for new, permissive interpretations of the law. The Soviet Union manufactured invitations to intervene in Hungary,[66] Czechoslovakia,[67] and Afghanistan.[68] The United States did the same respecting Vietnam, Grenada, and Panama.[69] They looked to the UN Charter for the language and the shared assumptions around their competition, and the UN Security Council offered a place and a process for communication. International lawyers of the Cold War period were loath to hold the United States to an authentic commitment to international law, given the appeal of realism's ideology.

When the United States decided to intervene militarily in Vietnam after nationalists defeated the French colonizers, fictions were concocted to provide legal cover. Officially, the United States recognized not one but two Vietnams. This way, South Vietnam could request US assistance in responding in lawful self-defense to attacks by North Vietnam. During the Kennedy administration, the CIA assassinated one South Vietnamese leader and replaced him with another to ensure US control.[70] The United States's international law position was developed by a new breed of international lawyers, influenced by both realism and the interest in instituting democracy and civil rights around the world. The University of Chicago's Quincy Wright refused to pretend Vietnam was two countries.[71] He condemned the US intervention as a violation of international law no different than British interference in the US Civil War. Yale Law School's professor of international law Myres McDougal, by contrast, was a champion of the US intervention in Vietnam because he believed the war would bring human dignity to the Vietnamese people.[72]

Surprisingly perhaps, the realists generally opposed the intervention. Morgenthau, Niebuhr, and Waltz were all outspoken in their opposition.[73] When the war went so terribly wrong, they were on the popular side, providing yet more credibility to their ideological stance. Their opposition was not based on any anti war sentiment. They opposed the reasons for the intervention. The United States aimed at promoting democracy through the war to block the rise of communism. Realists doubted that indirect strategy would work. They promoted intervention to directly enhance the perception of US military superiority. Their dispute with the Vietnam War's proponents was a foretaste of the post–Cold War split between liberal interventionist and neoconservative wars for human rights and democracy versus realist wars for military power.

In addition to their gain in opposing Vietnam, the realists had another boost to their prestige when the Soviet Union collapsed. It is often said that US military spending broke the other superpower. The story is more complicated and involves not only a failed economic system, but popular demands for human rights and environmental protection as well as the strength of national identity, the impact of technology, and more. George H. W. Bush was president and knew something about international law from his military service in World War II and from his role as ambassador to the United Nations. He was undoubtedly influenced by realism but had other sources to draw upon so that in 1991, the United States used its massive war machine for the first time since 1945, fully in compliance with the UN Charter. When Iraq invaded Kuwait on August 2, 1990, the United States succeeded in getting a unanimous Security Council resolution condemning the aggression against Kuwait the same day.[74] After months of sanctions and negotiation, the council then authorized a coalition to end the occupation and push Saddam's forces out of Kuwait. The authorization was to liberate Kuwait, nothing more. The coalition needed only 100 hours of combat to fulfill the mandate. Three decades later, Kuwait remains independent. The United States received generous financial contributions to the effort and even made money. President Bush declared a "new world order under the rule of law."[75]

In a great but barely appreciated paradox, realists, liberals, and neoconservatives failed to see the essential role of law in the Persian Gulf victory. They focused instead on the extraordinary power of the US military. Bill Clinton was elected president in 1992, and liberals and neoconservatives lobbied for interventions to promote human rights and democracy.[76] In 1998, neoconservatives organized as the "Project for a New American Century" wrote to President Clinton insisting that "removing Saddam Hussein and his regime from power needs to become … the aim of United States foreign policy."[77] Clinton authorized a continuous series of air attacks on Iraq for the eight years of his presidency – in violation of international law – but did not attempt regime change.

Instead of heeding the call of the neoconservatives, Clinton, in 1998, was listening to liberal interventionists. He ordered the use of significant, unlawful military force on at least five occasions. The greatest loss of life occurred in 1999 during 78 days of bombing in Serbia and Montenegro to force troops out of Kosovo. Twenty-thousand people died to accomplish that goal. Kosovo was the first significant use of military force since the drafting of the UN Charter in 1945 for which the United States issued no justification under international law.[78]

Clinton and many of his top advisers had attended elite US law schools in the 1960s and 1970s. It was a period of turning inward in the social upheaval caused by the Vietnam War, the civil rights movement, and the women's movement. Interest in international law at Harvard, Yale, Columbia, Stanford, Chicago, and other leading law schools dwindled, replaced by a new, heavy emphasis on US constitutional law and the US Bill of Rights.[79] When President Jimmy Carter was elected he signed numerous human rights treaties, launching, as Sam Moyn has argued, the era of human rights.[80] Louis Henkin, a law professor at Columbia and one of the most important legal scholars shaping the new interest in human rights, came from the world of US constitutional law, not international law. His approach to human rights was heavily influenced by the American Bill of Rights. He had not studied international law in law school nor had some of his followers, most notably Harold Koh, who would become dean of Yale Law School and State Department legal adviser under Obama.

International law was also disappearing from the curriculum of international relations departments. Developments, such as the Helsinki Movement that had spurred grassroots opposition to Soviet domination, was studied by American lawyers and international relations scholars alike, but they tended to see human rights largely in isolation from the larger body of international law of which it is a part. International relations theorists were educated not in international law but in realist theory. While some international relations scholars tried to understand international institutions, such as the United Nations, or human rights norms, they generally did so without considering international law. At the same time, realism was generating great profits for the "military-industrial complex." Small wonder it became so dominant. By the end of the Cold War, international relations scholars interested in human rights became advocates of the use of military force to respond to human rights crises and to replace authoritarian governments by imposing democratic ones.[81] Thomas Weiss, a professor at Brown University and a president of the International Studies Association, for example, published a stream of books advocating "military humanitarianism."[82] The very fact that the Clinton administration is associated with advances in international law is a sign of declining knowledge of what international law actually is.

Clinton's violations of the most important rule in international law – the prohibition on the use of force – likely has several explanations, including the triumph of realist faith in military force regardless of the law, the belief in American exceptionalism, meaning the United States is above the law, and the inward turn to US-style civil rights at the expense of basic knowledge of global law. Not only do liberal interventionists see their goals as morally superior to the principle prohibiting force,[83] they also contend that imposing human rights would be good for US security.[84]

The administration of Clinton's successor, George W. Bush, included prominent neoconservatives who ridiculed liberals but, as Mearsheimer observes, are difficult to distinguish from liberal interventionists. Neoconservatism also originated at the University of Chicago through the teaching of Leo Strauss. Charles Krauthammer called it "Democratic realism."[85] Its proponents have much in common with liberal interventionists but substitute democracy for human rights. Both groups hold out that "democratic peace" will be the outcome of the wars they promote.[86] Vice President Richard Cheney argued forcefully for using military force to impose weak democratic regimes in states so as to render them easily controllable by Washington. The similarity between neoconservatives and liberal interventionists is seen in the fact that noted human rights advocates and liberals, such as Michael Ignatieff and Anne-Marie Slaughter supported the Kosovo War and the 2003 Iraq War. While at Harvard University's Carr Center for Human Rights, Ignatieff referred to the Iraq War as a "humanitarian intervention."[87]

Barack Obama brought many Clintonites back to the White House when he succeeded Bush. Hillary Clinton became secretary of state and Harold Koh, legal adviser to the State Department. Clinton and Koh were both strong advocates of humanitarian intervention. Clinton pushed Obama to agree to intervene in Libya's civil war in 2011. In her own attempt in 2016 to become president, she promised to step up military force in Syria if elected. While Obama later said the Libya War had been a mistake,[88] Koh said that failing to intervene in Syria was Obama's real mistake.[89] Yet, the United States had no legal right to intervene in Syria, and more puzzling still, the advocacy to use military force in Syria's civil war ignored the tragic outcome of the excessive and, thus, unlawful use of force in Libya. President Obama had the humility to concede that Libya had been a failure.[90] He refused to order a comparable intervention in Syria. He did, however, authorize the arming and training of opposition forces, which also violated international law.

Former US ambassador to the United Nations Samantha Power, another person associated with Harvard's Carr Center for Human Rights, is a well-known advocate of military intervention for humanitarian purposes.[91] In August and September 2013, she called strenuously for using military force in Syria following the use of chemical weapons.[92] During an interview, she was asked whether a US attack on Syria would be "legal." She used terms that give the impression an attack would be lawful. She answered that it would be a "legitimate, necessary, and proportionate response."[93] These terms fail to explain, however, how attacking Syria does not violate Article 2(4) of the UN Charter. The only right to resort to force is reserved for self-defense to an armed attack (Article 51) or with Security Council authorization. She asserted moral notions as overriding the applicable legal principles. She wanted the United States to bomb, and predictably kill civilians, on the unproven hope that such killing would deter a man known to have no compunction in the commission of unspeakable crimes. According to realism, however, Syria's president Bashar al-Assad, like everyone else, is supposed to fear military force and thus to bow to the threat of a US military attack. Assad has bowed to neither the threat nor the reality of being attacked.

At the same time Power was arguing for a military attack on Syria, President Obama was authorizing hundreds of drone strikes outside armed conflict zones. These strikes defied the international law prohibiting the use of force as well as the human rights of the targeted individuals and people near them. Lawyers for the administration wrote memos with little merit as actual legal analysis. The argument that "imminent" to mean not immediate was the stuff of late-night television comedy.[94] In 2013, perhaps seeing the counterproductive results of widespread, lawless military attacks, Obama issued Presidential Policy Guidelines (PPG) to restrict drone attacks. PPGs do not have the force of law and do not bind future presidents.[95] Indeed, the PPG was a document reflecting arrogance and contempt for existing international law in substituting the administration's own constructed principles for the rules of the international community. Within days of his inauguration, unsurprisingly, Donald Trump provided the military with wide latitude to decide where and when to use military force, including drones.[96] The PPG was ignored, along with international law.[97]

US failure to promote the rule of law in the post–Cold War period was part of the context when, in 2014, Russia took control by military force of the Ukrainian province of Crimea. At the time of this writing, it remains the only successful act of conquest since the adoption of the UN Charter. It is a flagrant violation that signals a breakdown in the law prohibiting the use of force. The United States is now stationing more troops in NATO states and carrying out massive, costly exercises to counter further Russian aggression. Tensions with China appear to be rising steadily. There is talk of a new Cold War.

Realists see military competition with Russia and China as inevitable and the failures of the Kosovo, Afghanistan, Iraq, Libya, and Drone Wars as the highly predictable failure as a result of liberals and neoconservatives' misunderstanding nationalism. They are right that outside military aggression does not succeed in reengineering societies to honor human rights or establish successful democracy. Yet, the record of American history indicates it has been the realist belief in using force, regardless of legal restrictions, that has weakened the legal and moral barriers to using military force for policy objectives. Realists should accept the influence they have had. It is their faith in military force built upon vague, subjective, and unproven predictions about the efficacy of war that has led to liberal and neoconservative advocacy of intervention.

Not only have the realists undermined respect for the law on the use of force, but their contempt for these central rules has influenced a wider disregard of law. Belief in the material reality of military power is preferred over the abstract concepts of law. Moreover, realists need an unfettered president to make the balance-of-power decisions. The neoconservatives saw the need, too. Some of their leading legal minds, such as John Yoo, wrote passionately about the need for a strong president at the head of a "unitary executive."[98]

In an echo from the film, *A Man for All Seasons*, having cut down all the laws, Yoo now apparently thinks matters have gone too far with Trump.[99] Trump sees himself as extraordinarily powerful and free to act.[100] He twice attacked Syria, committing unlawful reprisals. The State Department provided no statement of legal justification. The then-UN Ambassador Nikki Haley repeated a pronouncement by Samantha Power, her predecessor, that the attacks following uses of chemical weapons were somehow "necessary." Trump also increased air strikes dramatically in the multiple military operations ongoing when he took office in 2017.[101] During his first seventy-four days in office, he ordered seventy-five drone strikes outside of battlefield zones.[102] The United States is implicated in war crimes in Yemen, a place where the United States has no legal right to even be fighting. The numbers of civilians killed in the anti-ISIS campaign in Iraq and Syria are generating the sort of anger that drove people to embrace ISIS in the first place. Trump threatened a preemptive nuclear strike if North Korea followed through on their nuclear weapons testing.[103]

Trump has managed to deeply disrupt the foreign and security policy consensus that has prevailed in Washington for many decades. He does not appear to hold any theoretical position, whether realist, neoconservative, liberal interventionist, or in support of the rule of law. Trump's consistent position is to follow his gut. When his presidency ends, the Americans may be ready to return to the principled and predictable path of the law. In addition, beyond any reaction to Trump, competition with China may restore the mirror to US conduct once held up by the Soviet Union. It is clearly within the US national interest to pursue a relationship with China based on respect for international law. Every bilateral concern is conditioned by law advantageous to the United States from trade, protection of intellectual property, maritime rights, human rights, environmental protection, and international dispute resolution.[104] China's military and economic strength may tempt its leaders to follow an exceptionalist stance as the United States has done. A centerpiece of post-Trump foreign and security policy should be to counter that temptation and to lead by example.

CONCLUSION

A small group of men conceived of the idea of a society under law—Washington, Adams, Jefferson, Madison, Jay – and an equally small group conceived of an ideology that is undermining the law– Morgenthau, Kennan, Niebuhr, and Waltz. The existential threat facing the United States as a result of the dominance of realist thinking is evident. The challenge now is to reverse realist influence and reestablish the rule of law as the definition of national security, including first and foremost respect for the prohibition on the use of force.

This chapter has sought to expose how realism took such a deep hold on the American – and now global– imagination. Realism is after all no more than an idea, a recent one without the pedigree or promise of "legalism-moralism." Indeed, realism is based on a myth that power is material. As Steinberg and Zasloff, drawing on Friedrich Kratochwil, so cogently put it, "Power is not material, but ideational, and the importance of power in the material sense depends critically on the social milieu in which the state exists. It is all ideas, all the way down."[105] Those ideas once gave pride of place to the rule of law and can do so again.

11

Rethinking the National Security State
from an Evolutionary Perspective: A Reconnaissance

David Sloan Wilson

Discussions of national security invariably focus on the need to evolve new practices to adapt to a rapidly changing and increasingly dangerous world. Yet, it is a curious fact that despite frequent use of the words "evolve" and "adapt" in the vernacular, policy experts seldom consult evolutionary theory as a source of insight for making the world a safer place.

They should. The reason they do not has nothing to do with national security per se, but broader trends in the history of ideas that largely confined evolutionary theory to the biological sciences during the twentieth century, leaving the many branches of the human social sciences and humanities to go their own ways. As a result, the academic expertise applied to national security or any other major policy area comes from an alphabet soup of disciplines that are poorly integrated with each other. As early as the 1970s, the geneticist Theodosius Dobzhansky (1973) could write, "Nothing in biology makes sense except in the light of evolution." The idea that the same theory might make sense of all aspects of humanity lies beyond the imagination of most academicians and policy experts. Yet, if such an integration is possible, then our enhanced ability to evolve new practices to adapt to a changing world could be transformational.

Such a transformation is not a future prospect but is already taking place, starting in the closing decades of the twentieth century. Today, there is a rapidly growing community of scientists, scholars, and policy experts who have expanded what Charles Darwin called "this view of life" in the final passage of *On the Origin of Species* to include all aspects of humanity. Their numbers are in the thousands, including many at the top of their respective professions and who publish in the most prestigious journals and university presses. Members of this community whose work relates to national security include Scott Atran (2016; Atran et al. 2017; Atran et al. 2014), Daniel Fessler (Fessler et al. 2017; Murray et al. 2017), Michele Gelfand (2018; Kruglanski et al. 2015; Lyons-Padilla et al. 2015; Webber et al. 2018a, b), Dominic Johnson (2004; Buhrmester et al. 2018), Anthony C. Lopez (2016), Rafe Sagarin (2012), Hammad Sheikh (Sheikh et al. 2016; Pretus et al. 2018), and Harvey

Whitehouse (2018). These, however, are still a tiny fraction of the worldwide academic and policy communities. Imagine how the average national security expert would react to this statement: "Nothing about national security makes sense except in the light of evolution."

The purpose of this chapter is to introduce the national security community to modern evolutionary thinking. It is divided into two sections. The first section introduces the major concepts that evolutionary theorists use to understand the natural world, which are equally useful for understanding all human-related topic areas and their policy applications. The second part concentrates on issues most relevant to rethinking the national security state. Obviously, this chapter can only be a reconnaissance – a preliminary survey. The more national security experts become familiar with "this view of life" in relation to their topic area, the faster a more thorough exploration can proceed.

DARWIN'S TOOLKIT

This section is a distillation of my book *This View of Life: Completing the Darwinian Revolution* (Wilson 2019), which should be consulted for a fuller treatment, along with the excellent work of the above-cited authors.

The Basic Core: Most people are familiar with the core of Charles Darwin's theory of natural selection:

1) Organisms vary in most of their properties;
2) Differences between organisms often make a difference in terms of their survival and reproduction; and
3) Offspring often resemble their parents (heredity).

When these three conditions apply, then the properties of organisms change over time. Traits that enhance survival and reproduction become more common. Organisms become adapted to their environments.

Seldom is a theory so powerful also so simple. One of the main insights is that the properties of organisms can be predicted without knowing anything whatsoever about their physical makeup. Instead, the relevant information is provided by knowledge about the organism's environment. For example, we can confidently predict that most organisms that live in deserts will be sandy colored to avoid being detected by their predators and prey. We can make this prediction for insects, snails, reptiles, birds, and mammals, even though they have different DNA and physical exteriors. We can make the prediction regardless of whether the sand color is white, tan, or black. As long as the physical makeup of organisms results in heritable variation in coloration, then it becomes a kind of malleable clay that is shaped by environmental forces relevant to survival and reproduction. This style of reasoning is called "natural selection thinking" or "adaptationist thinking," and it is one of the most important tools in Darwin's toolkit.

To say that adaptationist thinking is powerful does not mean that it always leads to the right answer or that all aspects of organisms are adaptive. Discerning the adaptive function of a trait is often more difficult than the example that I provided. Some traits of organisms are costly by-products of other traits without any function of their own. Adaptations to past environments can become maladaptive when the environment changes. And some variation is neutral with respect to survival and reproduction, so whatever evolves is a matter of chance. Natural selection thinking done right must take into account all of these possibilities.

Also, complete understanding of any particular product of evolution needs to go beyond its functional basis. Niko Tinbergen, who received the Nobel Prize in physiology in 1973 for his pioneering studies of animal behavior, noted that four questions need to be asked about any given trait: One, what is its functional basis (if any)? Second, what constitutes its physical mechanism? Third, how does the trait develop during the lifetime of the organism? Lastly, what is its phylogenetic history? (Tinbergen 1963; see Bateson and Laland 2013 for an appraisal and update). For example, the function of the human hand is to manipulate objects. Its physical basis consists of bones, tendons, and muscles put together in just the right way. It starts to develop during the fifth week of gestation, and it can be traced back to the fins of fish in our phylogenetic history. A fully rounded evolutionary approach requires addressing all four of these questions in conjunction with each other.

All very well, you might be thinking, but how can these four questions be related to national security in the twenty-first century?

Beyond Genetic Evolution: So complete is the restriction of evolutionary theory to the biological sciences that when anyone says the word "evolution," most listeners hear the word "gene." Yet, the third requirement for an evolutionary process – heredity – is not genes per se but any mechanism that causes offspring to resemble their parents. For example, offspring share the same language as their parents thanks to mechanisms that have nothing to do with genes, other than the genes that make language acquisition possible. As for language, so also for everything else that we associate with culture.

The reason that evolutionary biology became so gene-centric is a long and complicated story (see Wilson and Schutt 2016 and Wilson and Paul 2016 for the fields of sociology and anthropology, respectively). The most important point is that evolutionary thinkers have gone back to the basics by studying multiple mechanisms of inheritance that interact with each other (Jablonka and Lamb 2006). In addition to genetic mechanisms, there are epigenetic mechanisms (changes in the expression of genes rather than gene frequency), forms of social learning that exist in many species, and forms of symbolic thought that are distinctively human. These other mechanisms of inheritance are both *products* of genetic evolution and *evolutionary processes in their own right.*

To elaborate on symbolic thought as a mechanism of inheritance, we are such a cultural species that each of us relies on an elaborate system of beliefs and practices to make sense of the world around us. How we perceive the world and act on the basis of our perception is influenced by our symbolic systems at least as much as our genes. If we call your symbolic system your "symbotype" and how you act your "phenotype," then there is a symbotype-phenotype relationship similar to the geno-type-phenotype relationship long studied by evolutionary biologists. The elements of symbotypes can be configured in so many ways that they exist in almost infinite variety, similar to the many combinations of genotypes in sexually reproducing species. In short, our capacity for symbolic thought has become a full-blown inheritance system that operates alongside our genetic inheritance system. This is called dual inheritance theory, and it only started to develop during the 1970s (Richerson and Boyd 2005; Henrich 2015; Paul 2015; Deacon 1998; Wilson et al. 2014; Wilson and Hayes 2018).

Another crucial point is that evolution can be not only an intergenerational process but can also take place within the lifetime of an individual. The best-known example is the adaptive component of the vertebrate immune system, which involves the production of more than 100 million antibodies and the selection of those that successfully bind to antigens (Sompayrac 1999). Another example is the kind of open-ended learning made famous by B. F. Skinner. When a rat is placed in a Skinner box with a lever that delivers a food pellet when pressed, the rat begins by exploring its surroundings – in other words, by varying its behavior. When it presses the lever and receives the reward, it increases the frequency of that behavior, similar to the immune system amplifying the antibodies that bind to antigens. Skinner (1981) called this "selection by consequences" and stressed its similarity to genetic evolution. The behavior of a rat in a Skinner box can be predicted without knowing anything about its physical makeup. The environment of the Skinner box provides the relevant information. In this case, however, it is the history of reinforcement during the lifetime of the individual rather than the history of genetic evolution that matters.

Finally, evolutionary processes can be encoded in computer algorithms (Mitchell 1998). In the famous traveling salesman problem, the paths that a salesman can travel through a number (N) of cities becomes astronomical as N increases, defying an analytic solution to finding the shortest path. A way to proceed is by treating each path as a string, similar to a chromosome, selecting them for path length, and mutating and recombining them to create variation. This simulated evolutionary process might not find the very best solution, but it will find very good ones. Evolutionary computer algorithms are being employed in diverse sectors with increasing sophistication and lighting speed (O'Reilly 2017).

The bottom line is that when we go beyond genetic evolution, then most of the changes taking place around us and even within us can be seen as evolutionary processes, giving rise to each other and interacting with each other at a variety of spatial and temporal scales – all requiring a four-question approach for complete understanding. The relevance of this expanded view of evolution to national security in the twenty-first century – along with all other major topic areas – should be clear.

Multilevel Selection (MLS) Theory. Another crucial insight of evolutionary theory is that natural selection is based upon relative fitness. It does not matter how well an organism survives and reproduces in absolute terms – only in comparison to other organisms in its vicinity. To get a feel for relative fitness thinking, imagine playing the game of Monopoly, where the goal is to own all the properties and drive the other players into bankruptcy. If I were to offer you 100 extra Monopoly dollars at the beginning of a game, you would gladly accept. If I were to make the same offer, subject to the constraint that every other player gets 200 dollars, you would turn me down. It is relative, not absolute wealth that counts in the game of Monopoly. All of us are able to identify the context and behave appropriately.

Now imagine organizing a Monopoly tournament where the trophy goes to the team of players that collectively develops the properties the fastest. Now the competition is among teams rather than among members of a single team. If you imagine this scenario for only a moment, I think you will agree that *nearly every decision you make as a team player in a tournament will be different than when you play the regular game of Monopoly.*

This is the quickest way I know to introduce the concept of multilevel selection (MLS) theory (see Wilson 2015 for a concise book-length account). Social behaviors are almost invariably expressed in groups that are small compared to the total evolving population – such as a school of fish, a flock of birds, a troop of primates, or a human hunter-gatherer group. The natural selection that takes place within groups is like a single game of Monopoly, favoring individuals that maximize their relative fitness in ways that are often harmful for others and the group as a whole. For members of a group to function cooperatively as a team, there must be a process of selection among groups – like the Monopoly tournament – which must be strong enough to counteract the disruptive effects of selection within groups. As E. O. Wilson and I conclude a major review article titled "Rethinking the Theoretical Foundation of Sociobiology": "Selfishness beats altruism within groups. Altruistic groups beat selfish groups. Everything else is commentary" (Wilson and Wilson 2007).

To make matters more complex, life consists of a multitiered hierarchy of units, not just a two-tier hierarchy of individuals in groups. The logic of relative fitness applies at every rung of the hierarchy. In human terms, what is good for me can be bad for my family. What is good for my family can be bad for my clan. What is good for my clan can be bad for my nation. What is good for my nation can be bad for the earth. The general rule is this: Adaptation at any level of a multitiered hierarchy requires a process of selection at that level and tends to be undermined by selection at lower levels (Wilson and Wilson 2007).

This is profoundly different from the Christian worldview the preceded Darwin's theory, which assumed that nature is harmoniously designed from top to bottom by a benign and all-powerful creator. Early Enlightenment thinkers such as Isaac Newton may have emphasized science and reason over scripture, but they also assumed a natural harmonious order at all scales. Against this background, the prospect that the kind of functional order associated with an organism, such as an insect or a human implement like a watch might exist at small scales and then cease to exist at larger scales, was profoundly disturbing and undoubtedly accounted for reluctance to accept Darwin's theory. Even today, the idea of a "natural order" that self-organizes at large scales finds expression in the concepts of balance of nature in ecology, the invisible hand in economics, and complex adaptive systems in systems science (Gowdy et al. 2013).

From the perspective of MLS theory, it becomes crystal clear that what counts as adaptive in the evolutionary sense of the word frequently departs from what counts as moral and normative in human terms. Evolutionary adaptations are frequently good for me but not you, us but not them, and for the short term but not the long term. Almost everything that we call corruption is a form of cooperation at lower levels of a multitiered hierarchy that is disruptive at higher scales. Benefiting oneself becomes selfishness. Benefiting relatives becomes nepotism. Benefiting friends becomes cronyism. Societies can function at large scales, such as nations and potentially the entire earth, only by suppressing the potential for disruptive selection at lower scales. How did this happen over the course of human history, to the extent that it has, and how can we influence the balance between levels of selection in the future?

Major Evolutionary Transitions and The Human Evolutionary Story: Most animal societies exhibit a mosaic of cooperation and disruptive competition, depending upon whether a given trait evolved by lower-level versus higher-level selection. Some of them would be regarded as horror societies in human terms, with the strong exploiting the weak and no end in sight as long as within-group selection overpowers between-group selection.

Other animal societies are different. Mechanisms evolve that largely (never entirely) suppress the potential for disruptive within-group selection, so that between-group selection becomes the dominant evolutionary force. This is known as a major evolutionary transition (Maynard Smith and Szathmary 1995, 1999), and it results in societies that are so cooperative that they qualify as higher-level "superorganisms" in their own right. In fact, every entity that we currently call an organism, such as a bacterial cell, a nucleated cell, or a multicellular organism, is a result of a major evolutionary transition. The concept of society as an organism, which has a venerable history in philosophical and political thought as a metaphor, now stands upon a strong scientific foundation thanks to multilevel selection theory.

A society qualifies as an organism, not by being physically bounded but by the amount of cooperation among its members. A cancer-ridden organism is as physically bounded as when it was healthy, but its cells are now disruptively competing rather than cooperating with each other (Aktipis and Nesse 2013). On any given day, the members of a honeybee colony might be dispersed over an area of several square miles, but they remain beautifully coordinated because the colony has been the primary level of selection (Seeley 1995, 2010).

Only during the last few decades has it emerged that our species qualifies as one of evolution's newest major transitions. Our closest ape relatives exhibit some cooperation but a lot of disruptive competition within groups (chimps more than bonobos; Boehm 1999; de Waal 2013). Our distant ancestors found ways to suppress disruptive self-serving behaviors within groups, so that between-group selection became the dominant evolutionary force (Boehm 2011). Nearly everything distinctive about our species, such as our ability to cooperate with genetically unrelated individuals, our distinctive forms of cognition, and our capacity to transmit learned information across generations, can be seen as forms of cooperation and coordination that evolved by between-group selection (Wilson 2015).

At first, group selection took place in the context of relatively small groups, comparable to modern bands of hunter-gatherers, although these groups were nested within tribes of several thousand that were also units of selection. This was the social environment that resulted in most of our genetically evolved adaptations. Our culturally evolved ability to produce food led to an increase in group size, which initially outstripped our genetically evolved ability to suppress disruptive self-serving behaviors within groups. The result was a despotic phase of human history, ironically more like our primate ancestors than egalitarian small-scale human societies. However, cultural evolution is a multilevel process, no less than genetic evolution, and numerous major transitions of cultural evolution over the last 10,000 years have led to the scale of cooperation that we see today.

It is important to stress that cultural multilevel selection is not a smooth or continuous process and is not guaranteed to continue increasing the scale of cooperative society. Disruptive cultural evolution within groups is an ever-present danger, similar to the evolution of cancers within multicellular organisms. Also, cultural evolution in the past often (although not entirely) took the form of warfare, something that we do not want to emulate in the present or future. Peter Turchin (2015) provides a panoramic tour of human history from an evolutionary perspective in his book *Ultrasociety: How 10,000 Years of War Led to the Most Cooperative Species on Earth.*

Evolutionary Mismatch: So far, I have identified one major source of dysfunction in modern life: practices (such as corruption) that are adaptive in the evolutionary sense of the word but deviate from our normative goals (such as cooperation at the national and global scales). Another major source of dysfunction arises when organisms that are adapted to one set of environmental conditions are thrust into a new set of environmental conditions. In this case, they may behave in ways that are maladaptive in every sense of the word. This is known as evolutionary mismatch.

As an example from nature (Witherington 1997), when baby sea turtles hatch and dig their way to the surface of the beach, they must quickly make their way toward the sea or die from predation and dehydration. The mechanism that evolved to make this happen is an attraction toward light, a reliable cue, since from time immemorial reflected light from the sea makes it lighter than the inland. Until the addition of beach houses and street lights. There is nothing in the evolutionary history of sea turtles to cope with this particular environmental change. They simply perish and the population will go extinct unless subsequent evolution happens (probably not fast enough) or humans intervene with environmental policies such as lights out during the hatching season or brigades of volunteers to collect and hand carry them to the sea.

In many respects, our species is like the sea turtles, living in a contemporary environment that differs from our ancestral environment in countless ways, such as our diets, our movement patterns, and even our light regimes (Giphart and Van Vugt 2018). Our capacity for cultural evolution can solve some of these problems. For example, when our ancestors left Africa and migrated north, they culturally evolved clothing rather than genetically evolving fur. Yet, cultural evolution has mismatches of its own. All things considered, the advent of agriculture was a cultural adaptation that largely replaced hunter-gatherer societies, but the agricultural diet was less healthy than the hunter-gatherer diet, something that thousands of years of genetic evolution has not entirely erased (Lindeberg 2010). All evolutionary processes are subject to mismatches at their relevant scales. Think of a time when you experienced an environment that was very different from your upbringing. If you found it disorienting and not entirely pleasant, if you found yourself not knowing how to behave or behaving inappropriately, it was because you were experiencing mismatch with respect to your personal evolution and your particular culture. National security situations are likely to be chock full of mismatches, especially when they involve admixtures of cultures that were previously isolated from each other.

The conceptual tools in Darwin's toolkit might seem difficult to master: multiple evolutionary processes that give rise to and interact with each other, four questions that must be addressed for each process, and mismatches caused by recent environmental changes. But consider the alternative – an alphabet soup of academic disciplines without any unifying theoretical framework at all. The biological sciences are far more diverse than the human-related sciences. After all, we are only one species. Moreover, as I stated earlier, a synthesis for the human-related disciplines, comparable to what took place in the biological sciences during the twentieth century, is already in progress. Many of its leaders received their primary training in a human-related discipline and picked up their evolutionary expertise on their own (Glass, Geher, and Wilson 2012). The more national security experts learn about the synthesis in progress, the more they will be able to make their own connections to their particular area of expertise.

APPLYING DARWIN'S TOOLKIT TO TOPICS RELEVANT TO THE NATIONAL SECURITY STATE

The broad topic of this volume, the national security state, is a fuzzy set of specific topics, from extremists and environmental disasters that threaten security to deeply entrenched bureaucracies that prevent large-scale societies from adequately responding. Every topic can be approached from an evolutionary perspective in the same way that evolutionary biologists apply the same toolkit to the study of different species. This is a refreshing alternative to the Silo Effect, in which a specialized and isolated community forms around each problem. In this section, I will touch upon a few topic areas most relevant to the national security state, realizing that a deeper dive is needed in each case.

Before proceeding, it is important to acknowledge a predecessor. Rafe Sagarin was a young environmental scientist who was interning in Washington DC during the 9/11 terrorist attack in 2001. The event moved him to write *Learning from the Octopus: How Secrets from Nature Can Help Us Fight Terrorist Attacks, Natural Disasters, and Disease* (Sagarin 2012), which was praised by public figures of the day such as Gary Hart. Tragically, Sagarin was killed in a bicycle accident in 2015. His book remains an excellent resource on national security issues from an evolutionary perspective.

The Psychology of Security and Insecurity: Earlier I described the immune system and the kind of open-ended learning made famous by B. F. Skinner as evolutionary processes that take place during the lifetime of an individual organism. The variation and selection of antibodies is called the adaptive component of the immune system in contrast to the innate component, an elaborate set of modules that fight various threats without changing during the lifetime of the organism. For example, when you get a splinter, your immune system cells already present at the site release chemicals that increase blood flow to the area, make the vessels more porous so that fluid from the capillaries can leak out into the tissues, and stimulate the nerves, which we subjectively feel as pain. Other chemicals, called cytokines, diffuse outward and recruit additional cells to the site, much like the pheromones emitted by an angry wasp colony. The response will be much the same if you are eight or eighty. The innate and adaptive components of the immune system are designed to operate in close coordination with each other.

Much the same can be said about our behavioral and social response to threats outside our bodies, in addition to our immune system response to internal threats. When we are threatened, innate psychological circuits are triggered that radically alter how we think and act. As with the immune system, we are adapted to respond innately to different types of threat, such as disease contamination (Murray et al. 2017), starvation, predators, natural disasters, and human threats (Atran 2016; Atran et al. 2014; Kruglanski et al. 2015; Navarette and Fessler 2005; Lopez 2016; Pretus et al. 2018; Sheikh et al. 2016; Webber et al. 2018a, b; Whitehouse 2018). An entire branch of psychology called terror management theory has documented massive psychological shifts that are triggered by even subtle reminders of our mortality (Navarette and Fessler 2005).

A major axis of cultural variation runs from "tight" (strong norms enforced by punishment) to "loose" (weak norms with high tolerance for individuals following their own preferences). Tight cultures tend to be adaptive under conditions of existential threat because solidarity and coordinated action are at a premium. Loose cultures tend to be adaptive under safe and secure conditions because experimentation leads to new opportunities when the consequences of failure are not too great. It is not an accident that US security is most threatened by regions of the world that are themselves highly lacking in basic needs and social services. If these regions could be made more existentially secure, most of the national security threats to the United States would go away by themselves (Gelfand 2018; Webber et al. 2018; Lyons-Padilla et al. 2015; Kruglanski et al. 2015).

This includes religious fundamentalism. In a ground breaking book titled *Sacred and Secular: Religion and Politics Worldwide*, Pippa Norris and Ronald Inglehart (2011) show that fundamentalist forms of religion are concentrated in geographical regions of high existential threat (this includes vulnerable populations within the United States). In geographical regions that are existentially secure, religious believers become more tolerant and the society as a whole becomes more secular. The key to fighting religious extremism is to increase existential security. Also, it is the perception of insecurity that matters. Cultivating an atmosphere of fear, even in an otherwise safe and secure environment, can result in a psychological and cultural shift in the direction of solidarity within a group and intolerance toward other groups. Conversely, cultivating an atmosphere of safety, security, and trust can help to bring previously hostile groups together into a larger cooperative unit.

Many national security experts are no doubt aware of these trends – how could they not, when the trends are operating all around them? However, there is considerable added value to employing a fully rounded four-question approach, including the deep history of human psychology, mechanistic studies of cognitive and neural mechanisms, and how particular cultures have evolved to evoke the mechanisms in response to their environmental challenges.

Core Design Principles Needed by All Groups to Function as Adaptive Units.
The political scientist Elinor Ostrom received the Nobel Prize in economics in 2009 for showing that human groups are capable of managing their natural resources – avoiding the famous "tragedy of the commons"– if they possess eight core design

principles (CDPs). I worked with Ostrom and her associate Michael Cox for three years prior to her death in 2012 to generalize her core design principles approach from an evolutionary perspective (Wilson, Ostrom, and Cox 2013). The generalized version is highly relevant to national security issues, providing a good example of how Darwin's toolkit can transcend disciplinary silos.

Here are the eight CDPs in their generalized form.

1) *A strong sense of identity and purpose.* To function well, members of nearly any kind of group must know that they exist as a group, know who counts as a member, and know the value of the group's purpose.

2) *Fair distribution of costs and benefits.* Groups where some people do most of the work while others get most of the benefits are unsustainable. Group members must get in proportion to what they give.

3) *Fair and inclusive decision-making.* Groups where some individuals get to make the decisions while others have no say are unsustainable. A strict consensus process might not be necessary (and might be inefficient in some contexts) but decision-making must be sufficiently transparent and open for all members to have an opportunity for input and above all to regard the process as fair.

4) *Tracking agreed-upon behaviors:* There must be a way to monitor agreed-upon behavior, not only to detect instances of cheating, but also to make sure that everyone is coordinating their efforts in the right way to produce the desired joint outcome.

5) *Graduated response to transgressions and praise for good behavior:* Disruptive behaviors of all kinds – including failures of coordination in addition to myriad forms of passive free-riding and active exploitation – must be corrected, but the response need not start out harsh. Friendly reminders are enough to keep most people in solid-citizen mode, although it must be possible to escalate when necessary. Also, most people thrive on social recognition of good behavior. The general rule is this: abundant praise for good behavior coupled with mild punishment for bad behavior that escalates when necessary.

6) *Fast and empathetic conflict resolution.* In almost all groups, conflicts will occur and must be settled quickly in a way that is perceived as fair to all parties. The most effective conflict resolution procedures acknowledge that both sides of a dispute typically have a point of view with at least some legitimacy that should be respected, rather than declaring winners and losers.

7) *Authority to self-govern.* Although nearly all groups need the aforementioned design principles, this does not mean that the design principles can be implemented in a cookie-cutter fashion. Instead, the best implementations are highly context-specific and group members are in the best position to know what will work best. If they lack the authority to manage their own affairs, then this can become a major cause of dysfunction.

8) *Appropriate relations with other groups.* The same principles that are needed to govern relations among individuals within groups are also needed to govern relations among groups in a multigroup cultural ecosystem. In other words, the core design principles are scale-independent.

Ostrom's formulation of the CDPs was based on a school of thought within the discipline of political science, and she was almost entirely unknown to economists before winning their most coveted honor. Even after winning the Nobel Prize, her work remains largely confined to the study of common-pool resource groups, illustrating the problem of disciplinary silos that pervades the human-related academic disciplines and policy applications. To appreciate the generality of the CDPs, imagine trying to benefit yourself at the expense of others or your group as a whole in a group that strongly implements the CDPs. It would be very difficult. The CDPs suppress the potential for disruptive self-serving behaviors within groups, so that teamwork can proceed without interference. Stated in evolutionary terms, if a group is regarded as a miniature culture, then the CDPs accomplish a major transition for that culture, turning it into a superorganism.

Given the generalities of the core design principles, national security applications are everywhere. Consider the situation that General Stanley McChrystal describes in his book *Team of Teams: New Rules of Engagement in a Complex World* (2015). As commander of the Joint Special Operations Task Force during the Iraq War, he was faced with a new kind of enemy in Al-Qaeda, which consisted of small, largely autonomous teams of fighters who could strike anywhere at a moment's notice. The standard hierarchical command structure of the US military was ineffective at responding to this new threat. McChrystal's solution was to create small teams of his own and to grant them much more authority to act autonomously than they had before. McChrystal describes the training of elite groups such as the Navy SEALs as more about bonding their members to each other than individual strength and endurance. He even employs terms such as "group consciousness" that are evocative of a superorganism. Although McChrystal does not mention Elinor Ostrom in his book, he converges upon many of her insights and the teams that he created score high on all the CDPs.

But the creation of teams was not good enough because they operated within a rigid top-down superstructure. To solve this problem, McChrystal had to create *teams of teams,* illustrating the eighth CDP, that relations *between* groups need to be governed by the same principles as relations *within* groups. It is encouraging that McChrystal was able to succeed at creating teams of teams, despite working with highly classified information and the strong social identities of the lower-level units that made up the higher-level superorganism.

Or consider the book *National Security and Double Government* by Michael J. Glennon (2014), which describes a layer of government that operates underneath the Madisonian institutions of the president, Congress, and the courts.

This "Trumanite" network includes dozens of military, intelligence, diplomatic, and law enforcement agencies that have been forming since the Truman era (1945–1953) and are poorly integrated with each other, much less with the Madisonian institutions (illustrating the historical dimension of a cultural evolutionary process). There is nothing inherently sinister about these agencies. All large-scale societies require bureaucracies. But it is all too easy for each agency to acquire a life of its own and to become organized more to perpetuate and expand its own influence than to contribute to the common good of the nation and world. Something like a team of team approach is required, in which lower-level entities retain strong identities but also act as cooperative agents in a larger superorganism. This will never happen spontaneously and must be orchestrated, which will require a detailed knowledge of cultural multilevel selection theory.

Adapting to Change. Everyone will agree with the need for individuals and institutions to change in response to their rapidly changing environments. Currently, there are two dominant narratives for how to change. The first is the narrative of the invisible hand (laissez-faire), which claims that the pursuit of lower-level self-interest (typically conceptualized as the pursuit of wealth in a free-market economy) robustly benefits the common good. The second is the narrative of centralized planning, which claims that a group of experts can figure out and implement the best policies. Ironically, many critics of centralized planning at the scale of nations (pejoratively called socialism) employ it in their own organizations, such as business corporations with typical top-down management structures.

Both of these narratives can be seen to be fatally flawed from an evolutionary perspective (Wilson and Gowdy 2014). If multilevel selection theory tells us anything, it is that the pursuit of lower-level self-interest does NOT robustly benefit the common good. Even a moderately sized corporation is too complex to be designed by a group of experts, which is why command-and-control efforts are more likely to fail than succeed. There are simply too many unforeseen consequences.

Change efforts that work are almost always evolutionary in nature. Consider the Toyota Corporation, which is legendary for its adaptability in the automotive industry (Rother 2009). Workers are instructed to call attention to any dysfunction that occurs on the assembly line, no matter how small (in the old days, this involved pulling a rope hanging from the ceiling called an andon). Every dysfunction results in the formation of a small team to analyze and solve the problem. The team includes the workers most closely associated with the problem along with their managers, whose offices are located on the shop floor rather than the top floor. When the team comes up with a potential solution, it is implemented provisionally in a way that allows indirect effects to be monitored. Only when the overall effect of the solution is shown to be positive is it incorporated into the routine of the assembly plant. In this fashion, the assembly plant experiences continuous improvement in small steps.

There are dozens of examples of successful change methods comparable to Toyota, which succeed by employing variation-and-selection procedures. They have arisen in multiple sectors, such as business, environmental planning, and municipal governance. They are called by names such as "adaptive management" and "adaptive governance," in which the word adaptive is meant in a similar way as the adaptive component of the immune system. Nevertheless, they suffer from a number of limitations.

First, they almost always arise by happenstance. The originators stumble upon a variation-and-selection process without the guidance of any theory or coherent narrative. Second, the procedure typically spreads slowly to other organizations. While Toyota is widely admired and copied, it has taken more than 70 years for its practices to spread to the extent that they have. One problem is that even if one group wants to emulate the success of another group, it is difficult to know exactly what to copy. How a group behaves is different than the process that gave rise to its behaviors, which is much less visible and perhaps even inscrutable to members of the successful group. Third, the spread of any given successful variation-and-selection practice comes up against barriers, which might be geographical or cultural, beyond which is unknown and will never spread on its own. This is why there are dozens of such practices, most of them unknown to each other.

Collectively, these limitations signify that cultural group selection is taking place to a degree, but not nearly at the spatial and temporal scale that it needs to. The solution to this problem is to develop a coherent narrative about cultural evolution that can be easily understood by the average person (or policy expert) and applied to all kinds of groups and multigroup cultural ecosystems. The narrative must be grounded in the relevant science, including complex systems theory in addition to evolutionary theory. This provides a middle path between laissez-faire and centralized planning, and it is needed for national security as much – or even more – than any other policy area.

Accomplishing a Major Transition in Internet Age. As I mentioned earlier, when the scale of human society increased with the advent of agriculture, our genetically evolved ability to regulate social behaviors in small groups broke down and had to be supplemented by culturally evolved regulatory mechanisms. These evolved by cultural group selection, in opposition to disruptive cultural evolution within groups. Major events in human history such as the advent of writing, numerical systems, money, transportation systems, the printing press, and electronic communication had a major impact on the balance between levels of selection. Sometimes a new innovation made communication and cooperation possible at a larger scale than ever before (e.g., the telegraph). Yet, every innovation also provided an opportunity for some members of society – especially the elites – to gain at the expense of others. Subsequent cultural evolution was required to alter the balance between levels of selection with no guarantee that higher-level selection would prevail.

The newest manifestation of this multilevel dynamic is now taking place for electronic communication in all its forms, which can collectively be called the Internet Age. Before the advent of the Internet Age, a planetary superorganism, complete with a collective brain and nervous system, would have been theoretically impossible. Now it has become theoretically possible, but that does not mean that it will self-organize. Instead, it will require an intentional process of cultural evolution with the welfare of the planet as the explicit target of selection. Anything else will result in the cultural evolution of various lower-level units that are disruptive at higher scales (Wilson 2019).

While the Internet Age is a brave new world in some respects, in other respects it represents the eternal trade-offs that exist for all social interactions. Consider examples of social interactions on the Internet that result in benign outcomes, such as our ability to buy products from total strangers, climb into someone's car, or sleep in someone's home with a very low risk of misbehaviors on either side of the transaction. Cooperation is (largely) assured for these examples for the same reason that cooperation is (largely) assured in small groups, where everyone a) knows each other, b) knows the history of their interactions, c) is able to reward good behavior, and d) is able to punish misbehavior and/or exclude bad actors from future interactions. These same ingredients are lacking in examples of social interactions on the Internet that lead to pathological outcomes, such as hate speech and the propagation of misinformation. The solution to these problems requires implementing the same core design principles that are required for groups of all sorts and at all scales to function as prosocial units (Seaman and Wilson 2016).

While global cooperation is the goal that must be worked toward for the future, all current nations must also protect themselves against sworn enemies, large (e.g., another nation) or small (e.g., a terrorist cell). In addition to human threats, there are the threats of economic collapse, disease pandemics, and natural disasters. The need for a something analogous to the vertebrate immune system, with both innate and adaptive components, should be clear and will require a sophisticated knowledge of evolutionary theory.

CONCLUSION

In this chapter, I have attempted to introduce modern evolutionary theory to a diverse readership interested in the national security state. The need for such an introduction is based on broad trends in the history of ideas, which confined evolutionary theory to the biological sciences for most of the twentieth century. These trends started to reverse in the late twentieth century, resulting in a rapidly expanding community for whom everything associated with the words "human," "culture," "policy," and "biology" can be understood with the same conceptual toolkit. There is no doubt that "this view of life" will become the theoretical framework of choice for science, scholarship, and policy formulation in the area of national security, along with all other human-related topic areas. However, there is an urgent need for the paradigm shift to take place in a matter of years rather than decades because the problems requiring solution will not wait. I hope that this chapter will help to speed the transition.

After Thought

John Berger

The chapters presented in this volume inform us about the many dimensions of national security in this transformative time. An overriding question emerges about how a national security state can effectively protect the citizens and institutions of a liberal democracy from perceived threats. But the conversation becomes challenging and unfocused when tactics such as torture, indefinite detention, extraordinary rendition, secret government surveillance, and Muslim bans are put forth as necessary to counter contemporary threats. Not only are these practices declared necessary, but such national security methods are open-ended and expansive. Enemies of the nation are global but often stateless and perceived to be actively planning attacks on the homeland motivated by their hatred of our values. The mission creep of the Global War on Terror is the preservation of the much maligned but still accepted Dick Cheney 1% doctrine of preparing for the unknown but known 1% possibility of a credible threat. The message is clear: This is a new reality, get used to it. Vigilance is paramount even if liberal notions of freedom of speech, religious tolerance, presumption of innocence, and constitutional restraints on an overreaching government are somewhat abridged.

So, what is the real cost of national security today? As this volume is about to go into production, Freedom House, the nonpartisan advocacy organization that has long promoted democratic ideals around the world, issued its Freedom in the World 2019 report. The title of this new report is "Democracy in Retreat," with the subtitle "Challenges to American democracy are testing the stability of its constitutional system and threatening to undermine political rights and civil liberties worldwide." This stark evaluation from an organization that was founded to fight fascism, counter global communism, and oppose the oppression of authoritative governments provides a clear warning that what is being experienced in the name of security is not only unacceptable but also pernicious, pervasive, and persuasive, even to those who proclaim they are promoters of core liberal values such as freedom, equality, and tolerance. There is proof that a society that mistrusts the legitimacy of democratic institutions, does not value the rule of law, and accepts "alternative facts" and the denigration of journalists as "enemies of the people" is in decline. The cost then is clear – the result of an unexamined and unrestrained national security state is less democracy. Is this the price that must be paid to be safe, or does the premise of perceived threats and the government's reaction need to be reevaluated, discussed, and challenged?

The contributors to this volume operate as scholars and practitioners in these new realities. They understand that in a liberal democracy, speaking out and offering reasoned narratives that analyze the past and interpret the present provide the necessary voices to counter a questionable future. National security has become a defining issue of our times. It significantly influences the nature of government, the psychology of citizens, and the attitudes toward the outside world, friends, and enemies. The intent of the combined efforts of this book is that it will spark a deep national dialogue on whether fear can be allowed to be the catalyst for the erosion of a liberal order that took many generations to develop and nourish.

Notes

WHO'S CHECKING WHOM?

1. *National: Public Troubled by "Deep State,"* Monmouth University (2018), https://bit.ly /2F1Y4Cu.
2. John Dinges and Saul Landau, *Assassination on Embassy Row*, 1st ed. (New York: Pantheon Books, 1981).
3. DINA refers to Chile's secret police, the Dirección Nacional de Inteligencia, under Augusto Pinochet.
4. Michael J. Glennon, *Investigating the Intelligence Community: The Process of Getting Information for Congress*, in T. Franck (ed.), The Tethered Presidency (NYU Press, 1981), 140.
5. Michael J. Glennon, *Liaison and the Law: Foreign Intelligence Agencies' Activities in the United States*, 25 Harvard Int. L. J. 1 (Winter 1984).
6. Marbury v. Madison. 5 U.S. (1 Cranch) 137 (1803).
7. Marbury v. Madison. 5 U.S. (1 Cranch) 137 (1803).
8. The 9/11 Commission Report, National Commission on Terrorist Attacks upon the United States 420 (2004).
9. *Few See Adequate Limits on NSA Surveillance Program*, Pew Res. Ctr. (2013), https:// pewrsr.ch/2K8BRGS. ("Nearly half of Americans (47%) say their greater concern about government anti-terrorism policies is that they have gone too far in restricting the average person's civil liberties; 35% say their greater concern is that they have not gone far enough to adequately protect the country."); *Americans Divided in Views of Use of Torture in U.S. Anti-Terror Efforts*, Pew Res. Ctr. (2017), https://pewrsr.ch/2KGgg8r. ("Overall, 48% say there are some circumstances under which the use of torture is acceptable in U.S. anti-terrorism efforts; about as many (49%) say there are no circumstances under which the use of torture is acceptable."); *American Public, Foreign Policy Experts Sharply Disagree over Involvement in Global Economy*, Pew Res. Ctr. (2016), https://pewrsr.ch/2QZxvm4. ("Many Americans are skeptical that the advantages of economic globalization outweigh the disadvantages: 49% of the public said in an April survey that U.S. involvement in the global economy is bad because it lowers wages and costs jobs. That compares with 44% who said that global economic engagement is good because it opens new markets and creates opportunities for growth."); *NATO, U.S. Allies, the EU and UN*, Pew Res. Ctr. (2016), https://pewrsr.ch/2XBoAXN. ("Though U.S. allies are largely viewed positively, a sizeable minority of the public expresses some reserve over the broader question of how much allies' interests should be taken into account in U.S. foreign policy: While roughly

half (51%) say the U.S. should take into account the interests of its allies even if it means making compromises with them, a sizeable minority (42%) says the U.S. should follow its own interests, even when allies strongly disagree.").

10. Loch K. Johnson, *National Security Intelligence*, 1st ed. (Malden, MA: Polity, 2012).

11. Paul C. Avey and Michael C. Desch, *What Do Policymakers Want from Us? Results of a Survey of Current and Former Senior National Security Decision Makers'*, 58 Int. Studies Quarterly 227, 242 (2014).

12. The Federalist No. 51, at 357 (James Madison) (Benjamin Fletcher Wright ed., 1961).

13. The Federalist No. 51, at 357 (James Madison) (Benjamin Fletcher Wright ed., 1961).

14. The Federalist No. 51, at 357 (James Madison) (Benjamin Fletcher Wright ed., 1961).

15. Bruce Ackerman, *The Decline and Fall of the American Republic* (Cambridge, MA: Harvard University Press, 2010): 45.

16. Alfred F. Young, *The Democratic Republicans of New York: The Origins, 1763–1797*, 194–201 (Chapel Hill: University of North Carolina Press, 1967).

17. Michael A. Memoli, *Schiff Says Nunes Can't Lead Russia Inquiry and Be a Trump Surrogate*, L.A. Times, March 22, 2017, https://lat.ms/2noLq8D.

18. Timothy Rives, *Grant, Babcock, and the Whiskey-Ring*, 32 Prologue Magazine 143, 2000.

19. Donald C. Smaltz, *The Independent Counsel: A View from Inside*, 86 Geo. L. J. 2307, 1998.

20. Carroll Kilpatrick, *Nixon Forces Firing of Cox; Richardson, Ruckelshaus Quit*, Washington Post, October 21, 1973, at A01.

21. U.S. Const. art. II, § 3.

22. U.S. Const. art. II, § 1, cl. 1.

23. Scott Bomboy, *Aaron Burr's Trial and the Constitution's Treason Clause*, Constitution Daily, National Constitution Center, 2017, https://bit.ly/2WZgZYS .

24. Donald J. Trump (@realDonaldTrump), Twitter (February 17, 2018, 8:08 PM), https://bit.ly/2o7XQkX.

25. 28 U.S.C. § 531 (2018).

26. 28 U.S.C. § 509 (2018).

27. Caroline D. Krass, Constitutionality of Legislation Extending the Term of the FBI Director, US Department of Justice, 2011, https://bit.ly/2WsYgR5.

28. Michael S. Schmidt, *Comey Memo Says Trump Asked Him to End Flynn Investigation*, The New York Times, May 16, 2017, https://nyti.ms/2r031gm.

29. *Open Hearing with Former FBI Director James Comey before the Senate Select Committee on Intelligence*, 115th Cong. 36 (2017), https://bit.ly/2I8QPe5 [hereinafter *Comey Hearing*].

30. S. V. Date, *Giuliani: Trump Could Have Shot Comey and Still Couldn't Be Indicted for It*, Huffington Post, June 3, 2018, https://bit.ly/2HhvsUb.

31. Tim Hains, *Former CIA Official Phil Mudd Warns Trump: "Think Again" about War with Intel Community, "We're Going to Win,"* RealClear Politics, February 4, 2018, https://bit.ly/2ZfxQnF.

32. Michael Morrell, *Three Lessons from the Trump-Russia Episode (and One Is Actually Good News)*, Washington Post, May 17, 2017, https://wapo.st/2KEVdTx.

33. B. Kristol (@BillKristol), Twitter (February 14, 2017, 5:36 PM), https://bit.ly/2K782GR.

34. Mallory Shelbourne, *Schumer: Trump "Really Dumb" for Attacking Intelligence Agencies*, The Hill, January 3, 2017, https://bit.ly/2j7Ja4j.

35. John Cassidy, *Trump Isolates Himself with C.I.A. Attack*, The New Yorker, December 12, 2016, https://bit.ly/2K7sLdF.

36. Michael J. Glennon, *Security Breach*, Harper's Magazine, June 2017, 41–43, 2017.

37. Michael S. Schmidt, Mark Mazzetti, and Matt Apuzzo, *Trump Campaign Aides Had Repeated Contacts with Russian Intelligence*, The New York Times, February 14, 2017, https://nyti.ms/2kQXcac.
38. Greg Miller, Adam Entous, and Ellen Nakashima, *National Security Adviser Flynn Discussed Sanctions with Russian Ambassador, Despite Denials, Officials Say*, Washington Post, February 9, 2017, https://wapo.st/2KEaofP.
39. Donald J. Trump (@realDonaldTrump), Twitter (March 4, 2017, 3:35 PM), https://bit.ly/2nsBwk2.
40. Michael S. Schmidt and Michael D. Shear, *Comey Asks Justice Dept. to Reject Trump's Wiretapping Claim*, The New York Times, March 5, 2017, https://nyti.ms/2mTl1gm.
41. *Comey Hearing*, supra note 28, at 27.
42. Brandon Carter, *Trump Slams Former US Intel Leaders as "Political Hacks,"* The Hill, November 11, 2017, https://bit.ly/2AutpsU.
43. Donald J. Trump (@realDonaldTrump), Twitter (January 11, 2017, 4:48 PM), https://bit.ly/2l7094T.
44. Edmund Burke, Writings and Speeches, vol. VI (Boston: Little Brown, 1901): 319.
45. Roberto Stefan Foa and Yascha Mounk, *The Democratic Disconnect* 27 Journal of Democracy, 5, 7–8 (2016).
46. Foa and Mounk, *The Democratic Disconnect*, 12.
47. Adam Goldman and Nicholas Fandos, *F.B.I. Condemns Push to Release Secret Republican Memo*, The New York Times, January 31, 2018, https://nyti.ms/2E6MB5q.
48. *Comey Hearing*, supra note 28, at 32.
49. John Solomon, *Early Comey Draft Accused Clinton of Gross Negligence on Emails*, The Hill, November 6, 2017, https://bit.ly/2h81Rlj.
50. Intelligence Activities and the Rights of the Americans before the Senate Select Committee to Study Governmental Operations, 94th Cong. (1976), https://bit.ly/2EkpAI4.
51. Loch K. Johnson, *Spy Watching: Intelligence Accountability in the United States* (New York: Oxford University Press, 2018): xi.
52. Michael J. Glennon, *Making Friends with the FBI*, Le Monde Diplomatique, July 2018, https://mondediplo.com/2018/07/05fbi.
53. The Federalist No. 48, at 343 (James Madison) (Benjamin Fletcher Wright ed., 1961).
54. Abraham Lincoln, "Annual Message to Congress, Dec. 1, 1862," in *Collected Works of Abraham Lincoln* (Roy P. Basler ed., 1953): 537.

THE DEEP STATE AND THE FAILED STATE: ILLUSIONS
AND REALITIES IN THE PURSUIT OF SECURITY

1. "The end of history – or of liberalism?," *National Review*, October 27, 1989. Republished as "The end of history, again?" in John Gray, *Gray's Anatomy: Selected Writings*, London, Penguin Books, pp. 217–233, 2016.
2. Gray, *Gray's Anatomy*, p. 221.
3. This refers to the 2018 poisoning of Sergei Skripal, a former Russian military officer and double agent for UK intelligence, and his daughter Yulia in Salisbury, England.
4. I discuss the modernity of Al-Qaeda in my book, *Al Qaeda and What It Means to Be Modern*, New York, The New Press, 2003.
5. David Hume, "Of Civil Liberty," in *Moral and Political Philosophy*, London and New York, Hafner Press, p. 318, 1948.

6. I discuss the secularization of religious ideas in modern political movements in my books *Black Mass: Apocalyptic Religion and the Death of Utopia*, London, Allen Lane, 2007, and *Seven Types of Atheism*, New York, Farrar Straus and Giroux, chapter 4, 2018.

A TALE OF TWO COUNTRIES: FUNDAMENTAL RIGHTS IN THE "WAR ON TERROR"

1. Freedom House, FREEDOM IN THE WORLD 2018, Table of Country Scores, accessible at https://freedomhouse.org/report/freedom-world-2018-table-country-scores. Scores in earlier years since 2001 are the same for almost all these countries. However, critiques appear in the UN Human Rights Committee issues of concern in its concluding observations on the periodic reports of States Parties to the International Covenant on Civil and Political Rights. See, e.g., Concluding observations on the fourth periodic report of the United States of America, UN Doc CCPR/C/USA/CO/4, April 23, 2014 (citing, aside from issues concerning terrorism, racial disparities in the criminal justice system, racial profiling, death penalty issues, gun violence, excessive use of force by law enforcement officials, non-refoulement, trafficking and forced labor, rights of immigrants, and domestic violence, among other concerns); and Concluding observations on the seventh periodic report of the United Kingdom of Great Britain and Northern Ireland, UN Doc CCPR/C/GBR/CO/7, August 17, 2015 (citing, aside from issues concerning terrorism, racism and xenophobia, stop and search powers, nondiscrimination and gender equality, violence against women, self-inflicted deaths and self-inflicted harm in custody, termination of pregnancy in Northern Ireland, diplomatic assurances and non-refoulement, corporal punishment, immigration detention, legal aid, and juvenile justice, among other concerns).
2. Will Hutton, *In the Belhaj Case, Britain Set Aside the Rule of Law and Moral Principles*, The Guardian, May 13, 2018.
3. The UK Supreme Court, in a 3–2 ruling, upheld the disclosure order. Belhaj v. Director of Public Prosecutions, [2018] UKSC 33.
4. Ian Cobain et al., *Britain Apologises for "Appalling Treatment" of Abdel Hakim Belhaj*, The Guardian, May 10, 2018.
5. HC 1113, released June 28, 2018 (hereafter "ISC Report").
6. All-Party Parliamentary Group on Extraordinary Renditions, House of Commons, Press Release, November 28, 2018.
7. All-Party Parliamentary Group on Extraordinary Renditions, House of Commons, Press Release, pp. 2–3, November 28, 2018.
8. All-Party Parliamentary Group on Extraordinary Renditions, House of Commons, Press Release, pp. 2–3, November 28, 2018.
9. Report of the Senate Select Committee on Intelligence, *Committee Study of the Central Intelligence Agency's Detention and Interrogation Program*, 113th Cong., 2nd Session, S. Report 113–288, pp. xviii–xix, xxi, xxv, December 9, 2014, (hereafter "Senate Report").
10. Senate Report, p. xii.
11. Senate Report, p. xii.
12. Interrogation techniques such as "short shackling" violate the UN Convention against Torture and Other Cruel, Inhuman or Degrading Treatment or Punishment. *Conclusions and Recommendations of the Committee against Torture, United States of America*, UN Doc CAT/C/USA/CO/2, July 25, 2006, par 24.

13. The White House, Press Conference by the President, August 1, 2014.
14. Randall Mikkelsen, *U.S. Government Vows Not to Use "Waterboarding,"* Reuters, March 2, 2009.
15. James Risen and Sheri Fink, *Trump Said "Torture Works." An Echo Is Feared Worldwide,* New York Times, January 5, 2017.
16. James Risen and Sheri Fink, "Trump Said 'Torture Works,'" *New York Times,* January 5, 2017.
17. *UN International Convention for the Protection of All Persons from Enforced Disappearance,* December 20, 2006, entered into force, December 23, 2010, 2716 UNTS 3, art 2.
18. R v. Mullen [1999] 2 Crim App R 143, parts 40 and 45–46.
19. ISC Report, p. 83 par 181.
20. ISC Report, p. 83 par 181.
21. ISC Report, pp. 87–88 par 187.
22. ISC Report, p. 84.
23. A v. Secretary of State [2004] UKHL 56.
24. *Dangerously Disproportionate: The Ever-Expanding National Security State in Europe,* Amnesty International (2017), p. 20 and note 61, citing the Protection of Freedoms Act 2012, part 4, section 58.
25. R. (on the application of Al-Jedda) v. Secretary of State [2007] UKHL 58.
26. Id., par 130.
27. Al-Jedda v. UK, App. No. 27021/08, Judgment of July 7, 2011.
28. The issue of indefinite detention is now pending before a US District Court. In Al Hajj v. Trump, Case No. 09-cv-745 (RCL) (DDC), eleven Guantánamo prisoners in January 2018 filed a motion arguing inter alia that their indefinite detention is unconstitutional. See https://ccrjustice.org/home/what-we-do/our-cases/al-hajj-v-trump-o.
29. R (Abbasi) v. The Secretary of State for Foreign Affairs [2002] EWCA Civ 1598, par 64.
30. Rasul v. Bush, 542 US 466 (2004).
31. Hamdan v. Rumsfeld, 548 US 557 (2006) (a 5–3 decision); Boumediene v. Bush, 553 US 723 (2008) (a 5–4 decision).
32. See, e.g., Editorial, *The Court Retreats on Habeas,* The New York Times, June 13, 2012. (US Court of Appeals rules for the government in all nineteen habeas cases it has decided; US Supreme Court declines to hear seven habeas cases from Guantánamo.)
33. *Guantanamo by the Numbers,* Human Rights First, October 10, 2018.
34. A v. Secretary of State [2004] UKHL 56.
35. Id., par 223.
36. Id.
37. Senate Report, p. 22.
38. Senate Report, p. 22.
39. Senate Report, p. 27.
40. Senate Report, pp. 72, 93–94.
41. Senate Report, p. 30.
42. Jamie Doward, *Diego Garcia Guards Its Secrets Even as the Truth on CIA Torture Emerges,* The Guardian, December 13, 2014. The International Court of Justice, in response to a request by the UN General Assembly, issued an advisory opinion in 2019 on the legal status of Diego Garcia in light of claims by Mauritius of sovereignty over the Chagos Archipelago of which the island is a part. The Court ruled that the UK must terminate its administration of the archipelago as rapidly as possible. See www.icj-cij.org /en/case/169/advisory opinions.
43. Doward, *Diego Garcia Guards Its Secrets.*

44. *President Discusses Creation of Military Commissions to Try Suspected Terrorists*, The White House, September 6, 2006.
45. Executive Order 13491, January 27, 2009, section 4 (a): ("The CIA shall close as expeditiously as possible any detention facilities that it currently operates and shall not operate any such detention facility in the future.").
46. Charlie Savage, *Trump Poised to Lift Ban on C.I.A. "Black Site" Prisons*, New York Times, January 25, 2017.
47. Executive Order 13823, January 30, 2018, section 2 (d).
48. For background, see Hamdan v. Rumsfeld, 548 US 557 (2006).
49. See, e.g., *KSM: Over a Decade of Trials, Still No Justice*, Human Rights First, December 3, 2018.
50. *Guantanamo a "Kangaroo Court" – British Judge*, The Age (Australia), November 27, 2003.
51. *Britain Frees Five Citizens Sent Home from U.S. Jail*, Reuters, March 11, 2004.
52. Erie v. Tompkins, 304 US 64 (1938), overruling Swift v. Tyson, 41 US 1 (1842).
53. Remaining "pockets" of federal common law include at least (1) rights and duties of the US, e.g., Clearfield Trust v. US, 318 US 363 (1943) (rights and duties of US on commercial paper issued by federal government); (2) disputes between US constituent states, e.g., Milwaukee v. Illinois, 451 US 304 (1981); (3) international relations, e.g., Banco Nacional de Cuba v. Sabbatino, 398 (1964); and (4) admiralty, e.g., Am Dredging Co. v. Miller, 510 US 443 (1994). Jay Tidmarsh and Brian Murray, "A *Theory of Federal Common Law*," 100 Northwestern Univ. L. Rev., pp. 585, 585–86 (2006). Even in these pockets of national concern, however, federal common law starts with the assumption that the Congress by statute, not the courts by common law, articulates federal law. Milwaukee v. Illinois, 451 US, at 312–317.
54. A v. Secretary of State [2005] UKHL 71, par 64.
55. A v. Secretary of State [2004] UKHL 56, par 36.
56. R v. Bartle ex parte Pinochet [1999] UKHL 17 [2000] (Lord Millett). Customary international law is part of US common law as well. *The Paquete Habana*, 175 US 677 (1900). But as noted above, federal judges have scant remaining common law jurisdiction.
57. A v. Secretary of State [2005] UKHL 71, par 112.
58. Rasul v. Bush, 542 US 466 (2004).
59. Hamdan v. Rumsfeld, 548 US 557 (2006).
60. Boumediene v. Bush, 553 US 723 (2008).
61. Human Rights Act 1998, section 19.
62. A v. Secretary of State [2004] UKHL 56, par 41 (Lord Bingham).
63. See discussion in A v. Secretary of State [2005] UKHL 71, and R v. Bartle ex parte Pinochet [1999] UKHL 17 [2000].
64. See declarations attached to US ratification of the International Covenant on Civil and Political Right; the Convention against Torture and Cruel, Inhuman or Degrading Treatment or Punishment; and the International Convention on the Elimination of All Forms of Racial Discrimination. The US declarations are listed under each treaty on the UN treaty webpage, http:treaties.UN.org.
65. Civil and Political Covenant, and Race Discrimination Convention, See note 64 above.
66. UN Convention against Torture. The implementing Torture Victims Protection Act, Public Law 102–256 (1992), provides a civil damages remedy in US courts for torture, but only if committed "under actual or apparent authority, or color of law, of any foreign nation." Section 2 (a).
67. E.g., Belhaj v. Director of Public Prosecutions, [2018] UKSC 33.

68. E.g., Eur Ct Human Rts, Sunday Times v. UK, 2 EHRR 45, [1979] HER 1; *Observer and Guardian v. UK*, 14 EHRR 153, [1991] ECHR 1385.
69. E.g., A v. Secretary of State [2004] UKHL 56.
70. Human Rights Act 1998, sections 4, 8, 10.
71. A v. Secretary of State [2004] UKHL 56.
72. Human Rights Act 1998, section 4 (6).
73. See, generally, A. W. Brian Simpson, *Human Rights and the End of Empire: Britain and the Genesis of the European Convention*, Oxford University Press, 2001.
74. E.g., Eur Ct Human Rts, Sunday Times v. UK, 2 EHRR 45, [1979] HER 1; Observer and Guardian v. UK, 14 EHRR 153, [1991] ECHR 1385.
75. *Theresa May "Will Campaign to Leave the European Convention on Human Rights in 2020 Election,"* The Independent, December 30, 2016.
76. An exception was Hirst v. UK *(No. 2)*, ECHR 681 (2005), following which Britain took twelve years to comply only partially with an unpopular judgment holding that certain categories of convicted criminals had the right to vote. Owen Bowcott, *Council of Europe Accepts UK Compromise on Prisoner Voting Rights*, The Guardian, December 7, 2017.
77. Frederick Cowell, *A Strange Irony: How the EU Withdrawal Process Ended Up Saving The Human Rights Act*, London School of Economics and Political Science Blog, December 3, 2018 (http://blogs.lse.ac.uk/brexit/2018/12/03/a-strange-irony-how-the-eu-withdrawal-process-ended-up-saving-the-human-rights-act/).
78. E.g., US Secretary of State Madeleine Albright: "We are the indispensable nation. We stand tall and we see further than other countries into the future." NBC's Today Show, February 19, 1998.
79. UN International Covenant on Civil and Political Right; Convention against Torture and Cruel, Inhuman or Degrading Treatment or Punishment; and the International Convention on the Elimination of All Forms of Racial Discrimination.
80. Nicaragua v. US, 1986 ICJ Reports 14; Mexico v. US, 2004 ICJ 12.
81. Medellin v. Texas, 552 US 491 (2008).
82. There is considerable academic literature on the relationship of law and culture. E.g., Naomi Mezey, *Law as Culture*, 13 Yale J. L. & Human, 35 (2001).
83. Foreign Minister Jack Straw may have given oral authorization for MI6 to support the rendition of Mr. Belhaj and his wife. Cobain et al. *"Britain Apologises,"* note 4 above.

THE NATIONAL SECURITY STATE GONE AWRY: RETURNING
TO FIRST PRINCIPLES

1. The casualty figure is from Paul Waldman, "American War Dead, by the Numbers," *The American Prospect* (May 26, 2014), http://prospect.org/article/american-war-dead-numbers.
2. Stephen R. Weissman, "Congress and War: How the House and the Senate Can Reclaim Their Role," *Foreign Affairs* 96/1, pp. 132–145, January/February 2017; Richard S. Conley, ed., *Presidential Leadership and National Security: The Obama Legacy and Trump Trajectory*, New York: Routledge, 2018; Edward S. Corwin, *The President: Office and Powers, 1987–1957*, rev. edn., New York University Press, 1957; Louis Fisher, *President and Congress: Power and Policy*, New York: Free Press, 1972; Roger Z. George and Harvey Rishikof, eds., *The National Security Enterprise: Navigating the Labyrinth*, 2nd edn., Washington DC: Georgetown University Press, 2017; Michael J. Glennon, *Constitutional Diplomacy*, Princeton University Press, 1990;

Louis Henkin, *Foreign Affairs and the US Constitution*, 2nd edn., Oxford: Clarendon Press, 1996; Shoon Murray and Jordan Tama, *U.S. Foreign Policymaking and National Security*, Oxford Handbooks Online, Oxford University Press, 2015.

3. "U.S. Commitments to Foreign Powers," *Hearings*, Committee on Foreign Relations, U.S. Senate, p. 194, 1967.

4. Memorandum, Department of State, July 3, 1950; *Department of State Bulletin* 23, pp. 173–177, July 31, 1950.

5. *Congressional Record*, S7318, May 19, 1971.

6. "National Commitments," Report No. 91–129, Committee on Foreign Relations, US Senate, p. 20, April 16, 1969.

7. Arthur M. Schlesinger, *The Imperial Presidency*, Boston: Houghton Mifflin, p. 159–160, 1973; Marvin Kalb, *The Road to War: Presidential Commitments Honored and Betrayed*, Washington, DC: Brookings Institution Press, 2013; Arthur M. Schlesinger Jr., *War and the American Presidency*, New York: Norton, 2004.

8. The casualty figure is from, "American War Dead, by the Numbers," *The American Prospect* (May 26, 2014), http://prospect.org/article/american-war-dead-numbers; in addition to these fatalities, well over 300,000 Americans suffered wounds during the war – many of which were profoundly life-changing; Loch K. Johnson, "Political Alienation among Vietnam Veterans," *Western Political Quarterly*, 29, pp. 398–409, September, 1976.

9. Senator Frank Church (D-Idaho), "Of Presidents and Caesars: The Decline of Constitutional Government in the Conduct of American Foreign Policy," *Idaho Law Review* 6, p. 10, 1969; for Undersecretary Katzenbach's testimony, see *U.S. Commitments to Foreign Powers*, Hearings, Committee on Foreign Relations, US Senate, p. 82, 1967.

10. *Congressional Record*, 36187, November 6, 1973.

11. Quoted by Steven V. Roberts, "Aide Cites Reagan Foreign Policy Power," *New York Times*, p. A5, May 15, 1987.

12. William Pfaff, "A Radical Rethink of International Relations," *International Herald Tribune*, p. A16, October 3, 2002.

13. Raoul Berger, "The Presidential Monopoly of Foreign Relations," *Michigan Law Review* 71, p. 39, 1972).

14. Loch K. Johnson, *The Making of International Agreements: Congress Confronts the Executive*, New York University Press, 1984; *American Foreign Policy and the Challenges of World Leadership: Power, Principles and the Constitution*, Oxford University Press, 2015; Glen S. Krutz and Jeffrey S. Peake, *Treaty Politics and the Rise of Executive Agreements: International Commitments in a System of Shared Powers*, University of Michigan Press, 2009; Jeffrey S. Peake, *Obama, Unilateral Diplomacy, and Iran: Treaties, Executive Agreements, and Political Commitments*, Richard S. Conley, ed., pp. 142–171, *Presidential Leadership*; "Secret Law Is Bad Law," *New York Times*, p. A21, October 18, 2016.

15. "National Commitments," *Report No.* 91–129, Committee on Foreign Relations, US Senate, April 16, 1969.

16. "National Commitments," *Report No.* 91–129, Committee on Foreign Relations, p. 28, US Senate, April 16, 1969.

17. Karen J. Greenberg, *Rogue Justice: The Making of the Security State*, New York: Crown, 2016; Loch K. Johnson, *Spy Watching: Intelligence Accountability in the United States*, Oxford University Press, 2018.

18. For an analysis that is pessimistic about the chances that Madisonian checks and balances can stand up successfully against forces in Washington, DC, that favor government

authority centralized into the hands of the executive branch, see Michael J. Glennon, *National Security and Double Government*, Oxford University Press, 2015.

19. Jean Edward Smith, *Bush*, New York: Simon & Schuster, 2016, quoted by Peter Baker, "Presidential Biography As Scathing Indictment," *New York Times*, p. C1, July 4, 2016.

20. Jeffrey S. Peake, *Obama, Unilateral Diplomacy, and Iran: Treaties, Executive Agreements, and Political Commitments*, Richard S. Conley, ed., p. 150, *Presidential Leadership*.

21. Peter Baker, "A Coalition in Which Some Do More Than Others to Fight ISIS," *New York Times*, p. A18, November 30, 2015.

22. On these points, see Richard A. Clarke, *Against All Enemies: Inside America's War on Terror*, New York: Simon & Schuster, pp. 204, 229, and 237, 2004; Robert Jervis, *Why Intelligence Fails: Lessons from the Iran Revolution and the Iraq War*, Ithaca, NY: Cornell University Press, 2010; Loch K. Johnson, *The Threat on the Horizon: An Inside Account of America's Search for Security after the Cold War*, Oxford University Press, 2011.

23. For this theory of the presidency, John Yoo, *The Powers of War and Peace: The Constitution and Foreign Affairs after 9/11*, University of Chicago Press, 2010.

24. Michael V. Hayden, *Playing to the Edge: American Intelligence in an Age of Terror*, New York: Penguin, p. 68, 2016.

25. Louis Fisher, *President Obama: Constitutional Aspirations and Executive Actions*, University Press of Kansas, 2018.

26. George Packer, "Dark Hours: Violence in the Age of the War on Terror," *The New Yorker*, p. 74, July 20, 2015. ISIS, the Islamic State in Iraq and Syria, is also known just as the Islamic State; as ISIL, or the Islamic State of Iraq and the Levant; or, in Arabic, as *Dawlat* (The State) or as *Daesh*, another Arabic term viewed by ISIS members as insulting.

27. David J. Barron, *Waging War: The Clash between Presidents and Congress, 1776 to ISIS*, New York: Simon & Schuster, p. 419, 2016.

28. Barack Obama, "Barack Obama's Q&A," *Boston Globe*, p. A1, December 20, 2007. "The Talk of the Town," *New Yorker*, p. 35, September 22, 2014.

29. Opinion, "Legal Authority for Fighting ISIS," *New York Times*, p. A26, September 12, 2014.

30. Louis Fisher, *Military Initiatives by President Obama*, in Richard S. Conley, ed., p. 79, *Presidential Leadership*, 2017.

31. David J. Barron, *Waging War: The Clash Between Presidents and Congress, 1776 to ISIS*, New York: Simon & Schuster, p. 420, 2016.

32. Louis Fisher, "Military Initiatives by President Obama," Richard S. Conley, ed., p. 80, *Presidential Leadership*, 2017.

33. Speech, Senate floor, September 12, 2017.

34. "Meet the Press," *NBC*, February 4, 2018; Eric Schmitt, "Deep in the Desert, A Murky U.S. War Ramps Up," *New York Times*, p. A1, April 22, 2018; For evidence that the Trump administration was attempting to keep its military activities in Niger secret from the Congress, see Charlie Savage, Eric Schmitt, and Thomas Gibbons-Neff, "U.S. Kept Silent about Its Role in Another Gun Battle in Niger," *New York Times*, p. A9, March 15, 2018.

35. Thomas Gibbons-Neff and Eric Schmitt, "After Deaths, U.S. Weighs Withdrawing Commandos from Niger," *New York Times*, p. A6, September 3, 2018.

36. Jonathan Weisman, "An Obama Ally Parts with Him on War Powers," *New York Times*, p. A1, October 6, 2014.

37. Charlie Savage, "Is the U.S. Now at War with the Shabab? Not Exactly," *New York Times*, p. A11, March 15, 2016.

38. Bruce Ackerman, "Obama's Betrayal of the Constitution," *New York Times*, p. A26, September 12, 2014.

39. Justice Louis Brandeis, *Myers v. United States*, 272 US 52, 293 (1926).

40. Quoted in Ken Burns, *The Vietnam War*, PBS Documentary, 2017.

41. David E. Sanger, "Obama Sees an Iran Deal that Could Avoid Congress," *New York Times*, p. A4, October 20, 2014.

42. Quoted in "That's Not How It Went on the Deal with Iran," *New York Times*, p. A16, October 11, 2017.

43. For a reference to this base, Eric Schmitt, "Deep in the Desert, A Murky U.S. War Ramps Up," *New York Times*, p. A1, April 22, 2018.

44. Loch K. Johnson, *The Making of International Agreements: Congress Confronts the Executive*, New York University Press, 1984.

45. Loch K. Johnson, *The Making of International Agreements*, p. 202–203.

46. For one case study, see Scott Shane, *Objective Troy: A Terrorist, a President, and the Rise of the Drone*, New York: Tim Duggan Books, 2015.

47. Carol Morello, "Tillerson and Mattis Tell Senate Panel No Need for New War Authorization," *Washington Post*, p. A1, October 30, 2017.

48. Cited by Jack Thompson, "*Superpower Constrained*," Oliver Thränert and Martin Zapfe, eds., *Strategic Trends*, Zurich, Center for Security Studies, p. 17, 2018.

49. Mujib Mashal, "An Emotional Farewell to Afghanistan," *New York Times*, p. A8, September 3, 2018.

50. Jack Thompson, "Superpower Constrained," Oliver Thränert and Martin Zapfe, eds., *Strategic Trends*, Zurich, Center for Security Studies, p. 17, 2018.

51. Charlie Savage, "Lawmakers to Revisit 9/11 Law Authorizing Ever-Expanding War," *New York Times*, p. A19, October 29, 2017.

52. Bruce Ackerman, "Trump, Congress and Syria," *New York Times*, p. A23, April 8, 2018.

53. Cory A. Booker and Oona A. Hathaway, "A Syria Plan That Breaks the Law," *New York Times*, p. A23, January 24, 2018.

54. Editorial Board, "Syria Is Now Mr. Trump's War," *New York Times*, p. A22, January 20, 2018.

55. Peter Baker, "Talk of 'Mission Accomplished!' But Mission in Syria Is Unclear," *New York Times*, p. A1, April 15, 2018.

56. Press Conference, Department of Defense, April 13, 2018.

57. David S. Sanger and William J. Broad, "Pentagon Plan Would Expand Nuclear Policy," *New York Times*, p. A1, January 17, 2018.

58. Karoun Demirjian, "Senators Release Bipartisan Proposal to Reauthorize Use of Force against Non-State Groups," *Washington Post*, p. A1, April 17, 2018.

59. James Goldgeier and Elizabeth N. Saunders, "The Unconstrained Presidency," *Foreign Affairs*, p. 150, September/October 2018.

60. See unsigned editorial, "Doubtful Limits on Presidential Power," *New York Times*, p. A22, April 25, 2018.

61. Michiko Kakutani, "When History Repeats," *New York Times*, SR-4, July 15, 2018, who in the context of the Japanese-American internments cites Assistant Secretary of War John J. McCloy as saying at the time: "The Constitution is just a scrap of paper to me." The 20,000 children figure is from this same article.

62. Quoted in David E. Sanger and William J. Broad, "U.S. Chases Russia into New Arms Race as a Treaty Takes Effect," *New York Times*, p. A1, February 5, 2018.

63. Remarks, Senator James E. Risch, *National Public Radio*, June 6, 2018.

64. Nicholas Fandos, Plan to Thwart Russia, And Restive President, "Takes Shape in Senate," *New York Times*, p. A17, August 2, 2018.

65. "U.S. Senators Move Again to Block F-35 Sales to Turkey Over Russian Deal," *Radio Free Europe/Radio Liberty*, p. 2, June 22, 2018.

66. For the quote and the "pushback" prediction, see the unsigned editorial, "A Bogus Deal on Nafta," *New York Times*, p. A18, September 3, 2018.

67. See, for example, Clapper's reflections on these disputes: James R. Clapper, *Facts and Fears: Hard Truths from a Life in Intelligence*, Viking, pp. 362 and 379–380, 2018.

68. Aspen Institute Forum, Aspen, Colorado, July 20, 2017.

69. Loch K. Johnson, *Spy Watching: Intelligence Accountability in the United States*, Oxford University Press, p. 471, 2018.

70. Connie Bruck, "The Guantánamo Failure," *The New Yorker*, p. 34, August 1, 2016.

71. Loch K. Johnson, *America's Secret Power: The CIA in a Democratic Society*, Oxford University Press, 1989.

72. *The News Hour* (PBS) reported on an increase in drone attacks (February 26, 2018); Greg Jaffe, "Trump Administration Reviewing Ways to Make It Easier to Launch Drone Strikes," *Washington Post*, p. A1, March 13, 2017; Aisha I. Saad and Zoe A. Y. Weinberg, "Remember Guantánamo?" *New York Times*, p. A27, March 16, 2018; Joe Penney et al., "C.I.A. Expands Drone Missions Obama Curbed," *New York Times*, p. A1, September 10, 2018.

73. For a spirited debate by several experts on the question of whether autocratic rule could take root in the United States during the Trump years, see Cass R. Sunstein, *Can It Happen Here? Authoritarianism in America*, New York: HarperCollins, 2018; Charlie Savage, "Aggressive Push by White House for Legal Power," *New York Times*, p. A1, June 5, 2018; Benjamin Carter Hett, *The Death of Democracy: Hitler's Rise to Power and the Downfall of the Weimar Republic*, New York: Henry Holt, 2018.

74. Edward Gibbon, *The Decline and Fall of the Roman Empire*, New York: Viking, p. 85, 1952.

THE ILLIBERAL EXPERIMENT: HOW GUANTÁNAMO BECAME
A DEFINING AMERICAN INSTITUTION

1. Johan Steyn, *Democracy through Law: Selected Speeches & Judgments*, Routledge, p. 195, 2004.

2. *Guantanamo by the Numbers*, Human Rights First, 2018 (www.humanrightsfirst.org/sites/default/files/gtmo-by-the-numbers.pdf).

3. *Report of the Senate Select Committee on Intelligence* (SSCI Report), Committee Study of the Intelligence Agency's Detention and Interrogation Program, S.Rep., pp. 113–288, 2014.

4. John Gray, *Liberalism: Concepts Social Thought*, 2nd ed., University of Minnesota Press, 1995.

5. Alexander Casella, *The Politics of Prisoners of War*, The New York Times, May, pp. 28, 1972.

6. For the purposes of this chapter, I will generally refer to Guantánamo and the black sites collectively as "Guantánamo."

7. Cesare Beccaria, *Crimes and Punishments*, 1764.

8. Darius Rejali, *Torture and Democracy*, Princeton University Press, 2007.

9. *Report of the Senate Select Committee on Intelligence* (SSCI Report), Committee Study of the Intelligence Agency's Detention and Interrogation Program, S.Rep., pp. 68–70, 2014.

10. *President Meets with World Health Organization Director-General*, The White House Archives (Dec. 6, 2005) (https://georgewbush-whitehouse.archives.gov/news/releases/2005/12/20051206–1.html).

11. Bernard Harcourt, *The Counterrevolution: How Our Government Went to War against Its Own Citizens*, Basic Books, 2018.

12. Jay Bybee, Memorandum for Alberto R. Gonzales, Counsel to the President, *Standards of Conduct for Interrogation under 18 U.S.C. §§ 2340–2340A*, at p. 13 (Aug. 1, 2002) (www.justice.gov/olc/file/886061/download).

13. *Judgment Concerning the Legality of the General Security Service's Interrogation Methods*, HCJ 5100/94 ¶36 (Sept. 6, 1999).

14. Tbeish v. Attorney General, HCJ 9018/17 (Nov. 26, 2018).

15. *Report of the Senate Select Committee on Intelligence (SSCI Report)*, Committee Study of the Intelligence Agency's Detention and Interrogation Program, S.Rep., p. 11, 2014.

16. Authorization for the Use of Military Force, 115 Stat. 224.

17. *Letter to the Speaker of the House of Representatives and the President Pro Tempore of the Senate*, 37 Wkly. Comp. Pres. Doc. 1447 (Oct. 9, 2001).

18. *Report of the Senate Select Committee on Intelligence (SSCI Report)*, Committee Study of the Intelligence Agency's Detention and Interrogation Program, S.Rep., p. 81, 2014.

19. Senate Armed Services Committee Report (SASC Report), Inquiry into the Treatment of Detainees in U.S. Custody, at p. 38 (Nov. 20, 2008).

20. *Report of the Senate Select Committee on Intelligence (SSCI Report)*, Committee Study of the Intelligence Agency's Detention and Interrogation Program, S.Rep., pp. 21–23, 2014.

21. Harcourt, *The Counterrevolution*, p. 69.

22. Detention, Treatment, and Trial of Certain Non-Citizens in the War against Terrorism, p. 66, Fed. Reg. 57833 (Nov. 13, 2001); Presidential Memorandum, *Humane Treatment of Taliban and al Qaeda Detainees* (Feb. 7, 2002); *see also* Memorandum for Timothy E. Flanigan, Deputy Counsel to the President, from John C. Yoo, Deputy Assistant Attorney General, Office of Legal Counsel, *Re: The President's Constitutional Authority to Conduct Military Operations against Terrorists and Nations Supporting Them* (Sept. 25, 2001); Memorandum from Patrick F. Philbin, Deputy Assistant Attorney General, Office of Legal Counsel, to Alberto R. Gonzales, Counsel to the President, *Legality of the Use of Military Commissions to Try Terrorists* (Nov. 6, 2001); Memorandum to Alberto Gonzales, Counsel to the President, from Jay S. Bybee, Assistant Attorney General, Office of Legal Counsel, *Re: Application of Treaties and Laws to al Qaeda and Taliban Detainees* (Jan. 22, 2002); Memorandum for William J. Haynes II, General Counsel of the Department of Defense, from Jay S. Bybee, Assistant Attorney General, Office of Legal Counsel, *Re: The President's Power as Commander in Chief to Transfer Captured Terrorists to the Control and Custody of Foreign Nations* (Mar. 13, 2002); Memorandum to John Ashcroft, Attorney General, from Jay S. Bybee, Assistant Attorney General, Office of Legal Counsel, *Determination of Enemy Belligerency & Military Detention* (June 8, 2002).

23. *Former State Department Attorney-Adviser Bowker Visits Law and Security Colloquium*, NYU Law School (www.law.nyu.edu/news/bowker_colloquium).

24. Philippe Sands, *Torture Team*, Palgrave Macmillan, 35–36, 2008, in which Sands asked former Undersecretary of Defense for Policy Doug Feith about whether his memo arguing that the War on Terror detainees fell within a gap in the coverage of the Geneva Convention sought to remove the legal constraints on detainee treatment, particularly in the course of interrogation, and Feith responded, "That's the point."

25. Presidential Memorandum, *Humane Treatment of Al Qaeda and Taliban Detainees* (Feb. 7, 2002).

26. Detention, Treatment, and Trial of Certain Non-Citizens in the War against Terrorism, 66 Fed. Reg. 57833 § 2 (Nov. 13, 2001). This standard was first formalized in Deputy Secretary of Defense Paul Wolfowitz, Memorandum for the Secretary of the Navy, Order Establishing Combatant Status Review Tribunal (July 7, 2004). It was soon after adopted by the courts with its attendant implications. *See, e.g.*, Khalid v. Bush, 355 F.Supp.2d 311 (D.D.C. 2005).

27. For a largely accurate explanation of "bayat" and the role it played in Al-Qaeda, *see, e.g.*, Peter Bergen, *The Osama bin Laden I Know: An Oral History of Al Qaeda's Leader*, Free Press, 423–45, 2006.

28. Philip Bobbitt, *Terror and Consent: The Wars for the Twenty-First Century*, Anchor Books, 269, 2008.

29. Bobbitt, *Terror and Consent*, at p. 266

30. Memorandum for William J. Haynes II, General Counsel of the Department of Defense, from Jay S. Bybee, Assistant Attorney General, Office of Legal Counsel, *Re: The President's Power as Commander in Chief to Transfer Captured Terrorists to the Control and Custody of Foreign Nations*, at pp. 3–4 (Mar. 13, 2002).

31. Deputy Secretary of Defense Paul Wolfowitz, Memorandum for the Secretary of the Navy, Order Establishing Combatant Status Review Tribunal (July 7, 2004) (www .law.utoronto.ca/documents/Mackin/MuneerAhmad_ExhibitV.pdf).

32. In practice, no inmates were ever even given the "no longer an enemy combatant" determination. And on the few occasions where these tribunals reached that conclusion, the inmate was brought before another tribunal, sometimes multiple times, until the "enemy combatant" designation was confirmed.

33. Erving Goffman, *Asylums: Essays on the Social Situation of Mental Patients and Other Inmates*, Anchor Books, p. 76, 1961.

34. Erving Goffman, *Asylums*, p. 5.

35. Order CJCS (Jan. 2002) (www.esd.whs.mil/Portals/54/Documents/FOID/Reading% 20Room/Detainne_Related/08-F-0099_CJCS_Order_Jan-02.pdf).

36. For an excellent history of this period, *see generally* Karen J. Greenberg, *The Least Worst Place: Guantanamo's First 100 Days*, 2010.

37. Michel Foucault, *Discipline & Punish: The Birth of the Prison*, Vintage Books, 1975.

38. Aamer v. Obama, 742 F.3d 1023, 1039 (D.C. Cir. 2014).

39. This changed in a few marginal cases after the military commissions began securing convictions in 2007. The handful of inmates to be convicted were, with some exceptions, segregated from the general detainee population and, as a rule, subjected to harsher conditions of confinement for the duration of their sentences. In most cases, this was only a few months or a few years. The single exception was Ali Hamza al-Bahlul, who was given a life sentence in 2008 and held in varying kinds of "penal" detention thereafter. For much of this period, al-Bahlul was the sole "convict" in Guantanamo, meaning that he spent a significant portion of his sentence in de facto solitary confinement.

40. Carol Rosenberg, *Guantanamo Prisoners a Curious Varied Group*, Miami Herald, Jan. 20, 2002.

41. Greenberg, *The Least Worst Place: Guantanamo's First 100 Days*, p. 116.

42. Carol Rosenberg, *91 Guantánamo Captives Vastly Outnumbered by 2,000 Guards, Staff*, Miami Herald, Feb. 23, 2016.

43. This process is described in the AR 15–6 Investigation, Report on the Facts and Circumstances Surrounding the 8 September 2012 Death of Detainee Adnan Farhan Abd Latif (ISN US9YM-000156DP) at Joint-Task Force-Guantanamo

(JTF-GTMO) (Nov. 8, 2012) (www.southcom.mil/Portals/7/FOIA%20Docs/
   FOIA_RELEASE_AR2015-6_Mr_Adnan_Farhan_Latif_Investigation.pdf?ver=2017-08-
   15-095254-857).
44. GTMO Review, Joint Staff External Review of Intelligence Operations at Guantanamo
   Bay, Cuba (Sept. 10, 2002) (http://guantanamotruth.com/documents-on-guantanamo-as-
   americas-battle-lab-in-the-global-war-on-terrorism/).
45. Senate Armed Services Committee Report (SASC Report), Inquiry into the Treatment of
   Detainees in U.S. Custody, at p. 52 (Nov. 20, 2008).
46. *Report of the Senate Select Committee on Intelligence* (SSCI Report), Committee Study of
   the Intelligence Agency's Detention and Interrogation Program, S.Rep., 21, 2014.
47. Martin Seligman, *Learned Helplessness*, 23 Annual Rev. of Medicine 1, p. 407–12, 1972.
48. *Report of the Senate Select Committee on Intelligence* (SSCI Report), Committee Study of
   the Intelligence Agency's Detention and Interrogation Program, S.Rep., p. 2, 2014.
49. Senate Armed Services Committee Report (SASC Report), *Inquiry into the Treatment of
   Detainees in U.S. Custody*, at p. 42 (Nov. 20, 2008) (www.armed-services.senate.gov/imo/
   media/doc/Detainee-Report-Final_April-22-2009.pdf).
50. Gherebi v. Bush, 352 F.3d 1278 (9th Cir. 2003).
51. Al Odah v. United States, 321 F.3d 1134 (D.C. Cir. 2003).
52. Boumediene v. Bush, 553 U.S. 723 (2008).
53. *Boumediene*, 553 U.S. at 765.
54. *Boumediene*, 553 U.S. at 733.
55. *Guantanamo Habeas Scorecard*, Center for Constitutional Rights, 2012.
56. Al-Adahi v. Obama, 613 F.3d 1102 (D.C. Cir. 2010); Al-Bihani v. Obama, 590 F.3d 866,
   873 n. 2 (D.C. Cir. 2010).
57. Kiyemba v. Obama, 605 F.3d 1046, 1048 (D.C. Cir. 2010); Kiyemba v. Obama, 561 F.3d
   509, 516 (D.C. Cir. 2009).
58. Jack Goldsmith, *Power and Constraint: The Accountable President after 9/11*,
   W. W. Norton, 2012.
59. Esmail v. Obama, 639 F.3d 1075, 1078 (D.C. Cir. 2011) (Silberman, J., concurring).
60. Hamdan v. Rumsfeld, 548 U.S. 557 (2006).
61. *Hamdan*, 548 U.S. at 629-31.
62. *Press Conference of the President*, White House Archives, Sept. 15, 2006. (http://georgew
   bush-whitehouse.archives.gov/news/releases/2006/09/20060915-2.html).
63. Military Commissions Act of 2006, 120 Stat. 2600.
64. *Id.* § 5.
65. See, e.g., Al-Zahrani v. Rodriguez, 669 F.3d 315 (D.C. Cir. 2012); Hamad v. Gates, 732
   F.3d 990 (9th Cir. 2013).
66. Rasul v. Myers, 563 F.3d 527, 532–533 (D.C. Cir. 2009).
67. *Germany Is a Friend*, Interview with President George W. Bush, Spiegel, May 8, 2006
   (www.spiegel.de/international/interview-with-george-w-bush-germany-is-a-friend-
   a-414995.html).
68. Steven Lee Myers, *Bush Decides to Keep Guantanamo Open*, The New York Times, Oct.
   20, 2008.
69. Transcript, "Meet the Press," NBC News, June 10, 2007 (www.nbcnews.com/id/
   19092206/ns/meet_the_press/t/meet-press-transcript-june/).
70. *Sen. Barack Obama Delivers Remarks at the Woodrow Wilson Center on Terrorism*, CQ-
   RollCall Political Transcripts, Aug. 1, 2007.
71. E.O. 13492, Review and Disposition of Individuals Detained at the Guantánamo Bay
   Naval Base and Closure of Detention Facilities, 74 Fed. Reg. 4897 (Jan. 22, 2009); E.O.

13491, Interrogation of Individuals in U.S. Custody or Control in Armed Conflicts; Standards and Practices, 74 Fed. Reg. 4893 (Jan. 22, 2009).

72. *Remarks by the President on National Security*, The White House Archives, May 21, 2009 (https://obamawhitehouse.archives.gov/the-press-office/remarks-president-national-security-5-21-09).

73. Scott Shane, *No Charges Filed on Harsh Tactics Used by the C.I.A.*, The New York Times, Aug. 30, 2012.

74. Memorandum for the Attorney General Re: Applicability of Federal Criminal Laws and the Constitution Contemplated Lethal Operations against Shaykh Anwar Al-Aulaqi, at pp. 21–23 (Jul. 16, 2010); Al-Aulaqi v. Obama, 727 F.Supp.2d 1 (D.D.C. 2010); Al-Aulaqi v. Panetta, 35 F. Supp. 3d 56 (D.D.C. 2014).

75. Meshal v. Higgenbotham, 804 F.3d 417 (D.C. Cir. 2015).

76. Osorio-Martinez v. Sessions, 893 F.3d 153 (3d Cir. 2018).

77. Hernandez v. Mesa, 885 F.3d 811 (5th Cir. 2018).

78. Korematsu v. United States, 323 U.S. 214, 246 (1944) (Jackson, J., dissenting).

79. Charlie Savage, *Power Wars: The Relentless Rise of Presidential Authority and Secrecy*, Back Bay Books, 48, 2016.

80. *Presidential Press Conference*, The White House Archives, Apr. 30, 2013 (https://obama whitehouse.archives.gov/the-press-office/2013/04/30/news-conference-president).

81. Presidential Inaugural Address, White House Archives, Jan. 20, 2009 (https://obamawhite house.archives.gov/blog/2009/01/21/president-barack-obamas-inaugural-address).

82. Michael Birnbaum, *Russia's Vladimir Putin Strikes Harsh Tone During Marathon Annual News Conference*, The Washington Post, Dec. 20, 2012.

83. Ron Suskind, *The One Percent Doctrine: Deep Inside America's Pursuit of Its Enemies Since 9/11*, Simon & Schuster, 2006.

84. *Turkey Coup Anniversary: Erdogan Hails "Defenders of Nation,"* BBC News, Jul. 16, 2017.

NATIONAL SECURITY AND COURT DEFERENCE: RAMIFICATIONS AND WORRYING TRENDS

1. Margaret B. Kwoka, *The Procedural Exceptionalism of National Security Secrecy*, 97 B.U. L. Rev. 103, 2017; Stephen I. Vladeck, *The Demise of Merits-Based Adjudication in Post 9/11 National Security Litigation*, 64 Drake L. Rev. 1035, 1037, 2016; Susan N. Herman, *Ab(ju)dication: How Procedure Defeats Civil Liberties in the "War on Terror,"* 50 Suffolk U. L. Rev. 79, 2017; Joshua L. Dratel, *The Unique Challenges of Defending a Terrorism Prosecution*, 43 Litigation 2, Winter 2017 (www.americanbar.org/groups/litigation/publica tions/litigation_journal/2016-17/winter/the_unique_challenges_defending_terrorism_pro secution/); David E. Pozen, *Note: The Mosaic Theory, National Security, and the Freedom of Information Act*, 115 Yale L.J. 628, 2005.

2. Mohamed v. Jeppesen Dataplan, *Inc.*, 614 F.3d 1070 (9th Cir. Cal. 2010) at 1092 ("[W]e do not reach our decision lightly or without close and skeptical scrutiny of the record and the government's case for secrecy and dismissal . . . . We . . . acknowledge that this case presents a painful conflict between human rights and national security."); El-Masri v. United States, 479 F.3d 296 (4th Cir. 2007), cert. denied 552 U.S. 947 (2007) (upholding lower court's dismissal of suit on grounds that el-Masri, who alleged that he was kidnapped, illegally detained, and abused by the CIA, would not be able to make his case except by using evidence barred by the state secrets privilege); Arar v. Ashcroft, 585

F.3d 559 (cert. denied, June 14, 2010) at 565, 575, 578, and 580–581 (upholding lower court's dismissal of suit, on the basis that it would interfere with national security and foreign policy, by Canadian national who claimed he was sent by the United States to Syria, where he was tortured for one year until his release); see also cases brought by several former US detainees in Guantánamo, Iraq, and Afghanistan that were blocked on the same theory, which effectively would bar a suit brought by a CIA detainee on the same grounds: Rasul v. Myers, 563 F.3d at 527, 532 n. 5 (D.C. Cir. 2009); *In re Iraq and Afghanistan Detainees Litigation*, 479 F. Supp. 2d 85 (D.D.C. 2007) at 103–107, affirmed by Ali v. Rumsfeld, 649 F.3d 762 (D.C. Cir. 2011) at 765.

3. Joshua Dratel, *The Unique Challenges of Defending a Terrorism Prosecution* 43 Litigation 2, Winter 2017; Margaret B. Kwoka, *The Procedural Exceptionalism of National Security Secrecy*, 97 B.U. L. Rev. 103, 2017.

4. Richard L. Abel, *Law's Trials: The Performance of Legal Institutions in the US "War on Terror,"* Cambridge University Press, 2018.

5. Jonathan Hafetz, *Habeas Corpus after 9/11*, New York University Press, 2011; Steve I. Vladeck, *National Security Policy and the Role of Lawyering: Guantanamo and Beyond: The D.C. Circuit after Boumediene*, 41 Seton Hall L. Rev. 1451, 2011; Jasmeet K. Ahuja and Andrew Tutt, *Evidentiary Rules Governing Guantánamo Habeas Petitions: Their Effects and Consequences*, 31 Yale L. & Pol'y Rev. 185, 2012; Baher Azmy, *Executive Detention, Boumediene, and the New Common Law of Habeas, Executive Detention, Boumediene*, 95 Iowa L. Rev. 445, 2010. Cite also to the detention standard 2.0.

6. Seth Freed Wessler, *The Coast Guard's "Floating Guantánamos,"* *The New York Times*, November 20, 2017 (www.nytimes.com/2017/11/20/magazine/the-coast-guards-floating-guantanamos.html).

7. Boumediene v. Bush, 553 U.S. 723 (2008).

8. *Boumediene*, at 779.

9. Jasmeet K. Ahuja and Andrew Tutt, *Evidentiary Rules Governing Guantánamo Habeas Petitions: Their Effects and Consequences*, 31 Yale L. & Pol'y Rev. 185, 2012 (https://ylpr.yale.edu/sites/default/files/YLPR/ahuja_tutt_evidentiary_rules_governing_guantanamo_habeas_petitions-_their_effects_and_consequences.pdf).

10. Al-Bihani v. Obama, 590 F.3d 866, 878 (D.C. Cir. 2010).

11. Salahi v. Obama, 710 F. Supp. 2d 1, 6 (D.D.C. Apr. 9, 2010).

12. Al-Bihani v. Obama, 590 F.3d 866, 879 (D.C. Cir. Jan. 5, 2010).

13. Charlton v. FTC, 177 U.S. App. D.C. 418, 543 F.2d 903, 907 (1976) ("It suffices for present purposes simply to recall that in American law a preponderance of the evidence is rock bottom at the fact-finding level of civil litigation."); Linda Greenhouse, *The Mirror of Guantánamo*, *The New York Times*, December 11, 2013 (www.nytimes.com/2013/12/12/opinion/greenhouse-the-mirror-of-guantanamo.html).

14. Al-Adahi, v. Obama, 613 F.3d 1102, at 1105 ("The government stated that ... a preponderance standard is appropriate ... thus [we are] left with no adversary presentation on an important question affecting many pending cases .... Although we doubt, for the reasons stated above, that the Suspension Clause requires the use of the preponderance standard, we will not decide the question in this case.")

15. Stephen Vladeck, *D.C. Circuit after Boumediene*, 41 Seton Hall L. Rev. 1451, 1473, 2011. (Judge Silberman's statement in Esmail v. Obama, 639 F.3d 1075 (D.C. Cir. 2011) (per curiam) is remarkable because "one might fairly read it as suggesting that he – and at least some of his colleagues – are in fact reviewing the government's case only for 'some evidence,' rather than the 'more evidence than not' requirement of the preponderance standard.")

16. Jasmeet K. Ahuja and Andrew Tutt, *Evidentiary Rules Governing Guantánamo Habeas Petitions: Their Effects and Consequences*, 31 Yale L. & Pol'y Rev. 185, 191, 2012 (https:// ylpr.yale.edu/sites/default/files/YLPR/ahuja_tutt_evidentiary_rules_governing_guanta namo_habeas_petitions-_their_effects_and_consequences.pdf).

17. David E. Pozen, *Note: The Mosaic Theory, National Security, and the Freedom of Information Act*, 115 Yale L.J. 628, 2005.

18. Pozen, *Note: The Mosaic Theory*, 630.

19. Al-Adahi v. Obama, 613 F.3d 1102 at 1104-06.

20. Bensayah v. Obama, 610 F.3d 718 (D.C. Cir. June 28, 2010) (reversed denial of habeas after the government eschewed reliance upon certain evidence the District Court had considered and abandoned its position that Bensayah's detention was lawful because of the support he rendered al-Qaeda).

21. Al-Adahi v. Obama, 613 F.3d 1102 (D.C. Cir. July 13, 2010), cert. denied, 131 S. Ct. 1001 (2011), Salahi v. Obama, 625 F.3d 745 (D.C. Cir. Nov. 5, 2010), Hatim v. Gates, 632 F.3d 720 (D.C. Cir. Nov. 9, 2010), Uthman v. Obama, 637 F.3d 400 (D.C. Cir. Mar. 29, 2011), cert. denied, 132 S.Ct. 2739 (2012), Almerfedi v. Obama, 654 F.3d 1 (D.C. Cir. June 10, 2011), cert. denied, 132 S.Ct. 2739 (2012).

22. Latif v. Obama, 677 F.3d 1175 (D.C. Cir. Oct. 14, 2011), cert. denied, 132 S.Ct. 2741 (2012).

23. See, e.g., Stansbury v. Wertman, 721 F.3d 84, 93 (D.C. Cir. June 26, 2013); Co. Doe v. Tenenbaum, 127 F. Supp. 3d 426, 458 (D. Md. 2012); Estate of Parsons v. Palestinian Auth., 397 U.S. App. D.C. 236, 265, 651 F.3d 118, 147 (2011).

24. Kate Clark, *Waiting for Release: Will Afghans Cleared to Leave Guantanamo Get Out before Trump Gets In?* Afghanistan Analysts Network, January 14, 2017 (www.afghanistan -analysts.org/waiting-for-release-will-afghans-cleared-to-leave-guantanamo-get-out- before-trump-ge) ("Case files contain very little, or no evidence of wrongdoing, but rather fantastical allegations, based on hearsay, double hearsay (X said Y said Z was a terrorist), testimony obtained through torture and unverified and unprocessed intelli- gence reports . . . gross factual mistakes."). See also Latif v. Obama, 677 F.3d 1175, 1214 (D.C. Cir. Oct. 14, 2011) (Tatel, J. dissenting) (pointing to numerous inaccuracies in the intelligence reports upon which the government relies in Guantánamo cases).

25. Laura Pitter (Human Rights Watch), *The Dangers of Guantanamo*: Keeping It Open Makes Us Less Safe, *Foreign Affairs*, August 24, 2016 (www.hrw.org/news/2016/08/24/ dangers-guantanamo).

26. Fact Sheet: The Flawed Guantanamo Assessment Files, Human Rights First, December 2016, (www.humanrightsfirst.org/sites/default/files/JTF-GTMO- Assessments-Fact-Sheet.pdf).

27. Carol Rosenberg, *Victims of Mistaken Identity among the 10 sent from Guantánamo to Oman, Miami Herald*, January 17, 2017 (www.miamiherald.com/news/nation-world /world/americas/guantanamo/article127055319.html).

28. Carol Rosenberg and Tom Lasseter, *WikiLeaks: Secret Guantanamo Files Show U.S. Disarray, McClatchy Newspapers*, April 24, 2011 (www.mcclatchydc.com/news/special- reports/article24625636.html). ("The inclusion of information from such a highly ques- tionable group of men would seem to raise serious issues about a key piece of the 'mosaic' process at Guantanamo and the decisions that followed.") See also Richard L. Abel, *Law's Trials: Performance of Legal Institutions in the US "War on Terror,"* Cambridge University Press, 2018, 428.

29. Scott Shane, *From Inside Prison, a Terrorism Suspect Shares His Diary*, The New York Times, June 25, 2015 (www.nytimes.com/2015/01/26/arts/guantanamo-diary-by-

mohamedou-ould-slahi.html). ("Based on that history, the government . . . listed him as the most dangerous terrorist at Guantánamo.").

30. One of the more damning pieces of evidence countering the US government's narrative about Slahi's dangerousness was a letter written by one Slahi's former Guantánamo guards, Steve Wood, in April 2016. The letter was submitted to a US government review board deciding whether Slahi could be released from Guantánamo. "I had heard that the men I would be guarding were the worst of the worst and that they would hate me and everything the United States and I stood for . . . . In no way did I experience that with Mohamedou," Wood wrote to the board. "I would be pleased to welcome him in my home . . . . I do not have safety concerns if I were to do so. I would like the opportunity to eventually see him again." Mohamedou Slahi Guantanamo Periodic Review Board Hearing – Letter of Support from Slahi's Former Guard at Guantanamo, ACLU, April 16, 2016 (www.aclu.org/letter/mohamedou-slahi-guantanamo-periodic-review-board-hearing-letter-support-slahis-former-guard); Carol Rosenberg, *A Freed Guantánamo Prisoner and His Ex-Guard Meet Again in Remarkable Ramadan Reunion, Miami Herald,* June 11, 2018 (www.miamiherald.com/news/nation-world/world/americas/guantanamo/article212337644.html); Lulu Garcia-Navarro, Ned Wharton, and Clare Lombardo, *A Guantanamo Guard and His Detainee Reunite,* NPR, August 12, 2018 (www.npr.org/2018/08/12/637932193/a-guantanamo-guard-and-a-detainee-reunite-in-mauritania).

31. Tom Kludt, *Guantanamo Detainee's Diary Is the New York Times Best Seller,* CNN, January 29, 2015 (https://money.cnn.com/2015/01/29/media/guantanamo-diary-new-york-times-best-seller/).

32. Salahi v. Obama, 710 F. Supp.2d 1, 16 (D.D.C. 2010) granting habeas (The government showed that Salahi was an al-Qaeda sympathizer, perhaps a fellow traveler, and that he was in touch with al-Qaeda members but its proof "is so attenuated, or so tainted by coercion and mistreatment, or so classified, that it cannot support a successful criminal prosecution."), reversed after government appeal in Salahi v. Obama, 625 F.3d 745 (D.C. Cir. 2010).

33. Charlie Savage, *Investigators Said to Question How Detainee Died of Overdose,* The New York Times, November 28, 2012 (www.nytimes.com/2012/11/29/us/yemeni-detainee-at-guantanamo-died-of-overdose.html).

34. Abdah v. Obama, 2010 U.S. Dist. LEXIS 83596, at 39, 2010 WL 3270761. ("Latif's story is not without inconsistencies and unanswered questions, but it is supported by corroborating evidence provided by medical professionals and it is not incredible."), reversed by Latif v. Obama, 666 F.3d 746 (D.C. Cir. 2011), cert. denied Latif v. Obama, 567 U.S. 913, 132 S. Ct. 2741 (2012).

35. Latif v. Obama, 399 U.S. App. D.C. 1, 3, 666 F.3d 746, 748 (2011), cert. denied Latif v. Obama, 567 U.S. 913, 132 S. Ct. 2741 (2012).

36. Charlie Savage, "Investigators Said to Question How Detainee Died of Overdose," *The New York Times,* November 28, 2012. www.nytimes.com/2012/11/29/us/yemeni-detainee-at-guantanamo-died-of-overdose.html.

37. Charlie Savage, *Military Identifies Guantánamo Detainee Who Died,* The New York Times, September 11, 2012 (www.nytimes.com/2012/09/12/us/politics/detainee-who-died-at-guantanamo-had-release-blocked-by-court.html).

38. Laura Pitter, *After 16 Years, End Injustice at Guantanamo,* Huffington Post, reprinted at Human Rights Watch, January 10, 2018 (www.hrw.org/news/2018/01/10/after-16-years-end-injustice-guantanamo).

39. Al-Hajj v. Obama, "Memorandum" case 1:09-cv-00745, District Court for the District of Columbia, Document 1529, filed Jun 8, 2011, dated May 23, 2011, available at the Center for Constitutional Rights (https://ccrjustice.org/sites/default/files/attach/2017/02/2011-06-08_Al-Hajj_LamberthUnclassifiedMemorandumOpinion.pdf).

40. Al-Hajj v. Trump, Petitioner's Emergency Motion for an Independent Medical Evaluation and Medical Records, District Court for the District of Columbia, Case No. 09-cv-745(RCL), available at the Center for Constitutional Rights, September 6, 2017, at 3–4 (https://ccrjustice.org/sites/default/files/attach/2017/09/Emergency_Motion_for_Independent_Medical_Examination_Al_Hajj.pdf).

41. Al-Hajj v. Trump, Petitioner's Emergency Motion for an Independent Medical Evaluation and Medical Records, District Court for the District of Columbia, Case No. 09-cv-745(RCL), available at the Center for Constitutional Rights, September 6, 2017, at 3–4 (https://ccrjustice.org/sites/default/files/attach/2017/09/Emergency_Motion_for_Independent_Medical_Examination_Al_Hajj.pdf).

42. *CCR Seeks Outside Medical Evaluation for Ailing Guantánamo Client on Hunger Strike*, Center for Constitutional Rights, September 17, 2017 (https://ccrjustice.org/home/press-center/press-releases/ccr-seeks-outside-medical-evaluation-ailing-guant-namo-client).

43. *Gitmo Attorneys File Major New Challenge to Trump's Guantánamo*, Center for Constitutional Rights, January 11, 2018 (https://ccrjustice.org/home/press-center/press-releases/gitmo-attorneys-file-major-new-challenge-trump-s-guant-namo).

44. Carol Rosenberg, *Victims of Mistaken Identity among the 10 Sent from Guantánamo to Oman*, Miami Herald, January 17, 2017 (www.miamiherald.com/news/nation-world/world/americas/guantanamo/article127055319.html).

45. *The Guantanamo Docket, Countries of Citizenship*, The New York Times, last updated May 2, 2018 (www.nytimes.com/interactive/projects/guantanamo/detainees/by-country).

46. *The Guantanamo Docket, Transfer Countries*, The New York Times, last updated May 2, 2018 (www.nytimes.com/interactive/projects/guantanamo/transfer-countries).

47. Pardiss Kebriaei, *Life After Guantanamo: A Father and Son's Story*, Harper's Magazine (https://harpers.org/archive/2015/04/life-after-guantanamo/6/).

48. In response to the Japanese attack on Pearl Harbor during World War II, US President Franklin Roosevelt signed an executive order requiring Japanese Americans to move into relocation camps as a matter of national security. In Korematsu v. United States, 323 U. S. 214, 65 S. Ct. 193, 89 L. Ed. 194 (1944), the US Supreme Court upheld the executive order. After years of criticism, however, US president Ronald Regan finally signed the Civil Liberties Act of 1988 acknowledging that these detentions were wrong and motivated by "racial prejudice, wartime hysteria," rather than legitimate national security concerns. The Act provided those detained under the executive order with compensation. See *No More Excuses: A Roadmap to Justice for CIA Torture, Human Rights Watch*, December 1, 2015, at 105 (www.hrw.org/sites/default/files/report_pdf/us1215web.pdf). Finally, this year, the US Supreme Court overturned Korematsu v. United States, in Trump v. Hawaii, 138 S. Ct. 2392, at 2423 (2018).

49. *US: Prolonged Indefinite Detention Violates International Law*, Human Rights Watch, January 24, 2011 (www.hrw.org/news/2011/01/24/us-prolonged-indefinite-detention-violates-international-law).

50. Ryan Browne, Elise Labott, and Barbara Starr, *Trump Signs Order to Keep Guantanamo Open*, CNN, January 31, 2018 (www.cnn.com/2018/01/30/politics/trump-guantanamo-bay-reverse-obama/index.html).

51. Miranda v. Arizona, 384 U.S. 436, 86 S. Ct. 1602 (1966). (The Fifth Amendment of the US Constitution requires that law enforcement officials advise suspects of their right to remain silent and to obtain an attorney during interrogations while in police custody.)

52. Article 17 of the Third Geneva Convention (GC III). ("Every prisoner of war, when questioned on the subject, is bound to give only his surname, first names and rank, date of birth, and army, regimental, personal or serial number, or failing this, equivalent information.")

53. See, e.g., Philip Mudd, *Mirandizing Terrorists: Not So Black and White*, Washington Post, June 4, 2010 (www.washingtonpost.com/wp-dyn/content/article/2010/06/03/AR2010060303937.html). ("I sat at hundreds of briefing tables for nine years after Sept. 11, 2001, and I can't remember a time when Miranda impeded a decision on whether to pursue an intelligence interview."); *Issue Brief: Law Enforcement Interrogation of Terrorism Suspects*, Human Rights First (www.humanrightsfirst.org/sites/default/files/Law-Enforcement-Interrogations-Brief.pdf).

54. "Fair trial rights are safeguarded not only under human rights law but also under international humanitarian law. Willfully depriving a prisoner of war or other protected person of the rights of fair and regular trial constitutes a grave breach under the Third and Fourth Geneva Convention (Articles 130 and 147), and Additional Protocol I (Article 85.4(e) .... While today there can be no doubt that prisoners of war benefit from the entire panoply of fair trial rights, the question remains as to the point in time at which they start to be under the protection of these rights," which include "the right of the accused to be judged by an independent and impartial court (GC III, Art. 84(2); AP I, Art. 75(4); AP II, Art. 6(2)); the right of the accused to be promptly informed of the offences with which he/she is charged (GC III, Art. 104; GC IV, Art. 71(2); AP I, Art. 75(4)(a); AP II, Art. 6(2)(a)); and the right of the accused not to testify against himself/herself or to confess guilt (AP I, Art. 75(4)(f); AP II, Art. 6 (2)(f))." Robin Geiß, Name, Rank, Date of Birth, Serial Number and the Right to Remain Silent, 87 International Review of the Red Cross, December 2005, 730–731, and n. 28. The "Body of Principles for the Protection of All Persons under Any Form of Detention or Imprisonment" provides for the right of persons in custody to be assisted by a lawyer regardless of the type of detention involved and specifies that communication with counsel may not be denied for more than "a matter of days." Body of Principles for the Protection of All Persons under Any Form of Detention or Imprisonment, adopted Dec. 9, 1988, G.A. Res. 43/173, annex, 43 U.N., GAOR Supp. (No. 49A), U.N. Doc. A/45/49 (1990), principle 15. The Human Rights Committee has also specified that detainees should be afforded "prompt and regular access to counsel" to facilitate the effective review of the lawfulness of their detention, after explaining that the right to take proceedings for release from unlawful or arbitrary detention "applies to all detention by official action or pursuant to official authorization, including detention in connection with criminal proceedings, military detention [and] security detention." Human Rights Committee, General Comment No. 35, paras 40, 46.

55. Roberto Suro, FBI's "Clean" Teams Follow "Dirty" Spy Work, *Washington Post*, August 16, 1999 (www.washingtonpost.com/wp-srv/national/daily/aug99/dirty16.htm).

56. Charlie Savage, *U.S. Tests New Approach to Terrorism Cases on Somali Suspect*, The New York Times, July 6, 2011 (www.nytimes.com/2011/07/07/world/africa/07detain.html?module=inline).

57. Charlie Savage, *U.S. Tests New Approach to Terrorism Cases on Somali Suspect*, The New York Times, July 6, 2011 (www.nytimes.com/2011/07/07/world/africa/07detain.html?module=inline).

58. Two-tiered interrogations have been used in other cases, but only in these three known cases was it decided that it would be used prior to the US arrest of the suspect. Stephen I. Vladeck, *SYMPOSIUM: Terrorism Prosecutions and the Problem of Constitutional "Cross-Ruffing,"* 36 Cardozo Law Review, 709–710, 2014. For a list of other cases where the two-tier system has been used on detainees subject to US military and civilian detention. This includes John Walker Lindh, Jose Padilla, Ali Saleh Kahlal al-Marri, and Ahmed Ghailani in addition to Warsame, al-Liby and Khatallah.

59. Benjamin Weiser, *Terrorist Has Cooperated with U.S. Since Secret Guilty Plea in 2011, Papers Show,* The New York Times, March 25, 2013 (www.nytimes.com/2013/03/26/nyr egion/since-2011-guilty-plea-somali-terrorist-has-cooperated-with-authorities.html?modu le=inline); Adam Goldman and Benjamin Weiser, *How Civilian Prosecution Gave the U.S. a Key Informant,* The New York Times, January 27, 2017 (www.nytimes.com/2017/01/ 27/us/intelligence-gained-from-somali-terrorist-shows-value-of-civilian-prosecutions.html).

60. Charlie Savage, *U.S. Tests New Approach to Terrorism Cases on Somali Suspect,* The New York Times, July 6, 2011 (www.nytimes.com/2011/07/07/world/africa/07detain.html ?ref=politics); Peter Finn, *Somali's Case a Template for U.S. as It Seeks to Prosecute Terrorism Suspects in Federal Court,* Washington Post, March 30, 2013 (https://wapo.st /2WLHqwV).

61. Jason Ryan and Luis Martinez, *New Terror War Tactic? Alleged Al Qaeda-Linked Operative Secretly Held 2 Months on US Navy Vessel,* ABC News, July 5, 2011 (https:// abcnews.go.com/Blotter/ahmed-abdulkadir-warsame-secretly-held-months-navy-ship /story?id=14004812); Charlie Savage, *U.S. Tests New Approach to Terrorism Cases on Somali Suspect,* The New York Times, July 6, 2011 (www.nytimes.com/2011/07/07/world/ africa/07detain.html?ref=politics).

62. Benjamin Weiser, *Terrorist Has Cooperated with U.S. Since Secret Guilty Plea in 2011, Papers Show,* The New York Times, March 25, 2013 (www.nytimes.com/2013/03/ 26/nyregion/since-2011-guilty-plea-somali-terrorist-has-cooperated-with-authorities. html?module=inline); Adam Goldman and Benjamin Weiser, *How Civilian Prosecution Gave the U.S. a Key Informant,* The New York Times, January 27, 2017 (www.nytimes.com/2017/01/27/us/intelligence-gained-from-somali- terrorist-shows-value-of-civilian-prosecutions.html).

63. "Declaration & Memorandum of Law in Support of Motion to Suppress" (hereinafter "al-Liby Motion to Suppress"), at 11, United States v. Anas al Liby, 98-cr-1023 (LAK), Doc. 1743, Sept. 16, 2014.

64. Benjamin Weiser and Eric Schmitt, *U.S. Said to Hold Qaeda Suspect on Navy Ship,* The New York Times, October 6, 2013 (www.nytimes.com/2013/10/07/world/africa/a-ter rorism-suspect-long-known-to-prosecutors.html?_r=0); Adam Goldman, *Video Shows U.S. Abduction of Accused al-Qaeda Terrorist on Trial for Embassy Bombings,* The Washington Post, February 10, 2014 (https://wapo.st/2XZNt2u).

65. United States v. al Liby, "Motion to Suppress," Exhibit B. (In the 150-page indictment al-Liby is mentioned in "three paragraphs relating to conduct in 1993 and 1994, and nothing else," his lawyer said at al-Liby's arraignment. In those paragraphs, authorities alleged al-Liby met with al-Qaeda members about bombing the US Embassy in Kenya, which ended up happening five years later in 1998.); Deborah Feyerick and Lateef Mungin, *Alleged al Qaeda Operative Abu Anas al Libi Pleads Not Guilty,* CNN, October 15, 2013 (www.cnn.com/2013/10/15/justice/al-libi-case/index.html); Abu Anas al Liby, *al Qaeda Suspect Nabbed in Libya, Pleads Not Guilty to Terrorism Charges,*

CBS News, October 15, 2013 (www.cbsnews.com/news/abu-anas-al-liby-al-qaeda-suspect-nabbed-in-libya-pleads-not-guilty-to-terrorism-charges/).

66. United States v. al-Liby, al-Liby Motion to Suppress, at 11.
67. Al Liby Motion to Suppress, Exhibit A, Declaration of Support.
68. Al-Liby Motion to Suppress, at 11.
69. Benjamin Weiser and Michael S. Schmidt, *Qaeda Suspect Facing Trial in New York over Africa Embassy Bombings Dies*, The New York Times, January 3, 2015 (www.nytimes.com/2015/01/04/us/politics/qaeda-suspect-facing-trial-in-new-york-dies-in-custody.html); Christopher M. Matthews, *Libyan Seeks to Bar Self-Incriminating Statements from Bombing Trial*, Wall Street Journal, October 15, 2014 (www.wsj.com/articles/libyan-seeks-to-bar-self-incriminating-statements-from-bombing-trial-1413398405).
70. United States v. Khatallah, 275 F. Supp. 3d 32, 70 (D.D.C. 2017).
71. United States v. Khatallah, 275 F. Supp. 3d 32, 45 (D.D.C. 2017); Spencer S. Hsu, *Thirteen Days in the History of the Accused Leader of the Benghazi Attacks*, Washington Post, June 9, 2017 (https://wapo.st/2KXBXAZ).
72. United States v. Khatallah, "Transcript on Motions Hearing," Motion to Suppress Oral Argument, June 6, 2017, at 39–41, Case No. 1:14-cr-00141 (CRC) (Dist. Court. D.C.), Doc. 221, filed June 14, 2007, at 50, line 18. United States v. Khatallah, 275 F. Supp. 3d 32, 45 (D.D.C. 2017).
73. United States v. Khatallah, 275 F. Supp. 3d 32 (D.D.C. 2017).
74. United States v. Khatallah, 275 F. Supp. 3d 32, 45 (D.D.C. 2017); Spencer S. Hsu, *Thirteen Days in the History of the Accused Leader of the Benghazi Attacks*, Washington Post, June 9, 2017 (https://wapo.st/2KXBXAZ).
75. United States v. Khatallah, "Transcript on Motions Hearing," Motion to Suppress Oral Argument, June 6, 2017, pp. 39–41, Case No. 1:14-cr-00141 (CRC) (Dist. Court. D.C.), Doc. 221, filed June 14, 2007.
76. Pete Williams and Richard Esposito, *US Charges Libyan with Role in Deadly Attack on Benghazi Consulate*, NBC News, August 6, 2013 (http://investigations.nbcnews.com/_news/2013/08/06/19898418-us-charges-libyan-with-role-in-deadly-attack-on-benghazi-consulate?lite).
77. United States v. Khatallah, 275 F. Supp. 3d 32, 50; Karen DeYoung, Adam Goldman, and Julie Tate, *U.S. Captured Benghazi Suspect in Secret Raid*, Washington Post, June 17, 2014 (https://wapo.st/2XWKwj3).
78. Michael S. Schmidt and Eric Schmitt, *Suspect in Benghazi Attack Is Arraigned in U.S.*, The New York Times, June 28, 2014 (www.nytimes.com/2014/06/29/world/africa/libyan-suspected-in-benghazi-mission-attack-arrives-in-washington.html).
79. Spencer S. Hsu, *Libyan Militia Leader Gets 22-Year Sentence in Benghazi Attacks that Killed U.S. Ambassador*, Washington Post, June 27, 2018 (https://wapo.st/2RnuA7d).
80. United States v. Khatallah, "Transcript on Motions Hearing," Motion to Suppress Oral Argument, June 6, 2017, at 39–41, Case No. 1:14-cr-00141 (CRC) (Dist. Court. D.C.), Doc. 221, filed June 14, 2007. See also, United States v. Khatallah, 275 F. Supp. 3d 32 (D.D.C. 2017).
81. United States v. Khatallah, 275 F. Supp. 3d 32, 70 (D.D.C. 2017).
82. United States v. Khatallah, 275 F. Supp. 3d 32, 70 (D.D.C. 2017).
83. United States v. Khatallah, 275 F. Supp. 3d 32, 69 (D.D.C. 2017).
84. Spencer S. Hsu, *Libyan Militia Leader Gets 22-Year Sentence in Benghazi Attacks that Killed U.S. Ambassador*, Washington Post, June 27, 2018 (https://wapo.st/2RnuA7d). "Transcript on Motions Hearing," Motion to Suppress Oral Argument, June 6, 2017,

p. 11, United States v. Khatallah, 1:14-cr-00141 (CRC)(Dist. Court. D.C.), Doc. 221, filed June 14, 2007.

85. Miranda v. Arizona, 384 U.S. 436, 447, 86 S. Ct. 1602, 1613 (1966).
86. Miranda v. Arizona, 384 U.S. 436, 447, 86 S. Ct. 1614 (1966).
87. Miranda v. Arizona, 384 U.S. 436, 447, 86 S. Ct. 1602, 1624 (1966).
88. Fed. R. Crim. P. 5(a)(1)(B); See also 18 U.S.C. § 3501(c) (2012).
89. Corley v. United States, 556 U.S. 303, 307.
90. Corley v. United States, 556 U.S. 303, 308.
91. Corley v. United States, 556 U.S. 303, 309 and Upshaw v. United States, 335 U.S. 410, 413 (1948).
92. *Khatallah*, 275 F. Supp. 3d 32, 60.
93. *Khatallah*, 275 F. Supp. 3d 32, 59.
94. Seth Freed Wessler, *The Coast Guard's "Floating Guantánamos," The New York Times*, November 20, 2017 (www.nytimes.com/2017/11/20/magazine/the-coast-guards-floating-guantanamos.html).
95. Seth Freed Wessler, *The Coast Guard's "Floating Guantánamos," The New York Times*, November 20, 2017 (www.nytimes.com/2017/11/20/magazine/the-coast-guards-floating-guantanamos.html); Seth Wessler, *U.S. Coast Guard Detentions of Drug Smugglers "Violating International Law," and Canada May Be Complicit*, CBC, June 6, 2018 (www.cbc.ca/radio/thecurrent/coast-guard-detainees-canada-1.4673272). ("When it rained we were all soaked," said two of the detainees held on US Coast Guard ships who said they were forced to sleep outside. "They put cuffs on us, chained us up.")
96. Seth Freed Wessler, *The Coast Guard's "Floating Guantánamos," The New York Times*, November 20, 2017 (www.nytimes.com/2017/11/20/magazine/the-coast-guards-floating-guantanamos.html)
97. Seth Freed Wessler, *The Coast Guard's "Floating Guantánamos," The New York Times*, November 20, 2017 (www.nytimes.com/2017/11/20/magazine/the-coast-guards-floating-guantanamos.html)
98. Seth Freed Wessler, *The Coast Guard's "Floating Guantánamos," The New York Times*, November 20, 2017 (www.nytimes.com/2017/11/20/magazine/the-coast-guards-floating-guantanamos.html)
99. Seth Freed Wessler, *The Coast Guard's "Floating Guantánamos," The New York Times*, November 20, 2017 (www.nytimes.com/2017/11/20/magazine/the-coast-guards-floating-guantanamos.html)
100. Seth Freed Wessler, *The Coast Guard's "Floating Guantánamos," The New York Times*, November 20, 2017 (www.nytimes.com/2017/11/20/magazine/the-coast-guards-floating-guantanamos.html); Nick Miroff, *In Latin America, John Kelly Trained for a Job Serving Trump*, Washington Post, January 7, 2018 (https://wapo.st/2ZvWdO6).
101. Seth Freed Wessler, *The Coast Guard's "Floating Guantánamos," The New York Times*, November 20, 2017 (www.nytimes.com/2017/11/20/magazine/the-coast-guards-floating-guantanamos.html).
102. Seth Freed Wessler, *The Coast Guard's "Floating Guantánamos," The New York Times*, November 20, 2017 (www.nytimes.com/2017/11/20/magazine/the-coast-guards-floating-guantanamos.html).
103. Seth Freed Wessler, *The Coast Guard's "Floating Guantánamos," The New York Times*, November 20, 2017 (www.nytimes.com/2017/11/20/magazine/the-coast-guards-floating-guantanamos.html).

104. United States v. Mero, No. 4:17-CR-00067, 2017 U.S. Dist. LEXIS 180567 (E.D. Tex. Sep. 27, 2017), at 7 and 10.
105. United States v. Mero, No. 4:17-CR-00067, 2017 U.S. Dist. LEXIS 180567 (E.D. Tex. Sep. 27, 2017), at 9.
106. *Mero*, at 10, citing *Khatallah*, 275 F. Supp. 3d 32, 2017 U.S. Dist. LEXIS 130185, 2017 WL 3534989, at *14 (D.D.C. Aug. 16, 2017).
107. United States v. Mero, No. 4:17-CR-00067, 2017 U.S. Dist. LEXIS 180567 (E.D. Tex. Sep. 27, 2017), at 10–11.
108. United States v. Cheme-Ibarra, No. 14-cr-3305, 2016 U.S. Dist. LEXIS 189157 (S.D. Cal. June 3, 2016).
109. *Cheme-Ibarra*, 2016 U.S. Dist. LEXIS 189157, at 39–41. ("Defendants were tasked with showing that the process by which the indictment was secured violated due process in such a way that it was 'so grossly shocking and so outrageous as to violate the universal sense of justice,' yet they have fallen short of this high mark.")
110. *Cheme-Ibarra*, 2016 U.S. Dist. LEXIS 189157, at 39–41.
111. *Cheme-Ibarra*, 2016 U.S. Dist. LEXIS 189157, at 39–41.
112. United States v. Giler et al., "Transcript of Defendant's Motion to Suppress," Case No. 17-60032-CR-COHN, U.S.D.C. Southern Dist. Florida, Apr. 19, 2017, Doc. No. 59.
113. United States v. Giler et al., "Transcript of Defendant's Motion to Suppress," Doc. No. 59, at 35–36.
114. United States v. Giler et al., "Transcript of Defendant's Motion to Suppress," Doc. No. 59, at 33 and 36. Seth Freed Wessler, The Coast Guard's "Floating Guantánamos", The New York Times, November 20, 2017 (www.nytimes.com/2017/11/20/magazine/the-coast -guards-floating-guantanamos.html).
115. United States v. Giler et al., "Transcript of Defendant's Motion to Suppress," Case No. 17-60032-CR-COHN, U.S.D.C Southern Dist. Florida, Apr. 19, 2017, Document No. 59.
116. Seth Freed Wessler, *The Coast Guard's "Floating Guantánamos," The New York Times*, November 20, 2017 (www.nytimes.com/2017/11/20/magazine/the-coast-guards-floating-guantanamos.html); United States v. Khatallah, 275 F. Supp. 3d 32, 54 (D.D. C. 2017).
117. Seth Freed Wessler, *The Coast Guard's "Floating Guantánamos," The New York Times*, November 20, 2017 (www.nytimes.com/2017/11/20/magazine/the-coast-guards-floating-guantanamos.html).
118. Convention against Torture and Other Cruel, Inhuman or Degrading Treatment or Punishment (Convention against Torture), adopted Dec. 10, 1984, G.A. res. 39/46, annex, 39 U.N. GAOR Supp. (No. 51) at 197, U.N. Doc. A/39/51 (1984), entered into force June 26, 1987. International Covenant on Civil and Political Rights (ICCPR), adopted Dec. 16, 1966, G.A. Res. 2200A (XXI), 21 U.N. GAOR Supp. (No. 16), at 52, U.N. Doc. A/6316 (1966), 999 U.N.T.S. 171, entered into force Mar. 23, 1976, Arts. 7 and 10. See also Manfred Nowak, *U.N. Covenant on Civil and Political Rights CCPR Commentary*, 2nd ed., N.P. Engel, 2005), 164–66, para. 12 describing conditions and treatment which courts have found constitute cruel, inhumane, or degrading treatment, including, for example, deprivation of food together with other harsh treatment such as "incommunicado detention" and death threats, at 174, para 27, citing to the UN Standard Minimum Rules for the Treatment of Prisoners, which require prisoners have adequate floor space, cubic content for air for each prisoner, adequate sanitary facilities, non-degrading clothing, bed, and food; Brian Wilson, Human Rights and Maritime Law Enforcement, 52 Stan. J Int'l L. 243, Summer 2016, at 54, *citing* Australian Hum. Rts. Comm'n, Report of an Inquiry: Mr. Zacharias Manongga (September 2005),

in which the Australian Human Rights Commission found that Australia had violated ICCPR Article 10(1) in holding Indonesian fishermen for between sixteen days and one month in similar, though perhaps slightly better conditions, on Australian vessels in Darwin Harbour.

119. Nowak, at 245, para, 10 ("incommunicado" detention, for a few days "might be justified by the particular circumstances of the case, but in principle it constitutes a violation of the right of all detainees to be treated with humanity and dignity, as stipulated in [ICCPR] Art. 10(1). . . . Prolonged 'incommunicado' detention fairly soon reaches the threshold of cruel, inhuman and degrading treatment . . . and for a longer term, it even amounts to torture."

120. Seth Wessler, *U.S. Coast Guard Detentions of Drug Smugglers "Violating International Law," and Canada May Be Complicit,* CBC, June 6, 2018 (www.cbc.ca/radio/thecur rent/coast-guard-detainees-canada-1.4673272).

121. Seth Wessler, *U.S. Coast Guard Detentions of Drug Smugglers "Violating International Law," and Canada May Be Complicit,* CBC, June 6, 2018 (www.cbc.ca/radio/thecur rent/coast-guard-detainees-canada-1.4673272).

122. International Covenant on Civil and Political Rights (ICCPR), adopted Dec. 16, 1966, G.A. Res. 2200A (XXI), 21 U.N. GAOR Supp. (No. 16) at 52, U.N. Doc. A/6316 (1966), 999 U.N.T.S. 171, entered into force Mar. 23, 1976, art. 2.

123. Stephen I. Vladeck, *SYMPOSIUM: Terrorism Prosecutions and the Problem of Constitutional "Cross-Ruffing,"* 36 Cardozo Law Review, 709–710, supra, n. 58, 2014; See also, Jonathan Hafetz, *Detention at Sea: The Persistence of Territorial Constraints on Constitutional Rights, in Constitutionalism Across Borders in the Struggle against Terrorism,* eds. F. Fabbrini and V. Jackson, Elgar Publishing, 2016, 233, at 256–259.

124. Currently, however, under the *Ker-Frisbie* doctrine, the Supreme Court has held that a defendant's prior treatment will generally not provide grounds for dismissal of a criminal indictment. Hafetz, Detention at Sea, at 257. This does not preclude, however, a statutory remedy.

THE ZEALOTRY OF "TERRORISM"

* Attorney at Law, Durkin & Roberts, Chicago, Illinois. Fellow, The Center on National Security at Fordham Law. Distinguished Practitioner in Residence at the Loyola University Chicago School of Law, and Co-Director of its National Security and Civil Rights Program. BA, University of Notre Dame, 1968; JD University of San Francisco School of Law, 1973. Graduate Student at Large and Returning Scholar, University of Chicago, 2009–present. Law Clerk to the Honorable James Parsons, US District Judge for the Northern District of Illinois; Assistant US Attorney, Northern District of Illinois, 1978–1984. Fellow of the American College of Trial Lawyers. One of five lawyers selected nationwide to be a participant in the John Adams Project, a joint collaboration of the American Civil Liberties Union and the National Association of Criminal Defense Lawyers to provide civilian counsel in the case of United States v. Khalid Sheikh Mohammed, et al., before the Military Commissions Trial Judiciary, Guantánamo Bay, Cuba. *See* www.durkinroberts.com.

1. This chapter will be necessarily limited to domestic considerations. However, for a recent discussion of the impact US foreign policy and its constant preparation for and fighting of wars has on the erosion of civil liberties at home, see John

J. Mearsheimer, *The Great Delusion: Liberal Dreams and International Realities*, Yale University Press, 182–185, 2018.

2. On the "no" side, see, *e.g.*, Eric Posner and Adrian Vermuele, *Terror in the Balance: Security, Liberty, and the Courts*, Oxford University Press, 2007 (argues that the government should be given wide latitude to adjust policy and liberties in the times of emergency, emphasizing the virtues of unilateral executive actions and argue for making extensive powers available to the executive); on the "yes" side, see, *e.g.*, *Owen Fiss, A War Like No Other: The Constitution in a Time of Terror*, New Press, 2015 (argues in defense of traditional civil liberties under law and critiques judicial, legislative, and administrative abrogation of basic rights). See also Richard C. Leone and Greg Anrig Jr., ed., *The Wars on Our Freedoms: Civil Liberties in an Age of Terror*, Century Foundation, 2003 and Jules Lobel, *The War on Terrorism and Civil Liberties*, 63 U. Pitt Law Rev., 767, 778–790, 2002.

3. Certainly, from the standpoint of belief in an indulgent judiciary, the debacle of the polarized confirmation hearings over US Supreme Court Justice Brett Kavanaugh has not helped matters. Kavanaugh's prior appellate court opinions on executive authority in the Guantánamo litigation controversy do not bode well either.

4. Resubtitled *Archetype of the Apocalypse: Divine Vengeance, Terrorism, and the End of the World*, ed. George R. Elder, Open Court, 2002 for the paperback edition. Elder also wrote the book's introduction.

5. This letter was dated May 1995 and made available to the editor of Edinger's *Archetype* and set forth in full on page xvii of the Editor's Preface.

6. The irony that President George W. Bush would resort to the same "axis of evil" language in his 2002 State of the Union Address in describing Iran, Iraq, and North Korea would not have been lost on Edinger. See https://web.archive.org/web/20090502151928/http:/georgewbush-whitehouse.archives.gov/news/releases/2002/01/20020129–11.html.

7. Edinger, *Archetype*, xvii.

8. Edinger, xvii.

9. Edinger, xvii. Zealot is the term used by the Roman writer Flavius Josephus, translating the Hebrew kanai, to refer to a "fourth sect" of Judaism (the others were the familiar Pharisees, Sadducees, and the Essenes), freedom fighters, or fighters for national liberation against the Romans. Flavius Josephus, *The Antiquities of the Jews*, Bk. II, trans. William Whiston, Wilder Pubs., 2018. Edition was first published in 1737, and it is believed that Josephus wrote it circa 93–94 CE. They existed from about 4 CE to 70 CE, when the Romans destroyed the Second Temple and surviving Zealots made a last stand and committed group suicide on the Masada. Simon the Zealot is listed among the Apostles in Luke 6:15 and Acts 1:13.

10. Edinger, xvii.

11. See, *e.g.*, *The 9/11 Commission Report: Final Report of the National Commission on Terrorist Attacks Upon the United States*, W. W. Norton, 161, 2004. I limit comment on these events to declassified and publicly available sources, referring to my own participation only where necessary.

12. See Thomas Anthony Durkin, *Apocalyptic War Rhetoric: Drugs, Narco-Terrorism, and a Federal Court Nightmare From Here to Guantanamo*, 2 Notre Dame J. Int'l & Comp. L., 257, 2012, and Durkin, *Permanent States of Exception: A Two-Tiered System of Criminal Justice Courtesy of the Double Government Wars on Crime, Drugs & Terror* 50 Valparaiso University L. Rev. 419–492, 2016.

13. Durkin, *Apocalyptic War Rhetoric*, 257–281. Many of these very exceptional or emergency measures have now seeped into and have become normalized in routine federal criminal prosecutions. See Durkin, Permanent States of Exception, 461 and footnote 198 (citing

Stephen I. Vladeck, *Normalizing Guantanamo* 48 Am. Crim. Law Rev., 4, 1547–1572, 2011. ("Over the past decade, a growing chorus of courts and commentators has expressed concern that doctrinal accommodations reached in post-9/11 terrorism cases might spill over or 'seep' into more conventional bodies of jurisprudence.") See also DAVID DYZENHAUS, THE CONSTITUTION OF LAW: LEGALITY IN A TIME OF EMERGENCY Cambridge University Press, 23, 2006.

14. Carl Schmitt, *Political Theology: Four Chapters on The Concept of Sovereignty*, trans. George Schwab, University of Chicago Press, 2005 [1922, 1934, 2nd ed.].

15. Schmitt, 5.

16. Schmitt, 6.

17. Schmitt, 6.

18. Schmitt, 7, emphasis added.

19. Schmitt, 7.

20. Schmitt, 11–12.

21. Schmitt, 11–12.

22. When the Reichstag burned down under suspicious circumstances on Feb. 27, 1933, Hitler maneuvered the president, the World War I hero Paul von Hindenburg, into invoking Article 48, suspending the protections in the Constitution, and leading immediately to Hindenburg's sidelining and the circumvention of parliament. William Shirer, *The Rise and Fall of the Third Reich*, Simon and Schuster, 191–196, 1960; Alan Bullock, *Hitler: A Study in Tyranny*, rev. ed., Harper Torchbooks, 262–270, 1962.

23. Schmitt, *Political Theology*, 13, 32.

24. Schmitt, 33–34, 47–48, 68.

25. Giorgio Agamben, *State of Exception*, trans. Kevin Attell, University of Chicago Press, 2005.

26. Agamben, *State of Exception*, 21.

27. See Michael J. Glennon's thorough analysis of the continuation of these policies throughout the Obama Administration: *National Security and Double Government*, 5 HARV. NAT'L SEC. J. 1, 1, 2014 (introducing the "double government" theory); see also his MICHAEL J. GLENNON, NATIONAL SECURITY AND DOUBLE GOVERNMENT 4 (Oxford Univ. Press 2015). . Glennon's explanation of the underlying systemic causes of this phenomenon, notwithstanding very opposing political differences, certainly applies to the Trump Administration as well. For examples of comment on the same carry-over in the Trump Administration, see Donna Starr-Deelen, *Double Government, National Security Powers, and the Trump Administration* SSRN, Feb. 20, 2017, https://ssrn.com/abstract=2927314; A. Percy Sherwood, *Tracing the American State of Exception from the George W. Bush, Barack Obama, and Donald Trump Presidencies*, 8 W. J. Legal Stud. 1, 2018. As late as October 2018, President Donald Trump threatened to send the US Army to the border of Mexico to assist in halting the so-called Central American "migrant caravan" heading to the border to seek asylum – all in the name of national security. See Trump Considering Plan to Ban Entry of Migrants at Southern Border, Deny Asylum, *Washington Post*, Oct. 25, 2018. Purported national security concerns over the failure of Congress to approve the funding for the building of Trump's wall lead to a government shutdown. To make his national security point, President Trump scheduled a bipartisan Congressional meeting to resolve the shutdown in the Situation Room.

28. Agamben, *State of Exception*, note 24, at 3. The order itself is titled "Presidential Military Order, Detention, Treatment and Trial of Certain Non-Citizens in the War Against Terrorism."

29. See Al Warafi v. Obama, 716 F. 3d 627, 632 (D.C. Cir., 2013). This is a remarkable opinion for a number of reasons, not the least of which is the fact that the government submitted a letter from President Obama himself, 15, which contradicts his rather unequivocal

statements to the public, 15. The court accuses al-Warafi of "blinkered logic" for suggesting that it take the president at his unambiguous word. The opinion is worth reading in its entirety to see how absurd the mess at Guantánamo has made all things legal.

30. Agamben, *State of Exception*, note 24, at 3–4.
31. Agamben, note 24, at 4.
32. Agamben, note 24, at 4. While I would once never have dreamed it possible or appropriate, I chose to begin a reply brief in the Guantánamo case by citing Agamben's rather bold statement in its entirety. See Nasser v. Obama; Case 1:05-cv-00764-CKK, Document #261, filed on Jan. 18, 2017. Suffice it to say, it did not provoke a response from the court in denying the motion.
33. Agamben, note 24, at 32, citing Carl Schmitt, *Dictatorship*, trans. Michael Hoelzl and Graham Ward, Polity Press, 2014 [1921].
34. Agamben, note 24, at 32. For a discussion of dictatorship in the context of constitutional democracies, see the classic work of Clinton L. Rossiter, *Constitutional Dictatorship: Crisis Government in the Modern Democracies*, 1948. *See also* Sanford Levinson, *Constitutional Norms in a State Off Permanent Emergency* 40 Georgia Law Rev., 699, 2006. Rossiter asks a quite poignant question as to whether we might have an intelligent adult discussion about this topic so that "an intelligent decision might be made as to the very kind of political order in which we wish to live." Levinson, supra, at 701–702. My answer, now some twelve years later, is sadly in the negative: Thomas Anthony Durkin, *Apocalyptic War Rhetoric*, 466–467.
35. Agamben, *State of Exception*, § 1.8, 23.
36. Agamben, § 1.2, 3.
37. Bernard Harcourt, *The Counterrevolution: How Our Government Went to War against Its Own Citizens* Basic Books, 2018.
38. Harcourt, 222.
39. Harcourt, 222.
40. Harcourt, 223.
41. Harcourt, 223.
42. Harcourt, 222. Harcourt's analysis of Foucault's negotiation of relationships of power, his historical analysis of the turning of legally ambiguous acts into legal violations, and the continued pushing of boundaries of the law as wealth became increasingly mobile after the French Revolution is well worth reading in this context. See Harcourt, *The Counterrevolution*, note 35, at 224–226, citing Michel Foucault, *The Punitive Society: Lectures at the Collège de France, 1972–1973*.
43. Harcourt, 237.
44. Harcourt, 237, citing Karen Greenberg, *Rogue Justice: The Making of the Security State*, Crown, 2016.
45. Harcourt, 237, citing Greenberg, *Rogue Justice*.
46. Dyzenhaus, *The Constitution of Law*, note 3, at 6.
47. Dyzenhaus, 19.
48. Dyzenhaus, 19.
49. Our client, Abdul Latif Nasser, has been identified in GTMO as ISN #244. As the detainees were taken off the cargo planes that transported them from Afghanistan in 2002, they were assigned numbers in the order they were deplaned.
50. This was passed on Sept. 18, 2001, repeated annually thereafter and codified at 50 U.S.C. § 1541 (note). The AUMF stated that that the president may use "appropriate and necessary" force "against those nations, organizations, or persons he determines planned,

authorized, committed, [] aided[, or harbored] the terrorist attacks that occurred on September 11, 2001."

51. Suhail Abdu Anam v. Donald J. Trump, No. 1: 04-cv-00194 (D.D.C., July 11, 2018) (transcript), 36.

52. Suhail Abdu Anam v. Donald J. Trump, No. 1: 04-cv-00194 (D.D.C., July 11, 2018) (transcript), 36–37.

53. Suhail Abdu Anam v. Donald J. Trump, No. 1: 04-cv-00194 (D.D.C., July 11, 2018) (transcript), 63.

54. "It is an ongoing issue that the Court and all the judges who handle these cases would like to see resolved in some reasonable time frame." Suhail Abdu Anam v. Donald J. Trump, No. 1: 04-cv-00194 (D.D.C., July 11, 2018) (transcript), 70. To date, Judge Hogan has yet to rule.

55. For a far more detailed and inside baseball account of the law involving FISA and the tortured history of the government's interlocutory appeal of Judge Coleman's order to the Seventh Circuit Court of Appeals, see Durkin, Permanent States of Exception, 466–467. It is also recommended that for those unfamiliar with the use of classified evidence in the courts, or what has become known in some quarters as "secret evidence," review the Seventh Circuit's classified opinion, attached to the article. To this day neither the defense nor the public has any idea what factual basis underlies the court's conclusions. The mere visualization of a *formal* court opinion covered page after page by grease pencil is usually shocking to the uninitiated.

56. Durkin, *Apocalyptic War Rhetoric*, 421, 2012, noting that this insight was suggested by Professor David Dyzenhaus in his thoughtful work *The Constitution of Law*. Speaking in the context of the UK's Emergency Act of 1937, Dyzenhaus admits it possible that courts are no longer capable of doing their job of "maintaining the integrity of the legal order." David Dyzenhaus, *The Constitution of Law*, 23.

57. Durkin, Permanent States of Exception, 419–492. It is of no small consequence to this discussion that the Department of Justice Counterterrorism and Counterespionage Sections were taken out of the Criminal Division chain of command and merged into a newly created National Security Division as part of the USA PATRIOT Improvement and Reauthorization Act of 2006. This Act created the Senate confirmation position of Assistant Attorney General (AAG) for National Security. This chain of command bypasses the AAG of the Criminal Division and requires the approval of the Director of National Intelligence before the presidential recommendation for appointment. The AAG remains as a supervisory authority over the conduct of the case from its inception until its conclusion, including appeal.

58. Sadly, a frequent question defense lawyers ask each other, particularly those who do national security work, is how much longer we can keep banging our heads against the wall. This is not a rhetorical question, as the question that goes with the first one is whether we are becoming complicit in a system that has essentially become corrupt.

59. See, for example, a child pornography conviction based upon evidence seized under the Foreign Intelligence Surveillance Act (FISA): US. v. Gartenlaub, No. 16-50339 (9th Cir. Oct. 2, 2018, citation of unpublished opinion); see, also, Marcy Wheeler, *FISA Court Secrecy Threatens to Subsume Our Open Court System*, Motherboard, Dec. 14, 2017.

60. Osama bin Laden, *Declaration of War on the Americans Occupying the Land of the Two Holy Places*, 1996, www.mideastweb.org/osamabinladen1.htm. The two holy places are Mecca and Medina, both in Saudi Arabia. Up until 2003, the US had several military bases in Saudi Arabia, one quite close to Mecca, but withdrew these in deference to Muslim (but not bin Laden's) ill-feeling about the US military presence in that country.

In addition to this grievance, bin Laden listed others, including killing of Muslims by "your Zionist brothers" (Israel) in Lebanon, Israeli fiddling with the al-Aqsa Mosque in Jerusalem, the loss of al-Quds (Jerusalem itself), Iraqi deaths due to Clinton's sanctions against Iraq, and oppression of Palestinians. The language, addressed to believers, is rather fraught, but bin Laden's letter "To the American People," circulated on the internet, although invoking religion, is written is a sober and matter-of-fact way, but asks Americans to embrace the traditions, not of Islam, but of our own Founders, www .theguardian.com/world/2002/nov/24/theobserver.

61. Address to the Nation, Washington Post, Sept. 11, 2006 (Cong. Quarterly Transcriptions, 2006), www.washingtonpost.com/wp-dyn/content/article/2006/09/11/AR2006091100775.html (emphasis added). The "Clash of Civilizations" language comes from Harvard Professor Samuel P. Huntington's book, *The Clash of Civilizations and the Remaking of the World Order*, Simon and Schuster, 1998, arguing that Cold War of the "Free World" against "Communism" had been replaced with the clash of the "civilized" West and the uncivilized world of Islam, unironically repeating as if they were real the tropes that the Lebanese scholar Edward Said of Columbia University had exposed and demolished in his classic *Orientalism*, Vintage, 1979. Huntington said that "ideas of individualism, liberalism, constitutionalism, human rights, equality, liberty, the rule of law, democracy, free markets, [and] the separation of church and state" often have "little resonance in Islamic, Confucian, Japanese, Hindu, Buddhist or Orthodox cultures." Id., 40. That is, the rest of the world.

62. Gregory Jusdanis, *The Necessary Nation*, Princeton University Press, 31, 2001.

63. Peter Sahlins, *Boundaries: The Making of France and Spain in the Pyrenees*, University of California Press, 269, 1989.

64. Ernst H. Kantorowicz, *The King's Two Bodies: A Study in Medieval Political Theology*, Princeton University Press, 234, 1957.

65. Arno J. Mayer, *The Furies: Violence and Terror in the Frenchand Russian Revolutions*, Princeton University Press, 141, 2000.

66. Mayer, *The Furies*, 141.

67. Mayer, 151.

68. John Gray, *Seven Types of Atheism*, Farrar, Straus and Giroux, 2018.

69. Gray, *Seven Types of Atheism*, 71.

70. Edward Edinger, *The Creation of Consciousness: Jung's Myth for Modern Man*, Inner City Books, 9–10, 1988.

71. Edinger, *The Creation of Consciousness*, 9–10.

72. Edinger, 10.

73. Edinger, 10–11. W. B. Yeats' poem is quoted in the text. For our purposes the following lines are pertinent: "the falcon cannot hear the falconer, and the center cannot hold." Yeats writes, "Mere anarchy is loosed upon the world./The blood-dimmed tide is loosed, and everywhere/The ceremony of innocence is drowned;/The best lack all conviction, while the worst/Are full of passionate intensity."

74. Edinger, 174–177. His own words are quite a bit more graphic: "[T]he process of transformation of the God-image can take place only if its human participants are *conscious* of what is happening, because consciousness is the agency of transformation for God and man. There is, of course, no transformation of the God-image if we end up with nothing but a heap of ruins and a group of savages having to make the laborious climb to civilization all over again. But the God-image can incarnate in a way that averts mass destruction if there are enough individuals aware of the unfolding archetypal drama that is before us." Id.

75. Edinger, *The Creation of Consciousness*, 179.

REIMAGINING THE NATIONAL SECURITY STATE: ILLUSIONS
AND CONSTRAINTS

1. Robert Malley and Jon Finer, "The Long Shadow of 9/11 – How Counterterrorism Warps U.S. Foreign Policy," *Foreign Affairs*, July/August 2018, available at www .foreignaffairs.com/articles/2018–06-14/long-shadow-911. Mr. Malley is the president and CEO of the International Crisis Group, and during the Obama administration he served as special assistant to the president, White House Middle East coordinator, and senior adviser on countering the Islamic State. Mr. Finer served as chief of staff and director of policy planning at the US Department of State during the Obama administration. *See also* Alex Nowrasteh, "More Americans Die in Animal Attacks Than in Terrorist Attacks," *Cato at Liberty, The Cato Institute*, March 8, 2018, available at www .cato.org/blog/more-americans-die-animal-attacks-terrorist-attacks. ("One reason people fear terrorism so much is that it appears random and there is little one can do to avoid it.").
2. *See* John Mueller and Mark G. Stewart, "Public Opinion and Counterterrorism Policy," *The Cato Institute*, 2018, available at www.cato.org/publications/white-paper/public-opinion-counterterrorism-policy.
3. Peter Bergen, Albert Ford, Alyssa Sims, and David Sterman, "Terrorism in America After 9/11," *New America*, available at www.newamerica.org/in-depth/terrorism-in-america/what-threat-united-states-today/.
4. Estelle Sommeiller and Mark Price, "The New Gilded Age: Income Inequality in the U.S. by State, Metropolitan Area, and County," *Economic Policy Institute*, July 19, 2018, available at www.epi.org/publication/the-new-gilded-age-income-inequality-in-the-u-s-by-state-metropolitan-area-and-county/.
5. *Id.*
6. *Id.*
7. *Id.*
8. *See* "New visionaries and the Chinese Century Billionaires insights 2018," United Bank of Switzerland and PwC, 2018, available at www.ubs.com/global/en/wealth-manage ment/uhnw/billionaires-report/_jcr_content/mainpar/toplevelgrid/col1/innergrid/xcol1/ actionbutton.0920626462.file/bGluay9wYXRoPS9jb250ZW50L2RhbS9hc3 NldHMvd2ovZ2xvYmFsL3VobncvZG9jL3Vicy1wd2MtYmlsbGlvbmFpcmVzLWluc2lna HRzLTIwMTgucGRm/ubs-pwc-billionaires-insights-2018.pdf. *See also* www.ubs.com/glo bal/en/wealth-management/uhnw/billionaires-report.html (links to annual reports); David Brennan, "The Rich Get Richer: 2017 Was Best Year for Billionaires in Recorded History with U.S. Leading the Way," *Newsweek*, October 26, 2018, available at www.newsweek.com /rich-get-richer-2017-was-best-year-billionaires-recorded-history-us-leading-1188645.
9. *Id.*
10. *Id.*
11. *Id.*
12. *See* Richard J. Whelan, "Joseph P. Kennedy: A Portrait of the Founder (Fortune Classics, 1963)," *Forbes*, April 10, 2011, available at http://fortune.com/2011/04/10/ joseph-p-kennedy-a-portrait-of-the-founder-fortune-classics-1963/.
13. Eduardo Porter, "The Profound Social Cost of American Exceptionalism," *The New York Times*, May 30, 2018, available at www.nytimes.com/2018/05/29/business/ economy/social-cost-american-exceptionalism.html.
14. *Id.*

15. *Id.*
16. *Id.* Porter laments that "[t]he United States is one of the richest, most technologically advanced nations in the history of humanity. And yet it accepts – proudly defends, even – a degree of social dysfunction that would be intolerable in any other rich society." *Id.*
17. *Id.*
18. *Id.*
19. *Id.*
20. Eduardo Porter and Karl Russell, "It's an Unequal World. It Doesn't Have to Be," *The New York Times,* December 14, 2017, available at www.nytimes.com/interactive/2017/12/14/business/world-inequality.html.
21. *Id. See* Facundo Alvaredo, Lucas Chancel, Thomas Piketty, Emmanuel Saez, and Gabriel Zucman, "World Inequality Report 2018," World Inequality Lab, available at https://wir2018.wid.world/files/download/wir2018-full-report-english.pdf.
22. *Id.* Porter also notes that the United States has not set a good example: If the United States's trends continue, "by 2050 the few at the top of the pyramid would be drawing 28 percent of global income. The bottom half would get only about 6 percent." *Id.*
23. Brennan, "The Rich Get Richer," 2018.
24. Rana Foroohar, "US and China Must Find Ways to Control Their Elites," *Financial Times,* July 1, 2018, available at www.ft.com/content/24a64504-7ba9-11e8-bc55-50daf11b720d . *See also id.* (*citing* Mancur Olson's *The Rise and Decline of Nations* (Yale University Press, 1982), in which "the economist argues that civilisations tend to decline when the moneyed interests take over politics").
25. Brennan, "The Rich Get Richer," 2018.
26. A. Q. Smith, "It's Basically Just Immoral to Be Rich," *Current Affairs,* June 14, 2017, available at www.currentaffairs.org/2017/06/its-basically-just-immoral-to-be-rich.
27. *Id.* Smith explains that what he is "arguing about is not the question of how much people should be given, but the morality of their retaining it after it is given to them." *Id.*
28. Princeton University Press, 2017.
29. "Can Inequality Only Be Fixed by War, Revolution or Plague?" *The Economist,* September 10, 2018, available at www.economist.com/open-future/2018/09/10/can-inequality-only-be-fixed-by-war-revolution-or-plague?fsrc=scn/fb/te/bl/ed/howtofixinequalityopenfuture.
30. *Id.*
31. Grace Guarnieri, "Billionaires Earned Enough Money in 2017 to End Extreme Poverty Seven Times Over, Report Says," *Newsweek,* January 22, 2018, available at www.newsweek.com/billionaires-money-end-poverty-report-786675, *citing* "Reward Work, Not Wealth," January 2018, available at www.oxfam.org/sites/www.oxfam.org/files/file_attachments/bp-reward-work-not-wealth-220118-en.pdf.
32. *See* A. Q. Smith, "It's Basically Just Immoral to Be Rich," *Current Affairs,* June 14, 2017, available at www.currentaffairs.org/2017/06/its-basically-just-immoral-to-be-rich, *citing* www.forbes.com/sites/laurashin/2015/03/26/the-racial-wealth-gap-why-atypical-white-household-has-16-times-the-wealth-of-a-black-one/#1ebc0b181f45.
33. Dedrick Asante-Muhammad, Chuck Collins, Josh Hoxie, and Emanuel Nieves, "The Ever-Growing Gap," CFED Racial Wealth Divide Initiative and the Institute for Policy Studies, August 2016, available at https://ips-dc.org/wp-content/uploads/2016/08/The-Ever-Growing-Gap-CFED_IPS-Final-1.pdf.

34. *Id.* at 8.

35. *Id.* at 5.

36. *Id.*

37. *Id.*

38. Devah Pager and Bruce Western, *Race at Work – Realities of Race and Criminal Record in the NYC Job Market*, 2005, at 12, available at https://scholar.harvard.edu/files/pager/files/race_at_work.pdf.

39. *Id.* at 6.

40. *Id.*

41. *Id.*

42. *Id.*

43. *Id.* at 6.

44. Katharine Q. Seelye, "Devah Pager Dies at 46; Exposed Shocking Race Bias in the Job Market," *The New York Times*, November 9, 2018, available at www.nytimes.com/2018/11/08/obituaries/devah-pager-dead.html.

45. Tom Loveless, "Racial Disparities in School Suspensions," *Brookings*, Friday, March 24, 2017, available at www.brookings.edu/blog/brown-center-chalkboard/2017/03/24/racial-disparities-in-school-suspensions/; "How Well Are American Students Learning?" The 2017 Brown Center Report on American Education, Vol. 3, No. 6, March 2017, available at www.brookings.edu/wp-content/uploads/2017/03/2017-brown-center-report-on-american-education.pdf.

46. *See* US Sentencing Commission, *Demographic Differences in Sentencing: An Update to the 2012 Booker Report*, at 2, available at www.ussc.gov/sites/default/files/pdf/research-and-publications/research-publications/2017/20171114_Demographics.pdf. *See also id.* (Violence in an offender's criminal history does not appear to account for any of the demographic differences in sentencing. Black male offenders received sentences on average 20.4 percent longer than similarly situated white male offenders, accounting for violence in an offender's past in fiscal year 2016, the only year for which such data are available. This figure is almost the same as the 20.7 percent difference without accounting for past violence. Thus, violence in an offender's criminal history does not appear to contribute to the sentence imposed to any extent beyond its contribution to the offender's criminal history score determined under the federal Sentencing Guidelines.).

47. "Redlining" is defined "as a discriminatory practice by which banks, insurance companies, etc., refuse or limit loans, mortgages, insurance, etc., within specific geographic areas, especially inner-city neighborhoods." *See* dictionary.com. While redlining has been illegal for fifty years, the Trump administration has proposed relaxing the banking rules that prevent the practice. *See* Rachel Louise Ensign and Ryan Tracy, "Trump Administration Seeks to Change Rules on Bank Lending to the Poor," *The Wall Street Journal*, January 10, 2018, available at www.wsj.com/articles/trump-administration-seeks-to-change-rules-on-bank-lending-to-the-poor-1515624418.

48. *See* US Census Bureau, Quick Facts, as of July 1, 2017, available at www.census.gov/quickfacts/fact/table/US/PST045217. *See also* Besheer Mohamed, "New estimates show U.S. Muslim population continues to grow," *Fact Tank: News in the Numbers*, January 3, 2018, available at www.pewresearch.org/fact-tank/2018/01/03/new-estimates-show-u-s-muslim-population-continues-to-grow/.

49. *See* "Black Identity Extremists Likely Motivated to Target Law Enforcement Officers," available at www.documentcloud.org/documents/4067711-BIE-Redacted.html. *See also* Jana Winter and Sharon Weinberger, "The FBI's New U.S. Terrorist Threat: 'Black Identity Extremists,'" *Foreign Policy*, October 6, 2017, available at http://foreignpolicy

.com/2017/10/06/the-fbi-has-identified-a-new-domestic-terrorist-threat-and-its-black-identity-extremists/.

50. Daniel White, "Nearly 20% of Trump Fans Think Freeing the Slaves Was a Bad Idea," *Time*, February 24, 2016, available at http://time.com/4236640/donald-trump-racist-supporters/.

51. See Adam Serwer, "America's Problem Isn't Tribalism – It's Racism," *The Atlantic*, November 7, 2018, available at www.theatlantic.com/ideas/archive/2018/11/racism-not-tribalism/575173/.

52. A few years ago, the American Bar Association instituted an "Implicit Bias Initiative," *see* www.americanbar.org/groups/litigation/initiatives/task-force-implicit-bias.html. *See also* Sarah E. Redfield, ed., *Enhancing Justice: Reducing Bias* (ABA Book Publishing, 2017) (including chapters by Judge Bernice Donald, Court of Appeals for the Sixth Circuit, and Judge Mark W. Bennett, District Judge for the Northern District of Iowa). *See* https://shop.americanbar.org/ebus/store/productdetails.aspx?productid=273962668.

53. Mikhail Lyubansky, "Studies of Unconscious Bias: Racism Not Always by Racists," *Psychology Today*, April 26, 2012, available at www.psychologytoday.com/us/blog/between-the-lines/201204/studies-unconscious-bias-racism-not-always-racists; Keith Payne, Laura Niemi, and John M. Doris, "How to Think About 'Implicit Bias,'" *Scientific American*, March 27, 2018, available at www.scientificamerican.com/article/how-to-think-about-implicit-bias/.

54. Regarding the second question, A. Q. Smith provides a dramatic example:
       Larry Ellison of Oracle could put his $55 billion in a fund that could be used to just give houses to black families, not quite as direct "reparations" but simply as a means of addressing the fact that the average white family has a house while the average black family does not. But instead of doing this, Larry Ellison bought the island of Lanai.
    A. Q. Smith, "It's Basically Just Immoral to Be Rich," *Current Affairs*, June 14, 2017, available at www.currentaffairs.org/2017/06/its-basically-just-immoral-to-be-rich, *citing* Jon Mooallem, "Larry Ellison Bought an Island in Hawaii. Now What?," *The New York Times*, September 23, 2014, available at www.nytimes.com/2014/09/28/magazine/larry-ellison-island-hawaii.html?_r=0.

55. *See* Nathan J. Robinson, "Slavery Was Very Recent," *Current Affairs*, October 20, 2016, available at www.currentaffairs.org/2016/10/slavery-was-very-recent.

56. *See* www.abrahamlincolnonline.org/lincoln/speeches/inaug2.htm.

57. Richard Clarke, *Cyberwar* (HarperCollins: 2010); Mark Bowden, *Worm: The First Digital World War* (Grove Press: 2012); David E. Sanger, *The Perfect Weapon* (Crown: 2018); Zero Days (Magnolia Pictures: 2016). *See also* Phillip Bantz, "Risky Business: What's Worrying Execs in Different Regions of the World?," *New York Law Journal*, November 15, 2018, available at www.law.com/corpcounsel/2018/11/13/risky-business-whats-worrying-execs-in-different-regions-of-the-world/ (World Economic Forum's 12th annual "Regional Risks for Doing Business" study finds that "cyberattacks represented the No. 1 business risk in the United States, bumping the threat of terrorist attacks, which ranked first last year, down to second place.").

58. Rebecca Smith and Bob Barry, "America's Electric Grid Has a Vulnerable Back Door—and Russia Walked Through It," *The Wall Street Journal*, January 10, 2019, available at www.wsj.com/articles/americas-electric-grid-has-a-vulnerable-back-doorand-russia-walked-through-it-11547137112 .

59. *See, e.g.*, Alan Blinder and Nicole Perlroth, "A Cyberattack Hobbles Atlanta, and Security Experts Shudder," *The New York Times*, March 27, 2018, available at www.nytimes.com/2018/03/27/us/cyberattack-atlanta-ransomware.html.
60. Natasha Turak, "The Next 9/11 Will Be a Cyberattack, Security Expert Warns," *CNBC*, June 1, 2018, available at www.cnbc.com/2018/06/01/the-next-911-will-be-a-cyberattack-security-expert-warns.html.
61. James Patchett, Opinion, "Danger of a Cyberattack on New York," *The New York Times*, April 10, 2018, available at www.nytimes.com/2018/04/10/opinion/cyberattack-new-york.html.
62. Paul Mee and Til Schuermann, "How a Cyber Attack Could Cause the Next Financial Crisis," Harvard Business Review, September 14, 2018, available at https://hbr.org/2018/09/how-a-cyber-attack-could-cause-the-next-financial-crisis.
63. *See* Indictment, United States v. Netyksho, available at www.justice.gov/file/1080281/download.
64. Dustin Volz and Aruna Viswanatha, "FBI Says Chinese Espionage Poses 'Most Severe' Threat to American Security," *The Wall Street Journal*, updated December 12, 2018, available at www.wsj.com/articles/senate-sifts-evidence-of-chinese-cyberespionage-11544635251.
65. James Patchett, Opinion, "Danger of a Cyberattack on New York, *The New York Times*, April 10, 2018, available at www.nytimes.com/2018/04/10/opinion/cyberattack-new-york.html. *See also* Matt Palmquist, "The Risks and Costs of Cyber-Attacks," *Strategy + Business*, May 9, 2018, available at www.strategy-business.com/blog/The-Risks-and-Costs-of-Cyber-Attacks.
66. *See, e.g.*, Scott Holcomb, "Election Security Is an Immediate National Security Concern," *Just Security*, October 31, 2018, available at www.justsecurity.org/61293/election-security-national-security-concern/; Benjamin Dynkin, Barry Dynkin, and Daniel Garrie, "Hacking Elections: An Act of War?" *The New York Law Journal*, June 5, 2017, available at www.newyorklawjournal.com/printerfriendly/id=1202788705366. *See also* United States v. Internet Research Agency, 18 Cr. 32 (DLF) (D.D.C.), available at www.justice.gov/file/1035477/download; United States v. Netyksho, 215 (ABJ) (D.D.C.), available at www.justice.gov/file/1080281/download.
67. Scott Bomboy, "The Drama behind President Kennedy's 1960 Election Win," National Constitution Center, November 7, 2017, available at https://constitutioncenter.org/blog/the-drama-behind-president-kennedys-1960-election-win/; Jeffrey Toobin, Too Close to Call (Random House: 2001).
68. "The Panama Papers: Giant Leak of Offshore Financial Records Exposes Global Array of Crime and Corruption," International Consortium of Investigative Journalists, April 3, 2016, available at www.icij.org/investigations/panama-papers/.
69. Michael Chertoff and Eileen Donahoe, "Commentary: For Election Hackers, a New and More Dangerous Tool," *Reuters*, November 12, 2018, available at www.reuters.com/article/us-chertoffdonahoe-hacking-commentary/commentary-for-election-hackers-a-new-and-more-dangerous-tool-idUSKCN1NH1W2 (discussing "deep fake" videos).
70. *See* Paul Mozur, "A Genocide Incited on Facebook, with Posts from Myanmar's Military," *The New York Times*, October 15, 2018, available at www.nytimes.com/2018/10/15/technology/myanmar-facebook-genocide.html. Such incitement of a local population to commit genocide had previously relied on radio, as in Rwanda in 1994. Philip Gourevitch, *We Wish to Inform You That Tomorrow We Will Be Killed with Our Families* (Farrar, Straus and Giroux: 1998); Meghan Lyon, "Radio in the

Rwandan Genocide," *Duke University Libraries,* May 10, 2013, available at https://blogs.library.duke.edu/rubenstein/2013/05/10/radio-in-the-rwandan-genocide/.

71. Bruce Schneier, *Click Here to Kill Everybody: Security and Survival in a Hyper-Connected World* (W. W. Norton & Company: 2018).

72. *See* Sean Berg, "Utilizing the Human Element to Mitigate Today's Sophisticated Cyber Threat Landscape," *Atlantic Council,* November 14, 2018, available at www.atlanticcouncil.org/blogs/new-atlanticist/utilizing-the-human-element-to-mitigate-today-s-sophisticated-cyber-threat-landscape.

73. The Maginot Line was an "elaborate defensive barrier in northeast France constructed in the 1930s and named after its principal creator, André Maginot, who was France's minister of war in 1929–31." *See* www.britannica.com/topic/Maginot-Line. A reaction to German aggression in World War I, "unfortunately, the line covered the French-German frontier, but not the French-Belgian. Thus the Germans in May 1940 out-flanked the line." *Id.*

74. *See Verizon 2017 Data Breach Investigations Report,* 10th edn., at 3, available at https://enterprise.verizon.com/resources/reports/2017_dbir.pdf (Forty-three percent of data breaches in 2017 were "social attacks.").

75. *See* Dustin Volz, "Trump, Seeking to Relax Rules on U.S. Cyberattacks, Reverses Obama Directive," *The Wall Street Journal,* August 15, 2018, available at www.wsj.com/articles/trump-seeking-to-relax-rules-on-u-s-cyberattacks-reverses-obama-directive-1534378721 .

76. Dustin Volz, "Trump Move to Loosen U.S. Use of Cyberweapons Prompts Intrigue," *The Wall Street Journal,* August 16, 2018, available at www.wsj.com/articles/trump-move-to-loosen-u-s-use-of-cyber-weapons-prompts-intrigue-1534456712 .

77. *See, e.g.,* James Rainey, "The Trump Administration Scrubs Climate Change Info from Websites. These two have survived," NBC News, July 17, 2018, available at www.nbcnews.com/news/us-news/two-government-websites-climate-change-survive-trump-era-n891806; Jonathan M. Samet, and Alistair Woodward, "National Government Denial of Climate Change and State and Local Public Health Action in a Federalist System," Am. J. Public Health, April 2018, 108 (Supp 2), available at www.ncbi.nlm.nih.gov/pmc/articles/PMC5922214/.

78. *See* Department of Defense, *Climate Change Adaptation Roadmap,* June 2014, Foreword, available at www.acq.osd.mil/eie/downloads/CCARprint_wForward_e.pdf.

79. *Id.*

80. *Id.*

81. *Id.*

82. *Fourth National Climate Assessment – Volume II: Impacts, Risks, and Adaptation in the United States,* November 2018, available at https://nca2018.globalchange.gov/. *See also* Coral Davenport and Kendra Pierre-Louis, "U.S. Climate Report Warns of Damaged Environment and Shrinking Economy," *The New York Times,* November 23, 2018, available at https://nyti.ms/2zmesuU.

83. Daniel Farber, "From Surviving to Thriving – FEMA and Disaster Resilience," *Center for Progressive Reform Blog,* September 10, 2018, available at www.progressivereform.org/CPRBlog.cfm?keyword=FEMA.

84. Eric Levenson, "How Coastal Development and Climate Change Are Making Hurricanes More Costly," *CNN,* September 13, 2018, available at www.cnn.com/2018/09/12/us/hurricane-damage-cost-coast-development/index.html.

85. *Id. See also* Kara Dapena, "The Rising Costs of Hurricanes," *The Wall Street Journal*, September 29, 2018, available at www.wsj.com/articles/the-rising-costs-of-hurricanes -1538222400. *See also Roadmap* (Pentagon also "studying the implications of increased demand for our National Guard in the aftermath of extreme weather events.").

86. *See* John Schwartz and Richard Fausset, "North Carolina, Warned of Rising Seas, Chose to Favor Development," *The New York Times*, September 12, 2018, available at www.nytimes.com/2018/09/12/us/north-carolina-coast-hurricane.html.

87. Eric Levenson, "How Coastal Development and Climate Change Are Making Hurricanes More Costly," *CNN*, September 13, 2018, available at www.cnn.com/2018/ 09/12/us/hurricane-damage-cost-coast-development/index.html.

88. *Id.*

89. Troy D. Allen, "Katrina: Race, Class, and Poverty: Reflections and Analysis," *Journal of Black Studies*, Vol. 37, No. 4 (March 2007), 466–468, available at https://journals .sagepub.com/doi/abs/10.1177/0021934706296184; Eleanor Krause and Richard V. Reeves, "Hurricanes Hit the Poor the Hardest," *Brookings*, September 18, 2017, available at www.brookings.edu/blog/social-mobility-memos/2017/09/18/hurricanes-hit-the-poor-the-hardest/. *See also* Bill McKibben, "How Extreme Weather Is Shrinking the Planet," *The New Yorker*, November 26, 2018, available at www.newyorker.com/maga zine/2018/11/26/how-extreme-weather-is-shrinking-the-planet.

90. Somini Sengupta and Kendra Pierre-Louis, "Study Warns of Cascading Health Risks from the Changing Climate," *The New York Times*, November 28, 2018, available at www.nytimes.com/2018/11/28/climate/climate-change-health.html. *See* "The 2018 Report of the Lancet Countdown on Health and Climate Change: Shaping the Health of Nations for Centuries to Come," *The Lancet*, November 28, 2018, available at www.thelancet.com/journals/lancet/article/ PIIS0140-6736(18)32594–7/fulltext.

91. *Id.*

92. Climate change, regardless of the underlying cause, has historically been a harbinger of significant change and dislocation. *See, e.g.,* Eric H. Cline, *1177 B.C. – The Year Civilization Collapsed* (Princeton University Press, 2014); Geoffrey Parker, *Global Crisis* (Yale University Press, 2013).

93. *See* Bill McKibben, "How Extreme Weather Is Shrinking the Planet," *The New Yorker*, November 26, 2018, available at www.newyorker.com/magazine/2018/11/26/how-extreme -weather-is-shrinking-the-planet.

94. Joshua Hammer, "Is a Lack of Water to Blame for the Conflict in Syria?," *Smithsonian Magazine*, June 2013, available at www.smithsonianmag.com/innovation/is-a-lack-of-water-to-blame-for-the-conflict-in-syria-72513729/.

95. Colin P. Kelley, Shahrzad Mohtadi, Mark A. Cane, Richard Seager, and Yochanan Kushnir, "Climate Change in the Fertile Crescent and Implications of the Recent Syrian Drought," *Proceedings of the National Academy of Sciences*, March 17, 2015, 3241–3246, at 3241, available at www.pnas.org/content/pnas/112/11/3241.full.pdf. See also Peter H. Gleick, "Water, Drought, Climate Change, and Conflict in Syria," *Weather, Climate, and Society*, February 2014, available at https://journals.ametsoc.org /doi/pdf/10.1175/WCAS-D-13–00059.1 ("Water and climatic conditions have played a direct role in the deterioration of Syria's economic conditions" and are relevant to the conflict there.); Henry Fountain, "Researchers Link Syrian Conflict to a Drought Made Worse by Climate Change," *The New York Times*, March 2, 2015, available at www.nytimes.com/2015/03/03/science/earth/study-links-syria-conflict-to-drought -caused-by-climate-change.html.

96. *Id.*
97. *Id.*
98. *See* Hadil Mohamed, Moosa Elayeh, Lau Schuplen, "Yemen between the Impact of the Climate Change and the Ongoing Saudi-Yemen War: A Real Tragedy," Centre for Governance and Peace-building-Yemen, November 2017, available at https://docs .google.com/viewer?url=https%3A%2F%2Fwww.ru.nl%2Fpublish%2Fpages% 2F871321%2Fa_real_tragedy.pdf&fname=a_real_tragedy.pdf&pdf=true.   *See also* Amanda Erickson, "Yemen is on the brink of a horrible famine. Here's how things got so bad," *The Washington Post*, November 19, 2017, available at www .washingtonpost.com/news/worldviews/wp/2017/11/19/yemen-is-on-the-brink-of-a-horri ble-famine-heres-how-things-got-so-bad; Margaret Suter, "Running Out of Water: Conflict and Water Scarcity in Yemen and Syria," *Atlantic Council*, September 12, 2017, available at www.atlanticcouncil.org/blogs/menasource/running-out-of-water-conflict-and-water-scarcity-in-yemen-and-syria.
99. Jeffrey Collins, "'Nature's Mutiny' Review: Tracking History's Turbulence," *The Wall Street Journal*, March 1, 2019, available at www.wsj.com/articles/natures-mutiny-review-tracking-historys-turbulence-11551450505?mod=searchresults&page=1&pos=1, *reviewing* Philipp Blom, *Nature's Mutiny* (Liveright, 2019); Glenn D. Rudebusch, "Climate Change and the Federal Reserve," *Federal Reserve Bank of San Francisco Economic Letter*, Number 2019–09, March 25, 2019, available at www.frbsf.org/eco nomic-research/files/el2019-09.pdf. *See also* Steve Matthews, "Fed Researcher Warns Climate Change Could Spur Financial Crisis," *Bloomberg*, March 25, 2019, available at www.bloomberg.com/news/articles/2019-03-25/fed-researcher-warns-climate-change-could-spur-financial-crisis; Ellen Mitchell, "Pentagon Releases List of Military Bases Most at Risk to Climate Change," *The Hill*, March 27, 2019, available at https://thehill .com/policy/defense/436098-pentagon-releases-list-of-military-bases-most-at-risk-to-climate-change.
100. Matthew J. Belvedere, "Trump Asks Why US Can't Use Nukes: MSNBC," *CNBC.com*, August 3, 2016, available at www.cnbc.com/2016/08/03/trump-asks-why-us-cant-use-nukes-msnbcs-joe-scarborough-reports.html.
101. *See* John Bolton, "The Legal Case for Striking North Korea First," *The Wall Street Journal*, February 28, 2018, available at www.wsj.com/articles/the-legal-case-for-striking-north-korea-first-1519862374.
102. *See, e.g.,* Jonathan Cheng, "North Korea Keeping Up Work on Missile Sites, Report Says," *The Wall Street Journal*, November 12, 2018, available at www.wsj.com/articles/north-korea-keeping-up-work-on-missile-sites-report-says-1542039838; Geoff Brumfiel, "North Korean Denuclearization Plan Has Gone Nowhere since Trump Kim Summit," *NPR*, November 19, 2018, available at www.npr.org/2018/11/19/668625273/north-korea-denuclearization-plan-has-gone-nowhere-since-trump-kim-summit.
103. *See* Julian Borger and Martin Pengelley, "Trump Says US will Withdraw from Nuclear Arms Treaty with Russia," *The Guardian*, October 20, 2018, available at www .theguardian.com/world/2018/oct/20/trump-us-nuclear-arms-treaty-russia; Alex Leary and Peter Nicholas, "Trump Says U.S. to Withdraw from Nuclear Treaty with Russia," *The Wall Street Journal*, October 20, 2018, available at www.wsj.com/arti cles/trump-threatens-to-withdraw-u-s-from-nuclear-arms-treaty-with-russia -1540078280.
104. *See* Rick Gladstone, "In Bipartisan Pleas, Experts Urge Trump to Save Nuclear Treaty with Russia," *The New York Times*, November 8, 2018, available at www.nytimes.com /2018/11/08/world/europe/trump-russia-arms-treaty.html; Andrew Roth, "Fragmenting

Nuclear Arms Controls Leave World in a More Dangerous Place," *The Guardian*, January 3, 2019, available at www.theguardian.com/world/2019/jan/03/fragmenting-nuclear-arms-controls-leave-world-in-a-more-dangerous-place; Vladimir Isachenkov, "Putin Issues Ominous Warning on Rising Nuclear War Threat," *APNews*, December 20, 2018, available at https://apnews.com/deaa45c70d3c4da98410 d5a3ec309510 (Russian President Vladimir Putin "pointed at Washington's intention to walk away from the 1987 Intermediate-Range Nuclear Forces Treaty, or INF, and its reluctance to negotiate the extension of the 2010 New START agreement, which expires in 2021 unless the two countries agree to extend it. 'We are witnessing the breakup of the arms control system,'" he said.); Michael R. Gordon, "As One Arms Treaty Falls Apart, Others Look Shakier," *The Wall Street Journal*, December 7, 2018, available at www .wsj.com/articles/looming-demise-of-a-nuclear-treaty-threatens-to-upend-others -1544187603.

105. Peggy Noonan, "We Must Improve Our Trust," *The Wall Street Journal*, May 31, 2018, available at www.wsj.com/articles/we-must-improve-our-trust-1527808866.

106. *Id.*

107. *Id.*

108. *Id.*

109. *See* Mitchell Lerner, "The key factor in the rise of Trumpism that we continue to ignore," The Washington Post, January 2, 2019, available at www.washingtonpost.com /outlook/2019/01/02/key-factor-rise-trumpism-that-we-continue-ignore/.

110. *See, e.g.*, Suzy Hansen, "Unlearning the Myth of American Innocence," *The Guardian*, August 8, 2017, available at www.theguardian.com/us-news/2017/aug/08/unlearning-the-myth-of-american-innocence.

111. Les Moonves, at the time CEO of CBS, "reinforced the perception in February [2016]" that the media were cultivating and nourishing Trump because coverage of him improved ratings when Moonves "said at a conference in San Francisco that the Trump spectacle 'may not be good for America, but it's damn good for CBS.'" Callum Borchers, "Yes, Donald Trump Has Been Good for the Media Business," *The Washington Post*, October 25, 2016, available at www.washingtonpost.com/news/the-fix /wp/2016/10/25/yes-donald-trump-has-been-good-for-the-media-business. In 2016, Moonves received $69.6 million in compensation from CBS, and essentially the same in 2017. *See* George Szalai, "CBS CEO Leslie Moonves' Pay Virtually Unchanged at $69.3 Million for 2017," *Hollywood Reporter*, April 6, 2018, available at www .hollywoodreporter.com/news/cbs-ceo-leslie-moonves-pay-virtually-unchanged-at-693-million-2017-1093742. Apparently, the good of the country was not worth sacrificing a few million.

112. Tim Wu, "Be Afraid of Economic 'Bigness.' Be Very Afraid," *The New York Times*, November 10, 2018, available at www.nytimes.com/2018/11/10/opinion/sunday/fascism-economy-monopoly.html.

113. *Id.*

114. *Id.*

115. *Id.*

116. *Id.*

117. *Id.*

118. *Id.*

119. *Id.*

120. According to investopedia.com, "dark money refers to the funds donated to non-profit organizations that in turn spend it in order to influence elections. These nonprofit organizations can receive an unlimited amount of donations, and they're not required to disclose their donors." *See* www.investopedia.com/terms/d/dark-money.asp.

121. George Monbiot, "Dark Money Lurks at the Heart of Our Political Crisis," *The Guardian*, July 18, 2018, available at www.theguardian.com/commentisfree/2018/jul/18/dark-money-democracy-political-crisis-institute-economic-affairs. George Monbiot argues that

> [t]he techniques now being used to throw elections and referendums were developed by the tobacco industry, and refined by biotechnology, fossil fuel and junk food companies. Some of us have spent years exposing the fake grassroots campaigns they established, the false identities and bogus scientific controversies they created, and the way in which media outlets have been played by them. Our warnings went unheeded, while the ultrarich learned how to buy the political system.

122. Suresh Naidu, Eric A. Posner, and E. Glen Weyl, "Antitrust Remedies for Labor Market Power," *Harvard Law Review*, May 30, 2019, available at https://harvardlawreview.org/2018/12/antitrust-remedies-for-labor-market-power/.

123. *Id. See also* Jared Bernstein, "Why Real Wages Still Aren't Rising," Opinion, *The New York Times*, July 18, 2018, available at www.nytimes.com/2018/07/18/opinion/wage-stagnation-unemployment-economic-growth.html?smprod=nytcore-ipad&smid=nytcore-ipad-share ("Stagnant wages for factory workers and non-managers in the service sector – together they represent 82 percent of the labor force – is mainly the outcome of a long power struggle that workers are losing."); David Leonhardt, "The Monopolization of America," Opinion, *The New York Times*, November 25, 2018, available at www.nytimes.com/2018/11/25/opinion/monopolies-in-the-us.html.

124. Tim Wu, "Be Afraid of Economic 'Bigness.' Be Very Afraid," *The New York Times*, November 10, 2018, available at www.nytimes.com/2018/11/10/opinion/sunday/fascism-economy-monopoly.html.

125. *Id. See also* Steve Denning, "How To Fix Stagnant Wages: Dump The World's Dumbest Idea," *Forbes*, July 26, 2018, available at www.forbes.com/sites/stevedenning/2018/07/26/how-to-fix-stagnant-wages-dump-the-worlds-dumbest-idea/#5971a8ca1abc. ("The implications [of wage stagnation] are dire for global political stability: resentment among middle- and lower-class workers has already given rise to populist leaders in both the U.S. and parts of Europe. Unless the problem is solved, more trouble lies ahead.").

126. *See also* Chris Hedges, "The Coming Collapse," *Common Dreams*, May 21, 2018, available at www.commondreams.org/views/2018/05/21/coming-collapse. ("It is impossible for any doomed population to grasp how fragile the decayed financial, social and political system is on the eve of implosion.").

127. The United States's most recent cholera outbreak occurred in 1910–1911 in New York City. During the mid-nineteenth century, periodic cholera outbreaks in the United States sometimes claimed between two and six lives each day. *See* "The Most Dangerous Epidemics in U.S. History," available at www.healthline.com/health/worst-disease-outbreaks-history#1.

128. Perhaps the most potent proof of just how distant the dread of these deadly diseases has become in the US is the rise of an anti-vaccination movement – the equivalent of reacting to the extraordinary safety record of commercial aviation in the past decade by dispensing with maintenance and inspection of aircraft.

129. Robert Malley and Jon Finer, "The Long Shadow of 9/11 – How Counterterrorism Warps U.S. Foreign Policy," *Foreign Affairs*, July/August 2018, available at www.foreignaffairs.com/articles/2018–06-14/long-shadow-911.

130. *Id.*

131. *Id.*

132. Max Roser, Mohamed Nagdy, and Hannah Ritchie, "Terrorism," OurWorldInData.org, January 2018, available at https://ourworldindata.org/terrorism. Nor was the United States in the top ten countries in which terrorism attacks occurred either prior to 9/11 (from 1970 through 9/11) or afterward. *Id.*

133. Peter Bergen, Albert Ford, Alyssa Sims, and David Sterman, "Terrorism in America after 9/11," *New America*, available at www.newamerica.org/in-depth/terrorism-in-america/what-threat-united-states-today/.

134. Neta C. Crawford, "Human Cost of the Post-9/11 Wars: Lethality and the Need for Transparency," Brown University, Watson Institute for International & Public Affairs, November 2018, available at https://watson.brown.edu/costsofwar/files/cow/imce/papers/2018/Human%20Costs%2C%20Nov%208%202018%20CoW.pdf.

135. Erin Durkin, "'A National Emergency': Suicide Rate Spikes among Young US Veterans," *The Guardian*, September 26, 2018, available at www.theguardian.com/us-news/2018/sep/26/suicide-rate-young-us-veterans-jumps (more than 6,000 US military veteran suicides each year since 2008); Nese F. DeBruyne, Senior Research Librarian "American War and Military Operations Casualties: Lists and Statistics," *Congressional Research Service*, Updated September 14, 2018, available at https://fas.org/sgp/crs/natsec/RL32492.pdf. *See also* Dave Philipps, "In Unit Stalked By Suicide, Veterans Try to Save One Another," *The New York Times*, September 19, 2015, available at http://nyti.ms/1V1idqK.

136. *See* Eve Bower, "American Deaths in Terrorism vs. Gun Violence in One Graph," *CNN*, October 3, 2016, available at www.cnn.com/2016/10/03/us/terrorism-gun-violence/index.html. *See also* Nurith Aizenman, "Deaths from Gun Violence: How the U.S. Compares with the Rest of the World," *NPR*, November 9, 2018, available at www.npr.org/sections/goatsandsoda/2018/11/09/666209430/deaths-from-gun-violence-how-the-u-s-compares-with-the-rest-of-the-world (The United States has a higher rate of gun violence deaths than Afghanistan, Iraq, or Syria); Jacqueline Howard, "Gun Deaths in US Reach Highest Level in Nearly 40 Years, CDC Data Reveal," *CNN*, December 13, 2018, available at www.cnn.com/2018/12/13/health/gun-deaths-highest-40-years-cdc/index.html.

137. *See* Stimson Study Group, "Counterterrorism Spending: Protecting America While Promoting Efficiencies and Accountability," May 2018, at 7, n. 7, available at www.stimson.org/sites/default/files/file-attachments/CT_Spending_Report_0.pdf. *See also* Josh Katz and Margot Sanger-Katz, "'The Numbers Are So Staggering.' Overdose Deaths Set a Record Last Year," *The New York Times*, November 29, 2018, available at www.nytimes.com/interactive/2018/11/29/upshot/fentanyl-drug-overdose-deaths.html.

138. *See* Adrienne Roberts, "U.S. Road-Death Rates Remain Near 10-Year High," *The Wall Street Journal*, February 15, 2018, available at www.wsj.com/articles/death-rates-on-u-s-roads-remain-near-10-year-high-1518692401 (National Safety Council figures).

139. Betsy McKay, "U.S. Life Expectancy Falls Further," *The Wall Street Journal*, November 29, 2018, available at www.wsj.com/articles/u-s-life-expectancy-falls-further-1543467660 ("Data the Centers for Disease Control and Prevention ... show life expectancy fell by one-tenth of a year, to 78.6 years, pushed down by the sharpest annual increase in suicides in nearly a decade and a continued rise in deaths from powerful

opioid drugs like fentanyl."); Colin Dwyer, "U.S. Life Expectancy Drops Amid 'Disturbing' Rise in Overdoses and Suicides," *NPR*, November 29, 2018, available at www.npr.org/2018/11/29/671844884/u-s-life-expectancy-drops-amid-disturbing-rise-in-overdoses-and-suicides. ("More than 70,000 people died of drug overdoses last year alone, according to the CDC. That number marks a nearly 10 percent increase from 2016 and the highest ever in the United States for a single year. By comparison, only about 17,000 people died of overdoses in 1999, the earliest year for which the CDC offered data."), *citing* www.cdc.gov/nchs/data/databriefs/db329_tables-508.pdf#1.

140. "American Deaths in Terrorist Attacks, 1995–2016," University of Maryland, START National Consortium for the Study of Terrorism and Responses to Terrorism, November 2017, available at www.start.umd.edu/pubs/ START_AmericanTerrorismDeaths_FactSheet_Nov2017.pdf.

141. Jared A. Forrester, Thomas G. Weiser, Joseph D. Forrester, "An Update on Fatalities Due to Venomous and Nonvenomous Animals in the United States (2008–2015)," *Wilderness & Environmental Journal*, Vol. 19, No. 1: 36–44, March 2018, available at www.wemjournal.org/article/S1080-6032(17)30313-7/fulltext.

142. *Id. See also* Robert Malley and Jon Finer, Foreign Affairs, "The Long Shadow of 9/11– How Counterterrorism Warps U.S. Foreign Policy," July/August 2018, available at www.foreignaffairs.com/articles/2018–06-14/long-shadow-911 (Americans consider terrorism a principal threat "despite the fact that they were less likely to fall victim to a terrorist attack by a refugee than be hit by lightning, eaten by a shark, or struck by an asteroid.").

143. *See* Michael Harriott, "White Supremacists Killed More People in U.S. in 2017 than Muslims, Antifa and Kneeling NFL Players Combined," *The Root*, January 18, 2018, available at www.theroot.com/white-supremacists-killed-more-people-in-2017-than-musl-1822193008; Jennifer Hansler, "Terrorism Deaths Down in 2017, but Far-Right Terrorism Rising, Report Says," *CNN*, December 5, 2018, available at www.cnn.com /2018/12/05/politics/global-terrorism-index-2018/index.html ("The 2018 Global Terrorism Index found that deaths resulting from terrorism decreased 27% worldwide last year. Ninety-six of the 163 countries tracked by the index saw an improvement; 46 had declines. Sixty-seven countries had at least one death from terrorism in 2017 – a drop from 2016's record high rate of 79 countries, according to the report" by the Institute for Economics & Peace, "a nonpartisan think tank that develops metrics to study peace and its economic impact.").

144. Emily Atkin, "A Database Showed Far-Right Terror on the Rise. Then Trump Defunded It," *The New Republic*, January 3, 2019, available at https://newrepublic .com/article/152675/database-showed-far-right-terror-rise-trump-defunded-it.

145. Charles Kurzman, "Counting Terrorists: The Urgent Need for Comprehensive Data," *Lawfare*, January 23, 2018, available at www.lawfareblog.com/counting-terrorists-urgent-need-comprehensive-data. Charles Kurzman is a professor of sociology at the University of North Carolina at Chapel Hill.

146. Robert Malley and Jon Finer, "The Long Shadow of 9/11 – How Counterterrorism Warps U.S. Foreign Policy," *Foreign Affairs*, July/August 2018, available at www .foreignaffairs.com/articles/2018–06-14/long-shadow-911.

147. *Id.*

148. *Id.*

149. Neta C. Crawford, "Human Cost of the Post-9/11 Wars: Lethality and the Need for Transparency," Brown University, Watson Institute for International and Public Affairs, November 2018, at 1, available at https://watson.brown.edu/costsofwar/files/cow/imce/ papers/2018/Human%20Costs%2C%20Nov%208%202018%20CoW.pdf.

150. *Id. See also id.* ("For example, tens of thousands of civilians may have died in retaking Mosul and other cities from ISIS but their bodies have likely not been recovered.").

151. *Id.*

152. *See Costs of War – Figures,* Brown University, Watson Institute for International & Public Affairs, November 2018, available at https://watson.brown.edu/costsofwar/figures/ 2018/direct-war-death-toll-2001–480000.

153. *See, e.g., "War of Annihilation" – Devastating Toll on Civilians, Raqqa – Syria,"* Amnesty International, June 5, 2018, available at www.amnesty.org/download/ Documents/MDE2483672018ENGLISH.PDF; Micah Zenko, "America Is Committing War Crimes and Doesn't Even Know Why," *Foreign Policy,* August 15, 2018, available at https://foreignpolicy.com/2018/08/15/america-is-committing-awful-war -crimes-and-it-doesnt-even-know-why/; Declan Walsh, "U.N.-Brokered Hudaydah Truce Is Big Step in Yemen War," *The New York Times,* December 13, 2018, available at www.nytimes.com/2018/12/13/world/middleeast/yemen-ceasefire-un.html. ("A child dies every 10 minutes in Yemen from preventable causes, according to Unicef.").

154. And it continues, and even worsens, as these conflicts persist. *See, e.g.,* Mujib Mashal and Taimoor Shah, "At Least a Dozen Civilians Killed in Afghan and U.S. Operation," *The New York Times,* November 28, 2018, available at www.nytimes.com/2018/11/28/ world/asia/afghanistan-civilians-killed.html?smprod=nytcore-ipad&smid=nytcore-ipad-share; Mujib Mashal, "C.I.A.'s Afghan Forces Leave a Trail of Abuse and Anger," *The New York Times,* December 31, 2018, available at www.nytimes.com/2018/12/31/ world/asia/cia-afghanistan-strike-force.html?smprod=nytcore-ipad&smid=nytcore-ipad-share (C.I.A.'s Afghan forces have "operated unconstrained by battlefield rules designed to protect civilians, conducting night raids, torture and killings with near impunity, in a covert campaign that some Afghan and American officials say is undermining the wider American effort to strengthen Afghan institutions.").

155. Neta C. Crawford, "Human Cost of the Post-9/11 Wars: Lethality and the Need for Transparency," Brown University, Watson Institute for International and Public Affairs, November 2018, available at https://watson.brown.edu/costsofwar/files/cow/imce/ papers/2018/Human%20Costs%2C%20Nov%208%202018%20CoW.pdf.

156. *Id.*

157. *See* Stimson Study Group, "Counterterrorism Spending: Protecting America While Promoting Efficiencies and Accountability," May 2018, available at www.stimson.org /content/counterterrorism-spending-protecting-america-while-promoting-efficiencies-and-accountability.

158. *Id. See also id.* ("Of $18 trillion in discretionary spending between fiscal years 2002–2017, [counterterrorism] spending made up nearly 16 percent of the whole.[] At its peak in 2008, [counterterrorism] spending amounted to 22 percent of total discretionary spending. By 2017, [counterterrorism] spending had fallen to 14 percent of the total.") (footnote omitted).

159. *Id.*

160. *Id.*

161. *Id. See also* Dave Lindorff, "Exclusive: The Pentagon's Massive Accounting Fraud Exposed," The Nation, November 27, 2018, available at www.thenation.com/article/ pentagon-audit-budget-fraud/.

162. *Id.*
163. Eben Kaplan, "Homeland Security Technologies," Council on Foreign Relations, November 16, 2007, available at www.cfr.org/backgrounder/homeland-security-technologies.
164. Dana Priest and William M. Arkin, *Top Secret America*, (Little Brown, 2011). *See also* Paul Harris, "How Private Firms Have Cashed In on the climate of Fear since 9/11," *The Guardian*, September 11, 2011, available at www.theguardian.com/world/2011/sep/05/private-firms-fear-9-11.
165. Carl Schmitt, *Political Theology*, trans. George Schwab (University of Chicago Press, 1985), at 5.
166. Robert Malley and Jon Finer, "The Long Shadow of 9/11 – How Counterterrorism Warps U.S. Foreign Policy," *Foreign Affairs*, July/August 2018, available at www.foreignaffairs.com/articles/2018–06-14/long-shadow-911.
167. *Id.*
168. Gareth Porter, "America's Permanent-War Complex," *The American Conservative*, November 15, 2018, available at www.theamericanconservative.com/articles/americas-permanent-war-complex/. *See also* Robert Malley and Jon Finer, "The Long Shadow of 9/11 – How Counterterrorism Warps U.S. Foreign Policy," *Foreign Affairs*, July/August 2018, available at www.foreignaffairs.com/articles/2018–06-14/long-shadow-911. (The United States "is engaged in more military operations, in more places, against more such groups than ever before: in Afghanistan, Iraq, Libya, Niger, Somalia, Syria, Yemen, and the Sahel region, to name a few.").
169. *See* www.worldometers.info/geography/how-many-countries-are-there-in-the-world/. That total includes Taiwan.
170. Kelley Beacar Vlahos, "Targeted Killing, Donald Trump Style," *The American Conservative*, June 4, 2018, available at www.theamericanconservative.com/articles/targeted-killing-donald-trump-style/.
171. *See* Watson Institute for International and Public Affairs, Mapping a World from Hell: 76 Countries Are Now Involved in Washington's War on Terror," January 10, 2018, available at https://watson.brown.edu/costsofwar/news/2018/mapping-world-hell-76-countries-are-now-involved-washingtons-war-terror.
172. Nick Turse, "US Military Says It Has a 'Light Footprint' in Africa. These Documents Show a Vast Network of Bases," *The Intercept*, December 1, 2018, available at https://theintercept.com/2018/12/01/u-s-military-says-it-has-a-light-footprint-in-africa-these-documents-show-a-vast-network-of-bases/.
173. Gareth Porter, "America's Permanent-War Complex," *The American Conservative*, November 15, 2018, available at www.theamericanconservative.com/articles/americas-permanent-war-complex/.
174. *Id.*
175. *Id.*
176. *See* www.defense.gov. *See also* Paul Szoldra, "Trump's Pentagon Quietly Made a Change to the Stated Mission It's Had for Two Decades," *Task & Purpose*, June 29, 2018, available at https://taskandpurpose.com/pentagon-mission/.
177. *Id.*
178. Kelley Beacar Vlahos, "Targeted Killing, Donald Trump Style," *The American Conservative*, June 4, 2018, available at www.theamericanconservative.com/articles/targeted-killing-donald-trump-style/.
179. *Id.*

180. *Id. See also* Spencer Ackerman, "Trump Ramped Up Drone Strikes in America's Shadow Wars," *The Daily Beast*, November 25, 2018, available at www .thedailybeast.com/trump-ramped-up-drone-strikes-in-americas-shadow-wars.

181. Vlahos, "Targeted Killing, Donald Trump Style." *The American Conservative* article also complains that information is released only "in fits and starts to a public that is distracted by a 24-hour news cycle obsessed more with Stormy Daniels and Russia-gate than the fact that in places like Iraq and Syria, where we are not technically 'at war,' there were nearly 30,000 U.S.-led coalition airstrikes over the last four years." *Id. See also* Azmat Khan and Anand Gopal, "The Uncounted," *The New York Times Magazine*, November 16, 2017, available at https://nyti.ms/2hCRlq7 (reporting on civilian casualties in Iraq in coalition air strikes against ISIS); Daphne Eviatar, "US Military Admits It Killed Dozens More Civilians than Previously Acknowledged. Now What?" *Just Security*, August 22, 2018, available at www.justsecurity.org/60413/military-admits-killed-dozens-civilians-previously-acknowledged-what/ ("Repeatedly the U.S.-led Coalition used weapons and tactics in the battle that caused disproportionate civilian deaths and destruction."); Loren DeJonge Schulman, "Precision and Civilian Casualties: Policymakers Believe Drones Can Be Precise. That May Not Be Enough," *Just Security*, August 2, 2018, available at www.justsecurity.org/59909/precision-civilian-casualties-policymakers-drones-precise-enough/; Loren DeJonge Schulman, *Behind the Magical Thinking*, Center for a New American Security, July 31, 2018, available at www.cnas.org/publications/reports/behind-the-magical-thinking; *Agence France Presse*, "23 Civilians Killed in US Air Strike in Southern Afghanistan, UN Investigation Confirms," *South China Morning Post*, November 30, 2018, available at www .scmp.com/news/world/middle-east/article/2175841/23-civilians-killed-us-air-strike-southern-afghanistan-un ("Initial findings indicate that the vast majority of the victims were women and children," according to the UN.).

182. Louis Menand, "What Went Wrong in Vietnam," *The New Yorker*, February 26, 2018, available at www.newyorker.com/magazine/2018/02/26/what-went-wrong-in-vietnam.

183. Robert Malley and Jon Finer, "The Long Shadow of 9/11– How Counterterrorism Warps U.S. Foreign Policy," *Foreign Affairs*, July/August 2018, available at www .foreignaffairs.com/articles/2018–06-14/long-shadow-911.

184. *Id. See also* Associated Press, "The Hidden Toll of American Drones in Yemen: Civilian Deaths, " *Haaretz*, November 15, 2018, available at www.haaretz.com/middle-east-news /the-hidden-toll-of-american-drones-in-yemen-civilian-deaths-1.6656362.

185. Gareth Porter, "America's Permanent-War Complex," *The American Conservative*, November 15, 2018, available at www.theamericanconservative.com/articles/americas-permanent-war-complex/.

186. *Id.*

187. Sune Engel Rasmussen and Salah al-Batati, "Al Qaeda Bids for Revival in Yemen," *The Wall Street Journal*, November 22, 2018, available at www.wsj.com/articles/yemens-war-opens-way-for-al-qaedas-revival-1542895200.

188. David A. Love, "A State of Perpetual War," *Huffington Post*, March 18, 2010, available at www.huffingtonpost.com/david-a-love/a-state-of-perpetual-war_b_422616.html.

189. *See* Robert F. Worth, "What If PTSD Is More Physical Than Psychological?" *The New York Times Magazine*, June 10, 2016, available at https://nyti.ms/1TYYp6U. Researchers have found scarring in the brain arguably attributable to exposure to explosions not only on the battlefield but in training. *See* Ben Kesling, "Weapons Training Likely Causes Brain Injury in Troops, Study Says," *The Wall Street Journal*, April 30, 2018,

available at www.wsj.com/articles/weapons-training-likely-causes-brain-injury-in-troops-study-says-1525060860. As a result, "much of what has passed for emotional trauma may be reinterpreted, and many veterans may step forward to demand recognition of an injury that cannot be definitively diagnosed until after death." Robert F. Worth, "What If PTSD Is More Physical Than Psychological?" *The New York Times Magazine,* June 10, 2016, available at https://nyti.ms/1TYYp6U. Regardless of the treatment that may be developed, "the crude message that lurks, unavoidable, behind [the] discovery" is that "modern warfare destroys your brain." *Id.*

190. Shira Maguen and Brett Litz, "Moral Injury in the Context of War," National Center for PTSD, February 23, 2016, available at www.ptsd.va.gov/professional/treat/cooccurring/moral_injury.asp.

191. Aaron Pratt Shepherd, "For Veterans, a Path to Healing 'Moral Injury,'" *The New York Times,* December 9, 2017, available at www.nytimes.com/2017/12/09/opinion/for-veterans-a-path-to-healing-moral-injury.html. *See also* Maguen and Litz, "Moral Injury in the Context of War," 2016; Jonathan Shay, *Achilles in Vietnam: Combat Trauma and the Undoing of Character* (Simon and Schuster, 2010); Nancy Sherman, *Afterwar: Healing the Moral Wounds of Our Soldiers* (Oxford University Press, 2015).

192. Shepherd, "For Veterans." Jason Hoffman, "Veteran's Day Column: USMC Vet Says 'Don't Thank Me for My Service,'" *cincinnati.com,* November 11, 2018, available at www.cincinnati.com/story/opinion/contributors/2015/11/11/veteran-go-beyond-shallow-gestures/75569398/. *See also* "Military Veterans Respond to Our Cover Story about Moral Injury," *The New York Times Magazine,* June 21, 2018, available at www.nytimes.com/2018/06/21/magazine/moral-injury-readers-respond.html; C. J. Chivers, "The Fighter," *The New York Times Magazine,* December 28, 2016, available at http://nyti.ms/2iDkjRt; Phil Zabriskie, Opinion, "Haunted By Taking Lives," *The New York Times,* March 4, 2015, available at www.nytimes.com/2015/03/04/opinion/haunted-by-taking-lives.html.
    Joseph Goldstein, "U.S. Soldiers Told to Ignore Sexual Abuse of Boys by Afghan Allies," *The New York Times,* June 20, 2015, available at http://nyti.ms/1KrOuSM; Nicholas Kulish and Christopher Drew, "A Deadly Deployment, a Navy SEAL's Despair," *The New York Times,* January 19, 2016, available at www.nytimes.com/2016/01/20/world/asia/navy-seal-team-4-suicide.html; video presentation by former US soldier Mike Prysner, available at www.facebook.com/TheHamptonInstitute/videos/910288692454668/.

193. Alex Young, "Too Much Information: Ineffective Intelligence Collection," *Harvard International Review,* August 20, 2013, available at http://hir.harvard.edu/article/?a=10382.

194. *Federal Bureau of Investigation's Foreign Language Translation Program Follow-up,* US Department of Justice, Office of the Inspector General, Audit Division, Audit Report 05–33, July 2005, at v, available at https://oig.justice.gov/reports/FBI/a0533/final.pdf. (OIG's "July 2004 audit reported that the FBI's estimated counterterrorism audio backlog was 4,086 hours as of April 2004. In this follow-up review, according to this same method, we found that the counterterrorism audio backlog had increased to 8,354 hours as of March 2005.").

195. Alex Nowrasteh, "More Americans Die in Animal Attacks Than in Terrorist Attacks," *Cato at Liberty, Cato Institute,* March 8, 2018, available at www.cato.org/blog/more-americans-die-animal-attacks-terrorist-attacks.

196. *Id.*

197. *Id.*
198. *Id.*
199. *Id.*
200. *Id.*
201. Robert Malley and Jon Finer, "The Long Shadow of 9/11 – How Counterterrorism Warps U.S. Foreign Policy," *Foreign Affairs*, July/August 2018, available at www .foreignaffairs.com/articles/2018–06-14/long-shadow-911.
202. *Id.*
203. *Id.*

BEYOND THE COUNTERINSURGENCY PARADIGM OF GOVERNING: LETTING GO OF PREDICTION AND THE ILLUSION OF AN INTERNAL ENEMY

1. For biographical details on David Galula, see Ann Marlowe, *David Galula: His Life and Intellectual Context*, SSI Monograph, Aug. 2010, https://ssi.armywarcollege.edu/pubs/ display.cfm?pubID=1016; Grégor Mathias, *Galula in Algeria: Counterinsurgency Practice versus Theory*, trans. Neal Durando, Santa Barbara, CA: Praeger, 2011; A. A. Cohen, *Galula: The Life and Writings of the French Officer Who Defined the Art of Counterinsurgency*, Santa Barbara, CA: Praeger, 2012; for citations in paragraph, see David Galula, "Introduction" to *Counterinsurgency Warfare: Theory and Practice*, Praeger Security International, 2006 (this is also the epigraph to Grégor Mathias's book *Galula in Algeria*); Mathias, *Galula in Algeria*, 27; Ann Marlowe, *David Galula*, 27.
2. *Counterinsurgency Warfare*, 56.
3. US Army Field Manual 3–24/MCWP 3–33.5, FM 3–24, Washington DC: US Government Printing Office, Dec. 15, 2006 (henceforth "FM"). General David Petraeus oversaw and produced this edition of the field manual in 2006 while he was at Fort Leavenworth between tours of duty in Iraq. General Petraeus's field manual would be dubbed "King David's Bible." Paula Broadwell, *All In: The Education of General David Petraeus*, New York: Penguin Press, 59, 2012.
4. FM, 35.
5. FM, 36.
6. Opinion, "*I Am Part of the Resistance Inside the Trump Administration: I Work for the President but Like-Minded Colleagues and I Have Vowed to Thwart Parts of His Agenda and His Worst Inclinations,*" The New York Times, Sept. 5, 2018.
7. Deleuze and Guattari, *Anti- Oedipus: Introduction to Schizoanalysis*, Routledge, 293, 1991.
8. Deleuze and Guattari, *Anti- Oedipus*, 104.
9. Olivier Roy, *Jihadism: Radicalization of Islam or Islamization of Radicalism?*, Yale Law School, Feb. 3, 2017, https://law.yale.edu/yls-today/yale-law-school-videos/olivier-roy-jihadism-radicalization-islam-or-islamization-radicalism.
10. Bernard E. Harcourt, "*Muslim Profiles Post 9/11: Is Racial Profiling an Effective Counterterrorist Measure and Does It Violate the Right to Be Free from Discrimination?*" in Security and Human Rights, eds. Benjamin Goold and Liora Lazarus, Oxford: Hart Publishing, 2007.
11. Tom R. Tyler, *Why People Obey the Law*, New Haven: Yale University Press, 1990; Tom R. Tyler, "Trust and Democratic Governance," in *Trust and Governance*, eds. Valerie Braithwaite and Margaret Levi, New York: Russell Sage Foundation, 1998.

12. *See generally,* Bernard E. Harcourt, *Illusion of Order: The False Promise of Broken Windows Policing,* Cambridge: Harvard University Press, 166–175, 2001.

13. The NAACP Legal Defense Fund, for instance, has done a study in Mississippi looking at the cost of pretrial detention to the community in terms of lost income of the prisoners and loss of ability to support their families.

14. Friedrich Nietzsche, *On the Genealogy of Morals,* trans. Walter Kaufmann and R. J. Hollingdale, New York: Vintage Books, 72, 1989 [1887].

REESTABLISHING THE RULE OF LAW AS NATIONAL SECURITY

1. See "Memorandum for John Rizzo, Acting General Counsel of the Central Intelligence Agency, from Jay S. Bybee, Assistant Attorney General, Office of Legal Counsel, Re: Interrogation of al Qaeda Operative," August 1, 2002, www.justice.gov/sites/default/files/olc/legacy/2010/08/05/memo-bybee2002.pdf; and *Department of Justice White Paper on Lawfulness of a Lethal Operation Directed against a US Citizen Who Is a Senior Operational Leader of Al-Qaida or Associated Force,* www.documentcloud.org/documents/602342-draft-white-paper.html. For a study of why these two very different administrations bothered with legal analysis when the policies were set to violate the law, see Rebecca Sanders, *Plausible Legality, Legal Culture and Political Imperative in the Global War on Terror* (New York: Oxford University Press, 2018).

2. Twice President Trump ordered major military attacks on Syria without any reference to applicable international law governing the use of force. The Department of Justice's Office of Legal Counsel did issue a memo arguing that the president needed no congressional authorization for the second attack. See "April 2018 Airstrikes Against Syrian Chemical-Weapons Facilities," May 31, 2018, https://fas.org/irp/agency/doj/olc/airstrikes.pdf. Trump has asserted that he can appropriate almost $6 billion dollars to build a wall on the US-Mexico border without congressional approval by declaring a national emergency despite the lack of factual indicia of an emergency.

3. As will be discussed further below, focus on military force regardless of law has migrated from foreign policy to domestic policy. A persuasive example of the problem is seen in *War Comes Home, The Excessive Militarization of American Policing,* American Civil Liberties Union (2014), www.aclu.org/report/war-comes-home-excessive-militarization-american-police.

4. Evidence abounds of the Founding Fathers' knowledge of international law and its influence on their design of a new nation. See, e.g., Vincent Chetail, "Vattel and the American Dream: An Inquiry into the Reception of the Law of Nations in the United States," in *The Roots of International Law,* eds. Pierre-Marie Dupuy/Vincent Chetail (Leiden: Martinus Nijhof, 2014): 252; Mark Weston Janis, *The American Tradition of International Law: Great Expectations 1789–1914* (Oxford: Clarendon Press, 2004): chs. 1–3; and Arthur Nussbaum, *A Concise History of the Law of Nations* (New York: Macmillan, rev. ed., 1958): 161.

5. International law is the system of rules, principles, and processes governing relations at the interstate level. While widespread skepticism exists about the characterization of international law as law in the United States today for reasons that will be discussed below, in fact, international law features the two essential components of any true legal system: It has an authoritative method of law creation and the means to coercively sanction the violation of any rule. See, generally, Mary Ellen O'Connell, *The Power and Purpose of International Law, Insights from the Theory and Practice of Enforcement* (New York: Oxford University Press, 2008).

6. Even when Americans had developed sophisticated domestic law of their own, beyond international law and the law inherited from Great Britain and colonial legislatures, international law remains the primary law between the United States and Native Americans. Hurst Hannum, "Sovereignty and Its Relevance to Native Americans in the Twenty-First Century," *American Indian Law Review* 23 (1998/1999): 487.

7. Members of the military and government officials take an oath to support and defend the Constitution. The Constitution incorporates international law as part of US law. See, in particular, Louis Henkin, *Foreign Affairs and the United States Constitution* (Oxford: Clarendon Press, 2nd ed., 1996).

8. See ns 51–76 and accompanying text.

9. See ns 76–97 and accompanying text.

10. Attempts at non-violent resistance as a path to societal change in Kosovo, Libya, and Syria were crushed by proponents of armed struggle. Tunisia is, to date, a notable exception. In 2015, four organizations that led the national dialogue for peaceful change, the Tunisian Quartet, won the Nobel Peace Prize. Norwegian Nobel Committee, "The Nobel Peace Prize for 2015," available at www.nobelprize.org/nobel_prizes/peace/laure ates/2015/press.html.

11. Two prominent realists have heavily critiqued liberal interventionism without acknowledging realism's role in promoting the use of force. See John J. Mearsheimer, *The Grand Delusion Liberal Dreams and International Realities* (New Haven: Yale University Press, 2018): ch. 6; and Stephen M. Walt, *The Hell of Good Intentions: America's Foreign Policy Elite and the Decline of U.S.Primacy* (New York: Farrar, Straus, and Giroux, 2018).

12. See, e.g., Aziz Huq and Tom Ginsburg, *How to Save a Constitutional Democracy* (Chicago: University of Chicago Press, 2018); and Robin Wright, "Is America Headed for a New Kind of Civil War?," *New Yorker* (August 14, 2017), www.newyorker.com /news/news-desk/is-america-headed-for-a-new-kind-of-civil-war.

13. Thomas Jefferson drafted the 1776 Declaration of Independence with these aims in mind:

> When in the course of human events, it becomes necessary for one people to dissolve the political bonds which have connected them with another, and to assume among the Powers of the earth, the separate and equal station to which the Laws of Nature and of Nature's God entitle them, a decent respect to the opinions of mankind requires that they should declare the causes which impel separation. . . . as Free and Independent States, they have full Power to levy War, conclude Peace, contract Alliances, establish Commerce, and to do all other Acts and Things, which Independent States may of right do.

See also, Janis, *The American Tradition* (n. 4): 53–56.

14. Remarks during the drafting of the Constitution on June 30, 1787, quoted in James Brown Scott, *James Madison's Notes of Debates in the Federal Convention of 1787 and Their Relation to a More Perfect Society of Nations* (Oxford: Oxford University Press, 1918): 36. See also, Janis, *The American Tradition* (n. 4): 57.

15. Nussbaum, *A Concise History* (n. 4): 161.

16. For the leading history of international law on the use of force, see Stephen C. Neff, *War and the Law of Nations, A General History* (Cambridge: Cambridge University Press, 2005).

17. See John F. Murphy, *The United States and the Rule of Law in International Affairs* (Cambridge: Cambridge University Press, 2004); Richard W. Leopold, *The Growth of American Foreign Policy, A History* (New York: Alfred A. Knopf, 1962); Janis, *The American Tradition* (n. 4); and Nussbaum, *A Concise History* (n. 4).

18. For a definition of "rule of law" as limitation on government, see Brian Z. Tamanaha, *On the Rule of Law* (Cambridge: Cambridge University Press, 2004): 137.

19. A famous formulation of the concept is provided by the sociologist Max Weber. Max Weber, *Rationalism and Modern Society*, trans. and eds. Tony Waters and Dagmar Waters (New York: Palgrave Books 2015): 129–198.

20. John Adams included the phrase in the Massachusetts Constitution of 1780. See also Karen J. Greenberg, *Rogue Justice: The Making of the Security State* (New York: Crown Publishers, 2016): 4.

21. Janis, *The American Tradition* (n. 4): 59.

22. *The Federalist Papers*, ed. Clinton Rossiter (New York: New American Library, 1961): 43.

23. See the Chinese Exclusion Act of 1882, discussed in *The Chinese Exclusion Case*, 130 U.S. 581 (1889).

24. Leopold, *The Growth of American Foreign Policy* (n. 17): 54.

25. Ibid.

26. Treaty of Amity and Commerce between His Majesty the King of Prussia and the United States of 1785, http://avalon.law.yale.edu/18th_century/prus1785.asp.

27. Leopold, *The Growth of American Foreign Policy* (n. 17): 35.

28. Mary Ellen O'Connell, "Arbitration and the Avoidance of War: The 19th Century American Vision," in *The Sword and the Scales: The United States and International Courts and Tribunals*, ed. Cesare Romano (Cambridge: Cambridge University Press, 2009): 30.

29. See, generally, A. M. Stuyt, *Survey of International Arbitrations 1794–1970* (Leiden: A.W. Sijthoff/Dobbs Ferry, NY: Oceana, 2nd ed., 1972): ix.

30. Leopold, *The Growth of American Foreign Policy* (n. 17): 4–5.

31. Ibid., 36–40.

32. See, generally, John Fabian Witt, *Lincoln's Code, The Laws of War in American History* (New York: Free Press, 2012).

33. Tom Bingham, "The Alabama Claims Arbitration," *International and Comparative Law Quarterly* 54 (2005): 1; and Eric C. Bruggink, "The Alabama Claims," *Alabama Law Review* 57 (1996): 339, 342.

34. *See* J. Gillis Wetter, *The International Arbitral Process: Public and Private* (Dobbs Ferry, NY: Oceana, 1979): 57.

35. Yuval Shany, "No Longer a Weak Department of Power? Reflections on the Emergence of a New International Judiciary," *European Journal of International Law* 20 (2009): 73; David D. Caron, "War and International Adjudication: Reflections on the 1899 Peace Conference," *American Journal of International Law* 94 (2000): 4, 10; and Jean Allain, *A Century of International Adjudication: The Rule of Law and Its Limits* (The Hague: T. M.C. Asser Press, 2000): 14.

36. O'Connell, "Arbitration and the Avoidance of War," (n. 28), 30.

37. Evan Thomas, *The War Lovers, Roosevelt, Lodge, Hearst, and the Rush to Empire, 1898* (New York: Little, Brown, 2010): 59.

38. Ibid.

39. Anthony Giustini, "Compulsory Adjudication in International Law: The Past, The Present, and Prospects for the Future," *Fordham International Law Journal* 9 (1985): 213, 220.

40. R. P. Anand, *Studies in International Adjudication* (Dobbs Ferry, NY: Oceana, 1969): 2, citing Elihu Root, "Instructions to the American Delegates to the Hague Peace Conferences," in *Instructions to the American Delegates to the Hague Peace Conferences and Their Official Reports*, ed. James Brown Scott (1916): 79–80.

41. Begun as an outgrowth of the peace movement, the Constitution of the American Society of International Law adopted in 1906 states that the object of the society is "to foster the study of international law and to promote the establishment and maintenance of international relations on the basis of law and justice." The American Society of International Law, www.asil.org.

42. See United Nations Office of Legal Affairs, *Handbook on the Peaceful Settlement of Disputes*, UN Doc. OLA/COD/2394 (1992): 27n. 34; and "The Bryan Treaties," *New York Times* (June 13, 1927).

43. Mary Ellen O'Connell, "Elihu Root and Crisis Prevention," *Proceedings of the American Society of International Law* 95 (2001): 115–118.

44. Mearsheimer, *The Grand Delusion* (n. 11), 158.

45. Despite heavy criticism before joining the war of Britain's embargo of food deliveries bound for civilians in Germany and German-occupied territories, the United States participated in the starvation embargoes once in the fight. Eric W Osborne, *Britain's Economic Blockade of Germany, 1914–1919* (London: Frank Cass, 2004): 134; and G. J. Meyer, *The World Remade: America in World War I* (New York: Bantam, 2017).

46. O'Connell, "*Elihu Root*," (n. 43).

47. Oona Anne Hathaway and Scott Shapiro, *The Internationalists: How a Radical Plan to Outlaw War Remade the World* (New York: Simon & Schuster, 2017): Part II.

48. The Treaty Providing for the Renunciation of War of 1928, https://avalon.law.yale.edu /20th_century/kbpact.asp. Mary Ellen O'Connell, review of *The Internationalists: How a Radical Plan to Outlaw War Remade the World*, by Oona Anne Hathaway and Scott Shapiro, *Journal of Ethics and International Affairs* 32, no. 2 (June 2018).

49. The leading international law theorist at the time of the adoption of the Kellogg-Briand Pact, Hans Kelsen, called the treaty an instantiation of the Just War Doctrine, which was the development of natural law teaching and the source of international law's prohibition on the use of force. Hans Kelsen, *General Theory of Law and State*, trans. Anders Wedberg (Cambridge, MA: Harvard University Press, 1945): 333.

50. See Stephen C. Schlesinger, *Act of Creation: The Founding of the United Nations: A Story of Superpowers, Secret Agents, Wartime Allies and Enemies, and Their Quest for a Peaceful World* (Boulder, CO: Westview Press, 2003): 28–36. Mearsheimer refers to militant liberalism as "liberal hegemony." Mearsheimer, *The Grand Delusion* (n. 11): 152.

51. See, e.g., Telford Taylor, *The Anatomy of the Nuremberg Trials, A Personal Memoir* (New York: Alfred A. Knopf, 1992).

52. See German Basic Law (*Grundgesetz*) 1949, art. 25; and the Japanese Constitution of 1946, prmbl, art. 9, and art. 98.

53. Mary Anne Glendon, *A World Made New: Eleanor Roosevelt and the Universal Declaration of Human Rights* (New York: Random House, 2001).

54. E. H. Carr, *The Twenty Years' Crisis 1919–1939* (London: Macmillan & Co. 1939): 186.

55. Ibid., 188.

56. George Kennan, *American Diplomacy 1900–1950* (New York: Mentor, 1951). Some realists confuse the liberal promotion of individual human rights as a policy of support for international law. Mearsheimer, *The Great Delusion* (n.11): 4–6. When this promotion involves the use of military force, it violates a peremptory norm of international law, the prohibition on the use of force.

57. See Hans J. Morgenthau, "Positivism, Functionalism, and International Law," *American Journal of International Law* 34 (1940): 260.

58. "In the late 1940s and 1950s, Morgenthau's classical realism swept through the emergent discipline of international relations." Nicolas Guilhot, *After the Enlightenment:*

Political Realism and International Relations in the Mid-Twentieth Century (Cambridge: Cambridge University Press, 2017): 232. Daniel Philpott, "Moral Realism," *Review of Politics* 64 (2002): 378 (reviewing Christoph Frei, *Hans J. Morgenthau: An Intellectual Biography* (2001)).

59. Hans J. Morgenthau, *Politics among Nations: The Struggle for Power and Peace* (New York: Knopf 1948).

60. Others who promoted the strongman decider were Walter Lippman and Harvey Mansfield. Mansfield asked, "How can a government be both rational and representative? It is notorious that what is rational is not necessarily representative of the people and is unlikely to be so." Carl Friedrich, in *Constitutional Government and Democracy*, advocated constitutionally enshrining dictatorial powers within the executive to better combat the "state of universal emergency throughout the world" created by communists and fascists (with words that sound strikingly close to those justifying the Global War on Terror).

61. Paul Elie, "A Man for All Reasons," *The Atlantic* (November 2007). The article misleadingly uses the term "pacifism" in the sense of Christian anti war teaching. Only a few small Christian denominations are pacifist, the Quakers, Mennonites, and Amish. Most accept the use of force in self-defense. For more on Niebuhr, see also, Robin Lovin, *Reinhold Niebuhr and Christian Realism* (Cambridge: Cambridge University Press, 1995).

62. Elie, "A Man for All Reasons," (n. 61).

63. Guilhot, *After the Enlightenment* (n. 58): 223.

64. As Max Weber indicated, Protestantism, rationalism, and science are interrelated intellectual developments that collectively account for the period known as the Enlightenment. Many authors have examined this point; see, e.g., Charles Taylor, *A Secular Age* (Cambridge, MA: Belknap Press of Harvard University Press, 2007) and Brad S. Gregory, *The Unintended Reformation* (Cambridge, MA: The Belknap Press of Harvard University Press, 2012).

65. Guilhot, *After the Enlightenment* (n. 58): 222–223.

66. Charles Gati, *Failed Illusions: Moscow, Washington, Budapest, and the 1956 Hungarian Revolt* (Washington DC: Woodrow Wilson Center Press, 2006): 17, 232–233.

67. Philip Windsor and Adam Roberts, *Czechoslovakia 1968: Reform, Repression and Resistance* (New York: Columbia University Press, 1969): 102–111.

68. Mary Ellen O'Connell, "Soviet Prisoners in the Afghan Conflict," *Columbia Journal of Transnational Law* 23 (1985): 497–504.

69. Christopher C. Joyner, "The United States Action in Grenada: Reflections on the Lawfulness of Invasion," *American Journal of International Law* 78 (1984): 131–175, particularly 137–139.

70. For a general history of the origins of the US intervention in Vietnam, see Fredrik Logevall, *Embers of War: The Fall of an Empire and the Making of America's Vietnam* (New York: Random House 2012).

71. Quincy Wright, "Legal Aspects of the Viet-Nam Situation," *American Journal of International Law* 60 (1966): 750–769.

72. Oscar Schachter, "McDougal's Jurisprudence: Utility, Influence, Controversy," *American Society of International Law Proceedings* 79 (1985): 266, 271.

73. James Joyner, "Kenneth Waltz's Crucial Logic, Why the Scholar's Thought Continues to Have Enormous Influence," *National Interest* (May 16, 2013), https://nationalinterest.org/commentary/kenneth-waltzs-crucial-logic-8471.

74. United Nations Security Council Resolution 660 (August 2, 1990).

75. Mary Ellen O'Connell, "Enforcing the Prohibition on the Use of Force: The U.N.'s Response to Iraq's Invasion of Kuwait," *Southern Illinois University Law Journal* 15 (1991): 453, 456.

76. For the views of a prominent neoconservative on intervention, see Charles Krauthammer, "Democratic Realism: An American Foreign Policy for a Unipolar World," 2004 Irving Kristol Lecture, American Enterprise Institute, Washington DC (February 2004). Krauthammer vehemently opposed respect for international law as part of US foreign policy. See, e.g., Charles Krauthammer, "The Curse of Legalism: International Law? It's Purely Advisory," *The New Republic* (November 6, 1989): 44. He asks, "What can law mean in an international system so conspicuously unable and unwilling to control lawlessness?" Liberalism is a focus topic of intense debate at the time of this writing. In a review of three analyses of liberalism published in 2017–2018, David A. Bell defines the "liberal ideal" as "constructed around representative democracy, human rights and free-market capitalism complement by a strong social safety net." David A. Bell, "The Many Lives of Liberalism," *The New York Review of Books* (January 17, 2019): 24–27, 24. He confirms that liberals have long held the view that "if necessary, rights could be defended by force, from beyond the boundaries of the state in question." Ibid., 26. See, also, Maja Zehfuss, *War & the Politics of Ethics* (Oxford: Oxford University Press, 2018). While Zehfuss avoids the term "liberal," her critical analysis concerns Western arguments in favor of war to pursue liberal goals abroad. Ibid., 10 (n. 9).

77. Letter to President Bill Clinton, January 26, 1998, www.informationclearinghouse.info/article5527.htm.

78. Mary Ellen O'Connell, "The UN, NATO and International Law after Kosovo," *Human Rights Quarterly* 22 (February 2000).

79. O'Connell, *The Power and Purpose of International Law* (n. 5).

80. Sam Moyn, *The Last Utopia, Human Rights in History* (Cambridge, MA: Belknap Press of Harvard University Press, 2010): 160, 166.

81. Kenneth Roth, "Setting the Standard: Justifying Humanitarian Intervention," *Harvard International Review* (April 6, 2004), http://hir.harvard.edu/interventionismsetting-the-standard.

82. See, e.g., Thomas G. Weiss, *Humanitarian Intervention: Ideas in Action* (Malden, MA: Polity Press, 2nd ed., 2012).

83. Zehfuss, *War & the Politics of Ethics* (n. 76), 3.

84. Mearsheimer, *The Grand Delusion* (n. 11), chap. 6.

85. Charles Krauthammer, "In Defense of Democratic Realism," *The National Interest* (Fall 2004): 15, 16.

86. Mearsheimer, *The Grand Delusion* (n. 11).

87. See, e.g., Michael Ignatieff, "Ein Krieg kann gut sein, wenn er das kleinere Übel ist," *Die Tageszeitung* (Berlin, February 25, 2005): 12; Michael Ignatieff, "The Uncommitted," *NY Times* (January 30, 2005): 15; Michael Ignatieff, "Second Sober Thoughts," *Toronto Star* (March 26, 2004): A14; Michael Ignatieff, "Why Are We in Iraq? (And Liberia? And Afghanistan?)," *NY Times* (September 7, 2003): 38.

88. Elie, "A Man for All Reasons," (n. 61).

89. Harold Hongju Koh, *The Trump Administration and International Law* (Oxford: Oxford University Press, 2019).

90. Elie, "A Man for All Reasons," (n. 61).

91. See Evan Osnos, "In the Land of the Possible, Samantha Power Has the President's Ear, to What End?," *New Yorker*, December 22, 2014, www.newyorker.com/magazine/2014/12/22/land-possible. See Helene Cooper and Steven L. Myers, "Obama Takes Hard Line

with Libya after Shift by Clinton," *NY Times*, March 18, 2011, www.nytimes.com/2011/03/19/world/africa/19policy.html?pagewanted=all&_r=0.

92. "U.S. Ambassador Samantha Power Presses for Strike on Syria," *National Public Radio*, September 9, 2013, www.npr.org/2013/09/09/220586231/u-s-ambassador-susan-rice-makes-case-for-strikes-on-syria.

93. Ibid.

94. *Department of Justice White Paper on Lawfulness of a Lethal Operation Directed against a US Citizen Who Is a Senior Operational Leader of Al-Qaida or Associated Force* (n. 1).

95. Marcy Wheeler, "Are There Any Limits on Obama's Drone War, Really?," *New Republic* (August 9, 2016), https://newrepublic.com/article/135933/limits-obamas-drone-war-really.

96. Josh Berry, "Searching for Strategy: America's Military under Trump," *Harvard Political Review* (September 22, 2017), http://harvardpolitics.com/united-states/searching-for-strategy-americas-military-under-trump.

97. Ibid.

98. John Yoo, *Crisis and Command: A History of the Executive Power from George Washington to George W. Bush* (New York: Kaplan, 2009).

99. John Yoo, "Executive Run Amok," *New York Times* (February 6, 2017).

100. Trump's belief in his almost unrestrained power as president are indicated in both his assertion that he may pardon himself from criminal conviction and that he may declare a national emergency even in the absence of one. His belief would not be so worrisome were it not for the additional indications that the courts will defer to his judgment, as they have respecting presidential decisions regarding torture and targeted killing. Respecting the national emergency declaration and likely judicial deference, see Emma Green, "The Most Remarkable Thing about Trump's Proposed National Emergency," *The Atlantic* (January 11, 2019), www.theatlantic.com/politics/archive/2019/01/trumps-plan-declare-national-emergency/580144. But see, also, Quinta Jurecic, "Everyone Calms Down about that Declaration of National Emergency," *Lawfare* (January 9, 2019), www.lawfareblog.com/everyone-calm-down-about-declaration-national-emergency (arguing that US national emergency legislation will not lead to the authoritarian outcome infamously predicted by the Nazi legal theorist Carl Schmitt.)

101. Christopher Woody, "Trump Is Ordering Airstrikes at 5 Times the Pace Obama Did," *Business Insider*, April 4, 2017, www.businessinsider.com/trump-is-ordering-airstrikes-at-5-times-the-pace-obama-did-2017-4.

102. Ibid.

103. William M. Arkin et al., "U.S. May Launch Strike If North Korea Reaches for Nuclear Trigger," *NBCNews.com*, NBCUniversal News Group, April 13, 2017, www.nbcnews.com/news/world/u-s-may-launch-strike-if-north-korea-reaches-nuclear-n746366. Barbara Starr and Zachary Cohen, "US Military Updates Trump's North Korea Options," *CNN*, Cable News Network, June 30, 2017, www.cnn.com/2017/06/28/politics/north-korea-trump-military-options/index.html.

104. See, e.g., Ø. Tunsjø, *The Return of Bipolarity in World Politics, China, the United States, and Geostructural Realism* (New York: Columbia University Press, 2018), 1. "An era of unprecedented unipolarity has come to an end as China's rise has changed the underlying distribution of power in the international system. While China is not equal to the United States in power aggregate, it has narrowed the power gap significantly and vaulted into top ranking. Equally important, no other state is strong enough to serve as a competitor to these two. Since the top two states are now much more powerful than

any third state, the structure of the international system has changed from unipolarity to bipolarity." Ibid. See, also, Mearsheimer, *The Grand Delusion* (n. 11), 228–229.

105. Richard H. Steinberg & Jonathan M. Zasloff, "Power and International Law," *American Journal of International Law* (2006): 64, 82–83.

Select Bibliography

Aktipis, C. A., & Nesse, R. M. (2013). Evolutionary Foundations for Cancer Biology. *Evolutionary Applications*, 6(1), 144–159. http://doi.org/10.1111/eva.12034

Atran, S. (2016). The Devoted Actor: Unconditional Commitment and Intractable Conflict across Cultures. *Current Anthropology*, 57(S13), S192–S203. http://doi.org/10.1086/685495

Atran, S., Axelrod, R., Davis, R., & Fischhoff, B. (2017). Challenges in Researching Terrorism from the Field. *Science*, 355, 352–354.

Atran, S., Sheikh, H., & Gomez, A. (2014). Devoted Actors Sacrifice for Close Comrades and Sacred Cause. *Proceedings of the National Academy of Sciences of the United States of America*, 111(50), 17702–3. http://doi.org/10.1073/pnas.1420474111

Bateson, P., & Laland, K. N. (2013). Tinbergen's Four Questions: An Appreciation and an Update. *Trends in Ecology & Evolution*, 28, 712–718.

Boehm, C. (1999). *Hierarchy in the Forest: Egalitarianism and the Evolution of Human Altruism*. Cambridge, Mass: Harvard University Press.

Boehm, C. (2011). *Moral Origins: The Evolution of Virtue, Altruism, and Shame*. New York: Basic Books.

Buhrmester, M. D., Burnham, D., Johnson, D. D. P., Curry, O. S., Macdonald, D. W., & Whitehouse, H. (2018). How Moments Become Movements: Shared Outrage, Group Cohesion, and the Lion that Went Viral. *Frontiers in Ecology and Evolution*, 6, 54. http://doi.org/10.3389/fevo.2018.00054

Deacon, T. W. (1998). *The Symbolic Species*. New York: Norton.

de Waal, F. B. M. (2013). *The Bonobo and the Atheist : In Search of Humanism among the Primates*. New York: Norton.

Dobzhansky, T. (1973). Nothing in Biology Makes Sense except in the Light of Evolution. *American Biology Teacher*, 35, 125–129.

Fessler, D. M. T., Pisor, A. C., & Holbrook, C. (2017). Political Orientation Predicts Credulity Regarding Putative Hazards. *Psychological Science*, 28(5), 651–660. http://doi.org/10.1177/0956797617692108

Gelfand, M. J. (2018). *Rule Makers, Rule Breakers : How Tight and Loose Cultures Wire Our World*. New York: Scribner.

Giphart, R., & Van Vugt, M. (2018). *Mismatch: How Our Stone Age Brain Deceives Us Every Day (and What We Can Do about It)*. London: Robinson.

Glass, D. J., Wilson, D. S., & Geher, G. (2012). Evolutionary Training in Relation to Human Affairs Is Sorely Lacking in Higher Education. *EvoS Journal*, 4(2), 16–22.

Glennon, M. (2014). *National Security and Double Government*. Oxford and New York: Oxford University Press.

Gowdy, J., Dollimore, D., Witt, U., & Wilson, D. S. (2013). Economic Cosmology and the Evolutionary Challenge. *Journal of Economic Behavior & Organization*, 90(S), 11–20.

Henrich, J. (2015). *The Secret of Our Success: How Culture Is Driving Human Evolution, Domesticating Our Species, and Making Us Smarter.* Princeton: Princeton University Press.

Jablonka, E., & Lamb, M. (2006). *Evolution in Four Dimensions: Genetic, Epigenetic, Behavioral, and Symbolic Variation in the History of Life.* Cambridge, MA: MIT Press.

Kruglanski, A. W., Gelfand, M. J., Bélanger, J. J., Hetiarachchi, M., & Gunaratna, R. (2015). Significance Quest Theory as the Driver of Radicalization towards Terrorism *Resilience and Resolve: Communities against Terrorism.* London: Imperial College Press, 17–30. http://doi.org/10.1142/9781783267743_0002

Lindeberg, S. (2010). *Food and Western Disease: Health and Nutrition from an Evolutionary Perspective.* Hoboken, NJ: Wiley-Blackwell.

Lopez, A. C. (2016). The Evolution of War: Theory and Controversy. *International Theory*, 8(01), 97–139. http://doi.org/10.1017/S1752971915000184

Lyons-Padilla, S., Gelfand, M. J., Mirahmadi, H., Farooq, M., & van Egmond, M. (2015). Belonging Nowhere: Marginalization & Radicalization Risk among Muslim Immigrants. *Behavioral Science & Policy*, 1(2), 1–12. http://doi.org/10.1353/bsp.2015.0019

Maynard Smith, J., & Szathmary, E. (1995). *The Major Transitions in Evolution.* New York: W.H. Freeman.

Maynard Smith, J., & Szathmary, E. (1999). *The Origins of Life: From the Birth of Life to the Origin of Language.* Oxford: Oxford University Press.

McChrystal, S., Collins, T., Silverman, D., & Fussell, C. (2015). *Team of Teams: New Rules for Engagement in a Complex World.* New York: Portfolio.

Mitchell, M. (1998). *An Introduction to Genetic Algorithms (Complex Adaptive Systems).* Cambridge, MA: MIT Press.

Murray, D. R., Fessler, D. M. T., Kerry, N., White, C., & Marin, M. (2017). The Kiss of Death: Three Tests of the Relationship between Disease Threat and Ritualized Physical Contact within Traditional Cultures. *Evolution and Human Behavior*, 38(1), 63–70. http://doi.org/10 .1016/J.EVOLHUMBEHAV.2016.06.008

Navarrete, C. D., & Fessler, D. M. T. (2005). Normative Bias and Adaptive Challenges: A Relational Approach to Coalitional Psychology and a Critique of Terror Management Theory. *Evolutionary Psychology*, 3(1). http://doi.org/10.1177/147470490500300121

Norris, P., & Inglehart, R. (2011). *Sacred and Secular: Religion and Politics Worldwide.* Cambridge UK: Cambridge University Press.

O'Reilly, T. (2017). *WTF? What's the Future and Why It's Up to Us.* New York: HarperBusiness.

Paul, R. A. (2015). *Mixed Messages: Cultural and Genetic Inheritance in the Constitution of Human Society.* Chicago: University of Chicago Press.

Pretus, C., Hamid, N., Sheikh, H., Ginges, J., Tobeña, A., Davis, R., Vilarroya, O., Atran, S. (2018). Neural and Behavioral Correlates of Sacred Values and Vulnerability to Violent Extremism. *Frontiers in Psychology*, 9, 2462. http://doi.org/10.3389/fpsyg.2018.02462

Richerson, P. J., & Boyd, R. (2005). *Not by Genes Alone: How Culture Transformed Human Evolution.* Chicago: University of Chicago Press.

Rother, M. (2009). *Toyota Kata: Managing People for Improvement, Adaptiveness, and Superior Results.* New York: McGraw Hill.

Sagarin, R. (2012). *Learning from the Octopus: How Secrets from Nature Can Help Us Fight Terrorist Attacks, Natural Disasters, and Disease.* New York: Basic Books.

Seaman, J., & Wilson, D. S. (2016). #Freespeech. *Arizona State Law Journal*, 48(4), 1013–1041.

Seeley, T. (1995). *The Wisdom of the Hive.* Cambridge, Mass: Harvard University Press.

Seeley, T. D. (2010). *Honeybee Democracy*. Princeton: Princeton University Press.

Sheikh, H., Gómez, Á., & Atran, S. (2016). Empirical Evidence for the Devoted Actor Model. *Current Anthropology*, 57(S13), S204–S209. http://doi.org/10.1086/686221

Skinner, B. F. (1981). Selection by Consequences. *Science*, 213, 501–504.

Sompayrac, L. M. (1999). *How the Immune System Works*. Malden, MA: Blackwell Science.

Tinbergen, N. (1963). On Aims and Methods of Ethology. *Zeitschrift Für Tierpsychologie*, 20, 410–433.

Turchin, P. (2015). Ultrasociety: How 10,000 Years of War Made Humans the Greatest Cooperators on Earth. Storrs, CT: Baresta Books.

Webber, D., Babush, M., Schori-Eyal, N., Vazeou-Nieuwenhuis, A., Hettiarachchi, M., Bélanger, J. J., Moyano, M., Trujillo, H. M., Gunaratna, R., Kruglanski, A. W., Gelfand, M. J. (2018). The Road to Extremism: Field and Experimental Evidence that Significance Loss-Induced Need for Closure Fosters Radicalization. *Journal of Personality and Social Psychology*, 114(2), 270–285. http://doi.org/10.1037/pspi0000111

Webber, D., Chernikova, M., Kruglanski, A. W., Gelfand, M. J., Hettiarachchi, M., Gunaratna, R., Lafreniere, M., & Bélanger, J. J. (2018). Deradicalizing Detained Terrorists. *Political Psychology*, 39(3), 539–556. http://doi.org/10.1111/pops.12428

Whitehouse, H. (2018). Dying for the Group: Towards a General Theory of Extreme Self-Sacrifice. *Behavioral and Brain Sciences*, 41, 1–64. http://doi.org/10.1017/S0140525X18000249

Wilson, D. S. (2015). *Does Altruism Exist? Culture, Genes, and the Welfare of Others*. New Haven, CT: Yale University Press.

Wilson, D. S. (2019). *This View of Life: Completing the Darwinian Revolution*. New York: Pantheon/Random House.

Wilson, D. S., & Gowdy, J. M. (2014). Human Ultrasociality and the Invisible Hand: Foundational Developments in Evolutionary Science Alter a Foundational Concept in Economics. *Journal of Bioeconomics*, 17(1), 37–52. http://doi.org/10.1007/s10818-014-9192-x

Wilson, D. S., & Hayes, S. C. (2018). *Evolution and Contextual Behavioral Science: An Integrated Framework for Understanding, Predicting, and Influencing Behavior*. Menlo Park, CA: New Harbinger Press.

Wilson, D. S., Ostrom, E., & Cox, M. E. (2013). Generalizing the Core Design Principles for the Efficacy of Groups. *Journal of Economic Behavior & Organization*, 90, S21–S32. http://doi.org/10.1016/j.jebo.2012.12.010

Wilson, D. S., & Paul, R., Interview, "Cultural Anthropology and Cultural Evolution: Tear Down This Wall! A Conversation with Robert Paul," Evolution-Institute.com, 2016.

Wilson, D. S., & Schutt, R., Interview, "Why Did Sociology Declare Independence from Biology (and Can They Be Reunited)? An Interview with Russell Schutt" Evolution-Institute.com, 2016.

Wilson, D. S., & Wilson, E. O. (2007). Rethinking the Theoretical Foundation of Sociobiology. *Quarterly Review of Biology*, 82, 327–348.

Witherington, B. D. (1997). "The Problem of Photopollution for Sea Turtles and Other Nocturnal Animals." In J. R. Clemmons & R. Buchholz (eds.), *Behavioral Approaches to Conservation in the Wild*. Cambridge, UK: Cambridge University Press, 303–328.

Index